edition

13

Political Behavior
of the
American
Electorate

edition

13

Political Behavior
of the
American
Electorate

William H. Flanigan
University of Minnesota

Elizabeth A. Theiss-Morse
University of Nebraska, Lincoln

Nancy H. Zingale
University of St. Thomas

Michael W. Wagner
University of Wisconsin, Madison

Los Angeles | London | New Delhi
Singapore | Washington DC

Los Angeles | London | New Delhi
Singapore | Washington DC

FOR INFORMATION:

SAGE Publications, Inc.

2455 Teller Road

Thousand Oaks, California 91320

E-mail: order@sagepub.com

SAGE Publications Ltd.

1 Oliver's Yard

55 City Road

London EC1Y 1SP

United Kingdom

SAGE Publications India Pvt. Ltd.

B 1/I 1 Mohan Cooperative Industrial Area

Mathura Road, New Delhi 110 044

India

SAGE Publications Asia-Pacific Pte. Ltd.

3 Church Street

#10-04 Samsung Hub

Singapore 049483

Printed in the United States of America

Library of Congress Cataloging-in-Publication Data

Flanigan, William H.
Political behavior of the American electorate / William H. Flanigan, University of Minnesota, Nancy H. Zingale, University of St. Thomas, Elizabeth A. Theiss-Morse University of Nebraska, Lincoln, Michael W. Wagner, University of Wisconsin, Madison. — Thirteenth edition.

pages cm
Includes bibliographical references and index.

ISBN 978-1-4522-4044-2 (alk. paper)

1. Voting—United States. I. Title.

JK1967.F38 2015
324.973—dc23   2013038730

This book is printed on acid-free paper.

Acquisitions Editor: Charisse Kiino

Editorial Assistant: Davia Grant

Production Editor: Jane Haenel

Copy Editor: Linda Gray

Typesetter: C&M Digitals (P) Ltd.

Proofreader: Annie Lubinsky

Indexer: Michael Ferreira

Cover Designer: Scott Van Atta

Marketing Manager: Amy Whitaker

MIX
Paper from
responsible sources
FSC® C014174

14 15 16 17 18 10 9 8 7 6 5 4 3 2 1

Contents

a p p e n d i x

Survey Research Methods   294

Index   306

To

Nicholas, Christopher, Eleanor, Abigail, and all of our students

Tables and Figures

Tables

Figures

Acknowledgments

THIS IS the franchise that Bill Flanigan and Nancy Zingale built. We are honored and delighted to begin building on the wonderful work they have done over the first twelve editions of *Political Behavior of the American Electorate*. Indeed, the general structure, orientation, and even many of the words found in these pages are outright pilfered from Bill and Nancy. We are grateful for their work and thank them for the opportunity to put our stamp on this book.

We are grateful to the National Science Foundation (NSF), which funds our primary data source, the American National Election Studies (ANES). The NSF's willingness to champion ANES investigations of what people think, what they want, what they do, and how well they think our democracy is working is crucial to the understanding and improvement of the American experiment. The support of this important work has benefited tremendously from the innovative step taken by scholars at the University of Michigan six decades ago. The late Angus Campbell, at the time director of the Institute for Social Research at the University of Michigan, first opened the data archives of the Survey Research Center to outside scholars. This generous act was the beginning of a tradition of data sharing that has characterized this area of the social sciences ever since. The late Warren Miller, former director of the Center for Political Studies, expanded these archival activities through the creation of the Inter-university Consortium for Political and Social Research (ICPSR). The ICPSR, composed of more than five hundred academic and research institutions, has made available to an extensive clientele not only the archives of the Survey Research Center but also thousands of other major data collections. Scholars and students have benefited in incalculable ways from the ability to use these data for their own research. The study of political science has likewise benefited from the ability to verify, replicate, and build on earlier work.

A second consequential development grew out of the first. The Survey Research Center at the University of Michigan had begun its state-of-the-art biennial election surveys in 1948, the fruit of which was being made widely available through the ICPSR by the mid-1960s. The critical importance of this for scholarship was recognized and institutionalized in 1977, when the National Science Foundation agreed to fund the surveys of the ANES as a national research resource. Under this arrangement, intellectual control of the development of the surveys passed to an independent board, composed of scholars drawn from several universities, with input from the political science community more generally and with data freely available via download from its website.

This book relies heavily on these institutional innovations in two ways. First, we base our analyses primarily on the large quantities of survey data collected by the ANES and the aggregate data contained in the ICPSR Historical Archive. Second, several generations of scholars whose work we cite have similarly benefited from the availability of these resources. We are pleased to acknowledge our great debt to the individuals involved in both the ICPSR and the ANES who have contributed to the establishment of these resources and services. We must hasten to add that they bear no responsibility for the analysis and interpretation presented here. We can only hope that any weaknesses of this work will not reflect on the worthiness and excellence of the open archives that the ICPSR and the ANES provide.

Given the quick turnaround time from the point that the 2012 ANES data became available and our publication deadline, we relied on an enormous amount of thorough-but-quick research assistance from Ben Sayre. We greatly appreciate and admire his passion for learning, data, coding, and tinkering. We could not have finished the book without him.

As we began the process of making the book our own, we benefited from conversations with many wonderful friends and scholars who generously gave their time and perspectives regarding things for us to think about as we embarked on this journey. We thank Jim Baughman, Barry Burden, Kathy Cramer, Bill Flanigan, Amanda Friesen, John Hibbing, Carly Jacobs, Dona-Gene Mitchell, Randy Morse, Dhavan Shah, Kevin Smith, Sergio Wals, Rachelle Winkle-Wagner, and Nancy Zingale.

We also wish to thank our editor at CQ Press, Charisse Kiino, for asking us to come along on this adventure and for supporting us through it. We also thank Davia Grant, Jane Haenel, Linda Gray, Scott Van Atta, and Amy Whitaker for their quick, professional work that was instrumental in bringing the book to completion. It is a pleasure to work with such wonderful people who are committed to the study of American democracy and to the education of the citizenry.

E. T.-M.

M. W. W.

Introduction

IT MIGHT HAVE BEEN PREDICTABLE, but it was never going to be easy. Barack Obama, the nation's first African American president, faced a 2012 election cycle that included a very slowly growing economy, an unemployment rate above 8 percent, a highly polarized (some scholars even called it toxic and broken) divided government, an ongoing conflict in Afghanistan, and a Republican Party that nominated as his opponent a moderate former governor, Mitt Romney, a personally wealthy candidate who had won a statewide election in liberal Massachusetts. While pundits and commentators such as George Will, Dick Morris, Peggy Noonan, Glenn Beck, Ari Fleischer, Michael Barone, and others predicted a Romney victory right up until Election Day, the president won the popular vote by a margin of about 51 to 47 percent and a decisive Electoral College victory 332 to 206. The result was not a surprise to political scientists like Alan Abramowitz, James Campbell, Robert Erikson, Christopher Wlezien, and Brad Lockerbie, who predicted Obama's popular vote share within 1 to 1.5 percent up to one hundred days *before* the election, nor was it earth-shattering news to former *New York Times* forecaster Nate Silver, who correctly called the Electoral College results of all fifty states. Heck, using only a measure of *projected* growth in the gross domestic product, political scientist Seth Masket forecasted, in August of *2011* (long before it was even clear who Obama's opponent would be), that Barack Obama would receive 50.9 percent of the popular vote.[1] While the 2012 elections scored a victory for the scholars over the pundits, statistically oriented forecasters were not perfect. Some summertime forecasts relying on state economic data and federal jobs data predicted a narrow Romney win, but on balance, predictions made several months before the election, using data that virtually ignored campaign dynamics, got it right, while (mostly) conservative pundits got it wrong right up to Election Day—and in former

1

George W. Bush adviser and FOX News contributor Karl Rove's case, even after the election had been called for Obama on his own network.

Of course, elections are not contested in seemingly abstract quantitative economic models. Just as the most statistically dominant football team has to defeat what on paper is the weaker team on the field to get a win, political candidates must face the voters on Election Day if they want the chance to serve in public office. The day-to-day narrative of the 2012 campaign was an exciting one, filled with enormous rallies, tight polls, a hidden-video controversy, dramatic debates, high-profile gaffes, billions of dollars of advertising spending from candidates and super PACs, early voting, social media explosions, and high-tech voter persuasion and turnout operations.

The 2012 election season opened with a vulnerable president presiding over a sputtering economy. The 2010 midterm elections resulted in a historic, sweeping victory for the Republican Party as the GOP won an additional sixty-three seats to decisively take back majority status in the House of Representatives and narrowly missed taking the U.S. Senate. At the time of the 2010 midterms, President Obama's approval rating was at 41 percent. His hard-fought victory passing the Affordable Care Act, also known as "Obamacare," cost some members of his party their seats in Congress. The Tea Party's ability to select candidates to win some primary elections against more moderate GOP incumbents moved Republicans in Congress to the right ideologically, but also likely cost the party majority status in the Senate as extreme, Tea Party–supported candidates in Nevada and Delaware lost elections that Republicans were likely to win with more middle-of-the-road candidates. Unemployment was high, and confidence that the economy would improve was low. The conventional wisdom was that the president was in trouble.

Sensing a chance to win the White House, or at least to help shape the party's message, several longtime Republican politicians announced their intentions to run for president. In addition to Mitt Romney, who had unsuccessfully sought the Republican nomination in 2008, former House of Representatives Speaker Newt Gingrich, former Pennsylvania senator Rick Santorum, Texas governor Rick Perry, Texas congressman Ron Paul, Minnesota congresswoman Michelle Bachmann, former Minnesota governor Tim Pawlenty, businessman Herman Cain, former Utah governor and ambassador to China under President Obama Jon Huntsman, and others entered the race. Romney was the frontrunner from the beginning, but he was unable to walk away with the nomination. At one time or another, Romney, Gingrich, Santorum, Cain, and Perry topped the national primary polls. Romney held steady in the 20 to 30 percent range of support during the invisible and early primary seasons before beginning an upward surge that began in March and ended with him easily securing the Republican nomination for president.

Before Romney was able to earn 50 percent or more of the support of the nation's Republican primary voters, he and most of the other candidates participated in twenty debates. Rick Santorum and Ron Paul participated in all twenty; Romney and Gingrich missed the first debate but participated in the remaining nineteen. Some of the debates were contentious (with candidates sparring with each other or with the moderators); others were noteworthy for their focus on Barack Obama. In one memorable early exchange, Tim Pawlenty, one of the early favorites to challenge Romney, declined a chance to label health care reform as "Obamney Care" (a play on "Obamacare" and the health care plan Romney signed into law as governor of Massachusetts) before his campaign fizzled due to a lack of endorsements, fund-raising, and poll numbers. Michelle Bachmann won the Iowa Straw Poll, a nonbinding, peculiar contest that has no correlation with winning the presidential nomination, though it did give Bachmann some good early press (and Pawlenty some bad press).

Herman Cain, a former CEO of Godfather's Pizza, earned the highest poll numbers of any African American GOP presidential candidate in history. His catchy "9–9–9" tax plan and on-camera charisma gained him early media notoriety, but few in the Republican establishment took him seriously. Stories about past personal misdeeds surfaced, and Cain's candidacy faded away.

Rick Santorum, a strong conservative from Pennsylvania, who lost his reelection bid to the Senate to Bob Casey in 2006, gained media attention for his socially conservative positions on abortion and gay rights and for his penchant for wearing sweater-vests. His contempt for the media scored him some points with some primary voters, as did the work he put into the Iowa caucuses. Though Romney was declared the winner on the night of the caucus (January 3, 2012), Santorum was the actual (and narrow) victor.

After Romney won New Hampshire, where he has a home, Gingrich surged, winning the South Carolina primary. Romney and Santorum split the next few contests while Gingrich began to fade, save his victory in his home state of Georgia. Even so, a super PAC favoring Gingrich funded by Las Vegas casino magnate Sheldon Adelson kept Gingrich's campaign on television, helping to keep him in the race longer than he would have been able to in the pre-super PAC era. Adelson and his wife reportedly spent more than $30 million supporting Republican candidates (eventually including Romney) in 2012.

Romney, with a few exceptions, ran the table from that point forward. By far, the wealthy Romney was the best-funded candidate and the candidate who had received the most endorsements from party insiders, something scholars have shown is far more predictive of who wins a party's nomination than polling, fund-raising, momentum, debate savvy, or oratorical skills. This makes it difficult for a candidate like Paul or Santorum, who are beloved by small factions of the party, to win the nomination contest overall. Party insiders want a candidate who suits the party ideologically, but they also want someone who can win in November—neither Paul nor Santorum was considered to be a serious threat to Obama's reelection. Rick Perry was considered to be a serious threat given his status as governor of Texas, the position from which George W. Bush successfully launched his presidency, but he spectacularly flamed out in the debates after famously claiming he would eliminate three federal agencies when he could name only two (the Department of Commerce and the Department of Education). After trying in vain to recall the third and even getting some helpful suggestions from his Lone Star State rival Ron Paul, Perry finally admitted defeat with a now iconic "Oops." Indeed, a Google search of "Rick Perry Oops" yields over 426,000 results!

Mitt Romney, on the other hand, was a moderate Republican with a record of pro-choice views on abortion (though he later converted to a pro-life position and promised that he was a "severe conservative"), had won a statewide race in liberal Massachusetts, and had a record of working with a divided government to get things done. While he was not the first choice of many of the most ideologically committed Republicans, he was a candidate who, of everyone running, seemed to have the best chance to win. As the political science blog Mischiefs of Faction put it,

> Gingrich had a notably unsuccessful and short term as Speaker and hadn't held public office in over a decade. Santorum's initial election to the Senate was somewhat of a fluke and his 2006 drubbing in a swing state did not bode well for him. Bachmann was a member of the House. Cain was an eccentric businessman. Parties almost invariably nominate current or recent senators or governors, and of the prospective field, only Pawlenty, Daniels, Christie, Palin, Perry, and Romney fit the bill. Three of those (Daniels, Christie, and Palin) seemed hesitant to fully jump into the contest, and among the three that jumped in enthusiastically, two of them (Pawlenty and Perry) had serious campaigning problems. Once the two of them had functionally dropped, it was hard to see anyone but Romney getting it.[2]

Once Romney had sewn up the nomination, the "veepstakes" began. Though names such as Chris Christie, Ohio's Rob Portman, Florida's Marco Rubio, and Virginia's Bob McDonnell came up, Romney chose Paul Ryan, a congressman from Wisconsin with a reputation for being one of the intellectual leaders of the House of Representatives on budget issues.

The polls showed a close election, though those who aggregated polls (e.g., Nate Silver of the *New York Times* or pollster.com) showed a consistent lead for Barack Obama. In September, as the Romney campaign was hoping to build some momentum ahead of the first debate, *Mother Jones* magazine's website released a secret video taken at a small Romney fund-raiser. In the video, Romney can be seen saying,

> There are 47 percent of the people who will vote for the president no matter what. All right, there are 47 percent who are with him, who are dependent upon government, who believe that they are victims, who believe the government has a responsibility to care for them, who believe that they are entitled to health care, to food, to housing, to you-name-it. That that's an entitlement. And the government should give it to them. And they will vote for this president no matter what. . . . These are people who pay no income tax. . . . My job is not to worry about those people. I'll never convince them they should take personal responsibility and care for their lives.

The Obama campaign was quick to air ads using Romney's words against him, the news media engaged in what political scientist Larry Sabato has called "feeding frenzies," and Obama supporters who had been reported to be less than enthusiastic about their candidate after four years of governing were energized, reportedly bringing up the video unprompted when getting fund-raising calls from the Obama campaign. Another reason the video hurt Romney is that the things he said fit the narrative the Obama campaign had built about him as a member of the wealthiest 1 percent who did not care about the average American. Kathleen Hall Jamieson and Paul Waldman's book *The Press Effect* argues that the news media tend to overreport items that fit what journalists think the truth is about a candidate (i.e., highlighting George W. Bush's verbal stumbles but not Al Gore's in the 2000 presidential race).[3]

The Romney campaign was limping, by press accounts, into the first debate with Barack Obama. By nearly everyone's account, Romney won the first debate with a strong, attacking performance while critics contended that the president looked tired and defensive. Romney moved up in the daily tracking polls, but debate effects are usually short-lived, and they were once again in 2012. Romney never gained enough traction to overtake Obama for a sustained period of time. Meanwhile, the Obama campaign's, with its unprecedented use of "big data," was working hard to identify persuadable voters, find those who needed to be reminded to turn out to vote, and solicit those who were most likely to donate. The campaign's get-out-the-vote campaign, as it had in 2008, took Republicans by surprise. On Election Day, Obama won reelection comfortably.

Obama's win in 2012 came on the heels of two historic elections. The 2010 midterm elections were, by any definition of the word, humbling for the Democratic Party. Democrats lost a historic sixty-three seats in the House of Representatives, along with their majority control of that body, and six seats in the Senate. Americans were upset with the state of the economy, and many disapproved of Obama's handling of his first two years in office. Disenchantment with Obama within some sectors of the American public offered Republicans the opportunity to give the Democrats a shellacking. This historic low point for the Democrats was preceded by a historic high point for the party in the 2008 presidential election, when Americans elected to office the first African American president. On the way to the nomination, Obama defeated the first serious female candidate for president, Hillary Rodham Clinton, whose strong showing in the primaries represented another first. Riding a wave of disenchantment with the administration of President George W. Bush, Obama's victory was the largest popular vote margin since 1984. Obama was aided by high turnout and solid support from African Americans, higher than usual turnout among young people, and strong support and good turnout among Hispanic voters, giving him wins in Florida, North Carolina, New Mexico, and Colorado. The comfortable victory margin of 53 percent to 46 percent for Obama in 2008 was accompanied by gains in the House of Representatives and, even more impressively, in the Senate, where Democrats added three votes to their existing fifty-five-vote majority on Election Day. (A fifty-ninth vote was added three months later when Senator Arlen Specter of Pennsylvania switched from the Republican caucus to the Democratic, and a filibuster-proof sixtieth arrived in July when a recount in Minnesota was finally settled.) The gains in both the House and Senate were a continuation of the Democratic tide that began in the midterm elections of 2006. With the Democratic tide on his side, the new president took office buoyed by an outpouring of euphoria and hope for a new beginning, hopes tempered by the realization that tremendous challenges awaited: an economy and financial system in crisis, wars in Iraq and Afghanistan, and a bundle of campaign promises in need of attention.

The large Democratic victories in 2006, 2008, and 2012 and their large loss in 2010 need to be seen against a backdrop of the two preceding presidential elections in 2000 and 2004 that were, in contrast, very close and very polarizing. The presidential contest in 2000 between Vice President Al Gore and Texas governor George W. Bush was the closest in more than a hundred years. More remarkable, the election remained undecided for more than a month because of the uncertainty of the outcome in Florida. The voting was extremely close in Florida, and an alarming number of irregular procedures and events occurred both before and after the election that called into question the validity of many votes. An unprecedented series of political and legal steps eventually led to a 5 to 4 U.S. Supreme Court decision, *Bush v. Gore,* that ended the recount then in progress and effectively gave a narrow Electoral College victory to Bush. The legal maneuvering and the actions of officials in Florida and Washington, D.C., made those on both sides worry about the sanctity of the American electoral process and caused many on the Democratic side to feel that an election had been stolen from them.

Other electoral oddities occurred in 2000. For the first time since 1888, the popular vote winner was not the Electoral College winner. Gore was the popular vote winner by a margin of more than 500,000 votes, but he lost the Electoral College by four votes. Ralph Nader, a minor-party candidate with a small percentage of the popular vote, denied the presidency to a candidate who otherwise would have won. This had not happened since 1912. The results of the 2000 election also left the U.S. Senate evenly divided between the Democrats and Republicans, with the Republican vice president holding the tie-breaking vote. In the late spring of 2001, Senator James M. Jeffords of Vermont switched from Republican to independent and denied the Republicans control of the Senate. It was the first time that party control of the Senate had changed during a session.

Against this backdrop of close partisan division and lingering resentment over the election results, the horrific events of September 11, 2001, took place. In the immediate aftermath of the attacks, the nation and its political leadership united behind President Bush to face and fight the threat of terrorism. Bush's approval ratings in public opinion polls soared, at least temporarily. The war in Afghanistan, undertaken in the following months, and an array of homeland security measures were widely accepted by Congress and the public as necessary steps to take.

One might expect that the awfulness of the attacks and the outburst of patriotism that followed would have a lasting impact on the political divisions in the country, but they did not. Instead, partisan division in the nation returned to the level it had been in 2000. A crucial variable in solidifying these divisions was the Bush administration's decision to go to war in Iraq. Suspicions about the veracity of intelligence reports that Iraqi leader Saddam Hussein possessed weapons of mass destruction and concerns that Iraq was a distraction from the "real" war on terrorism in Afghanistan followed existing partisan divisions among the public.

In this highly charged political atmosphere entering the 2004 election cycle, the task of the Democratic Party was to choose a candidate to challenge President Bush. The intensity of the negative feelings toward Bush was perhaps best illustrated by the unusually high level of commitment of rank-and-file Democrats, Democratic activists, and elected officials to choose someone as their nominee who could beat him. When Senator John Kerry of Massachusetts won the Iowa caucuses, upsetting early front-runner Howard Dean, whose campaign imploded in the final days leading up to the caucuses, Democratic hunger for a winner was so great that other early states fell in line behind Kerry, and he had virtually wrapped up the nomination by early February—at the time, an unprecedented early date.

The outcome in 2004 was close—but not as close as 2000. Bush won the popular vote by almost three million, versus a loss by over a half million votes in 2000. The Electoral College was a close copy of 2000, with only Iowa, New Mexico, and New Hampshire changing columns.[4] In 2004, a slight change in voting in Ohio would have given the state to Kerry, making him the winner of the Electoral College while losing the popular vote nationwide. Thus, two elections in a row were extremely close in popular voting and in the Electoral College, with the possibility or actuality of the popular vote and the Electoral College vote diverging. Few elections in American history have been as close as 2000 and 2004.

Thus, the Obama victories in 2008 and 2012 came against a recent history of partisan polarization and close division. The president's calls for bipartisanship and a newfound respect for working together went unanswered in Obama's first term. Critics argued that Obama quickly abandoned any goals of an improved tone in Washington, while supporters complained that the president was too quick to give Republicans what they wanted at the beginning of a negotiation. On the one hand, Obama's first term came with some major successes: a nearly $800 billion economic stimulus, national health care reform, the confirmation of Justices Elena Kagan and Sonia Sotomayor to the Supreme Court, new banking regulations, permanent tax cuts for most Americans while raising taxes on Americans with the highest incomes, the killing of terrorist Osama bin Laden by Navy SEALs, and the stock market's nearly doubling from his first month in office to the first six months of his second term. On the other hand, his first-day-in-office executive order to close the detention center at Guantanamo Bay, Cuba, had still not been executed; unemployment remained above 8 percent; black unemployment was over 12.5 percent in August of 2013 (though it had steadily dropped); a terror attack on the U.S. Consulate in Benghazi, Libya, resulted in several deaths (including a U.S. Ambassador) and a major controversy; the emerging democracy spurred by the Arab Spring in Egypt was fledgling at best; the formerly routine raising of the debt ceiling became a weeks-long crisis; and many of his proposals were mired in a deeply divided legislative branch of government. Obama hoped the beginning of his second term would usher in more cooperation among lawmakers, but the early months of 2013 suggested that there was little room for compromise between the president and the House of Representatives.

The first edition of this book was published in 1967. The plan of the book then, as now, was to present basic analysis and generalizations about the political behavior of Americans. What was unknowable at the time was that a decade of political trauma was beginning for the American polity. Not only would some basic changes in political life take place in the late 1960s, but these changes would call into question some of the things political scientists thought they knew about the way Americans behave politically. The years since then have seen their quiet periods and their moments of political upheaval. Much has changed in the political landscape—the impeachment and forced resignation of presidents, the dismantling of the welfare state under Ronald Reagan, the Republican "revolution" in the House of Representatives in 1994, the focus on homeland security in the post–September 11 world, and the stunning election of the first African American president in U.S. history. Over the years since that first edition, however, we have been impressed with the overall continuity in the behavior of the electorate, even in the midst of significant changes in the political environment.

In this thirteenth edition, we continue to focus attention on the major concepts and characteristics that shape Americans' responses to politics: Are Americans committed to upholding basic democratic values? Who votes and why? How does partisanship affect political behavior? How and why does partisanship change? How do economic and social characteristics and group identities influence individuals' politics? How much influence do the mass media have on the electorate's attitudes and political choices? How do party loyalties, candidates' personalities, and issues influence voters' choices among candidates? Throughout the book, we place the answers to these and other questions in the context of the changes that have occurred in American political behavior over the past sixty years. Specifically, we are concerned with trends in voter turnout, the loss of trust in government that many citizens have expressed, and changes in voter attachment to political parties, coupled with an increasing polarization of political activists and elites.

A second major focus of this book is to illustrate and document these trends in American political behavior with the best longitudinal data available. We rely heavily, although not exclusively, on data from surveys conducted by the American National Election Studies (ANES). The ANES surveys, covering a broad range of political topics and offering the best time-series data available, have been conducted during the fall of every election year (except 2006 and 2010) since 1952. Unless otherwise noted, the data come from this extraordinarily rich series of studies. We hope that the numerous tables and figures contained in this book will be used not only for documenting the points made in the book but also for learning to read and interpret data. Students can also explore a much wider range of data from the ANES on its website at www.electionstudies.org. The data from the ANES and other studies are available for classroom use through the Inter-university Consortium for Political and Social Research (ICPSR). (To see the full range of political studies available to the academic community, visit the ICPSR website at www.icpsr.umich.edu.) An especially good introduction to the analysis of ANES data is a website at the University of California, Berkeley, that is open to all users: http://sda.berkeley.edu. One of our purposes is to provide an impetus for obtaining high-quality data to answer questions prompted, but not answered, by this book.

Notes

1. Seth Masket, "Using Economic Projections to Make Vote Projections," *Enik Rising* (blog), August 15, 2011, http://enikrising.blogspot.com/2011/08/using-economic-projections-to-make-vote.html.
2. Seth Masket, "Why the Republicans Had to Nominate a Flip-Flopper," *Mischiefs of Faction* (blog), May 29, 2012, http://mischiefsoffaction.blogspot.com/2012/05/why-republicans-had-to-nominate-flip.html.
3. Kathleen Hall Jamieson and Paul Waldman, *The Press Effect* (New York: Oxford University Press, 2003).
4. A reallocation of electoral votes following the 2000 census accounts for an additional switch of seven votes to the Republicans, as the population—and thus electoral votes—shifted from "blue" to "red" states.

Democratic Beliefs and American Democracy

POLITICS IS COMPLICATED. We want to believe it is not, that we just need to elect the right people and problems will be fixed. Ross Perot gained momentum in the 1992 presidential election in part because he suggested that fixing America's problems was relatively simple. According to Tom Luce, a Perot strategist, Americans viewed Ross Perot "as a problem solver, . . . a leader, . . . a guy who will get under the hood, fix the engine, hands on."[1] Many Americans liked the "I will easily fix it" message, and Perot walked away with 19 percent of the popular vote, the largest independent candidate vote percentage since Teddy Roosevelt ran as an independent in 1912. Americans' hopes in 2008 were similar, with many people believing that Barack Obama could step into the presidency, quickly change what was going wrong, and make things better. By 2012, some of Obama's luster had faded. He accomplished some of his major campaign promises from 2008, including health care reform, but many problems still remained. Americans entered the 2012 election season a bit more cynical but still with the hope that whoever was elected, the problems they were experiencing would be quickly fixed: unemployment, a weak economy, fractured relations with other nations, and so on. The questions people asked in 2012 were similar to the questions they asked in every recent election: Why can't the economy just be fixed? Why can't we have enough jobs for people who want to work? Why can't we just deal with our own problems and not be involved in the rest of the world? Why can't someone run for president who will just fix the problems?

What makes these wishes unrealistic is that the U.S. government is structured in such a way as to make it extremely difficult, if not impossible, for a president to take office and quickly right the wrongs. The president has to try to convince Congress to go along with him (and someday her), but members of Congress represent constituencies that are often very different from the national constituency of the president. Americans quickly get frustrated that the president hasn't accomplished his promises and angry at Congress for not getting anything done, yet this is the basic system the framers of the Constitution established and James Madison defended in Federalist 10. A representative democracy with many interests that is large and has a separation of powers and federalism will have a government less able to infringe on people's liberty. The structural aspects of politics today are even more complicated than they were in the late 1700s, what with political parties and a wildly different mass media environment. Americans often want quick fixes, but the chances of getting them are small.

The electoral system in the United States is another structural element that sets the context for people's attitudes and behaviors. In a representative democracy, citizens are autonomous actors with inherent political rights who choose their representatives in regular, free, and fair elections. We therefore need to understand the electorate's attitudes and behaviors as well as what leads them to think and behave as they do. But a representative democracy is more than its citizens and the people they elect to office. It is also the institutions that set the ground rules that constrain or promote certain attitudes and behaviors. The American electoral system is quite unique. The most obvious unique feature is the Electoral College, which no other country has for electing its president or prime minister, but there are many others as well. Campaign finance laws, state-level election laws, the old-media franchises and the new media, the primary system, the political parties, and more make up the institutions within which elections take place. To understand American electoral behavior, then, we must not only understand individuals' attitudes and behaviors but the impact the relevant institutions have on these attitudes and behaviors and on electoral outcomes.

Context is set not only by institutions but by events and the key actors themselves. The economy, always a huge factor in election outcomes, was weak but improving by the time Election Day arrived in November 2012. The war in Afghanistan continued even as Americans paid it less and less attention. Interest groups spent a great deal of money on political ads that tried to frame the issues and candidates in ways that would get people to vote along with the interest groups' interests. And the major parties and their candidates struggled fiercely to frame the election in a way that would help their candidate win. Whichever candidate wins the struggle over what issues are considered most important or how the issues and candidates are portrayed is more likely to win the presidency. In 2012, the winner was Barack Obama.

Throughout this book, we examine in depth the political behavior and attitudes of the American electorate while taking into account the context within which those behaviors and attitudes occur. In this chapter, we establish the "big picture" context by considering what democracy is, what demands it puts on its citizens, and specifically what makes elections democratic. We then focus on what Americans think of democracy and their own democratic system. Gauging Americans' beliefs and values about democratic processes and the people they elect to office sets the groundwork for what happens in specific elections.

Representative Democracy and Elections

What sets representative democracies apart from nondemocracies? The obvious answer is elections, but many nondemocracies or democracies that are just marginally so hold elections because elections are the currency of legitimacy in the modern world. To be a democracy, countries must have democratic institutions and share certain practices. According to Robert Dahl, the essential features of a democracy are as follows:

1. Elected officials

2. Free, fair, and frequent elections

3. Freedom of expression

4. Alternative sources of information

5. Associational autonomy

6. Inclusive citizenship[2]

The main ideas underlying this list are (a) that power must be broadly dispersed and not concentrated in the hands of a small number of people and (b) that democratic citizens must have the ability to influence political outcomes. For the latter to occur, citizens must have access to information, preferably accurate information, and the opportunity to voice their opinions and participate in the political sphere. Not everyone will get what they want in a democracy—majorities will tend to win over minorities—but they must have the opportunity to try to get what they want.

One aspect of democracy that Dahl highlights is "free, fair, and frequent elections." Elections are a basic component of a democratic political system. They are the formal mechanism by which the people maintain or alter the existing political leadership. At regular intervals, competitive elections give ordinary citizens the power to choose their leaders and, just as important, to throw them out of office. Although the choices available to voters in a general election may not be numerous or even particularly dissimilar, democratic systems must provide for competition, usually by means of political parties, in presenting alternative candidates. Political leaders and organizations must be able to compete for the support of voters, and voters should have leaders competing for their support.

Competitive elections require that all citizens must be free to participate fully in campaign activities before the election itself. Such campaign activities include the freedom to express one's views and the freedom to organize with others during the nominating phase and the campaign to make preferences known and to persuade others. Implicit in this is the freedom to receive information about the choices before the voters.

Citizens must be free to vote, and the right to vote should not be undermined by substantial economic or administrative barriers. No physical or social intimidation should take place. Citizens legally eligible to vote should have full and convenient access to polling places. The right to vote and the right to express one's choices freely require a secret ballot. In fair elections, the ballots cast should reflect the intention of the voters, and the votes should be counted accurately. Votes should be weighted equally in translating votes into representation.

Requirements for Free and Fair Elections

A democratic system requires political leaders to compete for public support in fair and free elections. For elections to be fair and free, they must meet the following conditions:

- Freedom of citizens to form or join organizations in support of candidates
- Freedom to express preferences
- Alternative sources of information
- Ability of new leaders to enter the system and compete for support
- Right to vote without administrative barriers or intimidation
- Votes counted fairly
- Votes translated into representation fairly

Americans take great pride in their democracy, but recent presidential elections provide an opportunity to reassess the extent to which the requirements for being fair and free have been met in the American political system. Elections in the twenty-first century have been close and intensely contested, and it is during extremely close elections that irregularities matter the most. Many observers have questioned how free and fair elections have been, especially in connection with the 2000 presidential election, but questions have been raised in other recent elections as well. From concerns about the role of money in politics to people being kept from voting to votes not being counted, there is good reason to keep an eye on what happens during elections.

The amount of money spent in presidential elections has increased astronomically. Not only do the candidates and major parties spend a great deal of time raising money, and spending it, an impressive array of independent, nonparty groups formed in support of specific candidates or interests also raise and spend money. Independent organizations and organizations that are only quasi-independent, in the sense that they are not truly independent of the parties or candidates, have been around for a long time. The number and vigor of these groups, such as Priorities USA and American Crossroads, are noteworthy. In 2008, the U.S. Supreme Court decided in a very close decision, 5 to 4, that corporations and unions had the same rights of political speech as individuals and therefore that funding of political ad campaigns in elections could not be limited. The *Citizens United v Federal Election Commission* decision potentially opened the door to more and more money coming into elections. Table 1-1 shows that in 2012, the combined total spending in the presidential race was over $2.3 billion, the highest amount in U.S. history. Candidate spending refers to the money the candidates raised and spent from small and large donors. National party spending is the money spent by the Democratic and Republican parties. Outside spending is the money relevant to *Citizens United.* Groups or individuals can spend money independently of the candidates and their campaigns and usually do so by running television ads that are often very negative. Because outside spending can take place without complete disclosure on the source of the funds, the amounts listed in Table 1-1 are necessarily conservative estimates.[3] Barack Obama and Mitt Romney had similar totals in their campaign spending, but Obama raised a bit more in individual contributions, whereas Romney received more spending support from the Republican Party and outside spending.

Campaign spending allows candidates, parties, and organizations the opportunity to get their message out to a wide audience. Television ads cost a great deal of money, for example. Candidates and organizations

TABLE 1-1   Campaign Spending in the 2012 Presidential Election

	Obama	Romney
Candidate spending	$683,546,548	$433,281,516
National party spending	$292,264,802	$386,180,565
Outside spending	$131,217,824	$418,610,490
Total	**$1,107,029,174**	**$1,238,072,571**

Source: OpenSecrets.org, available at http://www.opensecrets.org/pres12/index.php.

that do not have access to resources have a difficult time getting their voices heard. The Internet has opened up a way to get the message out quite cheaply, but the audience receiving these messages is usually small. Reaching a wide audience often takes a lot of money. Although the two major political parties are well funded, candidates seeking the presidential nomination through the primaries, minor-party candidates, and citizens with views not represented by the major parties may find themselves unable to get a wide hearing.

Given the vast amounts of money spent on political advertising in presidential election campaigns—much of it highly negative—the focus has often been on how to place limits on it. For years, the U.S. Supreme Court has ruled that issue advocacy by individuals or independent groups is protected by First Amendment guarantees, and now with *Citizens United*, corporations and unions are included under this protection. The Court and Congress have wrestled with the problem of placing limits on campaign spending but have been unable to come up with a solution that isn't interpreted by the Court as unconstitutional. One way to try to even the playing field in terms of resources is to have public funding of elections. People can choose to have $3 of their federal taxes be used for campaign financing. Because of the limits imposed on candidates who take public funding, candidates with deep pockets usually choose not to accept public funding, which again leads to the disparity in resources available to candidates.

Concerns have been raised in recent years about the concentration of ownership of mass media outlets in fewer hands. Although this has certainly happened, it is probably more than offset by the proliferation of new sources of information from cable and satellite television and the Internet. The availability of the Internet as a place for groups to "meet" has facilitated the ability to join with like-minded people in support of one's preferred candidate. In both 2008 and 2012, Barack Obama's campaign took the use of the Internet to a new level, as a way to raise funds, turn out crowds, and organize at the grassroots level as well as to provide information to his supporters. Mitt Romney also used the Internet to reach out to supporters and provide information. The problem likely is not whether a variety of information sources exists, but whether consumers can sort through them to find credible sources and whether they will avail themselves of varied and competing views. The decline of newspapers, with their higher journalistic standards for fact-checking, nonbiased reporting, and civility, makes this situation potentially worse.

Despite the tight competition between the two major-party candidates and the fairly open competition among candidates within the parties' primaries, the barriers to entry into the competition by other parties' candidates are severe. Although other candidates can get on the ballot and some get attention, such as Pat Buchanan and Ralph Nader in 2000 and Nader in 2004, the obstacles to competing effectively are serious. Third-party or independent candidates are almost always denied a place in the nationally televised debates, and the Electoral College is a huge obstacle for these candidates. The winner-take-all system used in all but two states means a third-party candidate can be highly popular but never win an Electoral College vote, a problem that is exacerbated by voters who like the candidate but do not want to "waste" their vote on a candidate who they think cannot win. Many of the rules governing elections in the United States are designed to weed out "nuisance" candidates and to limit attention to those with some degree of public support. Public financing, participation in the debates, and a place on the ballot all require demonstration of some minimum level of support. On an informal level, coverage of a candidate's campaign by the mass media also requires such a demonstration. Minor candidates are faced with a chicken-and-egg dilemma: they cannot gain access to these important resources unless they are competitive, but they cannot become competitive unless they have access to these resources.

Registering to vote has become easier in most states in recent years; in consequence, registration has increased. (We treat the topic of voter registration and turnout more fully in chapter 3.) Efforts also are evident in many states to make it easier for registered voters to vote by allowing vote by mail, easing restrictions on the use of absentee ballots, and setting up in-person, early voting opportunities. Administrative problems remain, however, and fall unevenly on the citizenry. For example, officials in some states have been slow to process new registrations so that individuals who have correctly followed registration procedures find themselves not registered when they get to the polling place. Thanks to the Help America Vote Act (HAVA) of 2002, voters who think they were registered but do not appear on the registration lists can cast a provisional ballot that will be sealed and held, but not counted, until the voter's eligibility to vote has been established. Another provision of HAVA was to mandate establishment of a statewide electronic database so problems of verifying registration can be resolved more quickly.

Nevertheless, as the competition between the two major parties has become closer and more intense, the willingness to use measures to restrict participation, discourage fraud, or both increases. These tendencies were at work in the presidential election in Florida in 2000 and in Ohio in 2004, both hotly contested states. An unusual registration problem in Florida in 2000 received a considerable amount of attention from the U.S. Commission on Civil Rights.[4] Before the 2000 election, the Florida state legislature contracted with a private firm to purge felons, who are not eligible to vote in Florida, from the registration lists, but this process removed many nonfelons due to inaccurate felon lists and computer mismatches of names. Some people were informed that they had been purged before the election, but the procedures for reinstatement were confusing. Others were not informed beforehand and arrived at their polling place only to be told that they were ineligible to vote. Not allowing eligible citizens to vote is a denial of fair access to a polling place. In Ohio in 2004, a bureaucratic decision led to not enough voting equipment available for voters in Cleveland and Columbus (areas with high Democratic concentrations). Voters had to stand in line, reportedly for hours, waiting to vote, and not everyone stuck around.

For elections to be free and fair, the marked ballot should accurately reflect the voter's intention and the vote should be counted accurately. Unfortunately, this standard is not always met. Voting devices can fail to record votes in various ways: on scanned ballots the choices might not be detected, and on most voting devices, the voter can inadvertently void the ballot by various kinds of inappropriate marking. (In party primary elections, in which voters are required to vote in only one party's races but the ballot form allows voting in more than one party primary, large percentages of the ballots are invalidated because people vote for candidates in more than one party.[5]) Voting machines do exist that detect such errors and give the voter another chance to cast a ballot correctly, but they are relatively expensive. Another provision of HAVA required that states give voters an opportunity to check and correct their ballots before the ballot is cast. It also mandated standards for voter systems (eliminating punch cards with their hanging chads) and appropriated funds to states to assist in their purchase. Among the requirements for an approved voting system is a "paper trail" to enable a recount process when necessary.

The counting of votes is overseen by representatives of the competing political parties, and they are expected to keep each other honest. Even so, standardizing procedures in different election districts is difficult. In Florida in 2000, election officials in different counties used different rules for determining the voter's intent on flawed ballots during the various phases of the recount. Some officials allowed votes to be counted if the voter's intention could be reasonably inferred from the marks or punches on the ballot. In other counties, even ballots with a clear declaration of intent—such as that of the frustrated voter who wrote "I want to vote for Gore" on the ballot—were disallowed.

A fair election must allow for a thorough and accurate recount to ensure that the official results faithfully reflect the voters' choices. All vote-counting procedures are susceptible to error and fraud, so the occasional authentication of official returns is crucial to maintaining the legitimacy of elections in general. Typically in the United States, recounts have uncovered a certain amount of clerical error and little fraud. The long-running recount in the 2008 Senate election in Minnesota revealed a net swing of only about five hundred votes out of three million cast (a small number, but enough to change the outcome from election night). It also revealed a surprising array of ways in which voters can spoil their ballots and substantial variation in the handling of ballots— especially absentee ballots—across different counties. Even after the HAVA provisions were in place, and in a state that was a pioneer in easing the burdens of voter registration, twelve thousand absentee voters did not have their ballots counted.

The election of 2000, in which the popular vote winner did not win in the Electoral College and did not become president, puts in stark relief the problem of translating votes into representation. How can votes be considered equal if the state in which they are cast determines how much influence they have in choosing the winner? The rationale lies in the nature of a federal system. States, as well as individual citizens, are actors in such a system, and their role was preserved in the Electoral College as a part of the price of establishing the Union. It is one of many ways in which the American system departs from a purely representative democracy. Electoral outcomes such as 2000 are rare, however. The only other presidential elections that resulted in a popular vote loser winning the Electoral College were those of 1876 and 1888.[6] If one wants to consider a far more perverse case of bad translation of votes into representation, one should look at the U.S. Senate, where the votes of 16 percent of the population can elect a majority of that body.

The challenge in a democratic electoral system is to be highly competitive without compromising the integrity of the election process. Many Americans were unhappy with the 2000 presidential election, with only half of the public in 2001 indicating that George W. Bush "won fair and square."[7] By 2004, little had changed in these feelings. Fifty percent thought the 2000 election was "fair," whereas 49 percent thought it was not—and most on both sides felt strongly. In contrast, only about 15 percent thought the 2004 election was unfair.[8] In 2012, people were asked in the American National Election Studies (ANES) survey how often the following had occurred in American elections: (a) votes are counted fairly, (b) journalists provide fair coverage of elections, (c) election officials are fair, (d) rich people buy elections, and (e) voters are offered a genuine choice at the ballot box. The response options were *very often, fairly often, not often,* and *not at all often.* Figure 1-1 shows the healthy democracy responses for each of the questions.[9] Looking at the most positive and positive responses combined, people believe overwhelmingly that votes are counted fairly (84 percent), that voters are given a genuine choice (80 percent), and that elections officials are fair (78 percent). Americans are much less likely to support the ideas that media coverage is fair (54 percent) and that the rich don't buy elections (only 32 percent). Using the higher standard of requiring the most positive response, none of these aspects of American elections reaches 50 percent. Americans appear to believe their election system has some integrity, but they remain skeptical, especially when it comes to the role money plays in politics.

FIGURE 1-1   Beliefs about the Integrity of American Elections, 2012

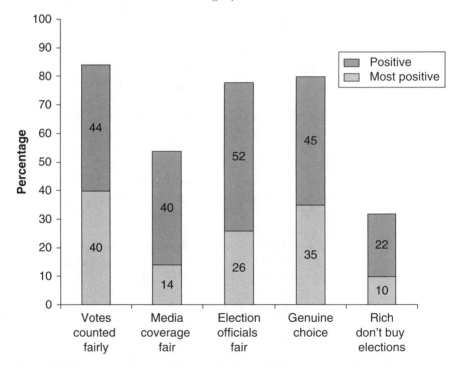

Source: 2012 American National Election Study, available at www.electionstudies.org.

Democratic Beliefs and Values

The United States has democratic structures well in place, but these structures can be used to pursue democratic or undemocratic goals. In democratic theory, much depends on the set of values and beliefs held by citizens that support democratic processes and institutions. Citizens need to accept the idea of rule by the majority and, equally, to believe that the rights of the minority should be respected. They should have some sense of their rights and obligations to participate in the political process, at a minimum through exercising the right to vote. The political elite—those who hold elected or appointed office and those who are informed about and engaged in politics—need to be willing to play by the democratic rules of the game and respect the will of the majority, even when it means the loss of their positions. In the remainder of this chapter, we examine the content of Americans' beliefs and values concerning democracy and assess them as a foundation for the maintenance of democracy.

System Support

Governments, whether democratic or nondemocratic, require some level of support from the public to stay in power. Their holding of power must be seen, in some sense, as *legitimate*. The source of that legitimacy could be the divine right of kings (in hereditary monarchies of the past), religious authority (as with the imams of present-day Iran), or the consent of the people (in modern democracies). An important element in maintaining legitimacy is the belief that officeholders gained their position through appropriate means (through fair and free elections in the case of democracies) and exercise their power according to prescribed procedures and within prescribed limits. In a simplified scenario, if the public in a democratic system believes in democratic values, it will support leaders who come to office through democratic elections and govern according to democratic procedures. Furthermore, it would withdraw support from any leader or would-be leader who attempts to gain office or govern by undemocratic means.

A complicating factor in the consideration of system support is the impact of governmental *effectiveness* on public perceptions of legitimacy. A tyrannical government that makes the trains run on time may gain some measure of legitimacy, despite abuse of persons and procedures. Conversely, a democratically elected government that governs by democratic procedures but is chronically unable to solve its nation's problems may lose its legitimacy. Its citizens might lose faith in democracy as a workable form of government and demand a different system. Support for a political system is thus a combination of belief in the rightness of a system of government and satisfaction with the way it is working.

On a relatively superficial level, Americans express strong pride in their country. In response to questions in public opinion polls, 96 percent say that they are proud to be American, 89 percent say they are very patriotic, and 89 percent characterize their love of America as "very strong" or "extremely strong." [10] As divisive as American politics is in the early 21st century, Americans still love their country. Almost four of five Americans (79 percent) said they feel very good or extremely good when they see the American flag, 71 percent said they love their country (and another 25 percent said they like it), and almost nine of ten (89 percent) said being an American is very or extremely important to them.[11]

When people are asked about their pride in the United States, they tend to offer political factors as examples. In other countries, people are much more likely to give nonpolitical reasons for their pride: their country's economy, culture, or physical beauty. They are not nearly as likely to say they are proud of their political system.[12] Americans not only give political reasons for their pride in the United States but also cite "freedom" or "liberty" as the aspect of their political system that makes them proud. Thus, not only is there strong patriotic pride in the nation, but a central democratic value also is a prominent feature of that sentiment.

Pride in the nation and its democratic form of government translates into high levels of political system support. Of the respondents in a national survey in 1995, 85 percent agreed that "whatever its faults, the United States still has the best system of government in the world." In 2000, more than half the public "would not change anything" in the American political system.[13] Pride in the political system has declined somewhat in recent years, reflecting both frustration with Washington and less confidence in the United States' place in the world. In 2009, people were asked if the U.S. political system was the best in the world compared to other industrialized countries. Only 19 percent said it was the best in the world, although another 31 percent said it was above average. Americans thought much more highly of the U.S. military—42 percent said it was the best in the world and 39 percent that it was above average—than its political system.[14] In 2010, people were again asked if they agreed that "whatever its faults, the United States still has the best system of government in the world." The percentage agreeing had dropped to 77 percent.[15]

Even with these declining numbers, Americans still think highly of their political system and its democratic form of government. The potential problem is that support for abstract notions of democracy and the political system does not mean people will support specific aspects of democratic political systems or the application of democratic principles. So it should not be surprising that respondents will agree to vague statements of system support while they endorse contradictory specifics. For example, 80 percent of the public say that the Constitution should not be amended.[16] However, majorities also believe that it should be changed to abolish the Electoral College or mandate a balanced budget. Almost certainly, none of these answers reveals how people would behave if faced with real choices on amending the Constitution. The importance of system support is that even when people are upset with Congress or the president, they support the basic democratic structures that are foundational to politics in the United States. In general, Americans do, although support for some nondemocratic options for the political system might be a cause for concern: the percentages of those answering fairly or very good were 14 percent for having army rule, 33 percent for having a strong leader, and 45 percent for having experts make decisions.[17]

Democratic Values

The beliefs and values supporting the American political system are variously referred to as the *American creed,* the *American consensus,* and the *American ethos.*[18] Among the most important values making up this creed are beliefs in *freedom, equality,* and *individualism.*

Social and political theorists make a distinction between the economic system and the political system. Most would say that the United States has, as an ideal, a democratic political system and a capitalist or free-market economic system. Ordinary citizens are more likely to mix the two and view freedom as a basic value in both. The freedom to own property, fundamental to a capitalist economic system, is considered by ordinary U.S. citizens to be as important as the right to vote, for example.

Although highly valued in American culture, freedom is not considered an absolute. People accept all kinds of limitations on their freedom. For example, when given a choice between government intervention and a wholly free market, Americans are clearly in favor of government activity. In the 2012 ANES, by a ratio of two to one, the public preferred strong government intervention to handle economic problems rather than depending solely on free-market operations. Similarly, majorities of the public support limiting the freedom to read pornography, to own guns, and to smoke cigarettes.

The widespread belief in equality similarly needs to be qualified. Americans believe in "equality before the law" and in "equal opportunity" but are largely uninterested in using government to promote economic and social equality. For example, the public agrees overwhelmingly (84 percent) with the proposition that "our society should do whatever is necessary to make sure that everyone has an equal opportunity to succeed," but a substantial minority (36 percent) of the public believes "we have gone too far in pushing equal rights in this country."[19] In many respects, the value placed on individualism undermines the commitment to equality. Most social groups exhibit widespread support for the idea that people can and should get ahead by virtue of their own hard work.

In her book *What's Fair?* Jennifer Hochschild distinguishes among social, political, and economic equality.[20] She finds that Americans wholeheartedly endorse equality in the social and political domains but not in the economic domain. It is at the intersection between the political and the economic domains that things get tricky. Americans believe that it is natural to have economic differentiation, with some people being wealthy and some being poor. They also believe that people should have equal rights before the law and that government policy should promote equality. When it comes to government policies designed to help the poor by redistributing wealth from the haves to the have-nots, Americans are conflicted. They support some government help to foster egalitarianism, but they accept inequality in the economic sphere. The bottom line is that Americans' support for equality depends on what kind of equality is being discussed.

Belief in Democratic Procedures

A distinction is often made between democratic *goals,* such as equality and individual freedom, and democratic *procedures,* such as majority rule; protection of the political rights of freedom of speech, press, and assembly; and due process of law. The distinction is an important one when the extent to which these ideals are supported within a political system is under consideration, because democratic goals can be pursued through undemocratic means or democratic procedures can be used for antidemocratic ends. Likewise, mass support may exist for democratic goals but not for democratic procedures, or vice versa.

A widely held and perfectly plausible expectation is that the American people support the values underlying democratic goals and procedures. At an abstract level this is true enough. American citizens overwhelmingly subscribe to the basic rules and goals of democracy when the commitment is kept vague. But as discussed above, the near-unanimous support for the democratic goals of freedom and equality disappears when specific applications of these concepts are considered. The same has been true for specific applications of democratic procedures, such as protection of free speech. Majorities historically have been happy to infringe on the right to speak, to organize, and to run for office of unpopular groups such as atheists, Communists, and the Ku Klux Klan.

The willingness to give disliked groups their basic constitutional rights is referred to as political tolerance. [21] Americans overwhelmingly support freedom of speech and assembly, for example, but they are much more reluctant to allow a noxious group, such as the Ku Klux Klan, to speak or assemble in a public place. So long as there is not a widespread consensus on which groups Americans believe are so noxious that they should not be given their rights, there will be enough people available to defend the rights of the noxious group to speak and assemble. The real problem occurs when a majority of Americans turns against a group and wants its rights taken away. Examples in U.S. history include the internment of people of Japanese descent during World War II and the treatment of suspected communists during the McCarthy Era in the early 1950s. The disparity between abstract democratic principles and their application in specific situations is a major concern for civil libertarians.

Political scientists have tried to figure out what increases or decreases political tolerance. Aside from demographic characteristics associated with tolerance (for example, education is related to more tolerance), the one factor that consistently and strongly affects tolerance is threat. [22] When people feel threatened, fear and anxiety override the abstract democratic principles, and people willingly remove the rights of the threatening group. The Japanese internment and the McCarthy Era are good examples of the role threat plays in increased intolerance. The threat caused by terrorism is another example. The September 11, 2001, attacks on the United States naturally led many Americans to feel highly threatened, and this perceived threat significantly increased their willingness to support policies that would infringe on the rights of Arab Americans. For example, almost a third of Americans (29 percent) supported the idea that Arabs and Arab Americans should be put under special surveillance by the U.S. government, and the more threatened people felt, the more they supported this policy. Threat also increased support for government surveillance of all Americans and of viewing security as more important than civil liberties. [23] Americans' willingness to sacrifice rights and freedoms in waging the war on terrorism can be seen in their support of the 2001 USA PATRIOT Act, which expanded the government's authority to monitor and regulate citizens. Initially, the public was about evenly divided over the provisions of the act, with between a quarter and a third believing it "goes too far" in restricting people's civil liberties and equal numbers thinking it does not go far enough. [24] By the fall of 2008, when the initial threat had receded, the American public was more concerned that the government would "restrict the average person's civil liberties" (51 percent) than fail to combat terrorism (31 percent). [25] By 2013, 46 percent said the government had gone too far in restricting civil liberties, and 39 percent said it had not done enough to protect the country from terrorist attacks.[26] Generally, the public is not supportive of the act's provisions directed at "ordinary citizens" but is supportive of activities directed at "terrorists." For example, in 2004, 71 percent disapproved of federal agents searching a U.S. citizen's home without informing the person, yet majorities supported a range of similar activities when the targets were "terrorists."[27] Of course, it is impossible to know ahead of time who the terrorists are.

When considering public support for civil liberties and other democratic values, it is essential to keep in mind the distinction between mass attitudes and those of the political, social, and economic leaders in American society who consistently support democratic principles more strongly than the general public. Support among leaders is usually so high that it is possible to conclude that the leaders in society defend and maintain democratic procedures. Consensus among leaders on democratic rights and values makes the weakness of the general public's support less seemingly problematic. Table 1-2 compares the responses of samples of the public with those of "political influentials" to questions about support for the "democratic rules of the game" in the 1960s and in 2004. In both time periods, the political influentials were consistently more likely to support maintaining civil liberties and democratic processes than a sample of the electorate.

Presumably, leaders are recruited and educated in such a way that they come prepared with, or develop, agreement on democratic procedures. Leaders apparently make decisions that maintain democratic practices, even without widespread public support. A somewhat less comforting possibility is that political elites are simply sophisticated enough to understand what the "correct" answer is to attitude questions dealing with democratic beliefs. The seemingly greater adherence to these values by the politically active would attest to the prominence of such norms in the mass political culture but would not necessarily suggest any great commitment or willingness to abide by these values. A third possibility exists that political leaders, like ordinary citizens, are willing to violate the rights of groups and individuals whom they particularly dislike or fear. Enough incidents of undemocratic behavior by public officials have occurred in recent decades—harassment of dissidents during the Vietnam War, "dirty tricks" to undermine the electoral process in 1972, surreptitious aiding of the Nicaraguan contras in violation of the law in the 1980s, and efforts to undermine the fair counting of ballots in Florida in 2000—to suggest no great depth of appreciation of democratic principles on the part of elites of either political party. Elected officials, who depend on the votes of their constituents, can be persuaded to infringe on a group's civil liberties if voters' voices are especially loud and consistent. The increasing incivility in Congress and the mass media that has accompanied the increased polarization of

TABLE 1-2   Political Influentials versus the Electorate, Responses to Items
Expressing Belief in Democratic Values, 1964 and 2004

Item	Percentage agreeing with item	
	Political influentials	General electorate
There are times when it almost seems better for people to take the law into their own hands rather than wait for the machinery of government to act. (1964)	13	27
The majority has the right to abolish minorities if it wants to. (1964)	7	28
I don't mind a politician's methods if he manages to get the right things done. (1964)	26	42
Almost any unfairness or brutality may have to be justified when some great purpose is being carried out. (1964)	13	33
People ought to be allowed to vote even if they can't do so intelligently. (1964)	66	48
The true American way of life is disappearing so fast that we may have to use force to save it. (1964)	13	35
Terrorists pose such an extreme threat that governments should now be allowed to use torture if it may gain information that saves innocent lives. (2004)	8	27
In order to combat international terrorism, [I favor] restricting immigration into the United States. (2004)	36	76

Sources: The 1964 data were adapted from Herbert McClosky, "Consensus and Ideology in American Politics," *American Political Science Review* 58 (June 1964): 365, Table 1. There were 3,020 influentials and 1,484 in the public sample for 1964. The 2004 data were taken from *Global Views 2004: American Public Opinion and Foreign Policy* (Chicago: Chicago Council of Foreign Relations, 2004), available at www.ccrf.org/globalviews2004. There were 450 influentials, including 100 members of Congress or their senior staff, and 1,195 in the public sample for 2004.

Note: Because respondents were forced to make a choice on each item, the number of omitted or "don't know" responses was, on average, fewer than 3 percent and thus has little influence on the direction or magnitude of the results reported in the table.

the society along political lines suggests that the democratic virtue of tolerance of one's opponent's views is in short supply among political elites today.

Reaction to the Supreme Court's decisions on flag burning illustrates several aspects of the role of political elites in supporting democratic values. Political dissidents have occasionally burned the American flag to protest policies or governmental actions with which they disagree. In retaliation, Congress and some state legislatures have passed laws making it a crime to desecrate the flag. The Supreme Court has consistently ruled these laws to be an unconstitutional infringement on free speech—classifying flag burning as "symbolic speech" and therefore protected by the First Amendment. Inevitably, such decisions provoke a public outcry and calls to amend the Constitution as a means to circumvent the Court's rulings and punish those who would burn the flag. In these circumstances, various political elites—the Court itself and some congressional leaders—support democratic values by resisting the popular passion for punishing flag burners. At the same time, other political leaders see an opportunity to exploit an issue that plays well among the public, because polls consistently show the public believes, by majorities of three or four to one, that there should be no right to burn or deface the U.S. flag.[28] In the past, proposed constitutional amendments to ban flag burning have been defeated once the issue became rephrased as "tampering with the Bill of Rights," thus demonstrating the generalized, if vague, support the public has for democratic values and the critical nature of elite leadership.

The widespread interest of political analysts in public opinion and democratic beliefs has been based partly on a somewhat mistaken impression. Stable democratic political systems have been assumed to rest on a nearly universal commitment to fundamental principles and their application, but the evidence is inconclusive. A democratic system cannot long survive widespread, intense hostility to democratic values, but positive belief in particular operating procedures among the public is probably unnecessary. Hostility to democratic procedures is fatal, whether among the leaders or the public, but support of specific procedures may prove essential only among leaders. Perhaps the public need not agree on basic principles so long as it does not demand disruptive policies and procedures.

Declining Trust in Government

In general, the public has considerable confidence in the *institutions* of government but not much in the *individuals* charged with operating these institutions. Thus, virtually no popular support is found for abolishing the presidency, the Supreme Court, or Congress, although disenchantment is widespread with the way the nation's political leadership is performing in the major branches of government. In June 2013, only 5 percent of the public had "a great deal" of confidence in Congress, 13 percent in the Supreme Court, and 19 percent in the presidency.[29] These confidence levels are lower than usual, but low levels of confidence, with some variations, have existed since the early 1970s and represent a noticeable drop from those of earlier years.

John R. Hibbing and Elizabeth Theiss-Morse argue, in their book *Congress as Public Enemy,* that it is the very openness to public scrutiny of congressional activities that generates the pronounced distaste for Congress in particular.[30] This may explain the higher level of confidence in the more secretive executive and Supreme Court decision making. In short, when the people see democracy in action, they do not like it very much. Democratic decision making entails serious and extensive debate and the willingness to compromise with opponents to reach solutions to problems. No one gets everything they want, but the majority coalition gets more of what it wants, and the minority gets at least something. Americans view debate as incessant bickering and compromise as selling out on principles, and they don't believe the conflict these processes represent is necessary. The government should just fix the problems, not waste so much time bickering about things. Since Congress puts these disliked democratic processes on show, Americans end up disliking Congress a great deal.

Figure 1-2 shows another indicator of declining public confidence in the political system. For years, the ANES has asked respondents whether they thought "the government in Washington could be trusted to do the right thing." There has been an overall decline from high levels in the 1950s and early 1960s to the point in the early 1990s where less than a third of the public believed the government would do what is right "all of the time" or "most of the time." Short-term reversals in this downward trend have been associated with policy successes or popular incumbents. President Ronald Reagan created an upbeat mood in the 1980s that translated into a modest restoration of confidence in government, as did the booming economy in the mid-1990s. After September 11, 2001, a *Washington Post* poll reported an upward spike in the level of trust in government, shown toward the right on Figure 1-2. Of the people questioned, 64 percent of the public said they trusted the government all or most of the time—a level that had not been seen since the early 1960s.[31] But commercial polls show that a month later the percentage dropped from 64 percent to 55 percent, with continuing decline thereafter.[32] By the fall of 2008, unhappiness with the Bush administration had sent the level of trust back to its previous low levels, and trust levels dropped even further in the first four years of the Obama administration.[33]

Because the most dramatic decline in trust in government officials occurred between 1964 and 1976, it is easy to blame the Vietnam War and the Watergate scandal. Although no doubt these were contributing factors, the decline in trust had already begun before Vietnam became an issue and continued after Richard M. Nixon's resignation from office. Furthermore, the pattern of declining trust extends to many nongovernmental institutions, such as the news media, schools, the professions,

FIGURE 1-2   Attitudes toward Politics and the Political System, 1958–2012

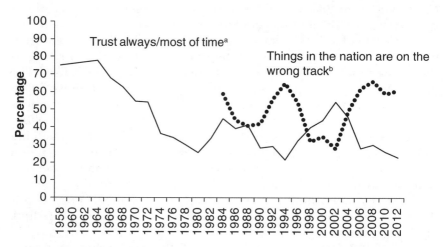

Sources: Trust data from American National Election Studies, available at www.election-studies.org, and from CBS News Poll, available at http://www.pollingreport.com/institut .htm. Wrong track data from NBC News/*Wall Street Journal* Poll, available at www .pollingreport.com (1996 to 2012), and from CBS News/*New York Times* Poll, the CBS News Poll database (1983 to 1994), available at http://www.cbsnews.com/2100-250_162-3362530.html/ (search for "wrong track" and the appropriate years).

[a] "How much of the time do you think you can trust the government in Washington to do what is right—just about always, most of the time, or only some of the time?"

[b] "All in all, do you think things in the nation are generally headed in the right direction, or do you feel that things are off on the wrong track?"

and people in general. It is paralleled by similar trends outside the United States in many of the developed nations of the world.

In recent years, commercial polling organizations have begun to track trust and confidence in government another way, by asking whether respondents "think things in the nation are generally headed in the right direction, or do you feel that things are off on the wrong track?" Although comparison with the years of high confidence in the 1950s and early 1960s cannot be made, responses to this question, also shown in Figure 1-2, indicate the increased support for government in the aftermath of September 11, followed by mounting concern over the direction of the country later in the Bush years. Even the hope represented by the early days of the Obama administration did not deflect the rising cynicism of the American people. Political strategists have come to use the responses to the "right track/wrong track" question as a kind of leading indicator of the electoral chances of the party in power; one can judge for oneself how well it reflects the closeness of the 2000 election, Bush's bigger victory in 2004, and the Democratic victories in 2006, 2008, and 2012.

The Role of the Citizen

Not only do Americans' support for democratic principles and views of their government matter; their views of their own role in the political system and of their fellow Americans also play an important part in democratic politics. A democratic system requires confidence in its institutions and processes. It also requires citizens who feel competent to involve themselves in politics.

Agreement or disagreement with statements such as "politics and government are too complicated for people like me to understand" or "I feel that I have a pretty good understanding of the important political issues facing our country" are used as indicators of internal political efficacy, the belief that people can have an effect on political outcomes. In the 2012 ANES, 66 percent of the respondents agreed that "politics is too complicated for people like me to understand," indicating a low sense of political efficacy, whereas 78 percent agreed that they felt they had "a pretty good understanding" of the issues of the day, which would indicate a higher level of internal efficacy. Obviously, different indicators produce different results. In any case, these indicators have yielded similar numbers over the years, so we can conclude that there have not been significant increases or decreases in citizens' sense of their own political competence. Internal political efficacy, however measured, is highly related to education, as one might expect.

Despite some apparent misgivings about their own political competence and the willingness of officeholders to listen, most Americans understand the basic obligations of citizens in a democracy. Most Americans consider voting a primary obligation, although whether this obligation is a duty or a choice remains up in the air. In 2008, about 85 percent of all adults said good citizens have a duty to vote in "every national election." In 2012, 45 percent said voting is a duty, and another 45 percent said voting is a choice.[34] Whether a choice or a duty, many Americans do not act on their commitment to the obligation to vote.[35] Although Americans also believe in the importance of informing themselves about political and governmental affairs, they readily concede that in most cases they personally are not as well informed as they should be. Even though there is some slippage between attitudes and behavior, citizens' perceptions of what a good citizen should do are related to their own political behavior.[36]

The most common form of political participation is exercising the right to vote. (We discuss voter turnout and other forms of participation in chapter 3.) Because the message or mandate of an election is seldom clear, specific policy concerns must be communicated to one's elected representatives via alternative routes. Contacting elected officials or writing a letter to the editor lets people more directly indicate their policy concerns. More intense forms of political activity, such as working on political campaigns, have remained much the same over this time period—although the levels of involvement have never been high. Many individuals who contribute financially to campaigns are not involved in any other way. When all forms of campaign activity—including financial contributions—are counted, somewhat more than 10 percent of the electorate is involved in some way.

Participation in voluntary associations—political and nonpolitical— has long been noted as an important contributor to democratic politics. Alexis de Tocqueville, writing in the nineteenth century, commented on Americans' proclivity toward joining organizations of all sorts. Not only do participants in voluntary associations learn useful political skills, but the existence of many organizations with overlapping memberships also has the potential to moderate conflict. People whose interests conflict on one set of issues may find themselves working as allies on another. Membership in organizations links people to each other and to their communities. For example, in his study of Italian states, Robert D. Putnam shows that the most significant difference between those with effective democratic politics and those without is the existence of a strong associational life.[37]

Given the importance of voluntary associations, Putnam has raised an alarm over what he refers to as the "declining social capital" in the United States. Americans, he argues, are now less likely to join organizations of all kinds—from bowling leagues to labor unions to political parties. He attributes this change to women in the workforce, increased residential mobility, and technological innovations such as television and the personal computer, all of which allow individuals to work and play in isolation.[38] Other scholars argue that the decrease in social capital is more related to the increasingly hectic and challenging nature of modern life. They argue that people are working longer and for less money, giving them less time to join civic organizations.[39]

In a major study of political participation in the United States, Sidney Verba, Kay L. Schlozman, and Henry E. Brady seem to counter Putnam's claim, finding organizational participation in America "lively and varied." [40] Comparing their data gathered in 1989 and 1990 with a similar study in 1967, they find a decline in some forms of political activity, such as membership in political clubs, but similar levels of participation in community activities and sizable increases in political contributions and contacting public officials about issues. Putnam would agree with the last contention, also noting increases in the membership in tertiary—or mass membership—organizations. Such organizations, however, usually do not involve the face-to-face interaction that fosters cooperation and builds community. The opportunities for networking via the Internet are only beginning to be explored in the context of building community. Although the Internet doubtless brings together like-minded people for a variety of purposes, early impressions suggest that these contacts are more likely to reinforce prejudices and incite intolerance against those with different views rather than moderate conflict and build bridges through cross-cutting interests, as envisioned by pluralist theorists.

Political scientists have studied extensively the impact voluntary association membership has on social capital. If being involved in voluntary associations increases social capital and social capital is essential for democratic political systems, then it is no wonder that so much emphasis has been put on getting people to volunteer. High school and college students are often required to do what might be called forced volunteering or service learning with the hope that they will learn to be more fully engaged in their communities when they are older and develop social capital. Putnam distinguished between bridging and bonding groups, with bridging groups made up of people of different backgrounds and bonding groups made up of very similar people. Bridging groups are better at increasing social capital because members must learn to trust those who are different from them. Bonding groups reinforce trust among similar others but do nothing to increase trust with those who are different. In a democracy, the kind of interpersonal trust that contributes to social capital necessarily involves trust in those who are different.

Most research on voluntary associations has focused on positive outcomes, but recent research has examined the "dark side" of social capital.[41] If many people tend to join homogeneous bonding groups rather than heterogeneous bridging groups, for example, then social trust does not extend to those who are different, leading to more distrust of outsiders and less social capital. Putnam found, in a later study, that people living in more heterogeneous communities—ethnically, racially, and religiously—are more fearful, less trusting, and less likely to volunteer.[42] Other research has found that people living in more heterogeneous communities are less likely to support paying taxes for community programs, such as garbage pickup, schools, and parks.[43] Since people tend to want to spend time with people like them, and therefore often join organizations made up of similar others, it is difficult to get people into situations in which they can develop social capital.

Verba, Schlozman, and Brady also conclude that the pattern of participation in America distorts the voice of the people. Those with education and money participate; the poor and uneducated do not. As a consequence, the interests of the affluent are well represented in government, and those of the less advantaged are not. Participation in religious institutions does not have this social class bias, and Verba, Schlozman, and Brady conclude that religious organizations are an important mechanism for developing political skills among the less advantaged citizenry.[44] In ongoing research, Putnam and David Campbell also cite the importance of religious communities in encouraging participation, finding that people active in religious networks are "better citizens" who vote more often, volunteer more, and give more to charitable purposes.[45]

One area that hasn't received much attention is Americans' views of their fellow citizens. The United States is a representative democracy, but it has some direct democratic processes within many states. For example, many states have initiatives and referendums that allow citizens to vote directly on policy options rather than relying on elected officials to make policy decisions. Perhaps Americans think more highly of their fellow citizens' judgment than the judgment of elected officials and would therefore prefer to see the expanded use of direct democracy. Hibbing and Theiss-Morse, in *Stealth Democracy*, asked people what they thought of the American people and if they preferred direct democracy over representative democracy.[46] They found that Americans were quite realistic about the capabilities of their fellow citizens, viewing them as more unselfish and united and less informed and intelligent than elected officials. They were also reluctant to hand political decision making to the people, questioning the time and effort it would take to have a direct democracy as well as the ability of Americans to make the right decisions. The bottom line seems to be that Americans don't think much of elected officials, but they also have reservations about the American people as well. Yet when it comes to assessing Americans' vote choices on Election Day, they are quite positive. Two-thirds of respondents say they have some or a great deal of confidence in the choices Americans make on Election Day.[47]

What Leads to Democratic Beliefs and Values?

A major question we have not yet addressed is why do some people hold beliefs and values that are supportive of democracy, whereas others do not. Given the importance of democratic beliefs in helping to sustain democracy, it is important to figure out what leads to prodemocratic beliefs. The primary answer offered by political scientists has been childhood socialization, which is the transmission of beliefs and values from one generation to the next. Alternative explanations have been offered, however, that include long-term factors such as personality and genetics and short-term factors such as context and people's reaction to that context.

Childhood Socialization

Most social groups, particularly those with distinctive sets of norms and values, make some effort to teach appropriate attitudes and expected behaviors to their new members. In most societies, the process of socialization is focused primarily on the largest group of new members: children. In a democracy, this would include teaching children the beliefs and values supportive of majority rule, tolerance for diverse opinions, and an understanding of the role of citizens as participants in the political process.

At a time when most learning about politics occurred in the home, the prevailing norms and values probably changed no faster than the attitudes of the adult population as a whole, in response to varied personal experiences and changing circumstances in the environment. In modern societies, other agents of political socialization also are involved, particularly the educational system and the mass media. To the extent that these institutions instill a different set of values and norms compared with those held by the adult population as a whole, an opportunity exists for changing the political culture. The prevalence of middle-class values among both teachers and the media in the United States has guaranteed that these orientations became and remain widespread in the population as a whole. As a more extreme example, under the Communist regimes in the People's Republic of China and, formerly, the Soviet Union, the official ideology dominated both the schools and the mass communications system. Massive changes in values took place within the span of a generation. (The fact that contrary attitudes survived the indoctrination attests to the multiplicity of agents of socialization, even in totalitarian states.) The worldwide availability of the Internet and the points of view it conveys mean that changes in political culture can occur rapidly even in traditional and authoritarian societies. The ideological movement that became the 1979 Islamic Revolution in Iran was spread via smuggled audiocassette tapes; challenges to that regime in 2009 were similarly organized through Internet communications. North Korea, a totalitarian state, not only outlaws Internet access, but also blocks access to outside information through other mass communication devices.

Research on the development of attitudes supportive of democratic goals and procedures via childhood socialization was popular in the 1950s and 1960s. Data collected in the 1950s by David Easton, Robert D. Hess, and others showed that children develop an affective attachment to the term *democracy* early (by about the third grade), but the concept acquires meaning much more slowly.[48] In 1999, an elaborate cross-national Civic Education Study directed by Judith V. Torney explored attitudes toward democratic culture among teenagers in twenty-eight countries.[49] The data in Table 1-3 display knowledge of the concept of democracy among American ninth graders. The top of Table 1-3 shows one-sided agreement that it is good for democracy "when everyone has the right to express their opinions freely" and "when citizens have the right to elect political leaders freely." Fifty-five percent believe the first item is "very good for democracy," and only 2 percent think it is "very bad for democracy." (When the "very good" and "somewhat good" responses are added together, the total is 83 percent, as shown in parentheses in the table.) These results reinforce the very strong support for the abstract principles of democracy among adults that we mentioned earlier.

Collectively, ninth graders are not nearly so sure of other tenets of democracy listed in Table 1-3. For example, only 24 percent believe it is very good for democracy for political parties to have different positions on issues or for newspapers to be free of government control. Young people may absorb the ambivalence that many adults, especially their teachers, feel toward political parties and a free press—a situation also reflected in the Easton and Hess studies forty years before. (In the 1999 study, teachers were divided half and half in thinking participation in political parties was a good idea in a democracy.) Ninth graders were fairly evenly divided on preventing newspapers from printing stories that might offend ethnic groups. They were even less supportive of the idea that the separation of church and state is a good idea in a democracy.

TABLE 1-3   Ninth Graders' Views on What Is Good and Bad for Democracy, 1999

	Percentage saying	
	Very bad for democracy	Very good for democracy
When everyone has the right to express their opinions freely	2 (9)	55 (83)
When citizens have the right to elect political leaders freely	5 (12)	61 (81)
When political parties have different positions on important issues	6 (25)	24 (59)
When newspapers are free of all government control	10 (37)	24 (51)
When people participate in political parties in order to influence government	10 (29)	22 (55)
When newspapers are forbidden to publish stories that might offend ethnic groups	19 (38)	27 (50)
When there is a separation between the church and the state	24 (49)	15 (32)

Source: U.S. Department of Education, National Center for Education Statistics, Civic Education Study, 1999, available at www.wam.umd.edu/~iea.

Note: The percentages in parentheses combine "very bad for democracy" responses with the "somewhat bad" and the "very good" with the "somewhat good."

During the elementary grades, children develop a set of attitudes toward their own roles as citizens. Initially, the emphasis is on obedience: the good citizen obeys the law, just as good children obey their parents. In the American socialization process, this is gradually replaced by a view of oneself as a more active participant in the political system: the good citizen is one who votes, and the government can be influenced through the voting process. Schools often hold a mock election as Election Day nears to help students understand the voting process. Schools, and specific teachers, vary dramatically, however, in how much they discuss the candidates and their issue stands with students to help them understand that they can think through their own vote choice and not simply rely on their parents' preferences. Because politics is such a divisive topic, many teachers stay away from discussing controversial topics in class. Diane Hess makes a strong argument for teaching students how to discuss controversial topics in classrooms so they are better prepared to handle political conflict as adults.[50] When divisive issues are not raised in the classroom, American children develop a low tolerance for conflict, believing, for example, that it hurts the country when political parties disagree.

In the past, younger voters were typically a bit more trusting of government than older voters. In the 1950s and early 1960s, when most of the major socialization studies were undertaken, young people entered adulthood with a strong affective feeling toward the government and a positive orientation toward themselves as participants in it. A study of high school seniors and their parents, carried out in 1965 by M. Kent Jennings, showed that trust and confidence in government were fairly high among the students.[51] As learning continues into adulthood, substantial modification of attitudes can occur through a variety of personal experiences with politics, new group membership, and the like. The original students in the Jennings study have been reinterviewed at intervals over the years. Their level of trust in government declined from 93 percent in 1965, to 67 percent in 1973, 51 percent in 1982, and 49 percent in 1997. The age disparity in trust, however, appears to depend on context. Using the mean level of trust in government, Figure 1-3 shows that in general, younger and older people share similar mean levels of trust in government over the years.[52] Yet there are certain periods when the young have been more trusting than older people, including the 1950s and early 1960s and the late 1980s through the 1990s. The overall message, though, is that trust has declined sharply since the early 1960s among people of all ages.

Alternative Explanations for Democratic Values and Beliefs

Socialization clearly plays a role in the extent to which people hold beliefs supportive of democracy. The more people are trained to hold prodemocratic beliefs, the more likely they are to do so. But other factors, both long-term and short-term, likely influence people's

FIGURE 1-3   Trust in Government by Age, 1958–2012

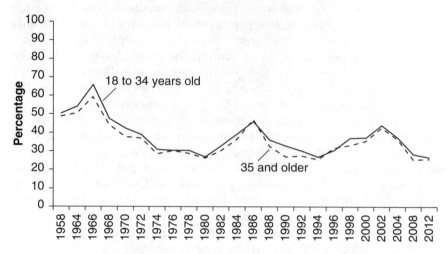

Sources: American National Election Studies, available at www.electionstudies.org.

democratic beliefs. Other factors that affect whether people are more or less democratic include such things as personality or genetic influences that come into play early in one's life and affect how people think about democracy throughout their lives. There are also things that happen in the immediate environment that can have an impact on people's responses. We start with the long-term forces and then discuss the short-term factors that influence democratic beliefs.

One area that has received increased attention in recent years is the impact of personality on political attitudes and behaviors, although political scientists have been interested in the impact of personality on politics for a very long time. People with different types of personalities definitely respond to the political world in different ways. Early research emphasized authoritarianism, dogmatism, and inflexibility as key predictors of such things as political intolerance and support for undemocratic political processes.[53] Perhaps not surprisingly, people who are more authoritarian and dogmatic, rigidly holding on to their opinions, are much less willing to give groups they dislike their basic civil liberties. For people who have a rigid and stereotypical view of the world, allowing disliked groups the opportunity to make public speeches, have their books in the library, and hold a march in a public square is anathema to their view of the world.

Drawing on more recent personality research in psychology, political scientists have examined the relationship between certain personality traits and support for various aspects of democracy. George Marcus and his colleagues studied the effects of personality traits on political tolerance. They found that three personality traits were related to tolerance: neuroticism, extraversion, and openness to experience. People high in neuroticism (or low in emotional stability, another term used for this personality trait) are more likely to feel worried, nervous, and insecure. People high in extraversion tend to be social, talkative, and optimistic. People high in openness to experience tend to be nontraditional, curious, and creative. Marcus and his colleagues found that neuroticism and extraversion were related to greater intolerance and openness to experience was related to greater tolerance.[54] Jeffrey Mondak examined the relationship between personality traits and support for democratic processes. He found that people were more likely to support democratic processes—specifically the need for members of Congress to compromise to get things done—if they were high in openness to experience and low in conscientiousness (responsible, self-controlled, and hardworking).[55]

These results suggest that people who are open-minded and open to new experiences are more likely to hold prodemocratic beliefs, whereas people who are more psychologically insecure and rigid are more likely to hold antidemocratic beliefs. There is a strong genetic basis for personality traits, although the environment can influence whether we are more or less, say, conscientious at any given time.[56] What this means is that people have basic individual traits, such as personality, that they bring into politics, and these are largely in place when they are born.

Genetics also influences people's bedrock principles of how society should work. Kevin Smith and his colleagues asked people a series of questions about what makes society work best. They found five different factors, or sets of beliefs, that constitute these bedrock principles: traditional values/moral codes; outgroups/rule breakers; role of group/individual; leadership; and absolutes. They found that people's responses to these bedrock principles were strong predictors of their attitudes concerning specific issues. They also found a strong genetic basis for the bedrock principles.[57] These bedrock principles have clear ramifications for beliefs relevant to democracy. For example, people who believe that society works best when leaders are obeyed and call the shots likely have different understandings about the functioning of democracy than people who believe society works best when leaders are questioned and forced to listen to others. The finding that there is a genetic basis for these beliefs highlights the long-term influence these beliefs have on how people view democratic politics.

The importance of long-term influences on democratic beliefs and values doesn't negate the impact of short-term forces on these same beliefs and values. As we discuss throughout this book, context matters. People are more likely to vote if someone rings their doorbell and asks them to vote. People's responses to issues are heavily influenced by how the issue is framed. And people's willingness to be politically tolerant depends on what the group is doing and how threatened they feel. After the terrorist attack on September 11, 2001, Americans who felt threatened were much more supportive of aggressive antiterrorism policies and infringing on the civil liberties of Arab Americans and Americans in general than were Americans who did not feel threatened.[58] The context of America after the 9/11 attacks led Americans who felt threatened to support having the government monitor the personal phone calls and e-mails of Americans, something they likely would have been loath to do before the attacks.

While threat matters a great deal in whether Americans support the basic democratic principles of freedom of speech, freedom of assembly, and due process, it is important to reiterate that Americans do support these values in the abstract. And when they are reminded of these principles, they are more likely to apply these principles in specific situations. Many Americans strongly dislike the Ku Klux Klan and eagerly approve taking away their basic civil liberties, but when they are reminded that a KKK rally is a free speech issue, they are much more likely to let them hold the rally.[59] Americans are also less likely to support undemocratic political processes when they are reminded of the democratic implications of their choices. When one of the authors of this book was conducting a focus group several years ago, the participants eagerly endorsed having government run like a business. It would be much more efficient and cost-effective than the current way government is run. After this discussion had gone on some time with many participants jumping in to say how great the business approach would be, one woman tentatively spoke up pointing out that businesses aren't democratic and so maybe it wasn't such a good idea. As soon as she said this, it was as if the other participants were suddenly stopped in their tracks. They quickly had to rethink what it meant to be a democracy, and as they did so, they came to the conclusion that having government run like a business would be a bad idea. Democracy, with all of its inefficiencies and messiness, was clearly preferable to a nondemocratic system.

Maintaining a Democracy

Belief in democratic ideals is essential to the preservation of a democratic system, both because such beliefs inhibit citizens from undemocratic actions and because the public will demand proper behavior on the part of political leaders. Belief that the system and its leaders meet democratic expectations in adhering to democratic procedures and responding to the wishes of the public is also important. A third factor is perhaps less obvious. A democratic system must meet some standard for effectiveness in solving societal problems. If not, the public may conclude that democracy does not work, that some other form of government—such as a dictatorship—is needed to maintain order, fend off an enemy, or provide economic well-being.

The United States is facing some big challenges at this point in its history. The threat of a terrorist attack looms constantly. The economy, while strengthening, remains weaker than most Americans would like. Income inequality is increasing at dramatic rates. Between 1979 and 2007, the top 1 percent of Americans saw their after-tax income grow 275 percent while the lowest 20 percent saw their after-tax income grow only 18 percent.[60] America's education system is less competitive internationally than was historically the case. With all of these challenges facing it, the government's ability to deal with such problems is hampered by the polarization that currently grips Washington. This polarization is not based simply on the parties trying to win political points but on deep-seated differences between the parties on how best to handle the problems. The unwillingness of political leaders to hammer out compromise solutions with the opposition, and the increased tendency of voters to throw out incumbents willing to compromise in primary elections, leads to stalemate.

When people's expectations are not met in the behavior of political leaders or in the experiences they have in the political process, disappointment, cynicism, or hostility may result. Americans hold high expectations for the political system and, as a consequence, are subject to considerable disenchantment with the performance of government and their own role in politics. Although no direct evidence on this point is available, nothing has been found to suggest that the value they place on the ideals of democracy, majority rule, or the importance of participation in politics has declined. Instead, events over the past thirty years have led to a larger perceived discrepancy between the specific American political institutions (and their incumbents) and the ideal.

Ideals, combined with the generally high expectations Americans hold for the political system, can lead to cynicism and mistrust of political leadership when scandals occur or policies fail to work. But another form of disenchantment operates at the individual level. The American ethos leads individuals to expect a wide range of conditions and values. They expect to enjoy freedom, justice, and equality; they expect to enjoy personal economic success; and they expect to be safe from violence.

Given the lack of sophistication in the public's understanding of democratic values and procedures, along with the declining levels of trust in government and its leaders, some uneasiness emerges about public support for American democracy—and perhaps for any democratic regime. Democratic theory implies that the public should demand values and procedures embodying democratic principles. The hope or expectation is that the public in a democratic society will insist on certain values and processes. A mass public demanding democratic values and procedures would provide strong support for a democratic regime. However, a democratic system could survive with much lower levels of support, given other conditions.

In our view, a distinction should be made between the factors necessary for establishing a democracy and those contributing to maintaining one. The example of contemporary Russia, to mention only one case, suggests that stronger public support probably is required for the successful launching of a new democracy than it is for maintaining an already established one. Possibly, preserving a regime simply requires that no substantial proportion of the society be actively hostile to the regime and engage in disruptive activities. In other words, absence of disruptive acts, not the presence of supportive attitudes, is crucial.

However, leaders' positive support for a political system is essential to its existence. If some leaders are willing to oppose the system, it is crucial that there be no substantial number of followers to which such leaders can appeal. The followers' attitudes, as opposed to their willingness to act themselves, may provide a base of support for antisystem behavior by leaders. In this sense, unanimous public support for democratic principles would be a firmer basis for a democratic system.

High levels of dissatisfaction, accompanied by lack of strong commitment to democratic values in the American public, appear to create some potential for public support of undemocratic leaders. However, as shown in subsequent chapters, many Americans feel an attachment to one or the other of the established political parties—an attachment that inhibits their embracing new political leaders. The parties and the public's attachment to them are often seen as preventing political change. They can also be seen as encouraging stability and preserving a democratic system by lessening the likelihood of a demagogue's rise to power.

Notes

1. David S. Broder, "Sen. Dole Defends Perot against Republican Charge of Demagoguery; Hill Races Seen as Potential Factors in Choosing a President," *Washington Post,* June 8, 1992, p. A10.
2. Robert A. Dahl, *On Democracy* (New Haven, CT: Yale University Press, 1998), 85.
3. "Outside Spending," OpenSecrets.org, http://www.opensecrets.org/outside spending/fes_summ.php.
4. U.S. Commission on Civil Rights, "Voting Irregularities in Florida during the 2000 Presidential Election," available at http://www.usccr.gov/pubs/vote2000/report/main.htm. See especially chap. 5.

5. In party primary elections, voting in both primaries invalidates up to one-third of the ballots.
6. Arguably, 1960 is another case.
7. Gallup Poll, April 20–22, 2001, Roper Center for Public Opinion Research.
8. 2004 American National Election Study.
9. The healthy democracy responses are those that reflect a positive view of elections. The most positive response for votes are counted fairly, media coverage is fair, election officials are fair, and voters are given a genuine choice is *very often* and the positive response is *fairly often*. For the rich buy elections question, the most positive response is *not at all often* and the positive response is *not often*.
10. "Opinion Roundup," *Public Perspective* 3 (May/June 1992): 7–9; and 2004 American National Election Study.
11. 2012 American National Election Study.
12. Gabriel Almond and Sidney Verba, *The Civic Culture* (Princeton, NJ: Princeton University Press, 1963). These patterns have been evident in cross-national public opinion polls since Almond and Verba first recorded them in 1963.
13. ABC News/*Washington Post* Poll, December 14–15, 2000, Roper Center for Public Opinion Research.
14. Pew Research Center for the People & the Press May 2009 General Public Science Survey, Final Topline, Questions Q.7.g and Q.7.b, http://www.people-press.org/files/legacy-questionnaires/528.pdf.
15. "Role of Government Survey," *The Washington Post*/Kaiser Family Foundation/Harvard University, October 2010, http://www.washingtonpost.com/wp-srv/special/politics/Post-Kaiser-Harvard-Role-of-Government-2010.pdf.
16. ABC News/*Washington Post* Poll, December 14–15, 2000, Roper Center for Public Opinion Research.
17. Wave 5 of the World Values Survey, Online Data Analysis, United States (2006), http://www.wvsevsdb.com/wvs/WVSAnalizeStudy.jsp.
18. For a major effort to capture this fundamental aspect of political culture, see Herbert McClosky and John Zaller, *The American Ethos* (Cambridge, MA: Harvard University Press, 1984).
19. 2012 American National Election Study.
20. Jennifer L. Hochschild, *What's Fair? American Beliefs about Distributive Justice* (Cambridge, MA: Harvard University Press, 1981).
21. For the major study of the 1950s, see Samuel Stouffer, *Communism, Conformity, and Civil Liberties* (Garden City, NY: Doubleday, 1955). See also James W. Prothro and Charles M. Grigg, "Fundamental Principles of Democracy: Bases of Agreement and Disagreement," *Journal of Politics* 22 (May 1960): 276–94; John L. Sullivan, James Pierson, and George E. Marcus, *Political Tolerance and American Democracy* (Chicago: University of Chicago Press, 1982).
22. James L. Gibson, "A Sober Second Thought: An Experiment in Persuading Russians to Tolerate," *American Journal of Political Science* 42 (July 1998): 819–50; George E. Marcus, John L. Sullivan, Elizabeth Theiss-Morse, and Sandra L. Wood, *With Malice toward Some* (Cambridge, England: Cambridge University Press, 1995).
23. Leonie Huddy, Stanley Feldman, Charles Taber, and Gallya Lahav, "Threat, Anxiety, and Support of Antiterrorism Policies," *American Journal of Political Science* 49 (July 2005): 593–608.

24. Gallup Poll, November 2003, Roper Center for Public Opinion Research.
25. CBS News/*New York Times* Poll, September 21–24, 2008, Roper Center for Public Opinion Research.
26. Quinnipiac University Poll, July 28–31, 2013, http://www.pollingreport.com/terror.htm.
27. Gallup, CNN, *USA Today* Polls, February 2004, Roper Center for Public Opinion Research.
28. In April 2000, the Freedom Forum found 25 percent agreed that "people should be allowed to burn or deface the American flag as a political statement" and 74 percent disagreed. The public was evenly divided on amending the Constitution to prohibit desecration of the flag. In a 2006 poll, a majority of the public (54 percent) opposed amending the Constitution to make it illegal to burn the flag. Gallup/*USA Today* Poll, June 2006. Both polls are available from the Roper Center for Public Opinion Research.
29. "Confidence in Institutions," Gallup, http://www.gallup.com/poll/1597/confidence-institutions.aspx.
30. John R. Hibbing and Elizabeth Theiss-Morse, *Congress as Public Enemy* (Cambridge, England: Cambridge University Press, 1995), chap. 3.
31. Stephen Barr, "Trust in Government Surges during Crisis," *Washington Post,* September 30, 2001, C02.
32. CBS News/*New York Times* Poll, October 25–28, 2001, Roper Center for Public Opinion Research.
33. 2008 and 2012 American National Election Study.
34. Ibid.
35. It is interesting to note that people who believe voting is a duty are much more likely to vote than people who think voting is a choice. According to the 2012 ANES data, 93 percent of people who very strongly believe voting is a duty voted compared to only 66 percent of those who very strongly believe voting is a choice.
36. Elizabeth Theiss-Morse, "Conceptualizations of Good Citizenship and Political Participation," *Political Behavior* 15 (December 1993): 355–80.
37. Robert D. Putnam, *Making Democracy Work: Civic Traditions in Modern Italy* (Princeton, NJ: Princeton University Press, 1993).
38. Robert D. Putnam, "Bowling Alone: America's Declining Social Capital," *Journal of Democracy* 6 (January 1995): 65–78.
39. W. Lance Bennett. "The UnCivic Culture: Communication, Identity, and the Rise of Lifestyle Politics," *PS: Political Science and Politics* 31 (December 1998): 740–61.
40. Sidney Verba, Kay L. Schlozman, and Henry E. Brady, *Voice and Equality: Civic Voluntarism in American Politics* (Cambridge, MA: Harvard University Press, 1995), 509.
41. See Jan W. van Deth and Sonja Zmerli, "Introduction: Civicness, Equality, and Democracy—A 'Dark Side' of Social Capital," *American Behavioral Scientist* 53 (January 2010): 631–39, and the rest of this special issue on social capital.
42. Robert D. Putnam, "E Pluribus Unum: Diversity and Community in the Twenty-First Century—the 2006 Johan Skytte Prize Lecture," *Scandinavian Political Studies* 30, no. 2 (2007): 137–74.

43. Alberto Alesina, Reza Baqir, and William Easterly, "Public Goods and Ethnic Divisions," *Quarterly Journal of Economics* 114 (November 1999): 1243–84.
44. Sidney Verba et al. *Voice and Equality: Civic Voluntarism in American Politics*, chap. 17.
45. Robert D. Putnam and David Campbell, *American Grace* (New York: Simon & Schuster, 2010).
46. John R. Hibbing and Elizabeth Theiss-Morse, *Stealth Democracy: Americans' Beliefs about How Government Should Work* (New York: Cambridge University Press, 2002), 109.
47. Elizabeth Theiss-Morse, *Who Counts as an American?* (New York: Cambridge University Press, 2009), 57–59.
48. The results of this study have been reported in several articles and in Robert D. Hess and Judith V. Torney, *The Development of Political Attitudes in Children* (New York: Anchor Books, 1968); and David Easton and Jack Dennis, *Children in the Political System: Origins of Political Legitimacy* (New York: McGraw-Hill, 1969).
49. See Stephane Baldi, Marianne Perie, Dan Skidmore, Elizabeth Greenberg, Carole Hahn, and Dawn Nelson, *What Democracy Means to Ninth-Graders: U.S. Results from the International IEA Civic Education Study*, National Center for Education Statistics, U.S. Department of Education, 2001, at nces.ed.gov/pubsearch/pubsinfo.asp?pubid=2001096.
50. Diane Hess, *Controversy in the Classroom: The Democratic Power of Discussion* (New York: Routledge, 2009).
51. The findings of this study are most extensively reported in M. Kent Jennings and Richard G. Niemi, *The Political Character of Adolescence: The Influence of Families and Schools* (Princeton, NJ: Princeton University Press, 1974); and M. Kent Jennings and Richard G. Niemi, *Generations and Politics* (Princeton, NJ: Princeton University Press, 1981).
52. The trust in government scale includes four measures consistently included in the American National Election Studies surveys: How much do you trust the government to do what is right? Is the government run by a few big interests or for the benefit of all the people? How much does the federal government waste tax money? How many government officials are crooked? The scale ranges from 0 (low trust) to 100 (high trust).
53. James L. Gibson, "Homosexuals and the Ku Klux Klan: A Contextual Analysis of Political Tolerance," *Political Research Quarterly* 40 (September 1987): 427–48; Herbert McClosky and Amanda Brill, *Dimensions of Tolerance* (New York: Russell Sage Foundation, 1983); John L. Sullivan et al., *Political Tolerance and American Democracy*.
54. George E. Marcus et al., *With Malice toward Some*.
55. Jeffrey J. Mondak, *Personality and the Foundations of Political Behavior* (New York: Cambridge University Press, 2010).
56. See, for example, Jeffrey J. Mondak, Matthew V. Hibbing, Damarys Canache, Mitchell A. Seligson, and Mary R. Anderson, "Personality and Civic Engagement: An Integrative Framework for the Study of Trait Effects on Political Behavior," *American Political Science Review* 104 (February 2010): 85–110.
57. Kevin B. Smith, Douglas R. Oxley, Matthew V. Hibbing, John R. Alford, and John R. Hibbing, "Linking Genetics and Political Attitudes: Reconceptualizing

Political Ideology," *Political Psychology* 32 (June 2011): 369–97; Carolyn L. Funk, Kevin B. Smith, John R. Alford, Matthew V. Hibbing, Nicholas R. Eaton, Robert F. Krueger, Lindon J. Eaves, and John R. Hibbing, "Genetic and Environmental Transmission of Political Orientations," *Political Psychology*, published electronically October 17, 2012. doi 10.1111/j.1467-9221.2012.00915.x.

58. See, for example, Leonie Huddy et al., "Threat, Anxiety, and Support of Antiterrorism Policies"; Leonie Huddy, Stanley Feldman, and Christopher Weber, "The Political Consequences of Perceived Threat and Felt Insecurity," *Annals of the American Academy of Political and Social Science* 614 (November 2007): 131–53.

59. Thomas E. Nelson, Rosalee A. Clawson, and Zoe M. Oxley, "Media Framing of a Civil Liberties Conflict and Its Effect on Tolerance," *American Political Science Review* 91 (September 1997): 567–83.

60. Congressional Budget Office, "Trends in the Distribution of Household Income Between 1979 and 2007" (October 2011), http://www.cbo.gov/publication/42729.

Suggested Readings

Almond, Gabriel, and Sidney Verba. *The Civic Culture.* Princeton, NJ: Princeton University Press, 1963. A classic study of political culture in five nations, including the United States.

Baldi, Stephane, Marianne Perie, Dan Skidmore, Elizabeth Greenberg, Carole Hahn, and Dawn Nelson. *What Democracy Means to Ninth-Graders: U.S. Results from the International IEA Civic Education Study.* Washington, DC: National Center for Educational Statistics, U.S. Department of Education, 2001. An interesting political socialization study as part of a multination project. For more information, see nces.ed.gov/pubsearch/pubsinfo.asp?pubid=2001096.

Herrnson, Paul S., Richard G. Niemi, Michael J. Hanmer, Benjamin B. Bederson, Frederick G. Conrad, and Michael Traugott. *Voting Technology: The Not-So-Simple Act of Casting a Ballot.* Washington, DC: Brookings Institution, 2008. An in-depth look at voting systems and their impact on voters' ability to vote as they intended and their confidence in voting.

Hetherington, Marc J. *Why Trust Matters: Declining Political Trust and the Demise of American Liberalism.* Princeton, NJ: Princeton University Press, 2005. An important study of the policy implications of declining trust.

Hibbing, John R., and Elizabeth Theiss-Morse. *Stealth Democracy: Americans' Beliefs about How Government Should Work.* Cambridge, England: Cambridge University Press, 2002. A provocative analysis of the public's attitudes toward American political processes.

Marcus, George E., John L. Sullivan, Elizabeth Theiss-Morse, and Sandra L. Wood. *With Malice toward Some.* Cambridge, England: Cambridge University Press, 1995. An innovative study of the public's tolerance of unpopular groups.

McClosky, Herbert, and John Zaller. *The American Ethos.* Cambridge, MA: Harvard University Press, 1984. An analysis of the public's attitudes toward democracy and capitalism.

Morrell, Michael E. *Empathy and Democracy: Feeling, Thinking, and Deliberation.* University Park: Pennsylvania State University Press, 2010. An intriguing examination of the role empathy plays in the functioning of democracy.

Putnam, Robert D. *Bowling Alone: The Collapse and Revival of American Community.* New York: Simon & Schuster, 2000. An analysis of the decline of participation in civic affairs.

Skocpol, Theda, and Morris P. Fiorina, eds. *Civic Engagement in American Democracy.* Washington, DC: Brookings Institution, 1999. A collection of readings on civic engagement in historical perspective.

Stimson, James A. *The Tides of Consent: How Public Opinion Shapes American Politics.* Cambridge, England: Cambridge University Press, 2004. Mainly about policy views and their impact, but also an interesting discussion of trust in government.

Verba, Sidney, Kay L. Schlozman, and Henry E. Brady. *Voice and Equality: Civic Voluntarism in American Politics.* Cambridge, England: Cambridge University Press, 1995. A survey of various forms of political participation, their determinants, and their impact on representative democracy.

Internet Resources

The website of the American National Election Studies, www.electionstudies.org, offers extensive data on topics covered in this chapter. Click on "Utilities" and then choose "The ANES Guide to Public Opinion and Electoral Behavior." Scroll down to "Support for the Political System." Some of the attitudinal data cover 1952 to the present. For every political item, there is a breakdown for each social characteristic in every election year.

If you have access through your school, click on "The Roper Center for Public Opinion Research." Click on "iPOLL Databank" and then follow the sign-in instructions, which have a keyword search capability. You will find hundreds—perhaps thousands—of items related to political culture from surveys taken from the 1930s to the present.

For a rich collection of data on American ninth graders, see the Civic Education Study, www.terpconnect.umd.edu/~jtpurta/.

C h a p t e r   T w o

Electoral Context and Strategy

"POLITICAL SCIENTISTS ARE KILLING the campaign narrative"; at least that is what Francis Wilkinson's column on Bloomberg.com in late September of 2012 claimed.[1] The tongue-in-cheek essay noted that as journalists were searching for misguided, but dramatic, narratives to promote about how Republican presidential nominee Mitt Romney's campaign could devise a new strategy to turn his fortunes around, political scientists had "established camp on the banks of the Web, from which [they take] aim at whatever diaphanous journalistic concoctions float past." Though political campaigns do affect the outcomes of elections and journalists do play an important role in informing the public and shaping expectations, Wilkinson's column cast a revealing light on the importance of understanding the factors that are *most likely* to explain campaign outcomes compared to the explanations created by media and political operatives for what happens on Election Day.

This chapter examines how economic and political conditions give us a baseline from which to understand elections in American politics, how the rules that govern elections can influence the outcome, and the basic strategic choices candidates and other interested groups make in an election season. Thus, this chapter serves as a lens through which we can think about how the political behavior of the American electorate works. Everything else that we analyze in this book—political partisanship, public opinion, group characteristics and social identity, the media, and the elements of individual vote choice—do not occur in a vacuum. Rather, they take place in a specific context, a context that, properly understood, can help us to make fairly accurate predictions about election results months before any ballots are cast. As is the case throughout the book, we will use examples from the 2012 election and data showing trends over time to illustrate our points.

48

The Fundamentals

Perhaps it was his experience as a basketball player. Perhaps it was his political instincts. Perhaps it was a keen understanding of electoral history. Or maybe it was just a public pander. Whatever it was, one of the most prescient predictions about the importance fundamental economic conditions would play in affecting the result of the 2012 presidential election was made by Barack Obama about one month into his first term as commander in chief. Obama told *Today*'s Matt Lauer, "If I don't have this [improving the economy] done in three years, then there's gonna be a one-term proposition."[2]

The popular punditry's understanding of the state of the economy suggested that a one-term proposition was a likely outcome in November of 2012. Even Charlie Cook of the venerable *Cook Political Report* wondered how the 2012 race between Barack Obama and Mitt Romney was close given that "incumbents generally don't get reelected with (economic) numbers" like those tied to the president's record.[3] However, a more complete understanding of the role that the most valuable indicators of the state of the economy, political partisanship, and presidential approval actually play in predicting election results suggested that—absent major campaign effects or a stunning, unpredictable event—President Obama would narrowly hold on to the White House. As we noted in the introduction of this book, one election forecast made in August of 2011, using a prediction about what economic growth would look like in 2012, predicted that Barack Obama would win 50.9 percent of the popular vote, just barely short of the president's actual total.[4] Recall that this prediction came before Mitt Romney was the Republican nominee and far before most Americans had ever heard of eventual vice presidential nominee Paul Ryan. In a world of campaign war rooms, instantaneous media coverage, billions of dollars of television advertising, dramatic debates, raucous campaign rallies, gaffes, special interest spending, and messaging, can a few elements of data correctly predict the winner of almost every election of the past 60 years months before any ballots are counted?

Historically, the American people have responded to a growing economy by awarding the incumbent or the incumbent's political party another term in the White House. A clear relationship exists between the growth in the nation's gross domestic product (GDP) (and/or the real disposable income per capita [RDI]) and the percentage of the two-party vote earned by the incumbent's party in presidential elections. People generally reward the occupant of 1600 Pennsylvania Avenue at the ballot box when the economy is on the rise. Figure 2-1 suggests a linear relationship with a growing GDP from January to

FIGURE 2-1   GDP Growth, Unemployment, and the Popular Vote for
             Presidential Candidates of the Incumbent's Party, 1952–2012

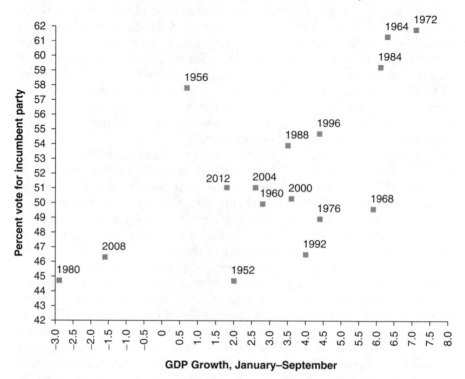

Source: GDP data from U.S. Department of Commerce Bureau of Economic Analysis, National
Economic Accounts, Gross Domestic Product, at http://www.bea.gov/national/; presidential voting data from John Woolley and Gerhard Peters, The American Presidency Project, at
http://www.presidency.ucsb.edu/elections.php.

September of the election year and an increase in the incumbent party's share of the two-party presidential vote. If we look at just 1956,
1964, 1972, 1980, 1984, 1992, 1996, 2004, and 2012 (the years the
incumbent president himself was seeking reelection), the relationship
is even stronger than it is for years when a presidential hopeful from
the same party is running for president.

    There are exceptions to this rule. Figure 2-1 shows that the econ-
omy was growing in 1976 when President Gerald Ford lost to Democrat
Jimmy Carter. In 1992, the economy was actually rebounding out of the
recession that doomed President George H. W. Bush's reelection bid
when Bill Clinton rode his "it's the economy, stupid" campaign strategy
and the strong showing of third-party candidate Ross Perot into the

Oval Office. But in general, a growing economy is good for the president seeking reelection. Indeed, of the sixteen presidential elections examined in Figure 2-1 only five saw the incumbent or incumbent's party earn less than 50 percent of the popular vote if the economy was growing at all.

Not all economic indicators are created equal, however. GDP and RDI are generally good estimators that help predict election results. Some popular data providing evidence about the economy is less well suited to the task of helping students of American politics understand elections. For example, hundreds of stories were written about how the nation's high unemployment in 2011 and 2012 spelled disaster for Obama. However, unemployment has what former *New York Times* election blogger Nate Silver called a "maddening" relationship with election results. For example, unemployment was relatively high (over 7 percent) for Ronald Reagan's popular and electoral vote thumping of Walter Mondale during Reagan's reelection victory in 1984. Unemployment *rose* from the beginning of the terms to Election Day for Dwight Eisenhower's 1956 reelection victory, Richard Nixon's reelection in 1972, and George W. Bush's reelection in 2004.[5] Unemployment actually dropped during Jimmy Carter's term, but he was not able to defend the White House from Ronald Reagan's advances.

Unemployment rates are certainly an important indicator about the health of the economy, but they are not highly correlated with presidential election results. Even so, a great deal of media coverage of the 2012 contest was quick to point out that one "reason" that Obama was in trouble was that no president in the post–World War II era had ever won reelection with an unemployment rate above 7.4 percent. Of course, and much to the dismay of both of the authors of this book, no one in the history of humankind has ever won any election after the Minnesota Vikings won the Super Bowl.[6] To wit, some claims are factually accurate without being substantively meaningful.

Gas prices are also a popular indicator of the state of the economy. Republican presidential primary candidate Newt Gingrich went as far as to promise that gas prices would drop to $2.50 per gallon if he were elected president, something that even HBO's *The Newsroom* mocked in its dramatic, fictional treatment of the 2012 campaign in which the anchorman character Will McAvoy pointed out the president does not control gas prices. On a more serious note, political scientist Andrew Gelman has argued that while rising gas prices can affect presidential approval, they are not a major player in predicting presidential elections.[7]

Amid frustrations of high unemployment, rising gas prices, a controversial stimulus bill, the political battle over health care reform, and an unpopular "bailout" of the nation's financial system, a growing economy was what President Obama had entering the 2012 reelection campaign.

When he had taken office in 2009, however, the economy was, by most accounts, in shambles. Consumer sentiment was nearly at an all-time low, the housing market was in a free fall, the auto industry had reached a crisis point, unemployment was almost at 10 percent, and the stock market had plunged about six thousand points over the previous three years. Though the nation's longest recession in the post-World War II era officially ended in June of 2009, many Americans thought that the nation was still experiencing negative economic growth nearly a year later.[8]

Moreover, the president's own Democratic Party had just experienced a shellacking during the 2010 midterm elections. Gone was the Democrats' majority in the House of Representatives; their filibuster-proof majority in the U.S. Senate was a distant memory as well. Senate Majority Leader Mitch McConnell, a Republican from Kentucky, noted that the filibuster would become standard operating procedure to combat the president's agenda and that "the single most important thing we want to achieve is for President Obama to be a one-term president."[9] However, the nation's GDP was on the rise in 2011 and 2012. Unemployment, though not highly correlated with election results, was also dropping. Consumer sentiment certainly did not skyrocket, but it did remain steady over the first three years of Obama's presidency, partially a reflection of a public that was not very confident that things would be getting better anytime soon. In 2011, Obama; Washington, D.C., more generally; and major players in the nation's financial district took rhetorical and protest fire from a group calling itself Occupy Wall Street— a group fed up with the growing gap between the top 1 percent (from an economic perspective) of Americans and everyone else.

Still, the economy was growing, which suggested a narrow victory for the Obama campaign, all else equal. But the state of the economy is not the only "fundamental" factor that helps us predict election results. Presidential approval plays a key role in forecasting elections. It should not be terribly surprising that public approval of the job the president is doing has something to do with whether the president gets a chance at a second term. Figure 2-2 shows the relationship between presidential approval in an election year and the incumbent party's share of the two-party vote. If you recall from Figure 2-1 that there were five elections in which a growing economy was not enough for the incumbent party to earn 50 percent of the popular vote, a quick look at Figure 2-2 highlights the fundamental importance of presidential approval as an independent indicator of presidential elections. In 1952, President Truman left office with a 32 percent approval rating, which helped drag down the effect of a growing economy and allowed Dwight Eisenhower to win the election. It is true that in 1992, President George H. W. Bush lost some support to the surprisingly strong third-party candidacy of Ross Perot, but he was also hurt by a dismal approval rating. Gerald Ford, who was appointed (not elected) to be vice president and ascended into the Oval Office after Richard Nixon resigned in disgrace, presided over a booming growth in GDP, but his pardoning of Nixon and problems with high inflation sank his approval rating and his bid for a presidential victory in his own right. Hubert Humphrey has been blamed for underperforming as a candidate, but his commander in chief, Lyndon Johnson, only had the approval of 41 percent of the country in 1968. The only other case, the election of 1960, is considered later in the section about strategy.

With respect to presidential approval in 2012, according to John Sides and Lynn Vavreck, President Obama had an advantage—an advantage that presidents normally would not have given the middling state of the 2011–2012 American economy. Sides and Vavreck used economic data to forecast what President Obama's approval rating would be throughout his first term and compared the predictions to what his approval rating actually was. They found that Obama's approval rating

FIGURE 2-2   Presidential Approval and the Two-Party Presidential Vote for the Incumbent Party, 1952–2012

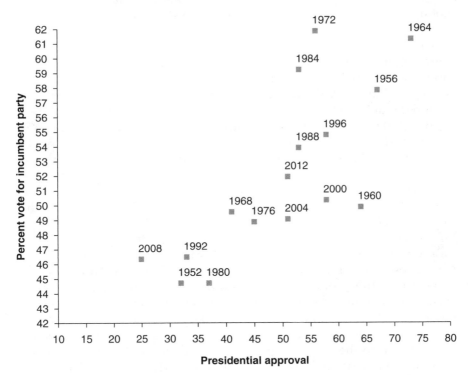

Source: Presidential approval and vote share data are from John Woolley and Gerhard Peters, The American Presidency Project, Presidential Job Approval, http://www.presidency.ucsb .edu/data/popularity.php.

was about three percentage points higher than it "should" have been, if the economic data were enough to correctly estimate public attitudes about the president's job performance.[10]

How did Obama overcome a sluggish economy to enjoy a higher approval rating than his average predecessor? In short, people liked him. Despite a bevy of broadcasts and print stories about a president who was cold, aloof, and not nearly as likable in person as he was when giving a speech to a large television audience, the public gave the president high marks on personal warmth and empathy. Obama also avoided quick boosts and drops in his approval rating, the major exception being the short-lived five-point bump he received after terrorist leader Osama bin Laden was killed.

In addition to the public's strong personal evaluations of the president, Obama's approval rating did not drop as much as many of his predecessors' ratings did in their first terms because of the increasing polarization of the American public. To be sure, Republicans did not approve of the job the president was doing, but Democrats were more united than normal in their approval of Obama's performance in office. This helped to keep his approval rating a bit higher than normal, strong enough to give him a good chance of winning reelection.

Additionally, Americans were not united in their belief that Obama was responsible for the sorry state of the economy. Many Americans were willing to blame former President George W. Bush for the economic woes befalling the country during Obama's first term. A Gallup survey in June of 2012 revealed that while 52 percent of Americans believed that Barack Obama deserved either a "great deal" or "moderate amount" of blame for the state of the economy, 68 percent said the same about Bush.[11] Thus, the normal blow that a sluggish economy might strike to a reelection campaign was blunted a bit, but only a bit. The fundamentals in 2012 forecasted an Obama victory, but a narrow one at best. The 2012 election was certainly a contest that could be decided by the quality of the campaigns, news coverage, and the behavior of the American electorate.

In addition to economic fundamentals and those related to approval of the president, political fundamentals can influence election results. This is especially the case in congressional elections. Putting election results into the proper context requires understanding the political structure heading into the election and the complexion of the electorate within electoral boundaries like a congressional district or a state.

For an example of the political structure's influence on elections, we can turn to the 2010 congressional contests. The Democratic Party went into the 2010 midterms with a solid majority, holding 255 seats in the 435 member House of Representatives. Democrats had taken back both houses of Congress in 2006 and brought their party back into the

White House in 2008. However, one political fundamental of congressional elections is that both success in previous elections and the size of a party's majority in a house of Congress tends to beget more vulnerable seats in the *next* election. For example, 48 Democratically represented house districts voted for John McCain in the 2008 presidential election. Districts in which the congressional representative is of a different party than the district's preferred presidential candidate are generally the hardest to hold in midterm contests.

These "swing districts" are an example of how the partisan complexion of a district can affect election results. Since they often have an incumbent who represents a district in which the majority of voters identify with the opposite political party, more qualified challengers are often inspired to enter the race. In competitive districts in 2010, the Republican Party fielded more quality challengers (those who have previously held elective office) than ever before. Over 39 percent of Democratic representatives holding competitive seats faced a quality Republican challenger in 2010, compared to 28 percent in 2008. Regardless whether an incumbent faces a quality challenger, the fundamental truth is that a district's general ideology holds great predictive power in congressional elections. As we noted in our supplement to this volume, *Political Behavior in Midterm Elections, 2011 Edition*,[12] simply knowing whether a congressional district voted for Barack Obama or John McCain, and nothing else, correctly predicted the results of 85 percent of the races for the House of Representatives in 2010.

The Rules of the Game

One of the authors likes to play pickup basketball with fellow faculty members, graduate students, and understanding undergraduates who don't mind a slower game consisting of older players with rapidly diminishing skills. He is most valuable to his team when the game rewards three-point baskets (rather than counting all baskets by ones, which is a conventional way of scorekeeping in pickup games). This is because he is slow-footed, middle-aged, and short. When the rules of the game reward long-distance shooting, the one element of the game in which he has some skill, his teams are more likely to win. The rules of the game are important in the confines of pickup basketball at public universities, but they are even more important (and more consequential!) in the world of elections.

Election rules affect access to the ballot, the ability to participate in debates, the schedule of primary elections, the date of the general election, who can run for office, and what type of vote is most important (the popular vote or that of the Electoral College). Rules are especially important in primary elections. The Democratic and Republican Parties award their delegates differently, which leads to different campaign strategies in primary elections for candidates of both parties. The Democrats award their delegates proportionately (so long as the candidate wins above 15 percent of the popular vote in the primary) so that a candidate who wins 35 percent of the vote would win 35 percent of the delegates. Thus, it is in a Democratic candidate's interest to campaign hard in every state in which she or he might win enough of the vote to earn some delegates. The Texas primary/caucus is so unique that even though Hillary Clinton won more votes than Barack Obama in the 2008 Texas primary, his strong performance in the caucus there resulted in Obama winning more delegates. Some analysts attributed Obama's defeat of Clinton to his campaign's more strategic understanding of the party's rules regarding the awarding of delegates, especially in states that held caucuses rather than primaries. Democrats also can win "superdelegates"—typically, lawmakers and high-ranking officials in the party. These superdelegates are not bound to the popular vote in their state's primary when deciding which candidate they will vote for at the Democratic National Convention.

Some Republican primaries are winner-take-all. That is, whoever wins the most votes gets all the delegates. Other Republican primaries elect to award delegates on a proportional basis. The different rules for these primaries can affect the number of visits a candidate makes to a state, the size of an advertising buy in that state, and the media momentum a candidate might enjoy (or suffer) after all the votes are counted.

Regardless of how delegates are awarded, Marty Cohen, David Karol, Hans Noel, and John Zaller have persuasively argued that party leaders typically unite behind a candidate and when they do, that candidate becomes the nominee. To be sure, there are times when party leaders stay on the sidelines, perhaps wary of the risk involved in supporting a candidate who falters, but in general, even in the era of primary elections and caucuses, "the party decides" who their nominee will be for president. Even though the rules of party nominations have changed a great deal, the somewhat hidden "fundamental" of endorsements from party insiders plays a crucial role in selecting nominees for president.

Perhaps no other rule shapes presidential campaigns as much as the awarding of Electoral College votes. Forty-eight states award electoral votes on a winner-take-all basis. Nebraska and Maine give a candidate two electoral votes for winning the state's popular vote and one electoral vote for each congressional district the candidate wins. In 2008, Barack Obama won the 2nd congressional district in Nebraska, but lost the Cornhusker State's popular vote and the contests in the 1st and 3rd congressional districts, giving him one electoral vote from

Nebraska to John McCain's four. Obama's 2008 campaign manager David Plouffe called the history-making result in Nebraska's 2nd district his favorite electoral vote.

Given the Electoral College's structure, candidates spend the most amount of time in swing states that possess a large number of electoral votes. Even the most casual observer of American politics can name a few of the states that regularly enjoy a high volume of candidate visits and an even higher volume of campaign advertising—states such as Ohio, Florida, Wisconsin, Pennsylvania, Indiana, Michigan, and Virginia. A candidate must win 270 electoral votes to become the president. However unlikely it may be, given that there are 538 total electoral votes up for grabs, a 269 to 269 stalemate is possible.

Table 2-1 shows that while there is a correlation between electoral votes and popular votes, these two measures of campaign success are not the same. For example, John F. Kennedy earned more electoral votes than Jimmy Carter did in 1976 and George W. Bush did in 2004 even though Kennedy won less of the popular vote. Bill Clinton won more

TABLE 2-1   Popular Vote Percentage and Electoral Vote Count for the Winning Presidential Candidate, 1952–2012

Year	Popular vote (%)	Electoral College votes
1952	54.9	442
1956	57.4	457
1960	49.7	303
1964	61.1	486
1968	43.4	301
1972	60.7	520
1976	50.1	297
1980	50.7	489
1984	58.8	525
1988	53.4	426
1992	43.0	370
1996	49.2	379
2000	47.9	271
2004	50.7	286
2008	52.9	365
2012	51.1	332

Source: John Woolley and Gerhard Peters, The American Presidency Project, available at http://www.presidency.ucsb.edu/data.

electoral votes in 1992 than presidents in seven other elections—all seven of whom got a higher percentage of the popular vote than he did. Of course, you will recall that Clinton's share of the popular vote was diminished as he beat President George H. W. Bush *and* strong third-party candidate Ross Perot in that election. One reason political scientists are far more skeptical about declaring that a winning presidential candidate has a "mandate" is that Electoral College blowouts, like the ones in 2012, 1996, 1992, and 1980, mask much narrower victories in the popular vote.

Campaign finance rules are also important to understand. Individuals are limited in the amount of money they can give to a campaign, but candidates face no such limit, in terms of how much they spend or how much they can give themselves. Some, notably John Kerry in 2004 and Mitt Romney in 2008, have spent substantial amounts of their own money in (unsuccessful) bids for the White House. Self-financed candidates have been more successful in congressional races; John Corzine of New Jersey spent about $62 million of his own money (more than half of it in the primary election) to get to the Senate in 2000. Despite Corzine's victory, self-funded candidates are by no means guaranteed victory. Wrestling mogul Linda McMahon has spent nearly $100 million in unsuccessful bids for U.S. Senate seats in Connecticut.

In fact, enormous campaign spending by incumbent members of Congress, whether they are self-financed or financed conventionally by individuals and PACs, is negatively correlated with vote totals. This is because the more a member of Congress has to spend to get reelected, the more likely it is that she or he represents a swing district, is facing a stiff challenge, or both. In other words, the more money one has to spend to hold onto a congressional seat, the more danger that seat tends to be in during an election. On the other hand, plenty of incumbents who spend a ton of money do win reelection, and spending too much money is far preferable than not having enough to compete.

Though the rules of the game are difficult to change, the times that they are altered introduce greater uncertainty into our ability to understand how elections will work. One example of a recent major change comes from a controversy commonly referred to as "Citizens United." The Federal Election Commission (FEC) had objected to the airing of *Hillary: The Movie*, a movie critical of Hillary Clinton, within 30 days of the 2008 presidential primaries. The FEC claimed that the movie, produced by a nonprofit organization called Citizens United, was electioneering and thus prohibited by law to air the movie that close to an election. As we discussed in chapter 1, the Supreme Court's decision in *Citizens United v. Federal Election Commission* determined that while corporations and unions are not literal humans, they do have the constitutional right to free speech afforded to "associations of persons." Thus, banning corporations and unions from spending money to engage in electioneering at any point in a campaign was unconstitutional.

Citizens United, and other subsequent decisions from the Court, opened the door to major spending from political action committees (PACs) and "super PACs" such as Restore Our Future (which supported Mitt Romney) and Priorities USA Action (which supported Barack Obama) to the tune of $142 million and $65 million, respectively, in 2012.[13] PACs are outside groups not officially connected with a campaign. Spending was up in congressional races too, though it should be noted that independent expenditures began their rapid rise after the Bipartisan Campaign Finance Reform Act (BCRA) in 2002 and not after *Citizens United*. Regardless, it is worth asking whether all the spending was consequential. The early returns on that question suggest that the increases in spending did not do much to affect the result of the 2012 presidential election. But these rule changes are relatively new; it may take the parties, corporations, unions, and interest groups some time to learn how to use the new rules in the most effective way possible.

Figure 2-3 shows the total presidential and congressional expenditures in millions of dollars from 1976–2012. Before the BCRA was passed, the average increase in spending from one congressional election to the next was $34 million. The average increase after BCRA was $83.75 million. As Figure 2-3 shows, the difference on the presidential side is even greater. Prior to the BCRA, presidential elections were $34 million more expensive than the one before. After the campaign finance reform passed, they were $667.67 million more costly!

Strategy

Even if candidates can accurately assess whether the economic, partisan, and structural fundamentals favor themselves or their opponents, candidates and their advisers need to develop and execute strategies designed to help them win elections. Increasingly, these strategies—at least at the presidential level—appear to be rooted in empirical evidence regarding what drives voter turnout, who is most likely to be persuaded to change their vote, and where the most efficient use of television advertising might be located.

Given the crucial role that economic conditions play in affecting presidential and congressional elections, successful candidates are more likely to rely on economic messages when the economic fundamentals favor them and focus on meeting other criteria when the prevailing economic headwinds are bad news for their campaigns.

FIGURE 2-3   Total Presidential and Congressional Campaign Expenditures (in Millions), 1976–2012

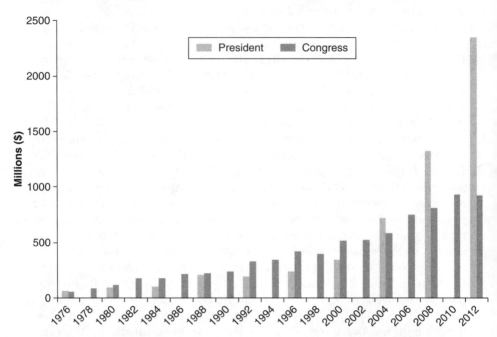

Source: Presidential campaign expenditures data from "Presidential Fundraising and Spending, 1976–2008," OpenSecrets.org, at http://www.opensecrets.org/pres08/totals.php, and for 2012 "2012 Presidential Race," OpenSecrets.org, at http://www.opensecrets.org/pres12/index.php; Congressional campaign expenditures data from "House Campaign Expenditures, 1974–2012," the Campaign Finance Institute, available at http://www.cfinst.org/data.aspx.

When candidates ignore a growing economy (recall Figure 2-1), as Vice President Richard Nixon did by focusing on foreign policy in his 1960 campaign against John F. Kennedy, opponents can use their media megaphone, as Kennedy did, to turn a potential strength into a problem area. Kennedy's focus on the decline in school quality, housing issues, and welfare helped propel him to victory, according to Lynn Vavreck.[14]

Candidates are often adept at ignoring issues they would rather not discuss in favor of issues that the campaign believes are a greater area of strength. As we note in chapter 7, candidates even do this in presidential debates, doing their best to reverse course on the topic of a question about a strategically disadvantageous issue to discuss an issue that fits the campaign's theme or area of strength.

Deciding on the issue content of campaigns is important at the congressional level as well. While constant press attention, millions of dollars in attack ads and the like make it difficult for presidential candidates to completely ignore a major issue on the campaign trail or in a debate, candidates in lower visibility races have a much easier time focusing on a small set of issues that are good for their campaign. Jamie Druckman and his colleagues have shown, via an analysis of campaign websites, a stunning lack of engagement between congressional campaigns on issues.[15] Simply put, candidates do not spend much time engaging in a back-and-forth debate over the same issues. Rather, they focus on an almost completely different set of issues, making it more difficult for the public to sort through which candidate is the best fit. Candidates tend to avoid engaging their opponent unless the issue is so salient to the voters that avoiding the issue would be campaign suicide.

How do candidates know upon which issues to base their campaigns? In chapter 7, we discuss the issue ownership and trait ownership hypotheses, which demonstrate that the public believes that one party handles particular issues better or exudes particular traits more than the other party. If candidates can get people to focus on the issues their party owns, they can improve their electoral outcomes. While it is difficult to steal issues from the opposing party, it is far easier to steal traits to improve their electoral fortunes. For example, though Democrats are viewed as the more empathetic party, George W. Bush ran for office in 2000 as a "compassionate conservative." While Republicans get higher marks from the public on the trait of strength, Barack Obama was fond of saying on the campaign trail, "We never throw the first punch, but we'll throw the last."[16]

In addition to searching for an issue focus, candidates work hard to get out the vote (GOTV). The Obama campaign's GOTV efforts in 2012 relied on the analysis of "big data," massive voter files that were merged with other bits of data exploring potential voters' previous voting behavior, party identification, spending habits, and, if known, favored candidate in 2012. After the campaign made predictions about which supporters were least likely to vote, they sent volunteers to knock on those people's doors, call them to remind them to vote, and send them mail that was tailored to their particular profile. The campaign even ran experiments to see whether volunteers were more successful at persuading undecided voters if the volunteer calling read a script about Obama's economic performance or asked the undecided voters which issues they wanted to discuss (the economic script performed better).

Candidates also must consider where to buy television advertisements and what to say in them. Contrary to advertisers who want to get their brand in front of as many eyes as possible, presidential campaigns are more interested in where their audience lives than in reaching the highest number of people. As you might have guessed, this means that candidates almost exclusively focus their advertising spending in a small number of states. In the last month of the presidential campaign, Barack Obama aired television ads in just over one-quarter of the country's media markets, ignoring the largest ones in New York City and Los Angeles. Mitt Romney aired ads in about one-third of the nation's markets over the course of the campaign, but his choices in the last month of the 2012 contest suggested that he spent money in places he should not have. In the summer and fall of 2012, Romney put ads up in 73 media markets, but was down to 50 in the final weeks of the campaign. Barack Obama aired ads in 62 markets, and was still airing them in 57 during the last month of the campaign.

Most congressional candidates who can afford television advertisements do not have to worry as much about where to air their ads. Many districts overlap into more than one media market, but typically, most of a district lies within a single market. Of course, the ranking of the market determines, in part, how expensive the advertisements will be. For example, in the 1st congressional district in Nebraska, the lone NBC station is in the Omaha media market, even though Omaha is located in the 2nd congressional district. Omaha is the 76th-ranked media market in the country, while Lincoln, located in the 1st district, is part of the 106th market, allowing Omaha stations to charge more for their ads. Thus, ads aired in 1st district races during the local and national news on the NBC affiliate reach far more voters who live outside the district than voters who live within the 1st district boundary while having the added problem of costing more precious campaign dollars.

The tone of the ads the candidates air is largely determined by the closeness of the race. A great deal of evidence shows that incumbents who are running against opponents who are not well-funded, have not held elective office, and so forth tend to air positive advertisements. Congressional incumbents typically air negative ads only in close races or after they have been attacked. However, well-financed candidates fearing future attacks may try to gain the upper hand by going negative first. In Wisconsin's 2012 senate race, Democrat Tammy Baldwin was on the air first with a series of ads blasting her opponent, Republican and former governor Tommy Thompson, as someone who is "not for you anymore." By the time Thompson got on the air to attack Baldwin, she had climbed ahead in the polls, eventually upsetting the popular Thompson in November.

In presidential races, the question is not whether to go negative, but how much. Kathleen Hall Jamieson makes a distinction between advertisements that purely attack the opponent and those that contrast the opponent's record or position on an issue with the candidate's own record or views.[17] Contrast ads made up about one-third of presidential advertisements from Barack Obama and Mitt Romney in 2012. Table 2-2 compares the tone of the advertising in the presidential races from 2004, 2008, and 2012 for a period from June 1 to October 21 in each election year. About 58 percent of Obama's ads were purely negative compared to about 50 percent of Romney's in 2012. Meanwhile, supporters of Obama and Romney saw little value in anything but negativity. Seventy-eight percent of ads aired by Democratic groups and 89 percent of ads from Republicans groups were purely negative.[18] Table 2-2 shows that Obama aired 15 percent more negative ads in 2012—a tighter race than 2008—and nearly 23 percent fewer positive ads. Romney was exactly as negative in 2012 as McCain was in 2008, but Romney aired more contrast ads and fewer positive ones than McCain.

Despite some of these differences, both Romney and Obama and McCain and Obama were more negative than anything else in their paid advertising. In 2004, John Kerry's strategy was to be positive. Over 55 percent of Kerry's ads were positive and only about 3 percent were purely negative. Most of Kerry's ads that said something bad about

TABLE 2-2   Tone of Presidential Campaign Advertisements, by Sponsor, 2004–2012 (June 1–October 21)

2012	Positive %	Contrast %	Negative %
Obama 2012	14.4	27.0	58.5
Romney 2012	20.4	30.0	49.2
Democratic groups	<1.0	21.7	78.2
Republican groups	2.9	8.0	89.2
2008	Positive	Contrast	Negative
Obama 2008	37.0	19.7	43.2
McCain 2008*	24.0	26.7	49.2
Democratic groups	4.0	32.7	63.3
Republican groups	0.3	1.0	98.7
2004	Positive	Contrast	Negative
Kerry 2004*	55.8	41.6	2.7
Bush 2004*	27.4	17.0	55.4
Democratic groups	0.3	14.4	85.3
Republican groups	14.8	39.7	45.5

Source: Percentages are based on an analysis of broadcast television and national cable spots. Totals in 2012 are based on ongoing Wesleyan Media Project coding of Kantar/CMAG presidential ad airings available at http://mediaproject.wesleyan.edu/data-access/. Totals for 2004 and 2008 are from the Wisconsin Advertising Project available at http://wiscadproject.wisc.edu/download.php.

*Coordinated party ads are included here.

George W. Bush also included contrasting elements of Kerry's plans for the future. With a growing economy and a reasonably popular president, this was a questionable strategy. President Bush, on the other hand, was more negative than Romney, McCain, and Obama in 2008, but slightly less negative than Obama in 2012.

Candidates also want to find new ways to reach voters, especially potential voters. The Obama campaign tried to reach out to young voters in a variety of ways in 2008 and 2012. Whether announcing Obama's choice of Joe Biden for his running mate to his supporters via text message, offering drawings for dinners with actors like George Clooney or Sarah Jessica Parker for those who donated to the campaign, or drawing for dinner with the president himself, the Obama campaign worked hard to energize potential donors. Both campaigns maintained a strong social media presence on their own websites, Facebook pages, and Twitter accounts. Candidates uploaded their advertisements and many video messages made by supporters to YouTube so that supporters could share the messages quickly and easily. Research from James Fowler shows that Facebook itself could be a mobilizer to vote.[19] Those people who received Facebook messages that it was Election Day or news that some of their friends had voted were more likely to turn out to vote themselves. Surely, campaigns will carefully study the findings from this research to figure out how to harness the potential power of social media in the 2014 midterm elections and the 2016 presidential election.

Campaigns spend an enormous amount of resources on advertising, but they also pay for pollsters, consultants, advance staff, administrative staff, yard signs, stickers, buttons, travel, and more. When one of the authors asked a top Obama campaign staffer about why the campaign was trying so many different strategies to reach voters, he replied, "We know that some of these things are working, but we aren't 100% sure about which ones they are. So we'll keep doing them all."

The Unexpected

Campaigns cannot plan for everything. Much of the day-to-day life of the campaign falls outside considerations of how closely the strategic messaging hews to the latest relevant economic data. Rather, campaigns spend a great deal of time responding to press inquiries, moves made by their opponent, and dealing with problems and opportunities they had not anticipated. It is highly unlikely that Barack Obama thought he would spend much of the last weeks of his last campaign talking about Big Bird, but after Mitt Romney said, "I'm going to stop the subsidy to PBS. . . . I like Big Bird. I like you [debate moderator and PBS anchor

Jim Lehrer]," the Internet was aflutter with Photoshopped pictures like the one of a laughing Romney with the caption, "Obama got bin Laden, I'll get Big Bird!" Obama struck while the iron was hot and inserted a paragraph about the oversized, yellow-feathered friend of *Sesame Street* watchers everywhere into his stump speech.

Sometimes, the unexpected events fit well with the theme a campaign is trying to portray. Though unemployment was high in 2012, it continued to drop throughout the summer and fall. Republicans argued that the unemployment rate was just another example of the failed promise of Obama's policies. Obama argued that the slow but sure recovery was proof positive that his policies were working and that to turn back now risked great peril for the nation. Indeed, the volunteer phone calls to undecided voters referenced above began by noting how difficult the situation the president inherited was and how long it had taken to begin digging out of the hole that the campaign claimed was caused by President Bush. While the administration could not directly control what the unemployment numbers would be each month, the slowly falling rate fit with their narrative about the economy.

In 2008, both Hillary Clinton in the Democratic primary campaign and John McCain and Sarah Palin in the general election painted a picture of then-Senator Obama as an elitist who was out of touch with "real Americans." When audio surfaced late in the primaries of Obama saying that some people would "cling to guns or religion or antipathy to people who aren't like them" in difficult times, his opponents were quick to jump on the gaffe as an example of the "real Obama." However, the kerfuffle did not affect Obama's campaign for long.

Of course, the cratering of the nation's economy was the major event of the 2008 campaign. John McCain filled in his own narrative that he was a "maverick" by suspending his campaign and calling for a postponement of a debate with Barack Obama. Obama countered that there are no timeouts for the president and that chief executives have to deal with many problems at once. McCain relented and participated in the debate, which helped amplify Obama's efforts to steal the "strength" trait owned by Republicans.

A few days before the 2004 election, Osama bin Laden released a video taking responsibility for the September 11 attacks against the United States. The video might have reminded voters that they gave high marks to President George W. Bush on his handling of the war on terror even though an increasing number of voters were critical of his leadership of the war in Iraq. Meanwhile, trying to drum up votes in Ohio, Bush's opponent John Kerry went hunting and was widely ridiculed for pandering to rural voters as the photos from that event showed Kerry, who had an F rating from the National Rifle Association, decked out in full camouflage, which was consistent with the Bush team's argument that Kerry was a flip-flopper who would say anything to get elected.

Perhaps the most well-known media event from the 2012 campaign was the secret video taken of Mitt Romney referring to the "47 percent" of voters who would not be voting for the Grand Old Party in 2012. The video and subsequent coverage fit into the Obama campaign's argument that Romney was a wealthy, heartless businessman who would leave middle America behind. Although Romney later offered an apology for the comment, it largely fell on deaf ears.

Understanding Fundamentals and Winning Elections

After billions of dollars of spending and nearly two years of campaigning, Barack Obama won every swing state but North Carolina. In fact, the swing states were not even that close. Except for Ohio, Virginia, and Florida, Obama won the hotly contested states comfortably. Obama won the popular vote by a margin suggested by most preelection forecasts that relied on fundamental economic data. The congressional elections largely followed suit as the Republicans comfortably held onto the U.S. House of Representatives as predicted and the Democrats maintained a slim majority in the U.S. Senate. This is not to say that the campaigns did not matter. Each campaign turned out an enormous number of voters, had evidence that they had persuaded fence-sitters to their side, and thought that they were going to win on Election Day. In the end, the Obama team had a better understanding of fundamentals, was more adept at using the rules of the game, and used unforeseen events to its advantage more than did the Romney campaign. In the remainder of the book, we take detailed looks at the context of these conclusions. We also engage in examinations, over time, of American political behavior and public attitudes. While the rest of the book analyzes American partisanship, public opinion, group identities and social characteristics, media use, and determinants of vote choice, keep in mind that each of those factors occurs in the context of the framework described in this chapter.

Notes

1. Francis Wilkinson, "Political Scientists Are Killing the Campaign 'Narrative,'" *Bloomberg.com*, September 28, 2012, http://www.bloomberg.com/news/2012-09-28/political-scientists-are-killing-the-campaign-narrative-.html.
2. Barack Obama, interview with Matt Lauer, *The Today Show*, NBC, February 2, 2009.

3. Quoted in John Sides, "Why Is It So Hard to Get the Fundamentals Right?" *The Monkey Cage* (blog), August 24, 2012, http://themonkeycage.org/2012/08/24/why-is-it-so-hard-to-get-the-fundamentals-right/.
4. Seth Masket, "Using Economic Projections to Make Vote Projections," *Enik Rising* (blog), August 15, 2011, http://enikrising.blogspot.com/2011/08/using-economic-projections-to-make-vote.html.
5. Nate Silver, "On the Maddeningly Inexact Relationship between Unemployment and Re-Election," *FiveThirtyEight* (blog), *New York Times,* June 2, 2011, http://fivethirtyeight.blogs.nytimes.com/2011/06/02/on-the-maddeningly-inexact-relationship-between-unemployment-and-re-election/?_r=0.
6. Something the Vikings have never done.
7. John Sides, "The Political Consequences of Gas Prices," March 12, 2012, *The Monkey Cage* (blog), http://themonkeycage.org/2012/03/12/the-political-consequences-of-gas-prices/.
8. Neil Irwin and Nia-Malika Henderson, "Obama Answers Skeptics after Recession Is Declared Officially Over," *Washington Post,* September 21, 2010, http://www.washingtonpost.com/wp-dyn/content/article/2010/09/20/AR2010092005999.html.
9. Chris Cillizza, "Kentucky Senate Race Spending Could Top $100 Million," *Washington Post,* August 11, 2013, http://articles.washingtonpost.com/2013-08-11/politics/41299737_1_state-alison-lundergan-grimes-elizabeth-warren-massachusetts-race.
10. John Sides and Lynn Vavreck, *The Gamble: Choice and Chance in the 2012 Election* (Princeton, NJ: Princeton University Press, 2012), e-book chapter "The Hand You're Dealt," made available before the book was published.
11. Frank Newport, "Americans Still Blame Bush More Than Obama for Bad Economy," *Gallup Politics,* June 14, 2012, http://www.gallup.com/poll/155177/Americans-Blame-Bush-Obama-Bad-Economy.aspx?utm_source=alert&utm_medium=email&utm_campaign=syndication&utm_content=morelink&utm_term=Politics.
12. Elizabeth Theiss-Morse, Michael W. Wagner, William H. Flanigan, and Nancy H. Zingale, *Political Behavior in Midterm Elections, 2011 Edition* (Washington, DC: CQ Press, 2011).
13. "Super Pacs," OpenSecrets.org, http://www.opensecrets.org/pacs/superpacs.php.
14. Lynn Vavreck, *The Message Matters: The Economy and Presidential Campaigns* (Princeton, NJ: Princeton University Press, 2009).
15. James N. Druckman, Cari Lynn Hennessy, Martin J. Kifer, and Michael Parkin, "Issue Engagement on Congressional Candidate Web Sites," *Social Science Computer Review* 28, no. 1 (2010): 3–23.
16. "Obama: 'We Don't Throw the First Punch, But We'll Throw the Last,'" *Huff-Politics Blog, Huffington Post,* October 6, 2008, http://www.huffingtonpost.com/2008/10/06/post_169_n_132323.html.
17. Kathleen Hall Jamieson, conversation with Bill Moyers, *Bill Moyers Journal,* PBS, February 29, 2008, http://www.pbs.org/moyers/journal/02292008/profile.html.
18. "2012 Shatters 2004 and 2008 Records for Total Ads Aired," Wesleyan Media Project, October 24, 2012, http://mediaproject.wesleyan.edu/2012/10/24/2012-shatters-2004-and-2008-records-for-total-ads-aired/.

19. Robert M. Bond, Christopher J. Fariss, Jason J. Jones, Adam D. I. Kramer, Cameron Marlow, Jaime E. Settle, and James H. Fowler, "A 61-Million-Person Experiment in Social Influence and Political Mobilization," *Nature* 489 (September 13, 2012): 295–98, available at http://www.nature.com/nature/journal/v489/n7415/abs/nature11421.html.

Suggested Readings

Issenberg, Sasha. *The Victory Lab: The Secret Science of Winning Campaigns.* New York: Crown, 2012. An accessible account of the "analytical revolution" in campaign management.

Shaw, Daron R. *The Race to 270: The Electoral College and the Campaign Strategies of 2000 and 2004.* Chicago: University of Chicago Press, 2006. A careful treatment of how and why Republicans and Democrats targeted specific media markets in presidential campaigns.

Sides, John and Lynn Vavreck. *The Gamble: Choice and Chance in 2012 Election.* Princeton, NJ: Princeton University Press, 2013. A fascinating empirical account of the 2012 campaign written and published largely in "real time"—at least by academic standards!

Theiss-Morse, Elizabeth, Michael W. Wagner, William H. Flanigan, and Nancy H. Zingale. *Political Behavior in Midterm Elections, 2011 Edition.* Washington, DC: CQ Press, 2011. A short and readable scholarly take on the 2010 midterm elections.

C h a p t e r   T h r e e

Turnout and Elections

I<small>N EVERY</small> election cycle, stories in the media question who and how many will vote. Are potential Obama voters in 2012 as fired up as they were in 2008? Are they fired up enough to vote? Can Mitt Romney get his base to the polls? Will Hispanics vote in higher numbers than expected? What about women? What about youth? Voter turnout is a major strategic concern for candidates running for office. Elections can be won or lost by getting one's supporters to the polls and keeping the opponent's supporters at home on Election Day. It is no surprise, then, that campaigns expend a great deal of time and energy in get-out-the-vote (GOTV) efforts to encourage their supporters to vote while trying to dampen enthusiasm for the opponent.

The activity surrounding GOTV efforts in any given election occurs against the backdrop of historically anemic turnout rates in the United States over the past fifty years. Turnout rates declined dramatically after 1960, leading many commentators to worry about the future of American democracy and many scholars to examine what was going on. Two major explanations were the focus of this research: institutional impediments to voting and individual-level attitudes that might increase or decrease turnout. We look at historical trends in voter turnout and at the institutional and attitudinal factors that affect whether people vote or not. We also address mobilization efforts by political parties and candidates and their impact on turnout.

While turnout is obviously important in a democracy, the American electorate can participate in many other ways that can have an impact on elections. Americans can donate money to a campaign, put a sign in their yard or a bumper sticker on their car, make telephone calls on behalf of a candidate, go door-to-door canvassing for a candidate, write letters to the editor supporting a candidate, and so on. We therefore examine in this chapter not only who votes but who gets involved more actively in campaigns.

Turnout in American Elections

One of the most persistent complaints about the current American electoral system is its failure to achieve the high rates of voter turnout found in other countries and common in the United States in the nineteenth century. U.S. voter turnout was close to 80 percent before 1900; modern democracies around the world frequently record similarly high levels. Turnout in the United States over the past one hundred years, in contrast, has exceeded 60 percent only in presidential elections, and it has exceeded that low threshold only twice since 1960.

These unfavorable comparisons are somewhat misleading. The *voting turnout rate* is the percentage of the eligible population that votes in a particular election (the number of voters divided by the number of eligible voters). This seems straightforward, but it isn't. As Michael McDonald and Samuel Popkin point out, most reports on voter turnout use the voting age population (VAP) as the denominator rather than the voting eligible population (VEP).[1] Not all people who are of voting age are eligible to vote because of state laws restricting voting to, for example, U.S. citizens and people who fulfill residency requirements. The voting turnout rate is ideally calculated taking into account all state-level restrictions. When the denominator includes the VAP rather than the VEP, the turnout rate appears lower than it actually is because the denominator is inflated. On the flip side, in some states, blacks, women, and eighteen-year-olds were given the right to vote before suffrage was extended to them nationwide by the Fifteenth, Nineteenth, and Twenty-Sixth Amendments to the U.S. Constitution. Since the Constitution originally left it up to the states to determine voter eligibility, states varied in who they let vote. Not including these groups in the denominator when they were actually eligible to vote within their states makes the turnout rate in earlier years appear higher than it actually was because of a deflated denominator.

Determining the numerator in the turnout rate is also surprisingly difficult. The total number of ballots cast throughout the country is unknown; some states report the total vote only for particular races. For example, not included are those who went to the polls but skipped the presidential race or who inadvertently invalidated their ballots. This "undercount" of votes cast also reduces the estimate of turnout. Most often, the number of votes cast for the highest office on the ballot is used as the numerator, but this method could miss some votes.

Michael McDonald, who runs the United States Election Project at George Mason University, has attempted to calculate turnout more accurately by correcting both the numerator and the denominator of the official figures on a state-by-state basis from 1980 through 2012. The turnout rate is slightly higher when total ballots cast, rather than total votes for the highest office, is used, but the difference is usually less than 1 percentage point. The most pronounced difference comes from using the VEP instead of the VAP, especially when looking at recent elections. The VEP-based turnout rate in the 1980s was about 2 percentage points higher than the VAP-based turnout rate. This difference increased to just under 5 percentage points in 2004, 2008, and 2012, largely due to both an increase in the number of noncitizens and an increase in the number of ineligible felons. In 1980, 3.5 percent of the U.S. population was made up of noncitizens, and just over 800,000 were ineligible felons. By 2012, 8.5 percent of the population was noncitizens, and 3.25 million were ineligible felons.[2] Rather than the official VAP turnout rate of 53.6 percent in 2012, the VEP turnout rate was 58.2. Turnout tends to be low in the United States compared to other established democracies, but it is not as low as official statistics suggest.

Despite the difficulties in estimating turnout, the data in Figure 3-1 show that dramatic shifts in the rate of voter turnout have occurred over time. During the nineteenth century, national turnout appears to have been extremely high—always more than 70 percent. The biggest drop in turnout occurred after 1896, especially in the South but also in the non-South. The steep drop in the South from 1900 to 1916 is in part attributable to the restrictions placed on African American voting and to the increasing one-party domination of the region. In many southern states, whoever won the Democratic primary won the general election, making turnout in the primary much more important than turnout in the general election.

Political maneuverings in the South, however, cannot explain the decline in turnout in the non-South that occurred at about the same time. While the Republican Party became dominant in the non-South, leading to less competition and therefore less interest in general elections, the Progressive-era reforms of the late 1800s and early 1900s likely affected turnout rates across the United States.[3] Party organizations in the latter part of the 1800s "delivered" or "voted" substantial numbers of voters, by party loyalists casting multiple votes, "voting tombstones" (dead people), or buying votes. The decline of stable party voting in the early twentieth century coincides with attacks on political corruption and party machines. These electoral reforms included the introduction of the secret, or Australian, ballot and the imposition of a system of voter registration.[4] Prior to the electoral reforms, voters were given distinctively colored ballots from their political party and openly placed

FIGURE 3-1   Estimated Turnout in Presidential Elections in the Nation, the
                South, and the Non-South, 1860–2012

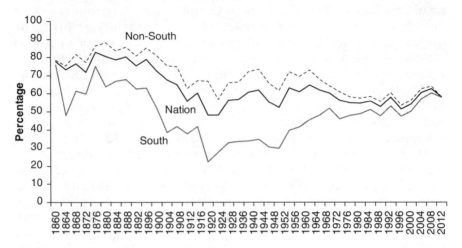

Sources: Curtis Gans, *Voter Turnout in the United States, 1788–2009* (Washington, DC: CQ Press, 2010) for the data from 1860 to 2010; Michael McDonald, United States Elections Project, http://elections.gmu.edu/voter_turnout.htm, for the data from 2012.

Note: The states included in the South were Alabama, Arkansas, Delaware, Florida, Georgia, Kentucky, Louisiana, Maryland, Mississippi, North Carolina, Oklahoma, South Carolina, Tennessee, Texas, Virginia, and West Virginia. All other states were counted as non-South. The data on southern states from 1864 were limited to only four states.

them in the ballot box. The Australian ballot provided for secret voting and an official ballot with all candidates' names appearing on it, thereby decreasing party control of voting. Without the color-coded ballots, the parties couldn't know for whom people voted, which meant they couldn't reward or punish people according to their vote. Voter registration requirements were another useful tool for combating corruption, by limiting the opportunity for fraudulent voting, but they also created an additional barrier to the act of voting that had the effect of decreasing the turnout of less motivated potential voters. The resultant weakening of party machines and increased honesty in electoral activities likely reduced turnout.

After reaching a low in the early 1920s, turnout in national elections increased steadily until 1940. A substantial—though temporary—drop in turnout occurred during World War II and its aftermath, and another decline took place from 1960 through the 1980s, before the recent slight uptick in the early years of the twenty-first century. Great differences in turnout among the states are concealed within these national data. Rates of voting in the South, as shown in Figure 3-1, were consistently low until recently, when they nearly converged with northern turnout, but state variation is still considerable. For example, states with the lowest turnout in 2012 were Hawaii at 44 percent and West Virginia at 46 percent. States with the highest turnout were Minnesota at 76 percent and Wisconsin at 73 percent.[5]

Variation in turnout is considerable not only from state to state but also from one type of election to another. Elections vary in the amount of interest and attention they generate in the electorate. As Figure 3-2 demonstrates, high-salience presidential elections draw higher turnout, whereas low-salience elections, such as off-year congressional elections, are characterized by turnout levels that are 10 to 20 percent lower. Even in a presidential election year, fewer people vote in congressional elections than vote for president. Primaries and local elections elicit still lower turnout. Most of these differences in turnout can be accounted for by the lower visibility of nonpresidential elections; when less information about an election is available to the voter, a lower level of interest is produced.

Voters and Nonvoters

While turnout rates vary across time and across states, political scientists are pretty clear on the demographic characteristics of those who vote and of those who stay away from the polling booth on Election Day.

FIGURE 3-2   Estimated Turnout in Presidential and Congressional Elections, 1860–2012

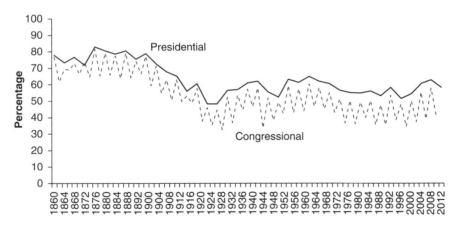

Sources: Curtis Gans, *Voter Turnout in the United States, 1788–2009* (Washington, DC: CQ Press, 2010) for the data from 1860 to 2010; Michael McDonald, United States Elections Project, http://elections.gmu.edu/voter_turnout.htm, for the data from 2012.

Campaign staffs care a great deal about who the voters and nonvoters are as well because what matters is not only whether people vote or not but whether the party's base is getting to the polls. We look at the voter turnout rates of various demographic groups in 2012 and compare these results to previous elections.

Socioeconomic status is a key predictor of turnout. People who are better educated, wealthier, and in more professional occupations consistently turn out to vote at a higher rate than those from a lower socioeconomic status. When respondents were asked in the ANES surveys from 1972 to 2008 if they voted in the previous presidential election, slightly over 90 percent of those with a college education or postgraduate degree said they voted compared to only about 65 percent of those with a high school education or less. In 2012, the exact same pattern emerges, with 93 percent of the college educated saying they had voted compared to only 76 percent of the high school educated. Granted, self-reported turnout in face-to-face and telephone surveys is always higher than actual turnout numbers, largely due to the social desirability problem of people not wanting to admit they did not vote when they know they should have.[6] And research suggests that the better educated seem to be more affected by the social desirability bias than the less educated and therefore are more likely to claim to have voted when they did not. Even taking into account exaggerated turnout numbers, education is highly related to voting for a variety of reasons, including having a better understanding of the voter registration process, having greater interest in and knowledge about politics, and being part of a more politically active social network.[7] Not surprisingly, family income plays out in much the same way. In the past 40 years, ANES data show that just under 90 percent of those in the top third of family income say they voted in the previous presidential election compared to just over 65 percent of those in the bottom third. The most recent presidential election was no different. Clearly, socioeconomic status matters in American elections.

The elections of 2012 fit the pattern of demographic shifts that have been taking place over the past sixty years. It used to be the case that men turned out to vote at a higher rate than women, sometimes by as much as 12 percentage points. As Figure 3-3 shows, this tendency reversed itself in 2004 when women began to vote at a higher rate than men. In 2012, however, women and men turned out to vote at almost the same rate (76 percent of women and 75 percent of men). Over the same time period, people living in the non-South were much more likely to vote than people living in the South. The comparatively low turnout in the South in the 1950s can be attributed to the efforts to keep African Americans from voting, such as the use of poll taxes and literacy tests. After passage of the Voting Rights Act of 1965, the difference in turnout between the South and the non-South diminished (see Figures 3-1 and 3-3).

FIGURE 3-3   Voter Turnout, by Gender and Region, 1952–2012

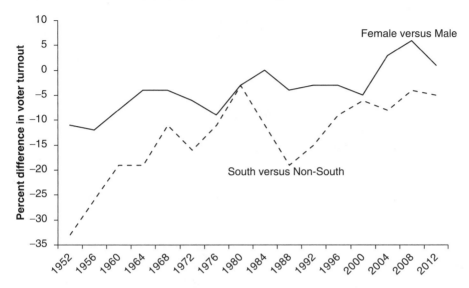

Source: American National Election Studies, available at www.electionstudies.org.

Note: The gender effect was calculated by subtracting the percentage of male voters from the percentage of female voters. Negative numbers therefore mean there were more male voters than female voters. Positive numbers mean there were more female voters than male voters. The region effect was calculated by subtracting the percentage of nonsouthern voters from the percentage of southern voters. Negative numbers mean there were more nonsouthern voters. Because nonsoutherners have outvoted southerners in this time period, there are no positive numbers.

In the past two presidential elections, turnout in the South has reached almost the same level as turnout in the non-South.

Race has long been a key factor when discussing turnout in the South. Whites discriminated against African Americans primarily but not exclusively in the South when it came to registering and voting. National turnout figures for African Americans consistently showed them voting at a much lower rate than whites because of these discriminatory practices that decreased African Americans' voting eligibility. When registration and voting laws that discriminated against blacks were removed, the turnout rate among African Americans increased. Figure 3-4 shows that while African Americans closed the distance with whites after the Voting Rights Act passed in 1965, they did not surpass whites in turnout until 2008, when Barack Obama first ran as the Democratic nominee for president. African Americans voted at an even higher rate than whites in 2012.

The ethnic group that has consistently voted at a level lower than whites is Latinos. Part of the reason behind these lower turnout rates is

FIGURE 3-4   Voter Turnout, by Race/Ethnicity, 1952–2012

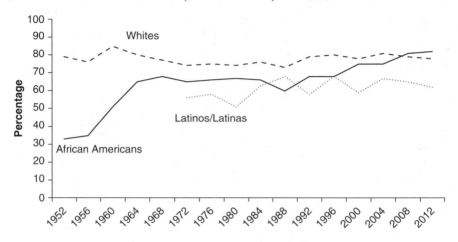

Source: American National Election Studies, available at www.electionstudies.org.

voter eligibility. In the past, some states gave noncitizens the right to vote, but today only citizens are allowed to vote in federal and state elections. Latino immigrants who are not U.S. citizens might be asked in a survey if they voted but they are not eligible to vote. Even taking eligibility into account, however, Latinos vote at a lower rate than whites and African Americans, as can be seen in Figure 3-4. One potential explanation is the possible language barrier some Latino voters might experience. A more likely explanation is that campaigns have been slow to target Latino voters. As the Latino population has grown in the United States and as the Latino vote has become more critical to election outcomes, the targeting of Latino voters will increase dramatically.

One demographic group that consistently gets a lot of attention for not voting is young people. People in the 18 to 34 age cohort consistently vote at a lower rate than older people, sometimes by 20 percentage points (see Figure 3-5). Even in a good year, such as 2004, youth turned out to vote significantly less than older people. Reported turnout was higher in all age groups in 2004 and 2008, in comparison to the late 1970s and the 1980s. The increase was most impressive among the youngest group of eighteen- to twenty-five-year-olds, whose turnout increased from 48 percent in 2000 to 64 percent in 2008 (data not shown). Turnout among younger people dropped in 2012.

There are many reasons why young people are less likely to vote than older people, including motivational and institutional factors. Young people often incorrectly think that politics doesn't have much of anything to do with their lives when in reality it does. Aside from the direct connection with certain issues, such as student loan rates, many laws debated by Congress have a big impact on young people, such as

FIGURE 3-5   Voter Turnout, by Age, 1952–2012

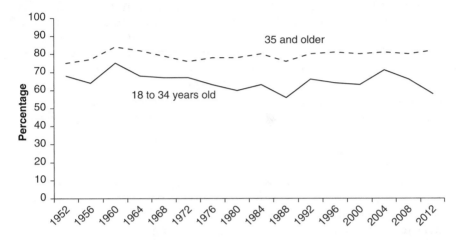

Source: American National Election Studies, available at www.electionstudies.org.

health care reform, the spending of money on defense versus social programs, and so on. A contextual factor that likely affects youth turnout is the attention, or lack of attention, they receive from the candidates running for office. Candidates know that young people vote at a much lower rate than older people and therefore often tailor their messages to older people to capture their votes. When candidates take the time to talk specifically to younger people, as Barack Obama did in 2008 and 2012, they are able to both increase youth turnout and gain much of their vote. Finally, much of the nonvoting among young people may be attributed to the unsettled circumstances of this age group rather than to simple disinterest in politics, although young people are slightly less interested than older people of similar educational levels. Military service, being away at college, geographic mobility with the possible failure to meet residence requirements, and the additional hurdle of initial registration, along with receiving less attention from candidates, all create barriers to voting for young citizens that are less likely to affect older ones. Efforts to promote voter registration have affected the young; as of 2012, about three-fourths of the youngest members of the electorate had registered to vote.

Institutional Impediments to Turnout

Political behavior, including whether people vote or not, takes place within a certain context. That context includes the institutional arrangements that make up the electoral system in the United States.

Would turnout be higher if elections were held on a weekend instead of a Tuesday? Would it be higher if the government automatically registered its citizens instead of having citizens take the initiative to get registered? Would it be higher if the United States had more competitive electoral districts? People have jobs, take care of families, and attend school, all of which make it difficult at times to fit politics into their already busy lives. The institutional arrangements surrounding elections can make it easier or more difficult for people to get to the polls. In essence, the easier it is to vote, the more people will turn out to vote.

Restrictions of Suffrage

Decisions about the institutional arrangements used in elections are inherently political and often partisan because they affect who can vote and how easily they can vote. After the Civil War, Republicans were eager to enfranchise African Americans, figuring that this new group of voters would vote Republican. In the early 1970s, Democrats were eager to enfranchise eighteen- to twenty-year-olds, figuring that they would vote Democratic. Reformers of all sorts encouraged the enfranchisement of women as a means of promoting their own goals. Women voters were seen optimistically as the cure for corruption in government, as unwavering opponents of alcohol, and as champions of virtue in the electorate. Expansions of the suffrage are quite rare, however, compared to attempts to restrict suffrage. The most notorious of these efforts was the effective disfranchisement of blacks in the southern states during the late nineteenth and early twentieth centuries.

Several techniques for disfranchising blacks were used after Reconstruction in the South, and from time to time some of these techniques were applied in the North on a more limited basis to restrict the electoral participation of immigrants. The most common methods included white primaries, the poll tax, literacy tests, discriminatory administrative procedures, and intimidation. In some southern states, only whites were allowed to vote in the party primary (the crucial election in one-party states), under the rationale that primaries to nominate candidates were internal functions of a private organization. In 1944, the U.S. Supreme Court ruled such white primaries unconstitutional on the ground that the selection of candidates for election is a public function in which discrimination on the basis of race is prohibited. The now-unconstitutional poll tax, whereby each individual was charged a flat fee as a prerequisite for registration to vote, was used for years and no doubt disfranchised both poor blacks and poor whites. The literacy test gave local officials a device that could be administered in a selective way to permit registration of whites and practically prohibit that of African Americans. Registrars could ask African Americans to read and interpret the state constitution, for example, and insist they had not done a satisfactory job, whereas they might ask whites only to sign their names. To remain effective over long periods of time, these and other similar administrative devices probably depended on intimidation or the use of violence against African Americans.[8] The outlawing of the poll tax through constitutional amendment and the suspension of literacy tests by the Voting Rights Act of 1965 and its extensions eliminated two important restrictions on the right to vote.

Felon disenfranchisement remains a major state restriction on suffrage, although there is great variation from state to state. In all but two states (Maine and Vermont), prison inmates cannot vote. In many states, convicted felons cannot vote until they have served their entire sentence—in other words, served their time in prison and completed probation or parole. In some states, a felony conviction entails a permanent forfeiture of voting rights. With the prison population growing, this amounts to a sizable restriction of the franchise. A study by the Sentencing Project estimates that in 2010, almost six million citizens were ineligible felons, compared to 3.34 million in 1996 and 1.17 million in 1976. This means that in 2010 approximately 2.5 percent of the voting age population was disenfranchised because of a felony conviction. Over 10 percent of the voting age population was disenfranchised in Florida, which has particularly strict laws.[9] African Americans are hit especially hard by felon disenfranchisement laws because of higher rates of incarceration among African Americans and because they tend to live in states that disenfranchise felons for life, even after they have served all of their sentence. The Sentencing Project study estimated that just under 8 percent of voting age African Americans are disenfranchised because of felony convictions, although certain states have much higher percentages (Virginia 20.4 percent, Kentucky 22.3 percent, and Florida 23.3 percent). The disenfranchisement rate of non-African Americans is 1.77 percent.[10]

Felon disenfranchisement clearly decreases the voting eligible population, but does it decrease voter turnout? This question is more difficult to answer. On the one hand, if the people who are disenfranchised because of a felony conviction would not have voted anyway, then voter turnout is not affected by these state laws. Felons often come from certain demographic groups—primarily young people, minorities, and the poor—that are less likely to vote. Felony disenfranchisement laws can affect voter turnout only if people who want to vote are not allowed to register and to vote because of their felon status. Based on these arguments, Thomas Miles has found that felon disenfranchisement laws do not affect state turnout rates.[11] Other scholars, however, have estimated a much larger impact. By matching felons and nonfelons on such characteristics as gender, race, age, and education, Christopher Uggen and

Jeff Manza estimate that just over a third (35 percent) of disenfranchised felons would have voted in presidential elections in recent years. They also find that a large proportion of these disenfranchised felons would vote for Democratic candidates.[12] In states with higher percentages of disenfranchised felons and in close elections, these disenfranchised non-voters could affect election outcomes. Putting felon disenfranchisement aside, some research shows that even being arrested (and not convicted) increases distrust in government and less attachment to the political system, leading to significantly lower turnout rates among those who have experienced the criminal justice system.[13] Even if states do not have severe felon disenfranchisement laws, they likely have citizens who do not vote in part because of their experiences with the criminal justice system.

Reforms and Institutional Impediments to Voting

Historically, the United States has stood out as being less voter friendly than many Western democracies. In many of these countries, governments maintain registration lists instead of placing the burden of registration on the individual. In the United States, citizens in all states but one—North Dakota—must register to be able to vote. States vary dramatically in how many days prior to the election people must register, ranging from Election Day registration in such states as Minnesota and Wisconsin, where people can register immediately prior to casting their vote, to registering thirty days in advance of the election in such states as Texas and Ohio. Virginia has a twenty-two-day deadline, California a fifteen-day deadline, Alabama a ten-day deadline, and Vermont a seven-day deadline. Not only must people register when they first vote, they must reregister each time they move. According to the U.S. Census Bureau, approximately 12 percent of Americans move in any given year.[14] College students are especially mobile. Regulations also typically cancel the registration of people who fail to vote in a few consecutive elections. With the various registration deadlines along with different rules concerning residency requirements set by each state, simply getting registered can appear daunting, and registration requirements raise the costs of political involvement, costs that a significant number of citizens choose not to assume.

Registering is much easier today than it was in the past, when people had to travel to the county seat to register, but this added step increases the costs of voting. Classic studies estimated that turnout in the United States would increase by 9 to 14 percent if people could register to vote on Election Day.[15] Because of concern over low voter turnout and the role registration requirements likely play in that low turnout, reformers have worked hard to make registering easier. In 1993, Congress passed the "motor voter" bill, which provides that registration forms will be available at various governmental agencies that citizens visit for other purposes. These include agencies where motor vehicles are registered and driver's licenses are obtained; however, because of a Republican-sponsored amendment, states are not required to provide them at unemployment and welfare offices. Because the unregistered tend to be poorer and less well educated, Democrats, who traditionally represent such groups, hoped (and Republicans feared) that reducing registration obstacles would increase the number of Democratic voters.

Many of the same political considerations were at play in the passage of the Help America Vote Act (HAVA) of 2002, which mandated that states provide provisional ballots for those citizens who believe they are registered to vote but whose names are not on the registration rolls. Congress passed HAVA in reaction to the voting debacle in Florida in the 2000 presidential election between Al Gore and George W. Bush. Aside from poorly designed butterfly ballots, hanging chads, and miscounted overseas absentee ballots,[16] some voters were turned away from polling places because they did not appear on the voter lists even though they insisted they were registered. At a primarily African American precinct in Fort Lauderdale, election workers turned away about one hundred people who came to vote because the voter list indicated they had not registered.[17] Similar scenes were played out across Florida. A provision in HAVA was designed to ensure that registered voters could vote by allowing people to cast a provisional ballot. If people show up to vote on Election Day and their name does not appear on the voter list, election workers must now offer them a provisional ballot. If they are registered, their vote will be counted. Much of the debate in Congress over this provision in HAVA involved the form of identification voters seeking to cast provisional ballots would need to produce at the polls. Republican legislators sought more rigid standards to prevent voter fraud; Democratic legislators generally argued for keeping the barriers to a minimum.[18]

Despite Republican fears that easing registration requirements would bring more Democrats to the polls, the main impact of making it easier to register seems to have been a decline in the percentage of people not registered to vote and a slight increase in the proportion of the officially registered who do not vote (see Figure 3-6). Overall, the effect has been relatively small. Failure to register prohibits voting, but registering does not ensure turnout. More of those only casually interested in politics and government register—because it is so easy. But when Election Day arrives, it takes the same amount of energy to get to the polling place as it always did.

Registration requirements are not the only institutional impediment to voting. Traditionally, voting in national elections has been done on just one day, the Tuesday after the first Monday in November,

FIGURE 3-6   Registration Status and Voter Turnout, 1952–2012

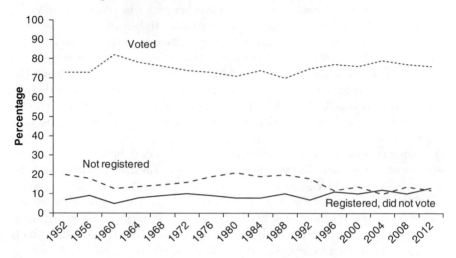

Source: American National Election Studies, available at www.electionstudies.org.

at polling sites located in the precincts near where people live. These polling sites are open at a set time, in many states from 7 a.m. to 7 p.m., although the opening and closing times vary state by state. Reformers have argued that having elections on a weekday, when many people work, could decrease turnout. Imagine having to commute an hour to and from work, which might involve leaving one's house at 6:30 a.m. and arriving back home at 6:30 p.m. The time available for voting can be narrow at best, especially since most voters have to vote in their own precinct on Election Day. The more inconvenient voting is for them, the less likely people are to vote.

To lessen the impact of these obstacles, reforms have opened up when and where people can vote by making it easier to vote through mail ballots, early voting, absentee ballots, and the use of voting centers. Some states mail ballots to registered voters and allow them to vote by mail. Oregon has pursued these possibilities most aggressively, with the entire electorate receiving mail-in ballots in statewide elections beginning in 2004. Other states have loosened the conditions under which voters can request absentee ballots. Still other states have set up systems for in-person early voting in the weeks prior to the election. Only 4 percent of votes cast in 1972 were early votes. The percentage of early votes rose to 31 percent in 2008 but dropped a bit to 24.5 percent in 2012.[19] Many people prefer to wait until Election Day to vote, and a fairly recent reform is specifically geared toward these voters. Election Day voting centers, located in convenient, high-traffic places, are designed to encourage people to vote when they are out doing what they would normally be doing, such as heading to work or shopping. People can simply select a voting center within their county and cast their vote there rather than having to make a special trip to a precinct polling site.[20]

If making voting more convenient is the answer to higher turnout, then the series of reforms put in place in recent years should lead to a significant increase in votes cast. The act of voting is much more convenient than it used to be, thereby lowering the costs associated with voting. Research on the impact of these reforms, however, has not shown the effects many reformers had hoped would occur. The people taking advantage of these reforms tend to be those who would vote anyway, it is just easier for them now. And these reforms have not increased substantially the turnout of underrepresented groups, such as people of color or young people.[21]

One reform that makes voting potentially less convenient is the requirement instituted by some states that voters provide an official form of identification to be able to vote. After the 2001 presidential election, states began passing voter ID laws in droves. According to the National Council of State Legislatures, thirty states have voter ID laws in place and three more states have passed voter ID laws.[22] The state laws vary, however. Some states require an official photo ID, whereas others simply require an official ID. What happens if people do not have an appropriate form of identification also varies by state. In some states, people who do not have an appropriate ID can vote using a provisional ballot but must bring their ID to election officials within a few days of the election to have their vote counted. Other states allow those without an acceptable ID to vote if they sign a voucher attesting to their identity or if a poll worker vouches for them. New voter ID legislation is introduced every year, including legislation to strengthen less strict laws.

A recent survey from the Pew Research Center found a large majority of Americans, 77 percent, favors the requirement that voters show a photo ID to be able to vote. Only one-fifth opposed this requirement. Republicans were more supportive than Democrats, 95 percent to 61 percent, but support for voter ID laws is widespread.[23] Supporters of voter ID laws worry about voter fraud, arguing that people who are ineligible to vote are casting ballots and potentially swaying election outcomes, whereas opponents worry about voter suppression, arguing that people who are eligible to vote but cannot afford a photo ID are being turned away from the polls. Little evidence exists that there is widespread voter fraud, especially of the type that a voter ID law would presumably stop. When Indiana passed its photo ID law among claims of widespread voter fraud, no cases of in-person fraud had been prosecuted, and a special investigation over almost two years of voter fraud in Texas led to only thirteen indictments, and six of these involved people helping friends with a mail-in ballot.[24] Fears of widespread voter fraud appear to be misplaced.

Similarly misplaced are fears that voter ID laws will significantly suppress turnout. Stephen Ansolabehere found that less than two-tenths of one percent (seven people out of four thousand) did not vote in 2008 because of voter identification problems. As we discuss in the next section, what drives voter turnout much more than voter ID laws is having an interest in politics and putting a priority on voting.[25] Research shows, however, that minorities are more likely to be asked to show identification at the polls than is the case for whites. Hispanics and African Americans are much more likely to be asked by poll workers to show some type of identification, especially photo IDs, even when there is no state law in place requiring identification to vote.[26] The unequal treatment of voters at the polls based on race raises serious concerns about voter ID laws. In *Shelby County v. Holder* (2013), the Supreme Court struck down a provision of the Voting Rights Act of 1965 that required nine states with a history of voting discrimination to get any changes in their election laws cleared by the U.S. Attorney General's Office. Immediately following this court decision, six of the nine states pushed for new voter identification requirements. States also moved to restrict early voting and same-day registration.[27]

Psychological Motivation, Genetics, and Turnout

Election processes and rules clearly play a role in encouraging or dampening voter turnout. Any obstacles increase the cost of voting, and even the smallest cost can cause people to find other things to do on Election Day. But many people vote even when obstacles and costs exist, just as many people do not vote even when voting is relatively easy. Attempts to make voting easier—voting by mail, early voting, absentee ballots—have not resulted in significantly higher turnout rates. Making the effort to register, to become informed about an upcoming election, and to cast a ballot demands a certain level of interest and engagement in politics that cannot be created simply by reducing institutional obstacles.

Some people are highly interested in politics, and they remain so over their lifetime. Political interest increases the likelihood of voting as well as the likelihood of seeking out political news and, not surprisingly, being informed about politics. When people are knowledgeable about politics, they are also more likely to vote. Understanding political issues and the differences between candidates and the political parties makes it more likely that people will more easily decide for whom to vote and therefore to make the effort to vote. Feeling strongly attached to a political party also increases the likelihood of voting, largely because strong identifiers care more about who wins.[28] Table 3-1 illustrates differences among unregistered citizens, registered nonvoters, and registered voters in terms of their level of interest in the election campaign, their political knowledge, and their partisanship. The registered nonvoters generally fall between the two other groups. In most years, a partisan impact is visible in the failure of potential voters to vote, with Republicans having greater representation among voters than they do in the electorate as a whole. Just as was the case in 2008, this did not happen in 2012. The nonvoters—both registered and unregistered—were disproportionately independents and the uninterested. If anything, Democrats in 2012 were slightly more likely to turn out to vote than their Republican counterparts.

Even though interest in politics is strongly correlated with voting, about half of those who say they have hardly any interest do vote in presidential elections (46 percent in 2012), suggesting that other factors are also at work. One of these is a sense of civic duty—the attitude that a good citizen has an obligation to vote. Many Americans see voting as an obligation of citizenship, and when they vote, they feel a sense of

TABLE 3-1   Interest and Partisanship of Registered Voters and Nonvoters and Unregistered Citizens, 2012

	Unregistered	Registered	
		Nonvoters	Voters
Very much interested	16%	15%	50%
Somewhat interested	36	47	38
Not interested at all	48	37	12
Total	**100%**	**99%**	**100%**
Strong Democrat	8%	11%	24%
Weak Democrat	14	20	12
Independent Democrat	16	22	14
Independent	30	17	6
Independent Republican	23	17	17
Weak Republican	5	11	12
Strong Republican	5	2	16
Total	**101%**	**100%**	**101%**
(*Weighted N*)	(226)	(245)	(1,444)

Source: 2012 American National Election Study, available at www.electionstudies.org.

gratification that overrides any cost of voting they might incur.[29] When voting is viewed as a civic norm, people with a strong sense of civic duty vote because of the intrinsic satisfaction they get from doing what they know is right or they vote because of extrinsic pressure to conform to a social norm. In a clever experiment, Gerber, Green, and Larimer found that when people were reminded of the obligation to vote, turnout increased by 1.8 percentage points compared to people who received no message. The biggest impact on turnout, however, came from people who were told that their neighbors would know whether they voted or not. In this case, turnout increased by over 8 percentage points.[30] Civic duty increases turnout not just because people feel good when they have done what they know they ought to do; it also increases turnout because people experience social pressure to vote. It should come as no surprise that polling places often hand out "I voted" stickers, allowing voters to publicly display the fact that they fulfilled their civic obligation to vote.

Political scientists have begun to wonder more recently if there are even deeper explanations for people's voting behavior, deeper in the sense that there might be a genetic component that leads people to vote or not to vote. Testing genetic influences is not easy, given that there is obviously not a gene for voting, but scholars have been able to use studies of twins to compare monozygotic twins (popularly known as identical twins, who share 100 percent of their genes) and dizygotic twins (popularly known as fraternal twins, who share only 50 percent of their genes, which is true for all biological siblings). We know that parents who vote are much more likely to have children who grow up to vote, and this is likely affected more by genetic influences than socialization influences. James Fowler and his colleagues found that over 50 percent of people's turnout behavior can be explained by genetic heritability, whereas about 35 percent can be explained by shared environment. Environment matters, but genes play a big role. The influence of genetics on voting might well occur through the large role they play in explaining attitudes related to turnout, such as interest, partisanship, civic duty, and political efficacy.[31]

Campaign Activity and Mobilization in American Elections

Our discussion of voter turnout thus far has implied that there are people who vote (sharing certain demographic characteristics such as higher education level and income, certain attitudes such as interest and civic duty, and certain genetics) and people who do not vote (those who do not share these characteristics). This is clearly not the case. Some people never vote, estimated to make up about 10 percent of eligible voters, and they are unlikely to go to the polls regardless what institutional rules are in place or what is done to get them to vote. Constant voters, about 25 percent of eligible voters, do not need to be prompted to go the polls, and they will overcome whatever obstacles might get in their way. They always vote. It is the remaining 65 percent who are the intermittent voters. They are more likely to vote in high-salience elections (e.g., presidential elections) and when voting is convenient. Since reforms have, in general, made voting easier, the trick now is to get these intermittent voters to vote regularly. Getting these voters to the polls is a target of mobilization efforts.[32]

Millions of dollars are spent by campaigns, partisan groups, and nonpartisan organizations to get people to the polls on Election Day. These GOTV efforts include door-to-door canvassing, leaflets, door hangers, direct mail, e-mail, and phone calls. In a series of field experiments, political scientists have tested the varying effects of these GOTV strategies to determine which lead to higher turnout.[33] Door-to-door canvassing, where campaign volunteers ring doorbells and ask the targeted individuals to be sure to vote, tends to be more effective than using the phone or mail. Personal, face-to-face requests elicit greater compliance than impersonal requests, but people also tend to follow through when they have made a commitment publicly.[34] People like to think of themselves as consistent, and the only way to be consistent after telling a canvasser that they will vote in the upcoming election is to vote. Given this logic, it makes sense that phone calls can be effective as well if there is a more personal touch involved—for example, when the call is made by volunteers or when professional phone banks use a more interactive and conversational approach rather than robotic calls.[35]

Major advances in GOTV efforts came into play in the 2012 presidential election with the use of "big data" and microtargeting. Both the Obama and Romney campaigns bought demographic data from companies that gather personal data on everything from shopping habits to financial problems. They gathered online data themselves on such things as social networks. As *New York Times* reporter Charles Duhigg wrote before the election,

> They have access to information about the personal lives of
> voters at a scale never before imagined. And they are using that
> data to try to influence voting habits—in effect, to train voters
> to go to the polls through subtle cues, rewards, and threats in
> a manner akin to the marketing efforts of credit card compa-
> nies and big-box retailers.[36]

The campaigns used the information to contact potential voters and apply targeted pressure to get them to vote, although appearing to know too much personal information can backfire by appearing creepy.

The Obama campaign was especially advanced in microtargeting. Jim Messina, Obama's campaign manager in 2012, set up campaign headquarters in Illinois and hired sixty data analysts to analyze all the data needed to microtarget. Being able to microtarget gave the Obama campaign a definite edge over the Romney campaign. In a story told by Messina, Obama volunteers were canvassing a neighborhood at the same time as Romney volunteers. The Romney volunteers knocked on every door on one side of the street, finding that half of the people were not home and the other half were Obama supporters. The Obama volunteers were told to knock on only two doors and to speak with certain people at those houses, people who fit the profile of being potential Obama supporters and who could be nudged to get to the polls on Election Day. Because of the analysis of big data, Messina said, the Obama campaign was able to target the houses of undecided voters who had a good probability of voting, and they were able to tell their volunteer canvassers what to say. The Obama volunteers knocked on the relevant doors, talked to the relevant people, and were able to move on to the next neighborhood while the Romney volunteers were still knocking on doors that would not elicit Romney voters.[37] The Obama campaign even ran experiments on volunteer phone calls to potential supporters to test whether it was more effective to control the message in the calls or let the voters talk about issues of their own choosing; the campaign persuaded more people to support Obama when sticking to the campaign script than when letting the voters lead the discussion.

Even if voter mobilization efforts were highly successful, turnout rates would not be consistently high across all elections. Context still matters. Good candidates, competitive races, and high-salience elections are more likely to bring out voters than are other, less invigorating races. In low-salience races, such as a local race for mayor or even a midterm congressional election, mobilization efforts are aimed at intermittent voters who vote frequently but not always and just need a nudge. Mobilization efforts to get people who only occasionally vote to the polls are more likely to be successful in high-salience elections.[38] GOTV campaigns can also be successful, as the Obama campaign found, by targeting probable voters who are undecided. The problem is that there are relatively few undecided voters in most recent elections, and this was especially the case in 2012. Defining undecided voters as those who stated in a survey that they were undecided and did not say they were leaning toward one candidate or the other when pushed, Larry Bartels and Lynn Vavreck found that only 5 percent of survey respondents were actually undecided in the months before the election. These undecided voters not surprisingly tended to identify as Independents and moderates, were not terribly knowledgeable about politics, and tended not to follow political news much.[39] While people might not be able to make a conscious decision, however, they often have implicit leanings toward one candidate or the other, and this unconscious preference is a good predictor of who they will actually vote for on Election Day.[40] Whether people are truly undecided or not, receiving personal contact from the Obama campaign clearly helped in getting out the vote.

Participation in Campaigns

Getting out the vote is what candidates need to do to win, but campaigns would be hard-pressed to get out the vote without a large amount of unpaid help. Candidates and political parties rely heavily on volunteers during the election season to do the canvassing, the stuffing of envelopes, and the calling of potential voters. They hope their supporters get out the word on their candidate by putting up yard signs or placing bumper stickers on their cars or talking to friends, relatives, and coworkers to drum up support for the candidate. And with the tremendous cost of campaigns, especially in recent years, campaigns want supporters' donations. Voting is a relatively easy way to participate in politics compared to the initiative and costs (in time and, for donations, money) associated with other types of campaign activity. Campaign activists have to be highly motivated both to figure out what they need to do to be involved and to participate in the activity. Most Americans are not motivated to be activists. A focus group participant summed it up nicely when she said, "When I leave here [the focus group discussion], when I walk out this door, I'm not going to volunteer for anything. I'm not going to get involved in anything. I mean I know this. I'm not going to pretend I'm some political activist. I'm lazy. I'm not going to do it. I'm too busy obsessing on other things going on in my life."[41] It comes as no surprise that fewer people are involved in campaign activities than vote.

Figure 3-7 shows Americans' involvement in various campaign activities over time. The first thing that stands out is that Americans are much more likely to try to influence other people in how they should vote than to be involved in other campaign activities. American National Election Studies respondents were asked, "During the campaign, did you talk to any people and try to show them why they should vote for or against one of the parties or candidates?" On average, about a third of the respondents said yes, they did try to influence people's votes. This percentage skyrocketed to just under 50 percent in the 2004 election and remained high in 2008 (at 43 percent). The percentage of those trying to influence other people's votes dropped to 40 percent in 2012, but this number was still higher than the average over the past sixty years. Making the effort to try to persuade people how to vote indicates a strong interest in the outcome of the election and enough knowledge about the campaign to be able to make an argument on behalf of a party or candidate. It is interesting to note that while voters are the most likely to try to influence others, people who end up not voting do so as well. In 2004, 54 percent of voters and 27 percent of nonvoters tried to influence others' votes. These percentages were 50 percent of voters and 22 percent of nonvoters in 2008 and 46 percent of voters and 20 percent of nonvoters in 2012. We can't know what the nonvoters had to say while trying to persuade other people, but we do know that in recent elections, a majority (58 percent) of nonvoters claimed to "care a good deal" about which party won the election. Granted, voters were more likely to care (90 percent), but it is clear that a lot of nonvoters care enough about the outcome of the election to want to persuade others for whom to vote. The other campaign activities are not as popular, with only 3 to 5 percent of Americans working on campaigns and just under 10 percent attending political meetings.

The second aspect of Figure 3-7 that stands out is the uptick in campaign participation in 2004 and 2008 and the downturn in 2012. Americans in 2004 were much more willing to influence others' votes, display a political button or sticker, and donate money than had been the case in most prior years. While 2008 witnessed a slight downturn

FIGURE 3-7   Campaign Participation, 1952–2012

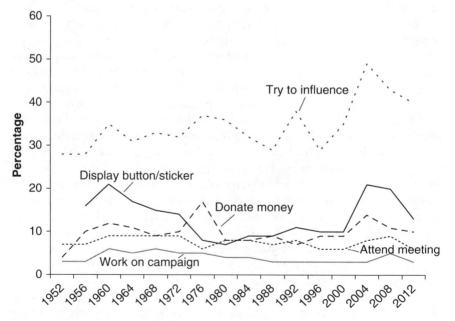

Source: American National Election Studies, available at www.electionstudies.org.

and 2012 a large downturn in these activities, Americans were still more engaged in these campaigns than usual. So what was it about 2004 that led to a pronounced increase in some types of campaign activity? Much of the commentary leading up to the 2004 election focused on an energized youth and upset Democrats who were still smarting after the 2000 election and the debacle in Florida. The closeness of the 2000 election led Democrats to emphasize the need for their followers to vote. The stepped-up efforts of Rock the Vote and Sean P. Diddy's "Vote or Die," both aimed at increasing youth turnout, and the large number of Democrats thinking that year's presidential election "the most important of their lifetimes" led to speculation that youth and Democrats would be much more engaged in 2004 than was usual.[42]

Figures 3-8 and 3-9 look at the differences in campaign activity between partisan groups and between youth and older people. Looking first at partisanship, it is Democrats who had the largest increases in activity between the earlier elections (1996 and 2000) and 2004 in terms of influencing others, displaying buttons or stickers, and donating money. Republicans started out at a higher level of participation than Democrats, but the data show that Democrats surpassed Republicans in 2004 in their rate of trying to influence others and in donating money, and they tied Republicans in displaying campaign paraphernalia. Participation levels generally stayed high in 2008, higher than in the previous years. Switching to youth, Figure 3-9 suggests that the pundits seemed

FIGURE 3-8   Party Identification and Campaign Participation, 1996–2012

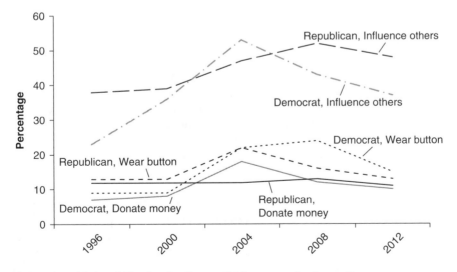

Source: American National Election Studies, available at www.electionstudies.org.

FIGURE 3-9   Age and Campaign Participation, 1996–2012

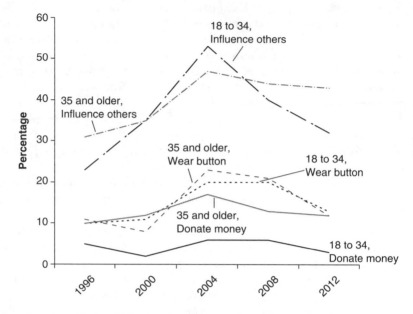

Source: American National Election Studies, available at www.electionstudies.org.

to have been right. Younger people (people eighteen to thirty-four years old) were significantly more involved in trying to influence others and in displaying buttons and stickers, especially in 2004. Older people (thirty-five and older) also experienced a significant increase in their participation. Both the young and older people experienced a drop in activity in 2008 but especially in 2012.

Electoral context matters, not just for voting but for other types of campaign activities as well. What happens in the political world—being upset about previous election outcomes, having GOTV efforts target certain groups of people—can influence people's behavior, making them more or less active in any given election.

A common theme among democratic theorists is the need for people to get more involved in politics. People need to vote, be informed about politics, participate in campaigns, and join organizations. The data throughout this chapter show that while many Americans achieve this standard of good citizenship, a great many do not. Political scientists have made significant advances in ascertaining what causes low participation rates and what can be done to increase citizens' engagement in the political system. Having people turned off of politics because of what they see happening in Washington in recent years does not help political scientists' efforts.

Notes

1. Michael P. McDonald and Samuel L. Popkin, "The Myth of the Vanishing Voter," *American Political Science Review* 95, no. 4 (2001): 963–74.
2. See http://elections.gmu.edu; and McDonald and Popkin, "The Myth of the Vanishing Voter."
3. On the one-party dominance argument, see E. E. Schattschneider, *The Semisovereign People* (New York: Holt, Rinehart, and Winston, 1960), especially chap. 5; and Walter Dean Burnham, "The Changing Shape of the American Political Universe," *American Political Science Review* 59 (March 1965): 7–28. On electoral manipulations and the subsequent electoral reforms, see Philip E. Converse, "Change in the American Electorate," in *The Human Meaning of Social Change*, ed. Angus Campbell and Philip E. Converse (New York: Russell Sage Foundation, 1972), 263–337. For an analysis that alters the estimates of turnout, see Ray M. Shortridge, "Estimating Voter Participation," in *Analyzing Electoral History*, ed. Jerome M. Clubb, William H. Flanigan, and Nancy H. Zingale (Beverly Hills, CA: Sage, 1981), 137–52.
4. Jerrold D. Rusk, "The Effect of the Australian Ballot Reform on Split-Ticket Voting: 1876–1908," *American Political Science Review* 64 (December 1970): 1220–38.
5. See Voter Turnout, United States Elections Project, http://elections.gmu.edu/voter_turnout.htm.
6. Allyson L. Holbrook and Jon A. Krosnick, "Social Desirability Bias in Voter Turnout Reports," *Public Opinion Quarterly* 74 (Spring 2010): 37–67.
7. Brian D. Silver, Barbara A. Anderson, and Paul R. Abramson, "Who Overreports Voting?" *American Political Science Review* 80 (June 1986): 613–24; Rachel Milstein Sondheimer and Donald P. Green, "Using Experiments to Estimate the Effects of Education on Voter Turnout," *American Journal of Political Science* 54 (January 2010): 174–89.
8. For a treatment of these and many additional topics, see J. Morgan Kousser, *The Shaping of Southern Politics* (New Haven, CT: Yale University Press, 1974). See also Jerrold D. Rusk and John J. Stucker, "The Effect of the Southern System of Election Laws on Voting Participation," in *The History of American Electoral Behavior*, ed. Joel Silbey, Allan Bogue, and William Flanigan (Princeton, NJ: Princeton University Press, 1978).
9. Christopher Uggen, Sarah Shannon, and Jeff Manza, "State-level Estimates of Felon Disenfranchisement in the United States, 2010," Sentencing Project, July 2012, available at http://www.sentencingproject.org/doc/publications/fd_State_Level_Estimates_of_Felon_Disen_2010.pdf.
10. Ibid.
11. Thomas J. Miles, "Felon Disenfranchisement and Voter Turnout," *Journal of Legal Studies* 33 (January 2004): 85–129.
12. Christopher Uggen and Jeff Manza, "Democratic Contraction? Political Consequences of Felon Disenfranchisement in the United States," *American Sociological Review* 67 (December 2002): 777–803, p. 786.
13. Vesla M. Weaver and Amy E. Lerman, "Political Consequences of the Carceral State," *American Political Science Review* 104 (November 2010): 817–33, p. 818.
14. Geographic Mobility/Migration, United States Census Bureau, U.S. Department of Commerce. http://www.census.gov/hhes/migration/data/cps/cps2012.html.

15. Raymond E. Wolfinger and Steven J. Rosenstone, *Who Votes?* (New Haven, CT: Yale University Press, 1980); G. Bingham Powell, "American Voter Turnout in Comparative Perspective," *American Political Science Review* 80 (March 1986): 17–43.

16. Henry E. Brady, Michael C. Herron, Walter R. Mebane Jr., and Jasjeet Singh Sekhon, "'Law and Data': The Butterfly Ballot Episode," *PS: Political Science and Politics* 34 (March 2001): 59–69; David Barstow and Don Van Natta Jr., "Examining the Vote; How Bush Took Florida: Mining the Overseas Absentee Vote," *New York Times,* July 15, 2001.

17. Mireya Navarro and Somini Sengupta, "Contesting the Vote: Black Voters; Arriving at Florida Voting Places, Some Blacks Found Frustration," *New York Times,* November 30, 2000.

18. *CQ Almanac Plus 2002* (Washington, DC: Congressional Quarterly, 2003), 143.

19. Michael McDonald, "The Return of the Voter: Voter Turnout in the 2008 Presidential Election," *Forum* 6 (December 2009): Article 4; "2012 Early Voting Statistics," United States Election Project, http://elections.gmu.edu/early_vote_2012 .html.

20. Robert M. Stein and Greg Vonnahme, "Engaging the Unengaged Voter: Vote Centers and Voter Turnout," *Journal of Politics* 70 (April 2008): 487–97.

21. See, for example, Adam Berinsky, "The Perverse Consequences of Electoral Reform in the United States," *American Politics Research* 33 (July 2005): 471–91; Jeffrey A. Karp and Susan A. Banducci, "Going Postal: How All-Mail Elections Influence Turnout," *Political Behavior* 22, no. 3 (2000): 223–39; Robert M. Stein and Greg Vonnahme, "Voting at Non-precinct Polling Places: A Review and Research Agenda," *Election Law Journal* 10 (October 2011): 307–11.

22. These numbers are accurate as of April 2013. "Voter Identification Requirements," National Conference of State Legislatures, http://www.ncsl.org/ legislatures-elections/elections/voter-id.aspx#State_Reqs.

23. "Broad Support for Photo ID Voting Requirements," Pew Research Center for the People and the Press, October 11, 2012, http://www.people-press.org/ 2012/10/11/broad-support-for-photo-id-voting-requirements/.

24. Chandler Davidson, "The Historical Context of Voter Photo-ID Laws," *PS: Political Science & Politics* 42 (January 2009): 93–96.

25. Stephen Ansolabehere, "Effects of Identification Requirements on Voting: Evidence from the Experiences of Voters on Election Day," *PS: Political Science & Politics* 42 (January 2009): 127–30; Jason D. Mycoff, Michael W. Wagner, and David C. Wilson, "The Empirical Effects of Voter-ID Laws: Present or Absent?" *PS: Political Science & Politics* 42 (January 2009): 121–26.

26. Ansolabehere, "Effects of Identification Requirements on Voting: Evidence from the Experiences of Voters on Election Day"; Lonna Rae Atkeson, Lisa Ann Bryant, Thad E. Hall, Kyle L. Saunders, and R. Michael Alvarez, "A New Barrier to Participation: Heterogeneous Application of Voter Identification Policies," *Electoral Studies* 29 (March 2010): 66–73.

27. Stephanie Condon, "After Voting Rights Act Ruling, States Tighten Voting Laws," *CBS News,* July 26, 2013, http://www.cbsnews.com/8301-250_162-57595695/after-voting-rights-act-ruling-states-tighten-voting-laws/; Adam Liptak, "Supreme Court Invalidates Key Part of Voting Rights Act," *New York Times,* June 25, 2013, http://www.nytimes.com/2013/06/26/us/supreme-court-ruling .html?pagewanted=all.

28. Markus Prior, "You've Either Got It or You Don't? The Stability of Political Inter-
est over the Life Cycle," *Journal of Politics* 72 (July 2010): 747–66; Markus Prior,
*Post-Broadcast Democracy: How Media Choice Increases Inequality in Political Involve-
ment and Polarizes Elections* (New York: Cambridge University Press, 2007);
Michael X. Delli Carpini and Scott Keeter, *What Americans Know about Politics and
Why It Matters* (New Haven, CT: Yale University Press, 1996); Larry M. Bartels,
"Partisanship and Voting Behavior, 1952–1996," *American Journal of Political Sci-
ence* 44 (January 2000): 35–50.

29. Angus Campbell, Philip E. Converse, Warren E. Miller, and Donald E. Stokes,
The American Voter (New York: John Wiley, 1960); Sidney Verba, Kay Lehman
Schlozman, and Henry E. Brady, *Voice and Equality* (Cambridge, MA: Harvard
University Press, 1995); Elizabeth Theiss-Morse, "Conceptualizations of Good
Citizenship and Political Participation," *Political Behavior* 15 (December 1993):
355–80.

30. Alan S. Gerber, Donald P. Green, and Christopher W. Larimer, "Social Pressure
and Voter Turnout: Evidence from a Large-scale Field Experiment," *American
Political Science Review* 102 (February 2008): 33–48.

31. James H. Fowler, Laura A. Baker, and Christopher T. Dawes, "Genetic Variation
in Political Participation," *American Political Science Review* 102 (May 2008):
233–48; Christopher T. Dawes and James H. Fowler, "Partisanship, Voting, and
the Dopamine D2 Receptor Gene," *Journal of Politics* 71 (July 2009): 1157–71;
Robert Klemmensen, Peter K. Hatemi, Sara Binzer Hobolt, Inge Petersen,
Axel Skythe, and Asbjørn S. Nørgaard, "The Genetics of Political Participa-
tion, Civic Duty, and Political Efficacy Across Cultures: Denmark and the
United States," *Journal of Theoretical Politics* 24 (June 2012): 409–27; Robert
Klemmensen, Peter K. Hatemi, Sara Binzer Hobolt, Inge Petersen, Axel
Skythe, and Asbjørn S. Nørgaard, "Heritability in Political Interest and Effi-
cacy across Cultures: Denmark and the United States," *Twin Research and
Human Genetics* 15, no. 1 (2012): 15–20.

32. The estimates of the percentages of those who never vote, the constant voters,
and the transient voters come from Adam Berinsky, Nancy Burns, and Michael
W. Traugott, "Who Votes by Mail? A Dynamic Model of the Individual-level Consequences of Vote-by-mail Systems," *Public Opinion Quarterly* 65 (June 2001):
178–97. See also Berinsky, "The Perverse Consequences of Electoral Reform in
the United States."

33. See, for example, Alan S. Gerber and Donald P. Green, "The Effects of Canvass-
ing, Telephone Calls, and Direct Mail on Voter Turnout: A Field Experiment,"
American Political Science Review 94 (September 2000): 353–63; Donald P. Green,
Alan S. Gerber, and David W. Nickerson, "Getting Out the Vote in Local Elec-
tions: Results from Six Door-to-door Canvassing Experiments," *Journal of Poli-
tics* 65 (November 2003): 1083–96; Alan S. Gerber, Donald P. Green, and
Christopher W. Larimer, "An Experiment Testing the Relative Effectiveness of
Encouraging Voter Participation by Inducing Feelings of Pride or Shame,"
Political Behavior 32 (September 2010): 409–22; Kevin Arceneaux and David W.
Nickerson, "Who Is Mobilized to Vote? A Re-Analysis of 11 Field Experiments,"
American Journal of Political Science 53 (January 2009): 1–16; David W. Nicker-
son, "Quality Is Job One: Professional and Volunteer Voter Mobilization Calls,"
American Journal of Political Science 51 (April 2007): 269–82.

34. Robert B. Cialdini and M. R. Trost, "Social Influence: Social Norms, Conformity, and Compliance," in *The Handbook of Social Psychology*, 4th ed., ed. D. T. Gilbert, Susan T. Fiske, and G. Lindzey (Boston: McGraw-Hill, 1998) 2:151–92; Robert B. Cialdini and Noah J. Goldstein, "Social Influence: Compliance and Conformity," *Annual Review of Psychology* 55 (2004): 591–621.

35. Shang E. Ha and Dean S. Karlan, "Get-Out-the-Vote Phone Calls: Does Quality Matter?" *American Politics Research* 37 (March 2009): 353–69; Nickerson, "Quality Is Job One."

36. Charles Duhigg, "Campaigns Mine Personal Lives to Get Out Vote," *New York Times*, October 14, 2012, p. A1.

37. Jim Messina (lecture at the Peter J. Hoagland Integrity in Public Service Lecture at the University of Nebraska-Lincoln, April 5, 2013), http://www.youtube .com/watch?v=N122vHLOO3E; see also Sasha Issenberg, "When It Comes to Targeting and Persuading Voters, the Obama Campaign Has a Massive, Insurmountable Advantage," *Slate*, October 29, 2012, http://www.slate.com/articles/ news_and_politics/victory_lab/2012/10/obama_s_secret_weapon_democrats_ have_a_massive_advantage_in_targeting_and.html.

38. Kevin Arceneaux and David W. Nickerson, "Who Is Mobilized to Vote? A Re-Analysis of 11 Field Experiments," *American Journal of Political Science* 53 (January 2009): 1–16.

39. Larry M. Bartels and Lynn Vavreck, "Meet the Undecideds," *Campaign Stops* (blog), *New York Times,* July 30, 2012, http://campaignstops.blogs.nytimes. com/2012/07/30/meet-the-undecided/.

40. Luciano Arcuri, Luigi Castelli, Silvia Galdi, Cristina Zogmaister, and Alessandro Amadori, "Predicting the Vote: Implicit Attitudes as Predictors of the Future Behavior of Decided and Undecided Voters," *Political Psychology* 29 (June 2008): 369–87; but see Malte Friese, Colin Tucker Smith, Thomas Plischke, Matthias Bluemke, and Brian A. Nosek, "Do Implicit Attitudes Predict Actual Voting Behavior Particularly for Undecided Voters?" *PLoS ONE* 7 (August 2012): e44130. doi:10.1371/journal.pone.0044130.

41. John R. Hibbing and Elizabeth Theiss-Morse, *Stealth Democracy* (New York: Cambridge University Press, 2002), 127.

42. E. J. Dionne Jr., "The Intensity Gap," *Washington Post,* October 26, 2004, p. A25.

Suggested Readings

Conway, M. Margaret. *Political Participation in the United States*. 3rd ed. Washington, DC: CQ Press, 2000. A good introduction to the study of turnout and other forms of political participation.

Lau, Richard R., and David P. Redlawsk. *How Voters Decide: Information Processing in Election Campaigns*. New York: Cambridge University Press, 2006. An innovative use of experiments shows how successful voters are at selecting the candidate closest to their own preferences.

Leighley, Jan E., ed. *The Oxford Handbook of American Elections and Political Behavior*. New York: Oxford University Press, 2010. An excellent series of articles looking at voter turnout and other aspects of American electoral behavior.

Manza, Jeff, and Christopher Uggen. *Locked Out: Disenfranchisement and American Democracy.* New York: Oxford University Press, 2008. An indispensable examination of felon disenfranchisement laws and their impact on American elections.

McDonald, Michael P., and Samuel L. Popkin. "The Myth of the Vanishing Voter." *American Political Science Review* 95, no. 4 (December 2001): 963–74.

Patterson, Thomas E. *The Vanishing Voter: Public Involvement in an Age of Uncertainty.* New York: Alfred A. Knopf, 2002. An analysis of political participation based on a huge, year-long survey in 2000.

Rosenstone, Steven J., and John Mark Hansen. *Mobilization, Participation, and Democracy in America.* New York: Macmillan, 1993. An analysis of the interaction among the strategic choices of political elites and the choices of citizens to participate in politics.

Rusk, Jerrold D., and John J. Stucker. "The Effect of the Southern System of Election Laws on Voting Participation." In *The History of American Electoral Behavior,* edited by Joel Silbey, Allan Bogue, and William Flanigan. Princeton, NJ: Princeton University Press, 1978. A sophisticated analysis of the disfranchisement of voters in the South in the nineteenth century.

Teixeira, Ruy A. *The Disappearing American Voter.* Washington, DC: Brookings Institution Press, 1992. A sophisticated and thorough analysis of the factors that have contributed to the decline in turnout in the United States and a discussion of the impact of proposed reforms.

Internet Resources

An important Web site for the analysis of aggregate turnout data is the United States Elections Project, elections.gmu.edu. Michael McDonald, the host of this website, uses strategies for reducing the error in turnout estimates and offers commentary on turnout.

The website of the American National Election Studies, www.electionstudies.org, offers data on turnout in both presidential and off-year elections since 1952. After clicking on "Utilities" and then on the link for tables and graphs under "The ANES Guide to Public Opinion and Electoral Behavior," scroll down to "Political Involvement and Participation in Politics." You also can examine turnout of numerous social groups from 1952 to the present.

Turnout and registration data for the nation and the states are available at the U.S. Census Bureau website, www.census.gov. Highlight "People" and click on "Voting and Registration."

Partisanship and Party Change

IF YOU ARE LOOKING to predict how someone is going to vote for president on Election Day and you can only learn one fact about that person before making your forecast, asking for that person's political partisanship gives you enough information to make a correct prediction nine times out of ten. As E. E. Schattschneider put it in his 1942 book *Party Government,* "Modern democracy is unthinkable save in terms of parties."[1] Political parties are organized coalitions working to win elections and govern. They structure public debate, dominate news columns and airtime, and continue to play a central role in American politics.

This chapter addresses *partisanship*—the sense of attachment or belonging that an individual feels for a political party—and offers a brief history of American parties, an examination of the implications partisanship has for political behavior, and an assessment of the factors that influence partisan change. In chapter 5, we pay some attention to how partisanship helps to shape and constrain public opinion. Chapter 6 spends time analyzing the social and group characteristics of partisans while chapter 7 considers, in part, how partisan identification influences media choice.

Party Loyalty

For a century and a half, the U.S. electorate has supported a two-party system of Republicans and Democrats in national politics. Such remarkable stability is unknown in other democracies. Within this stable party system, however, voter support for Republicans and Democrats has fluctuated widely, and significant numbers of voters occasionally, as in 1992, abandon the traditional parties to support third-party or independent candidates. The aggregate division of partisans in the electorate, shown in Figure 4-1, reveals a wide range of the structure of political conflict from 1952 to 2012, even in elections close together in time. While Democrats have outnumbered Republicans in the electorate for more than half a century, students of American politics know that holding the majority of partisans nationwide is not enough to promise victory at the ballot box. Moreover, the number of partisans in the electorate regularly vacillates. Years in which the total percentage of Democrats and Republicans drops a bit include elections with the third-party candidacies of George C. Wallace in 1968 and Ross Perot in 1992 and, to a lesser degree, 1996. Perot's 1992 showing of 19 percent was the largest percentage won by a third-party candidate since 1912. Although Ralph Nader's votes denied the presidency to Al Gore in 2000, his 2.7 percent of the popular vote was an unimpressive figure for a third-party candidate in recent years. Third-party candidates supporting the Green, Libertarian, and other parties garnered about 2 percent of the popular vote in 2012.

Despite variations in election outcomes and American voters' differentiated support for the candidates offered to them by the political parties, most voters have a basic and stable loyalty to one party or the other. This tendency of most individuals to be loyal to one political party makes the idea of partisanship, or *party identification* as it is often called, one of the most useful concepts for understanding the political behavior of individuals. After good survey data became available in the late 1940s, party identification assumed a central role in all voting behavior analysis.[2]

FIGURE 4-1   Partisan Division of Americans, 1952–2012

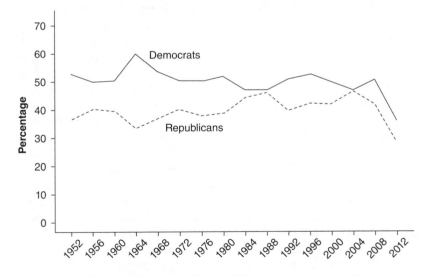

Source: American National Election Studies, available at www.electionstudies.org.

Party Identification

Party identification is a relatively uncomplicated measure determined by responses to the following questions:

- Generally speaking, do you usually think of yourself as a Republican, a Democrat, an independent, or what?

- [If Republican or Democrat] Would you call yourself a strong [Republican/Democrat] or a not very strong [Republican/Democrat]?

- [If independent] Do you think of yourself as closer to the Republican Party or to the Democratic Party?

Leaving aside for the moment the people who do not or cannot respond to such questions, this yields seven categories of participants in the electorate according to intensity of partisanship ranging from strong Democrat at one end to weak Democrat and independent-leaning Democrat to pure independent in the middle, to independent-leaning Republican and weak Republican to strong Republican on the other end.

Because this self-identification measure of party loyalty is the best indicator of partisanship, political analysts commonly refer to *partisanship* and *party identification* interchangeably. While many other influences are at work on voters in U.S. society, and partisanship varies in its importance in different types of elections and in different time periods, partisanship is the single most important influence on political opinions and voting behavior.

Partisanship represents the feeling of identification with and loyalty to a political party that an individual acquires—sometimes during childhood—and generally holds through life, often with increasing intensity. This self-image as a Democrat or a Republican is useful to the individual in a special way. For example, individuals who think of themselves as Republicans or Democrats respond to political information partially by using party identification to orient themselves, reacting to new information in such a way that it fits in with the ideals and feelings they already have. A Republican who hears a Republican Party leader advocate a policy has a basis in party loyalty for supporting that policy, apart from other considerations. A Democrat may feel favorably inclined toward a candidate for office because that candidate bears the Democratic label. Partisanship orients individuals in their political environment, although it may also distort their picture of reality. For good or ill, people often see the world through partisan-colored glasses.

Table 4-1 shows the stability of partisan conflict in the United States during the modern polling era. Democrats have held the party ID advantage, even in years such as 1956, 1972, 1980, and 1984, when Republicans ran away with the White House. One element of the data that jumps out is the fact that self-identified independents have nearly doubled since the time series began. Even so, independent partisan leaners are among the most loyal party voters. Indeed, after asking independents which party they lean toward, under 10 percent of the public reveals itself to be truly independent from the two major parties.

The dramatic role that the southern United States has played in American political history—from seceding from the Union to kick off the Civil War to the days of "solid South" Democratic presidential voting to a region where Republicans have the advantage today—merits a careful examination of partisanship in the South and non-South. Table 4-2 shows the impressive shifts in southerners' partisan loyalties, from a South that was almost twice as likely to identify as strongly Democratic compared to the non-South in 1952 to a region that displayed a significant loss of Democratic loyalty (but lack of gain for Republicans) by 1972 to one that is indistinguishable from the rest of the country across the party spectrum by 2012. We consider the changes in the South later, in the sections of the chapter dealing with party systems and realignment.

Partisanship is also interesting to political analysts because it provides a base against which to measure deviations in particular elections. In other words, the individual voter's long-standing loyalty to one party means that, "other things being equal," or in the absence of disrupting forces, he or she can be expected to vote for candidates of that party. Of course, campaigns are not conducted in a vacuum; Republican presidential candidates do not simply say to themselves, "Well, there are more Democrats than Republicans, and I'll never be able to convince any Democrats to vote for me, so I guess I'll bow out of the race now!" Nor do Democratic candidates say to themselves, "Well, looking at those party ID numbers, I see that there is no need to campaign, we have this in the bag!" Indeed, voters are responsive to a great variety of other influences that can either strengthen or weaken their tendency to support their usual party. Variations occur from election to election in such factors as the attractiveness of the candidates, the impact of foreign and domestic policy issues, and purely local circumstances. These current factors, often called *short-term forces,* may move voters away from their usual party choices. If the political predispositions of all the individuals in the electorate were added up, the result would be an "expected vote" or "normal vote."[3] This is the electoral outcome that would be expected if all voters voted their party identification. Departures from this expected vote in elections represent the impact of short-term forces, such as issues or candidates.

TABLE 4-1 Party Identification of the Electorate, 1952–2012

Party identification	1952	1956	1960	1964	1968	1972	1976	1980	1984	1988	1992	1996	2000	2004	2008	2012
Democrats	47%	44%	46%	51%	45%	40%	39%	41%	36%	35%	35%	38%	36%	32%	34%	34%
Independents	22	24	23	22	29	35	36	35	34	36	38	32	42	38	40	37
Republicans	27	29	27	24	24	23	23	22	28	28	25	29	20	29	25	25
Nothing, don't know	4	3	4	2	2	2	2	2	2	2	2	1	2	2	2	4
Total	**100%**	**100%**	**100%**	**99%**	**100%**	**101%**	**100%**	**99%**	**100%**	**101%**	**99**	**101%**	**100%**	**100%**	**101%**	**100%**
(*N*)	(1,377)	(1,442)	(1,540)	(1,247)	(1,186)	(965)	(1,930)	(1,109)	(1,622)	(1,418)	(1,848)	(1,286)	(1,301)	(948)	(1,820)	(1,946)

Source: American National Election Studies, available at www.electionstudies.org.

TABLE 4-2   Party Identification of the Electorate for the Nation, the Non-South, and the South, 1952–2012

The Nation

	1952	1956	1960	1964	1968	1972	1976	1980	1984	1988	1992	1996	2000	2004	2008	2012
Strong Democrats	23%	22%	21%	27%	20%	15%	15%	18%	17%	18%	18%	18%	19%	17%	19%	20
Weak Democrats	26	24	26	25	26	25	25	23	20	18	17	19	15	16	15	13
Independents	23	24	23	23	29	36	37	37	36	37	39	36	42	39	40	43
Weak Republicans	14	15	14	14	15	13	14	14	15	14	14	15	12	12	13	11
Strong Republicans	14	16	16	11	10	10	9	8	12	14	11	12	12	16	13	13
Total	100%	101%	100%	100%	100%	99%	100%	100%	100%	99%	99%	100%	100%	100%	100%	100%
(N)	(1,689)	(1,690)	(1,864)	(1,536)	(1,531)	(2,695)	(2,833)	(1,612)	(2,228)	(2,026)	(2,473)	(1,706)	(1,790)	(1,194)	(2,293)	(2,041)

The Non-South

	1952	1956	1960	1964	1968	1972	1976	1980	1984	1988	1992	1996	2000	2004	2008	2012
Strong Democrats	19%	19%	19%	23%	17%	13%	13%	15%	15%	16%	16%	17%	19%	15%	19%	20%
Weak Democrats	22	20	21	23	24	23	22	22	18	16	17	20	16	14	18	14
Independents	26	28	26	25	29	38	40	39	36	37	40	35	42	42	41	44
Weak Republicans	16	17	17	16	17	15	16	14	17	16	15	16	12	12	13	10
Strong Republicans	17	18	18	13	12	11	10	9	14	15	12	12	12	16	10	12
Total	100%	102%	101%	100%	99%	100%	101%	99%	100%	100%	100%	100%	101%	99%	101%	100%
(N)	(1,237)	(1,221)	(1,248)	(1,071)	(1,061)	(1,793)	(1,920)	(1,042)	(1,490)	(1,312)	(1,603)	(1,054)	(1,152)	(780)	(1,309)	(1,280)

(Continued)

TABLE 4-2 (Continued)

									The South								
	1952	1956	1960	1964	1968	1972	1976	1980	1984	1988	1992	1996	2000	2004	2008	2012
Strong Democrats	35%	31%	25%	36%	27%	17%	19%	23%	21%	21%	22%	21%	20%	19%	19%	21%
Weak Democrats	35	35	36	31	29	31	30	25	23	21	18	19	15	19	12	11
Independents	15	16	18	17	31	32	33	32	36	37	39	37	41	33	40	42
Weak Republicans	9	10	9	7	8	10	11	13	11	10	12	13	11	13	12	11
Strong Republicans	6	9	13	7	4	9	7	7	9	11	9	11	13	17	17	15
Total	100%	101%	101%	98%	99%	99%	100%	100%	100%	100%	100%	101%	100%	101%	100%	100%
(N)	(452)	(469)	(616)	(465)	(470)	(902)	(913)	(570)	(738)	(714)	(870)	(652)	(638)	(413)	(984)	(761)

Source: American National Election Studies, available at www.electionstudies.org.

In assessing the partisanship of the American electorate historically, we have no data to add up individual party identifications to find an expected vote. Survey data of this type have been available only for the past seventy-five years or so. For the period from 1824 to 1968, we base our estimates on the only available data—election returns for aggregate units.[4] These data cannot tell us about the voting patterns of individuals, but they do allow one to make assessments of party loyalty and temporary deviations from party by collections of voters. Even though the same set of individuals does not turn out to vote in each election, we use the election returns over the years to indicate the collective partisanship of the electorate. From these data, an estimate is made of the expected vote for the Democratic and Republican Parties. It is then possible to say, for example, that the electorate deviated from its normal voting pattern in favor of the Republican Party in 1904 or that the voters departed from their normal Democratic loyalty in 1952.

Jerome Clubb, William Flanigan, and Nancy Zingale's estimates of the expected vote nationwide in presidential voting for the Democratic Party from 1840 to 1968 and for the Republican Party from 1872 to 1968 are shown in Figures 4-2 and 4-3, respectively. The actual vote in these elections is also shown to indicate the amount of departure from underlying partisan patterns that occurred in each election.

FIGURE 4-2   Democratic Expected Vote in Presidential Elections, 1840–1968

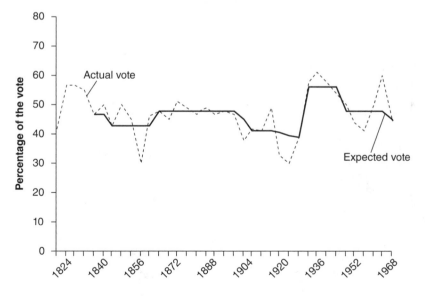

Source: Jerome M. Clubb, William H. Flanigan, and Nancy H. Zingale, *Partisan Realignment* (Beverly Hills, CA: Sage, 1980), 92–93, Table 3.1a.

The figures show the importance of Theodore Roosevelt's third-party candidacy in 1912 and the strength of Dwight Eisenhower in his races in 1952 and 1956.

For the more recent period, something similar to the normal vote technique developed by Philip E. Converse, which depends on individual-level survey data, can be used to create an expectation about vote choice in the absence of short-term forces. This technique uses party identification, expected defection rates, and turnout to generate an estimate of the normal vote. Our analysis (not shown) finds that the deviation of the actual Democratic vote meanders under the predicted Democratic normal vote, meaning that Democratic presidential candidates since 1968 have rarely done as well as would be expected, given the distribution of party identification. The elections of 2004, 2008, and 2012 were exceptions, as the Democratic candidates' performances matched Democratic partisan strength in the electorate. In elections in which a third-party candidate won a significant number of votes—1968, 1992, and 1996—both the Democratic and Republican candidates performed below what the normal votes would predict.

FIGURE 4-3   Republican Expected Vote in Presidential Elections, 1872–1968

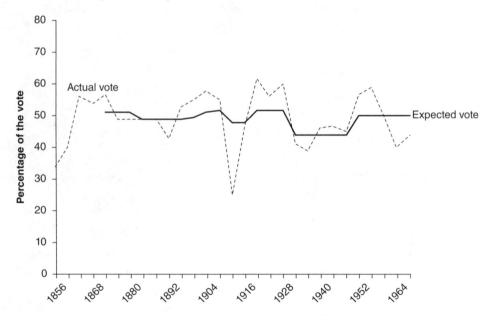

Source: Jerome M. Clubb, William H. Flanigan, and Nancy H. Zingale, *Partisan Realignment* (Beverly Hills, CA: Sage, 1980), 92–93, Table 3.1a.

Voting Behavior

The standard party identification question, used in almost all political surveys, asks respondents whether they are Republicans, Democrats, or independents and whether they are "strong" or "not very strong" Republicans or Democrats. The likelihood of voting loyally in support of one party varies with the strength of individuals' partisanship. The defection rates of strong and weak partisans in each presidential election since 1952 are shown in Figure 4-4. Declining party loyalty is apparent as the intensity of partisanship decreases. Strong partisans consistently support the candidate of their party at higher rates than do weak partisans. In most years, Republicans have been more loyal to their party than Democrats, although this is partly accounted for by southern Democrats who regularly deserted their party in presidential elections. By the end of the twentieth century, southern Democrats were no longer distinctive in this regard; previously defecting Democrats had become independents or Republicans.

Differences in candidate appeal affect the propensity to defect. Few Republicans deserted Dwight D. Eisenhower in the 1950s, Richard M. Nixon in 1972, or Ronald Reagan in 1984; many more left Barry Goldwater in 1964. Similarly, most Democrats were loyal to Lyndon B. Johnson in 1964 but abandoned George McGovern in large numbers in 1972.

Another potential cause of defection is attractive third-party candidates. In 1992, Ross Perot drew defectors from both parties, although more from the Republican side. Ten percent of strong Republicans and 25 percent of weak Republicans defected to Perot. Although few strong Democrats defected to Perot, 17 percent of weak Democrats did. John B. Anderson in 1980 and George C. Wallace in 1968 similarly account for part of the upsurges in defections in those years.

Historically, third-party candidates often have been viewed as "halfway houses" for partisans moving from one party to another. Not as dramatic for a partisan as defection to the opposition party, a vote for such a candidate may be a first step away from party loyalty or a temporary blip related to a party's nominee for president, economic conditions, or a positive response to an unusually effective third-party candidate. In any event, support for third parties and an increase in defection rates have generally been symptomatic of the loosening of party ties in eras of dealignment.

A different pattern—one of high party loyalty on both sides—was exhibited in the presidential elections of 1976, 1988, 1996, 2000, 2004, 2008, and 2012. In these elections, partisans of both parties remained loyal to candidates who were relatively balanced in their appeal. Contrary to much speculation before the election in 2012, Barack Obama

FIGURE 4-4   Defection Rates by Party Identifiers in Presidential Voting,
1952–2012

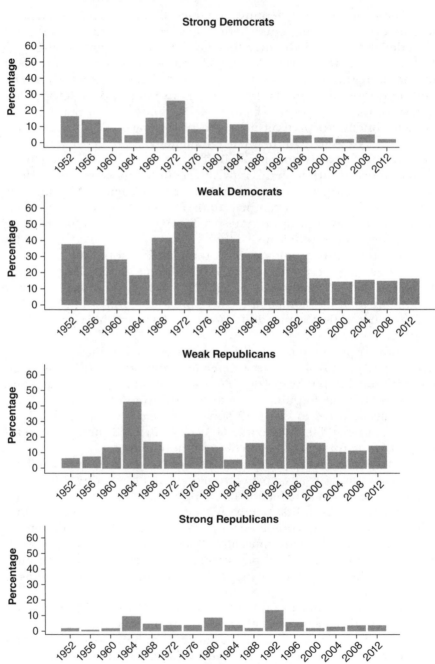

and Mitt Romney held onto their partisan bases very effectively. In the twenty-first century, the high degree of loyalty is also a reflection of partisan polarization.[5]

Although strong partisans vary in their loyalty from year to year depending on the candidates offered by their party, this tendency is much more pronounced among weak partisans. For example, the defection rate of strong Republicans falls in a narrow range from around 2 percent in a good Republican year to 10 percent in a bad year. In contrast, weak Republicans are almost as loyal as strong Republicans when an attractive Republican candidate is on the ticket, but nearly 50 percent defected in the disastrous 1964 election. The behavior of Democrats is similar, although both strong and weak Democrats are more likely to desert their party than are Republicans. Clearly, marked departures from the expected vote of a party are accomplished by wooing away the weaker partisans of the opposite party. Figure 4-4 shows that 2012 brought low defection rates for strong Republicans and historically low defection rates for strong Democrats. While weak partisans on both sides tended to hold the party line, their defection rates were higher than those of weak Republicans and Democrats in 2008.

The tendency of both strong and weak partisans to vote according to their party identification becomes even more pronounced as one moves down the ticket to less-visible and less-publicized offices. Figure 4-5 shows that this is a product of the dominant two-party system nationwide. Even highly successful third-party or independent candidates down the ticket are merely local disruptions that have virtually no impact on national patterns. (Data limitations from 2006 and 2010, years in which the ANES did not field a midterm survey, prevent the breaking down of partisans by strong and weak for the entirety of the congressional data.) The voting behavior of partisans in congressional races since 1952 differs from the presidential data in two significant ways. First, differences between the party loyalty of strong and weak partisans are usually smaller (not shown due to data constraints in 2006 and 2010). Second, the defection rate does not fluctuate from year to year nearly as much as in the presidential elections. Both differences are attributable to the lower visibility of congressional races. In a presidential election, the flood of available information means that a particularly attractive candidate or a stirring issue may touch the consciousness of the weak partisans, causing them to defect from traditional party ties; the firmly attached, strong partisans are more likely to resist. In the less-publicized congressional races, the information that might cause weak partisans to defect is less likely to even reach them. In the absence of information about the candidates and issues, weak partisans vote their party identification. The last two midterm races, in particular, have had historically low levels of partisan defection on both sides of the aisle.

FIGURE 4-5   Defection Rates by Party Identifiers in Congressional Voting,
1952–2012

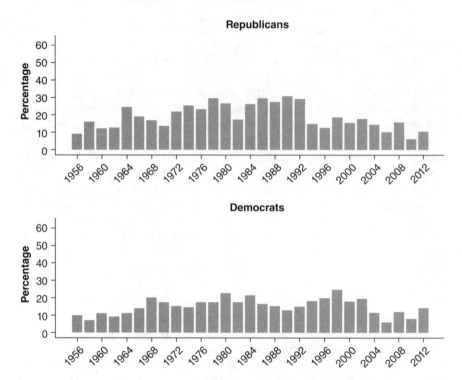

Sources: American National Election Studies, available at www.electionstudies.org. Data
for 2006 and 2010 from Pew Research Center, November 2006 Post-Election Survey and
November 2010 Post-Election Survey, available at people-press.org.

The intensity of partisanship affects political behavior beyond its
influence on the likelihood of voting for or defecting from a party's
candidate. Strong partisans are also more likely to vote in all kinds of
elections than are either weak partisans or independents. In fact, one
explanation sometimes offered for the low turnout in the late twentieth
century was the declining partisanship of the American public.[6] The
turnout rates of the various categories of partisans and independents
for three types of elections—presidential, off-year congressional, and
primary—are illustrated in Figure 4-6. Presidential primaries, despite all
their accompanying publicity and frenetic campaigning, typically have a
lower average turnout than off-year congressional elections. This is especially true in uncontested primaries, which often occur when an incumbent president is seeking reelection. With no opponents squaring off
against Barack Obama in 2012, fewer strong Democrats than strong

Republicans felt compelled to turn out to vote in the primaries. Even so, Figure 4-6 shows the power of strong partisanship, as strong Democrats voted at a higher rate than weak Republicans even though Republicans had a highly populated field of would-be nominees for their party.

In congressional voting, unlike presidential voting, Democrats were regularly more party loyal than were Republicans until 1994. This was both cause and effect of the recent disjuncture of national politics, whereby Republicans were stronger in presidential politics and Democrats dominated in congressional politics. Throughout the 1970s and 1980s the Republicans were able to field more attractive presidential candidates than the Democrats, leading more Democratic partisans to defect in presidential races. In contrast, congressional races saw Republican partisans often defecting to vote for a long-term Democratic incumbent running against token Republican opposition. The situation changed dramatically in 1994, when the Republicans gained control of the House of Representatives in part by fanning the flames of anti-incumbent,

FIGURE 4-6   Voting by Partisans and Independents in Presidential and Presidential
                         Primary Elections, 2012

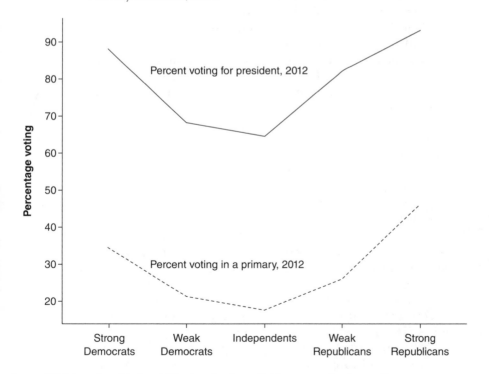

Source: 2012 American National Election Study, available at www.electionstudies.org.

anti-Democratic sentiment. Thereafter, with more Republican incumbents for whom to vote, Republican partisans were noticeably more party loyal than they had been in previous congressional elections. Even when the Democrats took back the House of Representatives in 2006, the percentage of GOP defectors in the electorate was low.

These ideas led Angus Campbell to suggest an intriguing theory of electoral change to explain the frequently observed phenomenon in American politics whereby the party winning the presidency almost always loses seats in the legislature in the next congressional election.[7] Because, the argument goes, presidential elections are usually accompanied by a high level of interest, large numbers of weak partisans and independents are drawn to the polls. Because weak partisans and independents are more easily shifted from one party to another, they add disproportionately to the vote for one presidential candidate, usually the winner. In congressional elections, these less-committed voters do not turn out, whereas relatively large numbers of intense partisans do. The strong party identifiers are not so likely to shift their vote away from their party. As a consequence, support declines in off-year congressional elections for the party that won the previous presidential election with disproportionately large numbers of less-interested voters.

Persuasive as Campbell's argument may be, it rests on some assumptions that may be questionable. First, it assumes that high-stimulus elections will be landslides—that is, it assumes that the short-term forces bringing the less-interested voter to the polls will work to the advantage of only one candidate. Even though this has often been the case, and it appears to have been so in 2008, for example, it is not invariable. The extremely close 1960 presidential election, with its emphasis on the religion (Catholicism) of Democratic candidate John F. Kennedy, was a high-turnout election, but different groups of voters were affected in different ways. Similarly, both George W. Bush and John Kerry benefited from the high turnout in 2004.

Second, Campbell's argument suggests that the less-interested voters who come to the polls to vote for the attractive presidential candidate will also vote for that party's candidate in congressional elections. In fact, the evidence shows that in many cases weak partisans who defect in presidential elections return to their own party in congressional elections or, in the case of Perot voters in 1992 and 1996, have no congressional candidates on the same ticket for whom to vote. In addition, independents often split their tickets instead of voting for the congressional candidate of the same party as their presidential choice. To some extent, the argument also rests on the assumption that independents are not only less partisan but also less informed, concerned, and interested in politics, a view that is frequently called into question.

Are Independents Apolitical?

Independents, who now account for more than one-third of the national electorate if leaners are included, are the most obvious source of additional votes for either party. Although partisans, especially weak partisans, sometimes abandon their party, year after year, independents are the largest bloc of uncommitted voters available to both parties. Theoretically, in the current closely divided electorate, the vote of the independents can easily determine the outcome of an election.

The independents' capacity for shifting back and forth between the major parties is shown in Table 4-3. Each party has, on occasion, successfully appealed to the independents, winning over a large majority to its side. In 1984, the independents voted almost two to one for Reagan over Walter F. Mondale, and Johnson held a similar advantage over Goldwater in 1964. During the years in which the Democrats had a clear advantage in partisan identifiers, Republicans had to win a healthy majority of the independent vote even to stay in close contention. This was the case in the elections of 2012 (Romney vs. Obama), 1976 (Jimmy Carter vs. Gerald R. Ford), and 1960 (Kennedy vs. Nixon). The election of George W. Bush in 2000 depended on, among other things, the substantial advantage he enjoyed over Al Gore among independents. Bush's reelection in 2004 was a different story as Democratic candidate Kerry handily carried the independent vote.[8] Obama matched Kerry's appeal to independent voters in 2008, though Mitt Romney scored more independent support than Obama did in 2012.

Third-party or independent candidates find unaffiliated voters a major source of votes. In 1992, 27 percent of the independents voted for Perot. His failure to hold those votes in 1996 turned his earlier, impressive showing into a minor story. In 1968, more than 20 percent of the independents gave their votes to Wallace, and in 1980, 14 percent voted for Anderson. Looking at the composition of third-party candidates' votes, more than half typically come from independents. Furthermore, independents may shift dramatically in voting for president and remain stable in voting for Congress.

On what basis do independents make their vote choices? Two views of independents have competed for popularity. The pundit's view is of an intelligent, informed, dispassionate evaluator of candidates and issues who, after careful consideration, votes for "the person, not the party." An alternate view—often attributed to scholars—is of an uninformed and uninterested voter on whom issue-oriented appeals is less effective. Further analysis will help determine who is right.

The first thing we need to do is make two distinctions among Independents. We note these distinctions and then drop them because they complicate the analysis and are usually ignored. First, important

TABLE 4-3   The Distribution of Votes for President by Independents, 1948–2012

	1952	1956	1960	1964	1968	1972	1976	1980	1984	1988	1992	1996	2000	2004	2008	2012
Democratic	34%	26%	46%	66%	26%	33%	46%	28%	34%	47%	43%	48%	46%	57%	58%	47%
Republican	66	74	54	34	57	67	54	58	66	53	30	36	54	42	42	50
Other candidate					17			14			27	15		1		3
Total	**100%**	**100%**	**100%**	**100%**	**100%**	**100%**	**100%**	**100%**	**100%**	**100%**	**100%**	**99%**	**100%**	**100%**	**100%**	**100%**
(N)	(261)	(303)	(298)	(219)	(281)	(481)	(537)	(299)	(424)	(357)	(574)	(283)	(344)	(245)	(499)	(428)

Source: American National Election Studies, available at www.electionstudies.org.

differences exist between nonpartisans who identify themselves as independents and those who lack any political identification. A sizable segment of the electorate answers the party identification question by saying that they identify themselves as nothing or that they do not know what they are. According to the coding conventions used by the American National Election Studies, most nonidentifiers are included with the independents, but important conceptual distinctions may exist between them and self-identified independents.[9] The two types of nonpartisans are included in Table 4-4. Those in one set identify themselves as *independents;* the others do not think of themselves in terms of political labels. Since 1972, between about one-sixth and one-third of the nonpartisans failed to identify themselves as independents. Even though the electorate generally has become more nonpartisan, it is not necessarily more independent. These situations present different implications for the political parties. Self-identified independents think of themselves as having a political identity and are somewhat antiparty in orientation. The nonidentifying nonpartisans have a less clear self-image of themselves as political actors, but they are not particularly hostile to the political parties. They are less self-consciously political in many ways.

Second, as we discussed earlier, within the large group of people who do not identify with either the Democratic or the Republican Party are many who say they "lean toward" one or the other. These leaners make up two-thirds of all nonpartisans, and they complicate analysis in a significant way. On crucial attitudes and in important forms of political behavior, the leaning independents look like partisans. Independents who lean toward the Democratic Party behave somewhat like weak Democratic partisans, and independents who lean toward the Republican Party behave like weak Republicans.[10] As can be seen in Figure 4-7, independent leaners are more similar to weak partisans than strong and weak partisans are to each other.

How appropriate, then, is it to include all independents in one category? On some characteristics, such as ideological self-identification and interest in public affairs, much more variation is evident within the three independent categories than between the several partisan categories. The differences between leaners and pure independents are often greater than those among Republicans or Democrats. Because the concept of "independent" embraces these three dissimilar groups, there is little wonder that some disagreement exists over what the true independent is like. As we briefly consider in chapter 5, some of these independents have ideological views on social and economic issues that directly contradict the views of other independents on the same issues. In any case, the point here is that independents are a very diverse group, and efforts to paint them with a broad brush and use that painting to make predictions is a fool's errand.

TABLE 4-4   Party Identifiers, Self-Identified Independents, and People Claiming No Preference, 1968–2012

	1968	1972	1976	1980	1984	1988	1992	1996	2000	2004	2008	2012
Identify with a party	69%	64%	63%	64%	64%	63%	61%	64%	59%	61%	60%	59%
Identify as independents	26	28	29	24	25	31	32	28	28	33	33	35
Have no preference	3	8	8	12	10	6	7	8	12	5	6	3
Don't know										1	1	2
Not ascertained					1							1
Total	**98%**	**100%**	**100%**	**100%**	**100%**	**100%**	**100%**	**100%**	**99%**	**100%**	**100%**	**100%**
(N)	(1,557)	(2,705)	(2,870)	(1,614)	(2,257)	(2,040)	(2,488)	(1,714)	(1,807)	(1,212)	(2,322)	(2,056)

Source: American National Election Studies, available at www.electionstudies.org.

FIGURE 4-7   Percentage of Turnout, High Interest, and Democratic Vote for
President by Partisanship, 2012

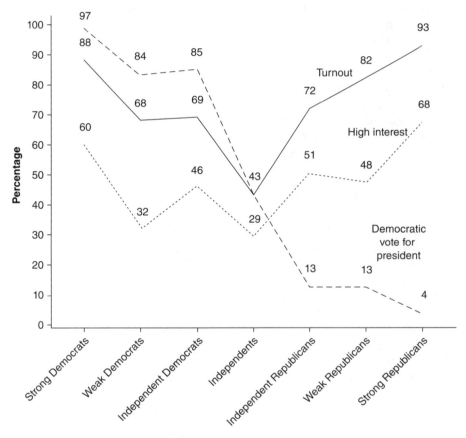

Source: 2012 American National Election Study, available at www.electionstudies.org.

In other words, as a consequence of including various types of people under the label "independent," making generalizations about the degree of political interest and information of independents is difficult. Some independents have considerable interest in politics, and others are apathetic. There are more informed, concerned voters among the leaning independents than among other nonpartisans, and the leaning independents are more likely to register and to vote. So are independents attentive or apathetic toward politics? The answer is, they are both.

To the student of contemporary American politics, these characteristics of the independent remain important because they determine the independent's susceptibility to political appeals. We and others have argued that the American electoral system is presently at a time when a fairly large group of potential voters has weak ties to the political parties. The argument is that, when a large portion of the electorate is either independent or exhibits more independent behavior, these people form a pool of potential recruits for one of the parties or a new party. Given the diverse nature of beliefs among the ranks of independents, the likelihood of the emergence of a third party that appeals to a majority of independents is unlikely. Indeed, between 2006 and 2008, anti-Bush and pro-Obama sentiment combined to move some previous independents to begin calling themselves Democrats, at the same time moving some Republicans into the independent category.

Partisans and Electoral Change

As we have said, the utility of the concept of the expected vote in part lies in providing a base against which to measure and analyze departures from the expected pattern. One type of departure is usually referred to as *deviating change:* the temporary deviations from normal party loyalty attributable to the short-term forces of candidate images or issues.[11] The amount of deviating change in an election tells how well a candidate or party did relative to the party's normal performance. In these terms, the Dwight D. Eisenhower victories in 1952 and 1956 and the Richard M. Nixon landslide in 1972 appear even more dramatic because they represent big Republican margins during a time when the Democratic Party held an advantage in party loyalists. These deviating elections involved substantial departures from the underlying strength of the two parties in the electorate.

Temporary deviating changes may be dramatic and reflect important electoral forces, but another type of change is of even greater interest. On rare occasions in American national politics, a permanent or *realigning change* in voting patterns occurs. In such instances, the electorate departs from its expected voting pattern but does not return to the old pattern afterward. The changes sometimes are large and durable enough to alter the competitive balance between the parties, with significant consequences for the policy directions of the government. Such a period of change is usually referred to as a *partisan realignment.*[12]

Electoral analysts usually discuss three major realignments in American history. One occurred during the time of the Civil War and the emergence of the Republican Party; another followed the depression of 1893 and benefited the Republicans; and the most recent followed the depression of 1929 and led to Democratic Party dominance. These abrupt changes in the expected votes of the parties can be seen in

Figures 4-2 and 4-3. Each realignment of partisan loyalties coincided with a major national crisis, leading to the supposition that a social or economic crisis is necessary to shake loose customary loyalties. But major crises and national traumas have not always led to disruptions of partisanship, suggesting that other political conditions must also be present for a crisis to produce a realignment. The nature of the realignment crisis has political significance, however, because it generally determines the lines along which the rearrangement in partisan loyalties will take place, as different segments of the electorate respond differently to the crisis and to attempts to solve it.

In general, realignments appear to happen in the following way. At a time of national crisis, the electorate rejects the party in power, giving a decisive victory to the other party—a victory that includes not only the presidency but also large majorities in both houses of Congress. The new party in office acts to meet the crisis, often with innovative policies that are sharp departures from the past. *If* the administration's policy initiatives are successful in solving the nation's problems (or at least if they are widely perceived as successful), then significant numbers of voters will become partisans of the new administration's party and continue voting for this party in subsequent elections, thus causing a lasting change in the division of partisan strength in the electorate. If the administration in power is *not* perceived as successful in handling the crisis, then in all likelihood the voters will reject that party in the next election, and its landslide victory in the previous election will be regarded, in retrospect, as a deviating election.

In a realignment, the people who become partisans of the new majority party likely are independents and previously uninvolved members of the electorate, not partisans of the other party. In other words, in a realignment few Democrats or Republicans switch parties. It appears more likely that independents drop their independent stance and become partisan. Thus, for a realignment to occur, a precondition may be a pool of people without partisan attachments who are available for realignment. This, in turn, suggests a longer sequence of events that forms a realignment cycle.

First there is the crisis that, if successfully handled, leads to a realignment. This initiates a period of electoral stability during which the parties take distinct stands on the issues that were at the heart of the crisis. Party loyalty is high during this period, both within the electorate and among the elected political leaders in government. However, as time passes, new problems arise and new issues gradually disrupt the old alignment and lead to greater electoral instability. During this period, often referred to as a *dealignment,* voters are much more susceptible to the personal appeals of candidates, to local issues, and to other elements that might lead to departures from underlying party loyalty. As the time since the last realignment lengthens, more and more new voters come into the electorate without attachments to the symbols and issues of the past that made their elders party loyalists. This group of voters, who have no strong attachments to either party, may provide the basis for a new realignment should a crisis arise and one or the other of the parties be perceived as solving it. One conceptual problem for the realignment perspective is its "either/or" nature. Declaring whether an election is or isn't a realigning one can mask slow but important shifts in the electorate. As campaigns become more sophisticated and ideologues sort themselves into the party that is best for them (see Chapter 5), dramatic realigning elections seem to be less common.

Party Systems and Realignments

Political historians often divide American electoral history into five *party systems*—eras that are distinguished from each other by the different political parties that existed or by the different competitive relationships among the parties.[13] The transition from one party system to another has usually been marked by a realignment.

The first party system, which extended from the 1790s until about 1824, saw the relatively rapid formation of two parties, the Federalists and the Jeffersonian Republicans. The issue that divided the parties most clearly was their attitude toward the power of the central government. The commercial and financial interests supported the Federalist position of increasing the authority of the central government, whereas Jeffersonian Republicans distrusted the centralizing and, in their view, aristocratic tendencies of their rivals. The parties began as factions within Congress, but before long they had gained organizations at the state and local level and had substantially broadened the base of political participation among the voting population. After 1815, competition between the two parties all but ceased as the Jeffersonian Republicans gained supremacy, moving the country into the so-called Era of Good Feelings.

The second party system is usually dated from 1828, the year of the first presidential election with substantial popular participation, which marked the resurgence of party competition for the presidency. Emerging ultimately from this renewed competition were the Democrats and the Whigs, parties that competed almost evenly for national power until the 1850s. Mass political participation increased, and party organizations were strengthened as both parties sought electoral support from the common people. Although the Democratic Party had come to prominence led by frontiersman Andrew Jackson, by the 1850s both Democrats and Whigs had adherents in all sections of the nation. Thus, when the issue of slavery broke full-force on the nation, the existing parties could not easily cope with the sectional differences they found within their ranks. As the Whigs and Democrats compromised or failed to act because of internal disagreements, a flurry of minor parties appeared to push the cause of abolition. One of these, the Republican Party, eventually replaced the floundering Whigs as one of the two major parties that would dominate party systems thereafter.

The intense conflicts that preceded the Civil War led to the basic regional alignment of Democratic dominance in the South and Republican strength in the North that emerged from the war and that characterized the third-party system. But the extreme intensity and durability of the partisan loyalties were also significantly dependent on emotional attachments associated with the war. The strength of partisan attachments after the Civil War was not lessened by the sharp competitiveness of the two parties throughout the system. Electoral forces were so evenly balanced that the Republican Party could effectively control the presidency and Congress only by excluding the southern Democrats from participation in elections. Once Reconstruction relaxed enough to permit the full expression of Democratic strength, the nation was narrowly divided, with the slightest deviation determining the outcome of elections.

The most dominant characteristic of the Civil War realignment was the regional division of party strongholds, but considerable Republican vote strength was found throughout much of the South and Democratic strength in most of the North. Especially in the North, states that regularly cast their electoral votes for Republican presidential candidates did so by slim margins. Within each region, persistent loyalty to the minority party was usually related to earlier opposition to the war. The intensity of feelings surrounding the war overwhelmed other issues, and the severity of the division over the war greatly inhibited the emergence of new issues along other lines. Thus, a significant feature of the Civil War realignment is its "freezing" of the party system.[14] Although later realignments have occurred and a fourth and fifth party system can be identified, after the Civil War the same two parties have remained dominant. New parties have found it impossible to compete effectively (although they may occasionally affect electoral outcomes). The subsequent realignments changed only the competitive position of these two parties relative to each other. Thus, although the choices were frozen following the Civil War, the relative strength of the parties was not.

Toward the end of the nineteenth century, Civil War loyalties weakened enough to allow new parties, particularly the Populists in the Midwest and South, to make inroads into the votes of both major parties. Following the economic recession of 1893, for which the Democrats suffered politically, the Republican Party began to improve its basic voting strength. In 1896, the formation of a coalition of Democrats and

Populists and the unsuccessful presidential candidacy of their nominee, William Jennings Bryan, resulted in increased Republican strength in the East and a further strengthening of the secure position of the Democratic Party in the South. Republican domination was solidified in the Midwest by the popularity of Theodore Roosevelt in the election of 1904. By the early twentieth century, competitive areas were confined to the border states and a few mountain states.

The realignment of 1896 and the fourth party system that followed are appropriately viewed as an adjustment of the Civil War alignment. Few areas shifted far from the previous levels of voting; most individuals probably did not change their partisanship. The issue basis of the alignment was economic. The Republicans advocated development and modernization while opposing regulation of economic activity. The Democrats supported policies intended to provide remedies for particular economic hardships. At a minimum these issues led the more prosperous, more modern areas in the North to shift toward the Republicans and the more backward, more depressed areas in the South to shift toward the Democrats. These tendencies are based on normal vote patterns and should not obscure the considerable variation in the vote for president during these years, particularly in the elections of 1912 and 1916.

Following the onset of the Great Depression in 1929 under a Republican president, Democrat Franklin D. Roosevelt rode the reaction to economic hardship to a landslide victory in 1932. In his first administration, Roosevelt launched a program of economic recovery and public assistance called the New Deal. The Democrats emerged as the majority party, signaling the start of the fifth party system. The New Deal realignment resulted in far greater shifts than the earlier realignment of 1896, because it moved many of the northern states from Republican to Democratic status. Because the policies of the Democratic administration during the New Deal appealed more to the working class than to the middle class, more to poor farmers than to prosperous farmers, these groups responded differently to Democratic candidates. The New Deal and the electorate's response to Roosevelt's administration considerably sharpened the social class basis of party support. Especially for younger voters during these years, class politics was of greater salience than it had been before or has been since.

This realignment resulted in adjustments in previous loyalties, but it did not override them completely. The New Deal coalition was based on regional strength in the South, which was independent of social class, and further reinforced an already overwhelming dominance in the region. The most incompatible elements in the New Deal coalition were southern middle-class whites, mainly conservative, and northern liberals, both white and black, and this incompatibility led to the later unraveling of the New Deal alignment. The erosion of the New Deal coalition occurred first in presidential voting with the departure of southern white voters from the Democratic Party. In 1964, the states of the Deep South were the only states carried by Republican candidate Barry Goldwater, a stark reversal of one hundred years of history. This pattern continued for the next four decades. Only when the Democratic candidate was a southerner (Jimmy Carter in 1976 and Bill Clinton in 1992 and 1996) did the Democrats have a chance to carry some southern states. In 2000, Gore, also a southerner, was given a chance of winning only two southern states—Florida and his home state of Tennessee. Ultimately, he won neither. (Of course, he was running against another southerner, George W. Bush.) However, Obama's success in winning Florida, North Carolina, and Virginia in 2008 and Florida and Virginia again in 2012 needs to be viewed against this recent history.

The departure of the South from the Democratic fold is the major reason for the decline of the New Deal coalition. To a degree, working-class whites in the North also have been attracted to the Republican Party on occasion, and middle-class voters—particularly those in service professions—have shifted toward the Democrats.

Survey data on party identification over the past fifty years yield evidence of the New Deal alignment, as well as its later deterioration (recall Table 4-1). In the early years of this period, the advantage that the Democrats enjoyed nationwide was largely a result of having an overwhelming Democratic majority in the South, as shown in Table 4-2. The increased strength of the Republicans in the South after 1964 led to a number of years of fairly even balance nationwide between Democrats and Republicans. Since 2006, the Democrats have gained an advantage over the Republicans, as Democrats increased their strength in the North.

Another important element regarding shifts in the New Deal alignment, also reflected in these tables, was the increase beginning in 1966 in the proportion of independents. Supporters of George Wallace in the South represented part of this increase initially, but an even larger portion is composed of young voters who, since the early 1970s, have not chosen sides in politics as quickly as their elders did. The increase leveled off in the 1970s, and although the proportions have fluctuated, the number of independents remains near its highest point since the era of survey research began. The 42 percent independent in 2000 is the largest proportion of independents in the history of the American National Election Studies.

The New Deal partisan realignment established in the 1930s remained intact longer in congressional voting. However, by the 1970s additional shifts in the New Deal alignment became evident, as conservative Republicans began to show strength in races for other offices in many parts of the South. Long-standing southern Democratic incumbents in Congress were safe from competition. As they stepped down, though, their seats were won more often than not by Republicans. Conversely, in some areas of the North moderate Republicans were replaced by liberal Democrats. In the 2008 congressional elections, not one Republican was elected to the House of Representatives from New England. These trends are shown in Figure 4-6, plotting the Democratic vote for Congress in the North and South since 1936. Clearly, Democratic strength in the South was crucial for the Democrats' control of the House of Representatives for much of this historical period.

We should be clear about what is changing and what is not. White southerners have always been conservative, especially on matters concerning race. From the Civil War until the 1960s, the Democratic Party was at least as conservative as the Republican Party on the crucial issue of race. When the national Republican Party took the more conservative position on race in 1964, white southerners began to vote for Republican presidential candidates; they continued to vote for southern conservative Democratic candidates in state and local races. Meanwhile, for the same reasons in reverse, newly enfranchised black southern voters were moving into the Democratic Party. Over the years, the positions of the two parties have become more clearly distinguished—the Democratic Party as the more liberal party on racial as well as economic issues, the Republican Party as the more conservative party. Particularly in the South, voters have changed their partisanship and their votes accordingly. Figure 4-8, showing the party identification of white voters, North and South, from 1952 to 2012, highlights the dramatic shift in the partisanship of white southerners over this period introduced in Table 4-2. The congressional elections of 1994 were perhaps the moment when the shift became complete. Even so, white Southern Democratic Party identifiers have continued to drop while non-Southern white Democrats have continued to fluctuate around the 40 percent mark. When the Republicans took control of the House of Representatives and Senate, their leadership was predominantly southern.

Are Conditions Right for a Realignment?

The decline of the New Deal coalition is best seen, we believe, as more of a process of conflict extension than of traditional dealignment.[15] Voter movement and electoral volatility have been in evidence since the 1960s. Furthermore, much of this movement has been a sorting-out process whereby some voters are finding their natural home in a political party that shares their views on issues that concern them most. Over this same time period, however, a sizable number of voters have found neither political party a congenial place and have chosen instead

FIGURE 4-8   Democratic Identification among Southern and Non-Southern
Whites, 1952–2012

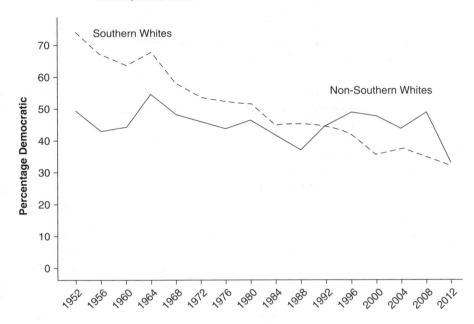

Source: American National Election Studies, available at www.electionstudies.org.

to become independent, not adopt a party identification in the first
place, or support independent candidates such as Perot or, to a lesser
extent, Nader. Through the 1990s, neither party was able to gather the
political support to take firm control of government or complete initiatives that would appear to solve societal problems and win converts to
their ranks. This sounds a lot like dealignment, so what gives?

Geoffrey Layman and Thomas Carsey have argued that what has
occurred in American politics can best be described not as dealignment
but as "conflict extension."[16] Along with other scholars, they show that
the New Deal divide between Republicans and Democrats has remained
on economic issues and that political conflict has been extended to
include issues of race and social issues like abortion and gay rights. As
Edward Carmines, Michael Ensley, and Michael Wagner have shown,
some Americans have liberal attitudes across these issues and are strong
Democrats, whereas others have conservative attitudes across these same
issues and are strong Republicans.[17] However, plenty of people have
views that are liberal on one set of issues and conservative on the other.
(We discuss this in greater detail in chapter 5.) Libertarians (conservative

on economic issues, liberal on social issues) and populists (the opposite of libertarians) regularly identify as partisans but are more likely to switch their party ID due to short-term forces, are more likely to cast split-ticket ballots, and are less likely to participate. Thus, while elite conflict has extended to a left-right divide across the panoply of political issues currently contested in Washington, the public continues to organize its attitudes separately across economic and social issues. In other words, the New Deal divide has weakened, but it still remains while at the same time the parties have adopted competing positions on a whole new set of issues that have pulled some people closer to the parties and pushed others further away. Those who have attitudes on social issues that match the positions offered by their political party have "extended" their conflict with the party on the other side of the aisle. Those who have attitudes on social issues that match one party and attitudes on economic issues that match the other have found themselves stuck in the middle, even though most (weakly) identify with a party.

Into this scenario rode a charismatic young candidate for president who promised change and won election in 2008 with the largest margin of victory in twenty-four years. His party increased the size of the majorities it had recaptured in both houses of Congress in 2006, giving the new administration control of all three branches of the federal government. Six months into the new Congress, the Democrats reached the magic number of sixty votes needed to shut off a filibuster in the Senate, after one switch of allegiance (Arlen Specter of Pennsylvania, who changed from Republican to Democrat) and one resolution to a long-running recount (Al Franken of Minnesota). Public opinion polls found fewer people who identified with the Republicans and more identifying with the Democrats. The new administration took office amid great euphoria, sky-high approval ratings, and an ambitious agenda of health care reform, energy independence, stopping climate change, and restoring international respect and prestige. Several of the ingredients for a realignment were there—a crisis (or crises); an electorate willing to throw the rascals out; a pool of voters without affiliation to either party, available for conversion; and unified control of government, giving the new administration the ability, in principle, to enact its policy agenda. Pundits argued that the opportunity was there for the new administration to capture the imagination of those available independents, turn them into Democrats, and change the partisan division in the country for the foreseeable future. The United States was poised for a true realignment and a new party system.

But . . .

As we contemplate this scenario, we need to keep in mind that many of the voters up for grabs in any given election have a series of issue preferences that do not match up perfectly with either party. Thus, long-term conversion of these voters is a difficult prospect. Carsey and Layman have also shown that people are willing to change their attitudes to align with their political party on issues that are not very important to them, but this has not occurred enough, nor has it been sufficiently durable, to result in a realignment.[18] Though the administration was moderately successful at enacting its policy agenda (with big victories, including health care reform, the auto bailout, and the economic stimulus plan), it also had some notable failures (failing to close the detention center at Guantanamo Bay, increase the minimum wage to $9.50/hr, and usher in a new era of bipartisan cooperation in Washington, D.C.). The Democrats' dramatic loss of seats in Congress in 2010 reflected, in part, the frustration of citizens over the unified government of Democrats not getting more accomplished, which also helped to prevent a cementing of a new and durable Democratic majority.

Partisan Change

Partisanship can be thought of as a basic attitude that establishes a normal or expected vote, an estimate about how individuals or populations will vote, other things being equal. However, partisanship itself is not unchangeable. Individuals may change not only their vote but also their long-term party identification from one party to another. More important, over extended periods of time, the partisan composition of the electorate may be altered as new voters of one political persuasion replace older voters of another. When the basic partisan division of the electorate changes, a partisan realignment occurs.

In the past, the absence of survey data limited analysis of realignments, but during the current period the individual processes of partisan change that underlie aggregate shifts in the partisan division of the electorate can be studied. These processes have been a matter of some controversy. One perspective holds that individual partisans are *converted* from one party to the other during a realignment. Other analysts, noting the psychological difficulty in changing long-held and deeply felt attachments, argue that such change probably comes about through *mobilization,* not conversion. In other words, the independents or nonpolitical individuals, perhaps predominantly young voters just entering the electorate without strong partisan attachments, fuel a realignment by joining the electorate overwhelmingly on the side of one party.

Some evidence on these points comes from the New Deal era. Although survey research was then in its infancy, some scholars have creatively used data from early surveys to try to answer these questions. Research by Kristi Andersen, reported in *The Changing American Voter,*

reveals high levels of nonvoting and nonpartisanship among young people and new citizens before the Great Depression.[19] Those uninvolved,
uncommitted potential participants entered the electorate in the 1930s
disproportionately as Democrats. Andersen's findings on the electorate
of the 1920s and 1930s support the view that realignments are based on
the mobilization of new, independent voters instead of on the conversion of partisans. In contrast, Robert S. Erikson and Kent L. Tedin argue
on the basis of early Gallup Poll data that much of the increase in the
Democratic vote in the 1930s came from voters who had previously
voted Republican.[20]

In the next section, we examine the processes of partisan change in
the contemporary period. Although we are in a better position to do so
than we were for earlier eras, efforts are still hampered by a scarcity of
panel data—that is, repeated interviews with the same individuals at different times. In most cases, it will be necessary to infer individual changes
from the behavior of different individuals over time.

Changes in Individuals over a Lifetime

Two types of change in partisan identification can be distinguished,
both of which have significant implications for political behavior. First,
an individual may change from one party to another or to independent
or from independence to partisanship. Such change is important if a
large proportion of the electorate shifts in the same direction at about
the same time. Second, an individual's partisanship may strengthen or
weaken in intensity. A long-standing hypothesis states that the longer
individuals identify with a party, the stronger their partisanship will
become.[21] In the electorate as a whole, the two types of change are not
necessarily related to one another, so the occurrence of one form of
change does not dictate or prevent the other. For example, recent
decades saw an increase in the number of independents in the electorate, which can be accounted for by young people not choosing a party
or by partisans moving to independence or both. At the same time, the
remaining partisans have become more firmly committed and more
party loyal, and polarization between the parties has increased.

Analysts have attempted to explain partisan change by referring
to three types of causal effects: (1) *period effects,* or the impact of a particular historical period that briefly affects partisanship across all age
groups; (2) a *generation effect,* which affects the partisanship of a particular age group for the remainder of their political lives; and (3) a
life-cycle effect, which produces changes associated with an individual's
age. In current political behavior, all three can be illustrated: a period
effect that resulted in increased independence in all age groups, a

FIGURE 4-9   Distribution of Independents, by Age Cohorts, 1952, 1972, 1992, and 2012

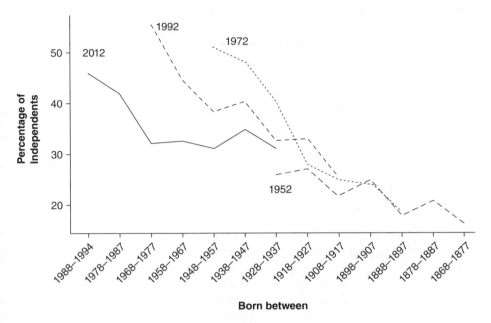

Source: American National Election Studies, available at www.electionstudies.org.

Note: The youngest cohort in each year includes only those old enough to vote.

generation effect that keeps Democratic partisan loyalty high in the generation that entered the electorate during the New Deal, and a life-cycle effect that yields greater independence among the young than among their elders.

The difference between 1952, 1972, 1992, and 2012 in the proportion of independents in various age groups is shown in Figure 4-9. The left end of each line reflects a higher rate of independence among the young in 1972, 1992, and 2012 when compared with 1952.

Each line reveals a downward slope to the right. This indicates that older individuals in each year were less likely to be independents compared with younger people in the same year (a life-cycle effect). By looking at the first point on the left of each line, the youngest respondents can be compared in each of the four years; the second point represents the second-youngest group; and so on. In general, the cohorts in the 1992 and 2012 surveys have higher levels of political independence at each age than the cohorts from the 1972 and 1952 surveys (a generation effect).

The change in particular age cohorts also can be examined using Figure 4-9.* The youngest cohort in 1972 was more than forty years old in 1992 and reveals a lower level of independence than it did when entering the electorate. By 2012, the cohort was more than sixty years old and had stayed about the same in its level of independence. At each point along the lines, the vertical distance represents an age cohort and shows the changing percentage of independents in that age cohort. Most age cohorts became more independent before 1980 and did not change much after that. This is a period effect.

Contrary to political folklore, little evidence exists that people become Republicans as they grow older—that is, that a life-cycle effect favors Republicans. Older members of the electorate were, for some years, more likely to be Republicans than younger members. The generation of young people who came of age before the Great Depression contained large proportions of Republicans, an understandable situation given the advantage the Republicans enjoyed nationally at that time. Relatively few members of this generation changed partisanship over the years, and these individuals constituted the older, more heavily Republican segment of the electorate. By the same token, the generation that entered the electorate during the New Deal was disproportionately Democratic. Because they also remained stable in partisanship, older voters looked increasingly Democratic as this generation aged.

However, when party voting is frequently disrupted, this reinforcement of partisanship may not occur. Even if the strength of partisanship does not increase with age, older partisans are less likely to abandon their party and become independents. This explains in part why older partisans are less likely to vote for independent or third-party candidates than are younger partisans. In 1992, 19 percent of the Republican and Democratic partisans aged twenty-five and younger voted for Perot, but only 11 percent of partisans aged forty-five and older voted for him. In 2000, Nader's vote, although small, was greatest among the young.

---

*In the absence of repeated observations of the same individuals over time, studying many aspects of change is impossible. The use of age cohorts is an analytical technique that attempts to assess individual change through the use of surveys of different individuals over the years. Individuals of a certain age are isolated in an early survey—say thirty- to forty-year-olds in 1960—and they are compared with forty- to fifty-year-olds from a 1970 survey. Thus, an age cohort can be compared at two different times. This technique has been used in several studies of partisanship. See, for example, Paul R. Abramson, "Generational Change in American Electoral Behavior," *American Political Science Review* 68 (March 1974): 93–105; David Butler and Donald Stokes, *Political Change in Britain: Forces Shaping Electoral Choice* (New York: St. Martin's Press, 1969), especially chaps. 3 and 11; and Philip E. Converse, *The Dynamics of Party Support: Cohort-Analyzing Party Identification* (Beverly Hills, CA: Sage, 1976).

Gradual changes in individual partisanship have not been assessed satisfactorily for the entire public because the few election studies based on repeated interviews of the same individuals have covered at most four years. Nevertheless, the possibility that individuals change their partisanship over longer time periods is of considerable interest. Speculation has focused on the possibility that the large number of young independents will become identified with one party or the other, thus creating a substantial shift in the overall partisan balance of the electorate. Obama's appeal to young people makes this appear a current possibility.

The best evidence of this type of change in the past comes from a major study of political socialization conducted by M. Kent Jennings. He surveyed a national sample of high school students and their parents in 1965, with follow-up interviews in 1973, 1982, and 1997.[22] This study provides a before-and-after picture of young people during the political traumas of the late 1960s and early 1970s, as well as later snapshots after a more quiescent period.

Table 4-5 shows the amount of change in partisanship between each wave of the study. As can be seen by looking at the highlighted

TABLE 4-5   Stability and Change of Partisanship, 1965–1997

		1973					1982		
		Dem.	Ind.	Rep.			Dem.	Ind.	Rep.
	Dem.	24	14	3		Dem.	23	9	3
1965	Ind.	7	24	5	1973	Ind.	8	32	7
	Rep.	3	9	10		Rep.	2	4	13
	Total = 99%		N = 952			Total = 101%		N = 924	

		1997		
		Dem.	Ind.	Rep.
	Dem.	23	7	2
1982	Ind.	5	27	5
	Rep.	4	10	17
	Total = 100%		N = 896	

Source: Youth-Parent Socialization Panel Study, 1965–1997, Youth Wave. Data provided by Inter-university Consortium for Political and Social Research.

Note: Dem. = Democrat; Ind. = Independent; Rep. = Republican. The highlighted cells (along the diagonal) represent those individuals who remained stable in their partisanship from one time period to the next. The off-diagonal cells represent individuals who changed their partisan identification.

cells, partisanship was least stable when the respondents were youngest, between 1965 and 1973. About two-thirds of the sample reported the same partisanship when interviewed in 1982 as in 1973 and, again, between 1982 and 1997. Most of the changes that did occur were between partisanship and independence; relatively few reported switching from Democrat to Republican or vice versa.

Changes across Generations

A shift in the partisan composition of the electorate owing to generational change is ordinarily a gradual one, because political attitudes, including partisanship, tend to be transmitted from parents to their children. Normally, more than two-thirds of the electorate identify with their parents' party if both parents had the same party identification. Adoption of parents' partisanship by their children is consistent with the notion of family socialization, but it is also consistent with the notion that political views are, in part, biological in nature. Children pick up the partisanship of their parents while young, but the parents' influence diminishes as the child comes into contact with other political and social influences during the teenage years. For most individuals, the political influence of their surroundings will be consistent with their family's political leanings, so the similarity between parents' and off-spring's partisanship remains strong. In contrast, people who remember their parents as having conflicting loyalties are more likely to be independents than either Democrats or Republicans. This is even more true of the children of parents without any partisan attachments. Thus, in each political generation a sizable number of voters lack an inherited party loyalty.

The Jennings study permits the empirical examination of the process of generational change because it allows a comparison of party identification for parents and their children. As can be seen in Figure 4-10, 58 percent of the seventeen-year-olds in 1965 had adopted the party identification of their parents. Of the high school seniors, 30 percent were Democratic and came from Democratic families. Another 10 percent of the seniors were Democratic but came from independent or Republican families. Although not explicitly shown in Figure 4-10, Democrats had a somewhat higher transmission rate than either Republicans or independents. Despite the higher transmission rate, there were so many more Democratic parents that their children also contributed substantial numbers to the independent ranks.

The latest wave of the Jennings study allows an examination of generational change in a more recent time, by comparing the partisanship of the 1965 high school seniors, now parents, with the partisanship

FIGURE 4-10   Party Identification of High School Seniors and Their
Parents, 1965

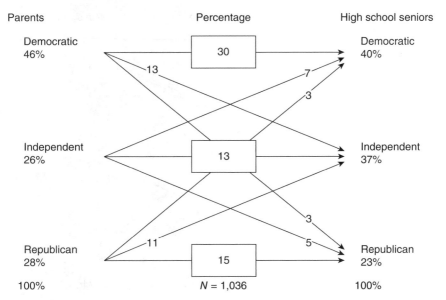

Source: Adapted from Paul A. Beck, Jere W. Bruner, and L. Douglas Dobson, *Political Socialization* (Washington, DC: American Political Science Association, 1974), 22.

Note: On the left of the figure is the distribution of the parents' party identification and on the right is their children's. The numbers in the three boxes highlight the percentages of the children who had the same party identification as their parents. The numbers on the remaining arrows show various amounts of change from their parents' partisanship by the children. For example, 7 percent of the total number of children had independent parents but became Democrats.

of their high school–age children (see Figure 4-11). (Not all the original 1965 students had children of that age in 1997, so the focus is on only a subset of those in the original sample reinterviewed in 1997. Therefore the distribution of partisanship of these parents will not be the same as for the whole 1997 sample covered in Table 4-5. The group of parents is somewhat less Democratic and more Republican than the full group.) Figure 4-11 suggests that parents transmitted their partisanship to their children at a lower rate in the 1990s than they had a generation earlier. Hidden in these numbers, however, are traces of a modest recovery in partisanship. Unlike 1965, the younger generation is only slightly more independent than the parents, and the number of children leaving their parents' parties for independence is about

FIGURE 4-11   Party Identification of High School Seniors and Their
Parents, 1997

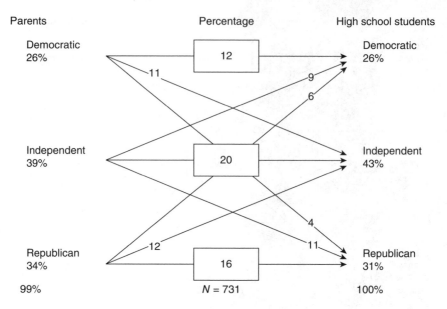

Source: Youth-Parent Socialization Panel Study, 1965–1997, Youth Wave. Data provided by
Inter-university Consortium for Political and Social Research.

equally offset by the children of independents adopting a partisanship.
In 1965, twice as many children opted for independence as moved
toward partisanship.

The Future of Parties and Partisanship

Since the 1970s, some political observers have commented on the
weakness of political parties, citing especially the overall increase in independents and the appeal of independent candidates, such as Anderson
in 1980 or Perot in 1992 and 1996. These factors, combined with declines
in trust and confidence in government, turnout, and attention to political news, have suggested to some that the American public has lost its
capacity to identify with political parties in a meaningful way. A corollary
would suggest there would likely never be another realignment because
political parties would not be able to attract new partisans to their camps.

A contrary point of view argues that many of these trends slowed or
stopped in the late 1970s, that partisan stability and party loyal behavior

since then have been nearly as high as in the 1950s. Analysts cite increases in party-line voting in Congress, sharper ideological division between the parties, and an increase in uncivil political discourse in the mass media and in Congress as evidence of the increased commitment to, as well as the polarization of, political parties.

So is partisanship becoming stronger or weaker? It seems to us that both these phenomena are occurring—in different parts of the electorate. On the one hand, among political elites and party activists, the polarization and hostility are becoming greater. On the other hand, a large pool of individuals remains who do not strongly identify with either of the major parties and for whom the increased intensity of the partisan debate is off-putting.

The close competitiveness of recent presidential elections has raised the intensity of feelings about politics. In 2004 and again in 2008, almost half the public reported trying to influence other people's votes. This is a substantial increase over percentages reported in any election in the past fifty years. Higher percentages than in previous elections reported having a strong preference for their presidential choice and caring who won the election. However, this does not seem to translate to stronger partisanship. The percentage of strong party identifiers has not increased in twenty years and is not as high today as it was in the 1950s and early 1960s. The percentage of people who call themselves "extremely liberal" or "extremely conservative" has not increased either and is generally a small fraction of the population.

A sizable segment of the electorate distrusts political parties, preferring divided government to keep either party from doing too much. The 2008 American National Election Study found that a majority of the public (51 percent) preferred to see divided control of government, though a Gallup survey just four years later saw that number drop to 23 percent.

For at least some of these nonparty people, the problem with the parties is the same partisan and ideological intensity that has been increasing. They see the party elites and activists as extreme in their views, whereas they see themselves as moderate. They view party conflict in Washington as divisive and contributing to, instead of solving, the country's problems. These are the people attracted to Romney's record of bipartisanship and Obama's appeal to postpartisanship. For such people, heightened partisan debate is unlikely to move them to embrace a political party. Becoming more engaged in political discussion, turning out to vote, and trying to influence the views of others are not unimportant aspects of the public's behavior, and they may signal changes in the partisan feelings of American citizens. However, the largest changes in partisan behavior are among leaders and political activists.

Notes

1. E. E. Schattschneider, *Party Government* (New York: Farrar & Rinehart, 1942), 1.
2. The most important research cited on party identification is in Angus Campbell, Philip E. Converse, Warren E. Miller, and Donald E. Stokes, *The American Voter* (New York: Wiley, 1960), 120–67. For an updated treatment, see Michael S. Lewis-Beck, William G. Jacoby, Helmut Norpoth, and Herbert F. Weisberg, *The American Voter Revisited* (Ann Arbor: University of Michigan Press, 2008), chaps. 6 and 7.
3. For the most important statement of these ideas, see Philip E. Converse, "The Concept of a Normal Vote," in *Elections and the Political Order,* ed. Angus Campbell, Philip E. Converse, Warren E. Miller, and Donald E. Stokes (New York: Wiley, 1966), 9–39.
4. This discussion and data presentation are based on earlier work by the authors of the first twelve editions of this book, William H. Flanigan and Nancy H. Zingale, "The Measurement of Electoral Change," *Political Methodology* 1 (Summer 1974): 49–82.
5. Larry Bartels argues that partisan loyalty has been steadily increasing since its nadir in 1972, but this trend has been overlooked by analysts focusing on the weakness of the political parties. See Larry Bartels, "Partisanship and Voting Behavior, 1952–1996," *American Journal of Political Science* 44 (January 2000): 35–50.
6. Paul R. Abramson and John H. Aldrich, "The Decline of Electoral Participation in America," *American Political Science Review* 76 (September 1982): 502–21.
7. Angus Campbell, "Surge and Decline: A Study of Electoral Change," in *Elections and the Political Order,* ed. Angus Campbell, Philip E. Converse, Warren E. Miller, and Donald E. Stokes (New York: Wiley, 1966), 40–62.
8. Had Bush adviser Karl Rove not implemented his strategy to turn out the vote among Christian conservatives in safe Republican states in the South, Bush would have again lost the popular vote nationwide, while winning in the Electoral College.
9. Arthur H. Miller and Martin P. Wattenberg, "Measuring Party Identification: Independent or No Partisan Preference?" *American Journal of Political Science* 27 (February 1983): 106–21.
10. John Petrocik, "An Analysis of Intransitivities in the Index of Party Identification," *Political Methodology* 1 (Summer 1974): 31–47.
11. This and most discussions of the classification of elections are based on the work of V. O. Key and Angus Campbell. See V. O. Key, "A Theory of Critical Elections," *Journal of Politics* 17 (1955): 3–18; and Angus Campbell, "A Classification of Presidential Elections," in *Elections and the Political Order,* ed. Angus Campbell, Philip E. Converse, Warren E. Miller, and Donald E. Stokes (New York: Wiley, 1966), 63–77.
12. This and the following discussion draw heavily on Jerome M. Clubb, William H. Flanigan, and Nancy H. Zingale, *Partisan Realignment: Voters, Parties, and Government in American History* (Boulder, CO: Westview Press, 1990). See especially chaps. 5 and 8.
13. See, for example, William N. Chambers and Walter Dean Burnham, eds., *The American Party Systems: Stages of Political Development* (New York: Oxford University Press, 1975).

14. This concept was developed by Seymour Martin Lipset and Stein Rokkan in their discussion of the development of the European party systems in *Party Systems and Voter Alignments* (New York: Free Press, 1967), 1–64.
15. Some analysts have argued that the movement of white southerners into the Republican Party and that of blacks and some northern whites into the Democratic Party constitutes a realignment and should be regarded as the start of a new party system. Disagreement arises about when this realignment occurred. Some date it from the 1960s, with the start of Republican dominance in presidential voting; others view it as a Reagan realignment of the 1980s.
16. Thomas M. Carsey and Geoffrey C. Layman. "Changing Sides or Changing Minds? Party Identification and Policy Preferences in the American Electorate," *American Journal of Political Science* (2006) 50: 464–77.
17. Edward G. Carmines, Michael J. Ensley, and Michael W. Wagner, "Political Ideology in American Politics: One, Two, or None?" *The Forum* 10, no. 4 (2012): 1–18.
18. Carsey and Layman, "Changing Sides or Changing Minds?"
19. Norman H. Nie, Sidney Verba, and John R. Petrocik, *The Changing American Voter* (Cambridge, MA: Harvard University Press, 1976), chap. 5.
20. Robert S. Erikson and Kent L. Tedin, "The 1928–1936 Partisan Realignment: The Case for the Conversion Hypothesis," *American Political Science Review* 75 (December 1981): 951–62.
21. Philip E. Converse, *The Dynamics of Party Support: Cohort-Analyzing Party Identification* (Beverly Hills, CA: Sage, 1976).
22. The parents were also reinterviewed in 1973. By 1997, many of the original high school seniors were parents of high school–age students. The study also interviewed the children of the original sample, creating a second set of parent-child interviews to compare with the original data from 1965. See Figure 4-11.

Suggested Readings

Burnham, Walter Dean. *Critical Elections and the Mainsprings of American Politics.* New York: W. W. Norton, 1970. An early, important statement of the electoral realignment perspective.

Campbell, Angus, Philip E. Converse, Warren E. Miller, and Donald E. Stokes. *The American Voter.* New York: Wiley, 1960. The classic study of public opinion and voting behavior in the United States.

Clubb, Jerome M., William H. Flanigan, and Nancy H. Zingale. *Partisan Realignment: Voters, Parties, and Government in American History.* Boulder, CO: Westview Press, 1990. A conceptualization of realignments that emphasizes both electoral behavior and political leadership.

Green, Donald, Bradley Palmquist, and Eric Schickler. *Partisan Hearts and Minds: Political Parties and the Social Identities of Voters.* New Haven, CT: Yale University Press, 2004. A strong argument for party identification as a social-psychological orientation and a powerful determinant of vote choice and political attitudes.

Keith, Bruce, David B. Magleby, Candice J. Nelson, Elizabeth Orr, Mark C. Westlye, and Raymond E. Wolfinger. *The Myth of the Independent Voter.* Berkeley: University of California Press, 1992. An effort to reaffirm the importance of party identification in an era of increasing numbers of independents.

Lavine, Howard G., Christopher D. Johnston, and Marco R. Steenbergen. *The Ambivalent Partisan: How Critical Loyalty Promotes Democracy.* New York: Oxford University Press, 2012. A fascinating analysis of partisans' willingness to view the world accurately and pay attention to issues and how this contributes to good democratic citizenship.

Lewis-Beck, Michael S., William G. Jacoby, Helmut Norpoth, and Herbert F. Weisberg. *The American Voter Revisited.* Ann Arbor: University of Michigan Press, 2008. A rich reanalysis of the themes from the classic work using mainly 2000 and 2004 data.

Nie, Norman, Sidney Verba, and John Petrocik. *The Changing American Voter.* Cambridge, MA: Harvard University Press, 1976. A major revisionist analysis of public opinion and voting behavior emphasizing the decline of partisanship.

Niemi, Richard G., and Herbert F. Weisberg, eds. *Controversies in Voting Behavior.* Washington, DC: CQ Press, 2001. A collection of sophisticated articles on major topics in political behavior and public opinion.

Wattenberg, Martin P. *The Decline of American Political Parties: 1952–1988.* Cambridge, MA: Harvard University Press, 1990. A thorough analysis of the changing patterns of partisanship in recent decades.

Public Opinion and Ideology

*P*UBLIC OPINION—the collective attitudes of the public, or segments of the public, toward the issues of the day—is a significant component of American political behavior. Public opinion polls are an ever-present feature of American public life and contemporary journalism. You can scarcely flip on the TV or read a story online without being inundated with the latest poll telling us what the American people think about issues ranging from whether abortion should be legal to the role that race played in the highly publicized killing of African American teenager Trayvon Martin in the George Zimmerman murder trial to attitudes about the name given to Prince William and Princess Catherine's first son. Understanding the nature, measurement, and content of public opinion is crucial to explaining American political behavior. The questions then arise: Are Americans informed, issue-oriented participants in the political process? Do they view problems and issues within a coherent ideological framework? Which issues divide Democrats and Republicans? Are people's preferences related to their behavior? These questions address the nature, quality, and influence of American public opinion.

A *political ideology* is a set of fundamental beliefs or principles about politics and government: what the scope of government should be, how decisions should be made, what values should be pursued. In the United States, the most prominent ideological patterns are those captured by the terms *liberalism* and *conservatism*. Although these words are used in a variety of ways, generally liberalism endorses the idea of social change and advocates the involvement of government in effecting such change, whereas conservatism seeks to defend the status quo and prescribes a more limited role for governmental activity. Another common conception of the terms portrays liberalism as advocating equality and individual freedom and conservatism as endorsing a more structured, ordered society. These two conceptions of liberalism and conservatism clash when considering differences in people's preferences about economic and social issues. That is, modern conservatives generally prefer that the government stay out of the deep management of economic issues while preferring that the government be more activist in regulating social issues. For example, conservatives generally want the government to relax business regulations and to outlaw abortion and define marriage traditionally. Contemporary liberals generally prefer more aggressive business regulations, but want a government that stays out of abortion and does not define marriage.

"Ideological" views on social and economic issues are not always joined in the political thinking of Americans. That is, some Americans have views on economic issues, relating to the government's role in managing the economy, that are generally liberal or generally conservative, and some Americans have opinions on social issues, relating to the government's weighing in on what is morally right or wrong, that are broadly liberal or conservative. However, there is no law or general psychological principle that requires Americans to have views that are consistently liberal or conservative across both dimensions. What's more, some people have attitudes that are moderate on these issues; still others just don't care. Thus, the ideological landscape of American public opinion certainly contains those who are either liberal or conservative across both economic and social issues, but it also contains those who are conservative economically and liberal socially (libertarians), those who are liberal economically and conservative socially (populists), and those who fall somewhere in between (moderates).[1]

Despite these ambiguities, most commentators on the American political scene, as well as its active participants, describe much of what happens in terms of liberalism or conservatism. And with good reason. The news media routinely chronicle political debate as a contest between Republicans and Democrats in government. At the federal level, there is a clear "left-right" divide between Republicans, who are on the ideological right, and Democrats, who are on the ideological left. Indeed, Republicans and Democrats in the U.S. Congress are now more polarized in their roll call voting behavior than they were in the years immediately following the Civil War![2] Furthermore, most political history and commentary treats the Democratic Party as the liberal party and the Republican Party as the conservative one. Although considerable ideological variation remains in both parties, the trend in recent years is toward greater ideological distinctiveness between the two parties both at the elite and mass levels.[3] Candidates of both parties attempt to pin ideological labels on opposing candidates (usually candidates of the other party, but sometimes within their own). In recent years, *liberal* has been portrayed more negatively than *conservative,* and some candidates for office portray themselves as "progressive" or use other such terms to avoid the liberal label.

Analysts of American political history pay special attention to those rare periods when a single-issue dimension dominates the public's views of governmental policy. Periods such as the Civil War or the New Deal revealed deep divisions in the public, paralleled by a distinctiveness in the issue stands of the political parties. Electoral realignments of voters are forged by unusually strong issue alignments, and during such times a close correspondence can be expected between attitudes on the relevant issues and partisanship.

At other times, highly salient issues may capture the attention of the public, but they are likely to cut across, rather than reinforce, other issue positions and party loyalties. If the parties do not take clearly differentiated stands on such issues and if party supporters are divided in their feelings toward the issues, party loyalty and the existing partisan alignment are undermined. On the other hand, if parties do take clear but competing positions on such issues, they run the risk of alienating some of their supporters. In a complex political system such as that of the United States, new, dissimilar issue divisions accumulate until a crisis causes one dimension to dominate and obscure other issues.

The most consistent and the most distinctive ideological difference between the parties emerged during the New Deal realignment. It focused on domestic economic issues, specifically on the question of what role the government should take in regulating the economy and providing social welfare benefits. These issues still underlie the division between the parties. Since the 1930s, the Democratic Party has advocated more government activity, and the Republican Party has preferred less. Historically, American political parties have not been viewed as particularly ideological, in part because other issues—such as racial or social issues—have cut across the economic dimension and blurred distinctions between the parties.

For example, in the 1940s and 1950s, the Republican Party was at least as liberal on race (i.e., supportive of civil rights legislation) as was the Democratic Party, with its strong southern base. Similarly, in the 1970s the two parties were both divided internally on the issue of abortion. Currently, immigration has the potential to be a cross-cutting issue, though it seems to divide Republicans more than it does Democrats. What makes the two parties especially interesting today is that they are in the rare historical position of being quite consistent and ideologically distinctive. The two parties have become more ideologically polarized over a broader range of issues, and their supporters seem to have sorted themselves out, as increasing numbers of Democrats have liberal positions on social and economic issues while more and more Republicans have conservative positions on them.[4]

In this chapter, we consider public opinion on several important issues and explore the relationship of social characteristics and partisanship to these opinions. (We focus on the relationship between social characteristics and partisanship in chapter 6.) We look at the extent to which Americans have a political ideology representing a coherent set of fundamental beliefs or principles about politics that serves as a guide to current political issues, much as partisanship does. Finally, we briefly consider the impact of public opinion on political leaders.

The Measurement of Public Opinion

The commercial opinion-polling organizations have spent more than seventy years asking Americans about their views on matters of public policy. Most of this investigation has taken one of two forms: (1) asking individuals whether they "approve or disapprove of" or "agree or disagree with" a statement of policy or (2) asking individuals to pick their preference among two or more alternative statements of policy. This form of questioning seriously exaggerates the number of people who hold views on political issues. People can easily say "agree" or "disapprove" in response to a question, even if they know nothing at all about the topic. If given the opportunity, many people will volunteer the information that they hold no views on specific items of public policy. For example, during the 2011 showdown between President Obama and congressional Republicans over raising the debt ceiling, about 35 percent of those polled by Gallup said they did not know enough about the issue to have an opinion.[5] In contrast, in the past several decades less than 5 percent of all adults had no opinion on issues such as abortion or the death penalty. More typically, in recent years approximately 10 percent of the electorate has had no opinion on major issues of public policy. Philip E. Converse has shown, in addition, that a number of those individuals who appear to have an opinion may be regarded as responding to policy questions at random.[6] One reason for this is that many people form opinions during a telephone survey off the "top of their heads," usually based on the most recent or salient information about the issue they can immediately recall.[7]

The lack of opinion and information on topics of public policy can be explained in several ways. In general, the factors that explain nonvoting also account for the absence of opinions. Individuals with little interest in or concern with politics are least likely to have opinions on matters of public policy. Beyond this basic relationship, low socioeconomic status is associated with a lack of opinion on issues. Low income and little education create social circumstances in which individuals are less likely to have views and information on public policies.

Some issues of public policy, such as abortion or the death penalty, are relatively easy to understand; others may be much more difficult, requiring individuals to face complex considerations. Edward G. Carmines and James A. Stimson have argued that different segments of the public respond to "hard" issues that involve calculation of policy benefits and "easy" issues that call for symbolic, "gut responses." Relatively unsophisticated, uninterested members of the electorate respond to "easy" issues; the more sophisticated, most interested citizens take positions on "hard" issues.[8]

It is no simple matter to describe the distribution of opinions in the American electorate because no obvious, widely accepted method has been established to measure these opinions. Asking different questions in public opinion polls will elicit different answers. Even on the issue of abortion, on which most people have views, the distribution of opinions can be substantially altered by asking respondents whether they approve of "killing unborn children" as opposed to "letting women have control over their own bodies." Furthermore, unlike reports of voting behavior, no direct means exist to validate measures of opinions. As a consequence, descriptions of public opinion must be taken as more uncertain and more tentative than those drawn from the discussion of partisanship.

The mode of public opinion gathering can also affect the distribution of opinions. The results from surveys asking Americans who they planned to vote for in the presidential election varied substantially based on whether the survey was a phone survey using random-digit dialing of landlines, included cell phone numbers, was conducted on the Internet, or was administered face-to-face. Partisan labels also affect people's opinions. Paul Sniderman and John Bullock found that adding words like "Democrats say" or "Republicans say" to an issue position increased individual ideological constraint. That is, liberals were more likely to agree with a position when it carried a Democratic Party label and conservatives were more likely to favor preferences with a Republican Party endorsement.

Domestic Economic Issues

The collapse of the financial sector in the fall of 2008 and the actions of both the Bush administration and the incoming Obama administration to stimulate the economy and to bail out and then reregulate banks and insurance companies brought cries of "socialism" from conservative politicians and commentators. Highly partisan debate over President Barack Obama's health care plan reminded Democrats of the failure of the Clinton administration's health care plan in 1993.

This failure helped usher in the loss of the House of Representatives to the Republicans in 1994 and promises of a "conservative revolution" that would reduce government involvement in the economy and cut support for various social programs. In similar fashion, Ronald Reagan's victory in 1980 and his administration's subsequent slashing of taxes and social programs was portrayed as a reversal of fifty years of economic liberalism. Elections have consequences, and in policy terms there have certainly been consequences of Republican or Democratic victories. In terms of public opinion, however, broad and continuing public support remains for many governmental initiatives, regardless of election outcomes. As George W. Bush discovered when he proposed privatizing Social Security after winning reelection in 2004, long-standing programs that appear to benefit "deserving" segments of the population are difficult to "reform" because they enjoy widespread support.

The responses to public opinion questions, and public opinion itself, can be affected by political rhetoric and election slogans. For example, the General Social Survey asks a long series of questions on whether spending on various programs is "too much, not enough, or about right." Over the years, sizable proportions of the public have said that too much is being spent on "welfare." At the same time, even larger proportions have said not enough is being spent on "assistance to the poor."[9] Clearly, years of anecdotes about "welfare queens" and promises to "end welfare as we know it" have had their effect on the way particular programs are perceived, if not on the public's general willingness to use government as an instrument for social purposes.

Figure 5-1 shows the distribution of attitudes toward spending for different governmental purposes, using data collected by the General Social Survey from 1973 to 2008. The form of these questions—whether too much or too little is being spent on a problem—elicits answers that reflect the attitude of the respondents, the wording of the question as noted previously, and the current state of public policy. Thus, a period of cutbacks in public spending, such as in the 1980s, would be expected to produce more responses of "too little" even if public attitudes about the ideal level of such spending had not changed. Figure 5-1 shows a drop in negative attitudes toward welfare spending after the Reagan administration slashed these programs, as well as a rise in proportions saying "too much" was being spent in the 1990s, when both political parties promised welfare reform. The implementation of those reforms, in turn, led to a sharp drop since 1996 in the proportion believing too much is being spent. Attitudes favorable toward spending on the environment showed a steady increase during the 1980s, as environmental programs were being curtailed, and then a gradual increase in the late 1990s and the first decade of the twenty-first century, which paralleled increased attention to climate change concerns. Support for more

FIGURE 5-1 Attitudes toward Domestic Spending, 1973–2008

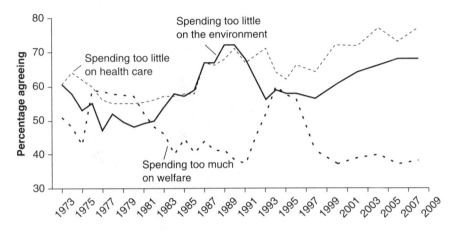

Source: National Opinion Research Center, *General Social Surveys, 1972–2008, Cumulative File,* available at www.norc.org/GSS/GSS+Resources.htm.

spending on health care has been high for several decades. Overall, Figure 5-1 shows fairly widespread willingness to support government spending on domestic social programs.

Perhaps not surprisingly, examining how different social groups think about major political issues reveals some fairly dramatic differences in what people want from the government. Figure 5-2 is based on a question in the 2012 American National Election Study (ANES) that offers respondents a choice between "cutting spending and decreasing services" and "increasing services and increasing spending." We look at responses to this question for several social categories, using race and ethnicity, education, and religion as variables. The pattern in the figure is not difficult to describe. The least economically secure—blacks, Hispanics, and less well-educated whites—support government services most strongly. The groups most distinctively in favor of cutting spending and services are white Protestants and Catholics.

Favoring services over spending cuts represents the type of choice in governmental policy that characterized the New Deal. Thus, it would be reasonable to expect a dramatic difference between Democrats and Republicans on such an issue. Economic issues have divided Democrats and Republicans since the 1930s, whereas other issues have been of only temporary significance for the parties. As a consequence, the relationship in Table 5-1 showing that Democrats disproportionately favor increased government services and Republicans prefer cuts is no surprise. Strong Democrats favor increased services over a reduction in spending by a margin of 65 percent to 16 percent; strong Republicans

FIGURE 5-2   Attitudes toward Cutting Spending versus Increasing Government
              Services, by Race, Ethnicity, Religion, and Education, 2012

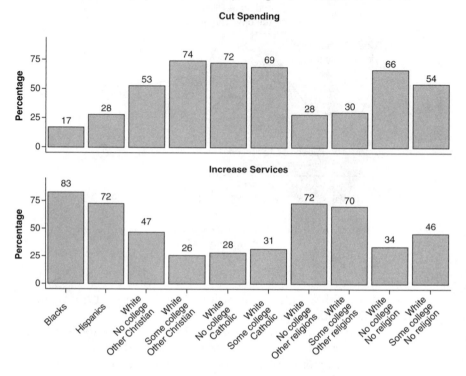

Source: 2012 American National Election Study, available at www.electionstudies.org.

are just the opposite, favoring a reduction in spending over increased
services by a margin of 68 percent to 6 percent. This basic pattern has
existed for decades, but it is also important to observe that noticeable
proportions of Democrats and Republicans hold opinions opposed by a
majority of their fellow partisans.

Rising health care costs have been a concern for years and took
center stage in the first year of the Obama administration. Reforming
the health care system was also attempted early in the Clinton administration, when President Bill Clinton appointed First Lady Hillary Rodham Clinton to head a group to develop a proposal for a national health
care program. The managed competition program eventually proposed
was not the national health care program favored by the most liberal
advocates, but the ensuing debate was cast in terms of governmentally
mandated and regulated programs versus private insurance companies

TABLE 5-1   Attitudes toward Cutting Spending versus Increasing Government Services, by Party Identification, 2012

	Strong Democrats	Weak Democrats	Independents	Weak Republicans	Strong Republicans
Favor cutting spending	6%	18%	45%	62%	68%
Neutral	29	35	29	29	15
Favor increasing government services	65	47	26	10	16
Total	**100%**	**100%**	**100%**	**101%**	**99%**
(*Weighted N*)	336	219	755	205	246

Source: 2012 American National Election Study, available at www.electionstudies.org.

with individual choice in health care providers. Ultimately, the Clinton administration lost the battle in Congress and in the arena of public opinion. Initially in 1992, the public favored a governmental insurance plan, 44 percent to 24 percent, over private insurance plans.[10] After health insurance and pharmaceutical companies and the American Medical Association launched an extensive advertising campaign featuring a middle-American couple, "Harry and Louise," worrying about the government taking away their choice of doctor, the Clinton program went down in defeat. In 1996, public sentiment had reversed, with 40 percent of the ANES sample saying they thought medical expenses should be paid by private insurance plans and 34 percent opting for a governmental plan. In the 2008 campaign, health care was again an issue, and the public was again tilting in favor of a government program, with 48 percent in favor of a government plan and 34 percent preferring private health insurance.[11] As the debate in Congress geared up, Harry and Louise returned to the airwaves, sixteen years older, and this time supporting a health care reform package. After the successful passage of the Affordable Care Act, known as Obamacare by political opponents and the news media, health care was again front and center in the 2012 presidential election. While the law contains many popular provisions, opinion of the entirety of the act is more negative than positive. Even so, Table 5-2 shows the durability of partisan divisions on health care issues as Democrats continued to favor government-sponsored health insurance and Republicans strongly favored private health insurance in 2012.

TABLE 5-2   Attitudes on Health Care, by Party Identification, 2012

	Strong Democrats	Weak Democrats	Independents	Weak Republicans	Strong Republicans
Favor governmental health insurance	61%	55%	39%	16%	8%
Neutral	20	23	20	15	9
Favor private health insurance	19	22	41	69	83
Total	**100%**	**100%**	**100%**	**100%**	**100%**
(*Weighted N*)	368	236	812	267	253

Source: 2012 American National Election Study, available at www.electionstudies.org.

Racial Issues

Race and attitudes associated with race hold a prominent place in American political history. For many years after Reconstruction, little overt public attention was paid to racial issues. The South was allowed to impose its system of segregation on its black population by law, while informal, de facto methods created much the same system of separate neighborhoods leading to segregated schools in the North. After integration became a major national and international focal point of attention in the 1940s and 1950s, a number of significant developments in the political attitudes of the public occurred. First, during the past fifty years southern blacks have become a concerned, involved, politically motivated group. Removing the legal barriers to voting in the South has enabled the black population in southern states to command the attention of politicians at the ballot box and in state legislatures and governors' mansions.

Second, large numbers of southern whites have adjusted their opinions to accept the realities of the new legal and political position of blacks. The public, as a whole, has come to support the general principle of racial equality. The recent near-unanimity on this point means that Americans no longer support policies and practices that discriminate against racial groups, and making political appeals based on blatant racism is no longer consistent with the dominant political culture.

At the same time, the public has not moved significantly closer to supporting government programs designed to improve the economic and social position of racial groups. Northern, as well as southern, whites have consistently opposed busing for the purposes of integration.

More than 80 percent of whites oppose affirmative action on behalf of racial minorities, and less than half support the federal government enforcing fair employment practices. The proportion of the public supporting various forms of governmental action to aid blacks is shown in Table 5-3. In contrast to the near-unanimity of support for "letting black and white children go to school together," less than half the public supports positive actions on the part of government to improve the social and economic position of blacks.

The lack of connection between broad principle and policy implementation has been the focus of both political debate and scholarly disagreement. One side argues that opposition to programs to aid blacks is based on opposition to government activities in general and, in particular, programs that benefit a subgroup of society.[12] This position, often referred to as "racial conservatism," is seen as stemming from a general philosophical commitment to limited government and a belief in individualism. The attitudes, it is argued, are based on principles, not racism.

The other view argues that opposition to policy proposals to use governmental programs to aid the social and economic circumstances of blacks and other minorities stems from racial hostility, even though racial conservatives may have learned to cloak their racism in acceptable philosophical language. To complicate the matter further, scholars take different views of how racial hostility expresses itself in political attitudes. Scholars have used three dimensions of racial hostility to explain white support for or opposition to government policies regarding race:

1. Racial resentment (the feeling that blacks are getting more than they deserve) or racial disapproval (the feeling that blacks do not live up to certain value expectations like working hard, etc.).[13] These contentions are often referred to as "symbolic racism."

2. Group conflict (zero-sum conflicts over scarce resources).[14]

3. Social dominance (protection of the status quo by a dominant group).[15]

These dimensions of racial hostility can be interrelated and may reinforce one another. It is difficult to separate them or to be confident in measuring them or evaluating which dimension contributes the most to racial attitudes. Measuring racial attitudes is especially tricky because social norms in twenty-first-century America dictate against making explicitly racist statements and people want to give answers to survey interviewers that are socially desirable. Interpreting racial attitudes can also be tricky. Although these dimensions are often labeled as if they were positive or negative in content, they have both pro-black

TABLE 5-3   Public Attitudes on School Integration and Employment
Practices

		Whites	
	Blacks	South	Non-South
Do you think the government in Washington should see to it that white and black children go to the same schools or stay out of this area as it is not the government's business? (2000)			
Government should see to it	78%	39%	50%
Not government's business	17	54	45
Other, don't know	5	7	5
Total	100%	100%	100%
(N)	(137)	(255)	(604)
There is much discussion about the best way to deal with racial problems. Some people think achieving racial integration of schools is so important that it justifies busing children to schools out of their own neighborhoods. Others think letting children go to their neighborhood schools is so important that they oppose busing. Where would you place yourself on this scale, or haven't you thought much about this? (1984)			
Bus to achieve integration	29%	4%	7%
Neutral	15	4	8
Keep children in neighborhood schools	56	92	85
Total	101%	101%	101%
(N)	(165)	(390)	(502)
Should the government in Washington see to it that black people get fair treatment in jobs or is this not the federal government's business? (2008)			
Government should see to it	89%	36%	50%
Not government's business	10	61	46
Other, don't know	2	4	5
Total	101%	101%	101%
(N)	(165)	(390)	(502)
Some people say that because of past discrimination, blacks should be given preference in hiring and promotion. Others say that such preference in hiring and promotion of blacks is wrong because it gives blacks advantages they haven't earned. What about your opinion—are you for or against preferential hiring and promotion of blacks? (2008)			
For preferential treatment of blacks	50%	8%	13%
Against preferential treatment	45	88	82
Other, don't know, refused to say	5	4	5
Total	100%	100%	100%
(N)	(241)	(699)	(948)

Source: American National Election Studies, available at www.electionstudies.org.

and anti-black extremes. In other words, if a black person believes strongly that black people are not getting what they deserve, racial resentment may be involved just as much as when a white person believes that blacks are getting more than they deserve.

To connect these dimensions with attitudes about policies designed to provide governmental aid to minorities, it seems reasonable to assume that people must view potential beneficiaries of government aid as deserving. How deserving blacks and other minorities are viewed by white Americans may depend on whether blacks are seen as individually responsible for their position or whether they are seen as victims of social and economic forces beyond their control. Presumably, whites who believe that blacks can improve their situation through their own efforts will not view them as deserving of special government programs on their behalf. This basis of opposition would fit the symbolic racism perspective. Whites who see social structures and conditions imposing special hardships on blacks regardless of their individual efforts will view blacks as deserving of special assistance.

Even if blacks are viewed by whites as deserving of government assistance, special programs may be opposed if whites see these programs as coming at the expense of whites. Another similar basis for opposition to programs for blacks would be the expectation that the status quo, which favors whites, would be disrupted, which would be undesirable from the point of view of whites. These objections are examples of the group conflict and social dominance perspectives.

A racial conservative might make the argument that there once was a time when all the relevant democratic principles were on the side of helping blacks but that more recently such principles work both ways. Blacks should have an equal chance to get an education, find a job, and so forth, but they should not be given advantages over other deserving people. Indeed, this was the argument that the majority of the Supreme Court used in its 2013 decision overturning key provisions of the Voting Rights Act that had required federal approval when states with a history of racial discrimination wanted to change voting procedures. However, great differences are found in the perceptions of blacks and whites about whether or not blacks have an equal chance in American society.

Racial attitudes have had a profound effect on the American political landscape. In their book *Issue Evolution*, Carmines and Stimson argue that an evolution of the racial issue since the early 1960s has led increasingly to the Democratic Party being perceived as the liberal party on civil rights issues and the Republican Party being perceived as the conservative party.[16] They see this distinction as the dominant perception of the parties in the eyes of the public, representing a fundamental redefinition of the issue alignment that has characterized the parties since the New Deal.

Before the 1960s, Republicans (the party of Abraham Lincoln) were seen as more progressive on civil rights than Democrats, particularly in light of the strongly segregationist cast to the southern wing of the Democratic Party. Carmines and Stimson show that a change occurred during the 1960s and 1970s, when the elites of the two parties—members of Congress, presidential candidates—as well as party activists became distinctive in their racial views. The Democratic Party became dominated by northern liberals advocating stronger governmental action to ensure equal rights. At the same time, the leadership of the Republican Party became racially conservative—that is, opposed to government intervention to ensure equal rights for minorities. As the elites and activists sorted themselves into distinct groups on the basis of their attitudes toward racial issues, the perceptions that the mass public held of the parties followed suit. Increasingly through the late 1960s and 1970s, Carmines and Stimson argue, the partisan choices of individual citizens fell in line with their attitudes on racial questions.

The role of race and racial issues in American politics is not always easy to trace, however. Because certain issues that are not explicitly stated in terms of race are nevertheless symbols of race in the minds of some people, candidates can make appeals based on racist attitudes without using racial language. For example, "law and order" may mean "keeping blacks in their place" to some, "welfare" may carry racial overtones, and so on.[17]

Furthermore, the lack of support among whites for policies that target assistance to blacks gives both parties an incentive to avoid embracing such policies, according to Donald R. Kinder and Lynn M. Sanders.[18] Republican leaders can oppose these policies and win support from their overwhelmingly white constituency, particularly southern whites. But Democratic leaders also have an incentive to avoid endorsing policies that would help blacks, so as not to alienate white support.

If race is not an issue to be openly discussed in political campaigns, then uncovering the political significance of race in people's attitudes and perceptions of the political parties becomes difficult. On the whole, straightforward efforts to capture distinctive party images along racial lines do not succeed. Although more than half of the public believe there are differences in what the parties stand for, typically only a small percentage characterize the differences in racial terms. Overwhelmingly, when people articulate differences between the parties, it is in terms of symbols and issues associated with the New Deal realignment. This in all likelihood reflects the lack of overt discussion of racial issues by the political leadership of either party. In fact, Paul Kellstedt has shown that shifts in mass opinion on racial attitudes have begun to mirror shifts on economic attitudes, suggesting that ideological opinions about race have "fused" onto economic preferences.

In 2008, with the first black candidate nominated by a major party, race was an issue whether anyone talked about it or not. From Bill Clinton's remarks downplaying a black candidate's win in the South Carolina primary, to the Rev. Jeremiah Wright's videotaped sermons, to Obama's March 18 speech on race, to the increased black turnout and overwhelming support for Obama on Election Day in 2008 and 2012, race was an often unspoken but constant presence throughout the campaign. In retrospect, it needs to be remembered that Obama did not have the unanimous support of black Democratic activists in the primaries. Former president Clinton was highly popular among blacks during and after his presidency, and Hillary Clinton benefited from that association. And early on, Obama was seen in some circles as "not black enough," given his mixed racial heritage and his upbringing by his white mother and grandparents. Once nominated, any Democratic presidential candidate can count on around 90 percent of the black vote in the November election. After Obama's nomination, he received not only virtually unanimous support from black voters, but high enthusiasm and turnout as well in both 2008 and 2012.

While explicit examples of race negatively affecting Barack Obama's candidacy were few and far between, research examining people's implicit, or "automatic," responses to race showed that those with an implicit preference for whites over blacks were more likely to support John McCain in 2008 and Mitt Romney in 2012, highlighting how complicated it is to untangle how racial attitudes affect public preferences and voting behavior.

Social Issues

One of the more emotional aspects of the polarization of the two political parties over the past two decades has been conflict over so-called traditional values. Issues such as abortion; gay rights, including gay marriage; pornography; and sex education and prayer in the public schools have risen in prominence in recent years. Common wisdom positions Democrats on the liberal side and Republicans on the conservative side of these "culture wars," as they are often called, but significant numbers of leaders and followers in both parties are not so easily placed. Like the process of sorting that occurred over racial issues in the 1960s and 1970s, a similar sorting over traditional values has been occurring more recently. The Republican Party, especially, has had a difficult time portraying itself as a "big tent" that welcomes a wide range of people with varying beliefs, but people who are pro-life or opposed to gay marriage have also come to feel uncomfortable in the Democratic Party.

Certainly, one of the most potent of these social issues is abortion. The 1973 Supreme Court decision in *Roe v. Wade* immediately generated a polarized response, turning election races in some areas into one-issue campaigns. Forty years later, intact dilation and extraction, far more commonly known as "partial birth" abortion, is a hot-button issue, and both sides in the abortion debate gird for battle over any anticipated retirement from the U.S. Supreme Court.

One of the difficulties in examining public opinion on abortion lies in the responses that different question wording elicits. Although responses to the same question are similar over time, different phrasing of questions produces differing proportions of "pro-choice" or "pro-life" answers. In the following analysis, we use data from the ANES, which has used the same question in each survey since 1980.

The public's views on abortion are associated with several personal characteristics, most notably age, education, and religion. No matter what combination of characteristics is examined in the general public, invariably more than half of the people in the ANES surveys support the right to abortion under at least some circumstances. The two response choices at the pro-life end of the continuum are that abortion should never be permitted and that abortion should be permitted only in cases of rape or incest or to save the life of the mother. The first is a more extreme position than many pro-life advocates would take; the second includes circumstances that have been explicitly rejected by pro-life advocates in and out of Congress. The most extreme pro-choice alternative offered is that by law a woman should always be able to obtain an abortion as a matter of personal choice. We have used the most extreme category at either end of the continuum to indicate pro-life and pro-choice positions.

In simple terms, older people are generally more likely to be pro-life than younger people, and the less educated are less supportive of legal abortion than are the better educated. Given the frequent labeling of abortion as a "women's" issue, it is worth noting that there is relatively little difference in the views of women and men, although women are more likely than men to take the extreme positions on both the pro-choice and pro-life sides.

Perhaps surprisingly, given the Roman Catholic Church's clear position in opposition to abortion, little difference is found between Catholics and Protestants in their positions on abortion. This is true even when the frequency of church attendance is taken into account. Figure 5-3 shows the percentages taking the most extreme pro-life position and the most extreme pro-choice position for Catholics and Protestants with different frequencies of church attendance. Among both Catholics and Protestants, opposition to abortion declines as church attendance declines, but the percentages expressing pro-choice and pro-life sentiments are quite similar for the Catholic and Protestant groups. Regular churchgoers among Catholics are about as pro-life as Protestant regular churchgoers. Catholic occasional attenders are more likely to be pro-choice than Protestants who attend church infrequently.

FIGURE 5-3   Attitudes toward Abortion among Catholics and Protestants, by
Frequency of Church Attendance, 2012

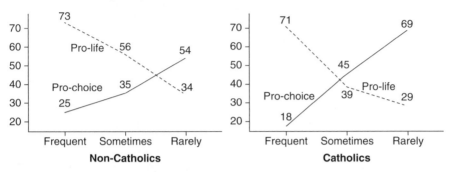

Source: 2012 American National Election Study, available at www.electionstudies.org.

Underlying this change is another trend—a smaller proportion of all Catholics claim to be regular churchgoers. Regardless of their religious denomination, the figure also shows that those who are faithful churchgoers are also more pro-life.

The data in Figure 5-3 mask the different attitudes on abortion among Protestant groups, especially among whites. Table 5-4 divides white mainline Protestants from born-again Christians and compares them with white Catholics and those with no religious affiliation, again controlling for frequency of church attendance. The born-again Protestants who regularly attend church are about as pro-life as the Catholics who regularly attend. However, the mainline Protestants who regularly attend church are considerably more pro-choice than the frequent attenders of other faiths. Because most mainline Protestant churches take a position of individual moral responsibility on the question of abortion, the pro-choice stance of many of their adherents is not unexpected.

Table 5-5 divides Hispanic respondents to the 2012 American National Election Study by the same factors as Table 5-4 divides whites. Keep in mind that the number of respondents is far smaller for this group; thus, while it is unwise to generalize from Table 5-5, the data imply that for born-again Hispanics, the frequency with which one attends church is not so important when it comes to explaining general views on abortion. Table 5-6 examines a similarly smaller sample of citizens, African Americans. Again, the number of respondents is comparatively small to white respondents, but the data suggest that being born-again has a different relationship with abortion attitudes for black Americans than being born-again does for Hispanics. Fifty-six percent of

TABLE 5-4 Whites' Views on Abortion, by Religion and Frequency of Church Attendance, 2012

	Catholics			Non-Catholic Born-Again Christians			Other Non-Catholic Christians			No affiliation
	Frequent	Sometimes	Rarely	Frequent	Sometimes	Rarely	Frequent	Sometimes	Rarely	
Pro-life	32%	11%	5%	29%	20%	2%	28%	5%	2%	6
Pro-life, with exceptions	48	32	13	44	41	42	36	37	23	16
Pro-choice, with limitations	10	21	16	20	16	7	16	16	29	19
Pro-choice	10	36	66	7	20	50	17	42	46	59
Other, don't know	0	1	0	0	3	0	3	0	0	0
Total	100%	101%	100%	100%	100%	101%	100%	100%	100%	100%
(Weighted N)	82	77	65	166	132	56	47	90	93	360

Source: 2012 American National Election Study, available at www.electionstudies.org.

Note: Frequent = "every week"; Sometimes = "almost every week" and "once/twice per month"; Rarely = "few times per year."

TABLE 5-5   Hispanics' Views on Abortion, by Religion and Frequency of Church Attendance, 2012

	Catholics			Non-Catholic Born-Again Christians			Other Non-Catholic Christians			No affiliation
	Frequent	Sometimes	Rarely	Frequent	Sometimes	Rarely	Frequent	Sometimes	Rarely	
Pro-life	13%	10%	3%	24%	4%	48%	41%	8%	7%	3%
Pro-life, with exceptions	39	26	28	52	42	31	41	41	3	21
Pro-choice, with limitations	4	25	26	11	30	7	0	19	0	16
Pro-choice	23	39	43	10	24	14	6	31	91	58
Other, don't know	22	1	0	3	0	0	12	0	0	1
Total	**101%**	**101%**	**100%**	**100%**	**100%**	**100%**	**100%**	**99%**	**%**	**99%**
(*Weighted N*)	16	30	20	33	13	2	3	10	4	55

Source: 2012 American National Election Study, available at www.electionstudies.org.

Note: Frequent = "every week"; Sometimes = "almost every week" and "once/twice per month"; Rarely = "few times per year."

TABLE 5-6 Blacks' Views on Abortion, by Religion and Frequency of Church Attendance, 2012

	Catholics			Non-Catholic Born-Again Christians			Other Non-Catholic Christians			No affiliation
	Frequent	Sometimes	Rarely	Frequent	Sometimes	Rarely	Frequent	Sometimes	Rarely	
Pro-life	0%	57%	7%	17%	18%	9%	6%	28%	3%	13%
Pro-life, with exceptions	45	11	8	27	33	18	5	16	12	17
Pro-choice, with limitations	33	5	11	17	7	14	0	11	8	7
Pro-choice	22	24	74	39	42	57	88	45	78	62
Other, don't know	0	3	0	0	0	2	0	0	0	2
Total	**100%**	**100%**	**100%**	**100%**	**100%**	**100%**	**99%**	**100%**	**101%**	**101%**
(*Weighted N*)	3	8	7	52	43	23	6	15	32	31

Source: 2012 American National Election Study, available at www.electionstudies.org.

Note: Frequent = "every week"; Sometimes = "almost every week" and "once/twice per month"; Rarely = "few times per year."

black born-again frequent churchgoers are pro-choice. This might reflect the political activism of black churches, activism that tends to support the Democratic Party, which holds a pro-choice position on abortion. The largest block of black Americans with pro-life attitudes are Catholics.

A candidate's position on abortion has become a litmus test for presidential hopefuls in both parties ever since the 1970s. Not surprisingly, then, a fairly strong relationship exists between partisanship and views on abortion, as can be seen in Table 5-7. Perhaps more unexpected is that the relationship is not stronger. Sizable minorities of both Republicans and Democrats take positions contrary to the stand of their party. This is one of several ways in which the polarization of the political activists and elites of the parties is not reflected in the rank and file.

TABLE 5-7   Attitudes on Abortion, by Party Identification, 2012

	Strong Democrats	Weak Democrats	Independents	Weak Republicans	Strong Republicans
Never permit abortion	9%	4%	12%	11%	21%
Permit only in special cases	17	22	29	32	40
Permit for other reasons	14	18	19	22	19
Always permit as a woman's right	59	55	39	34	22
Total	**99%**	**99%**	**99%**	**99%**	**102%**
(*Weighted N*)	405	257	872	213	267

Source: 2012 American National Election Study, available at www.electionstudies.org.

Note: The full text of choices is as follows:

1. By law, abortion should never be permitted.

2. The law should permit abortion only in case of rape, incest, or when the woman's life is in danger.

3. The law should permit abortion for reasons other than rape, incest, or danger to the woman's life, but only after the need for the abortion has been clearly established.

4. By law, a woman should always be able to obtain an abortion as a matter of personal choice.

The issue of gay marriage has become very contentious in recent years, with some states banning gay marriage through legislative actions or referenda and others moving toward legalizing it. In 2004, the issue was suddenly injected into the presidential campaign when the Supreme Court of Massachusetts ruled that denying gays and lesbians the right to marry was unconstitutional in that state, and when the mayor of San Francisco began issuing marriage licenses to gay couples. This was a no-win situation for the Democrats and their presidential candidate, given that the American public opposed gay marriage by a two-to-one margin at the time. Because proposed bans on gay marriage were on the ballot in several states that year, the issue also served to energize conservative voters in safe Republican states, thus raising George W. Bush's popular vote margin. President Obama famously "evolved" to a position of support for gay marriage, following growing public sentiment favoring such a position. In 2013, the Supreme Court ruled that the federal government could not define marriage as being between one man and one woman, striking down the Defense of Marriage Act signed by former President Bill Clinton.

Over time, the American public has become more tolerant of the idea of gay marriage or, at least, civil unions for gay couples. This is another social issue that has a fairly strong relationship with partisanship, as can be seen in Table 5-8. Democratic partisans are more accepting of the idea than Republicans, although a substantial minority of Democrats oppose it. Since 2008, strong Republicans' support for gay marriage has grown from 9 percent to 14 percent, and strong Democrats' support is up to 55 percent, from 46 percent in 2008. Weak Republican support is unmoved over the same time period, and weak Democrats' support of gay marriage jumped 15 points to 63 percent in 2012.

TABLE 5-8   Attitudes toward Gay Marriage, by Party Identification, 2012

	Strong Democrats	Weak Democrats	Independents	Weak Republicans	Strong Republicans
Allow gay marriage	55%	63%	44%	28%	14%
Allow civil unions	26	22	37	45	35
Do not allow either	19	15	19	27	51
Total	**100%**	**100%**	**100%**	**100%**	**100%**
(*Weighted N*)	402	256	867	212	267

Source: 2012 American National Election Study, available at www.electionstudies.org.

Homeland Security and Terrorism

Since September 11, 2001, the eight-hundred-pound gorilla of American public opinion has been terrorism. Not only have the events of that day been seared into people's memories, but the fear of future terrorist attacks remains pervasive—although concern has ebbed a little as time passes without another attack. In the fall of 2011, a CBS News poll found that 83 percent of the public believed that the threat of terrorism will always exist, though more than half also believed that an attack was not likely in the next few months.[19]

A wide-ranging survey in 2004 on Americans' perceptions of the threat of terrorism showed that concerns about a terrorist attack focus on chemical and biological weapons as the most worrisome.[20] Terrorism is seen as multifaceted, taking many possible forms with a wide array of possible targets. Even without another attack, many years will pass before substantial numbers of the public have no personal memory of September 11, so the feelings and issues surrounding terrorism will be around for a long time.

Terrorism is a "valence" issue—that is, one in which virtually every citizen of the United States agrees that it is bad—as opposed to a "position" issue, which some support and others oppose. At one level, terrorism is also an "easy" issue, in the sense that Carmines and Stimson use the term. It is easy, on a gut level, to understand what happened on September 11 and to find it abhorrent. Beyond this, however, the terrorist threat becomes more complicated—a "hard" issue—as one tries to imagine who might be terrorists, what motivates them, and what array of possible weapons they might use. Even more difficult is assessing the steps proposed and taken to thwart terrorists. Do they work? Are they cost-effective? How would one know?

More than most other international issues, the threat of terrorism involves domestic policies aimed at preventing terrorist attacks, such as security searches at airports and on mass transit systems. Most initial survey research in this area has focused on the public's reaction to the USA PATRIOT Act. Among the roughly 80 percent of the public who had heard of the act, opinion was fairly evenly divided between those who saw it as a necessary tool for finding terrorists and those who thought it went too far and threatened civil liberties.[21] These responses were strongly influenced by partisanship. Only 15 percent of Republicans thought it went too far, while 53 percent of Democrats held that view when George W. Bush was president.

Up to some unknown point, Americans are willing to see their civil liberties compromised if they believe doing so will help prevent terrorism, even though three-fourths of the public has little confidence that the government will use personal information, gained through antiterror measures, appropriately.[22] Respondents are more willing to sacrifice the civil liberties of others than their own. For example, a CBS News poll in the spring of 2005 found that 56 percent of the public was willing to have government agencies monitor the telephone calls and e-mails of Americans the government finds suspicious; only 29 percent favored allowing this monitoring of "ordinary Americans."[23] These views are driven by partisanship as well. In 2013, with Democrat Barack Obama serving as commander in chief, 49 percent of Republicans supported the federal government's monitoring Americans' phone calls, while 58 percent of Democrats did.

Typically, important valence issues such as terrorism have components that can be treated as position issues when segments of the public and their leaders hold differing views. So while everyone is opposed to terrorism, dissimilar views can be held about how well President George W. Bush handled the war on terrorism or whether the Iraq war made the United States more or less safe from terrorism. As might be expected, the positions people take on these matters are related to partisanship.

Using data from the 2008 ANES, Figure 5-4 shows the relationship between party identification and three attitudes toward terrorism. In 2008, Democrats were likely to believe that the war in Iraq increased the terrorist threat; Republicans were not. Republicans were likely to approve of the government's handling of the war on terrorism; Democrats were not. Even views on spending money on the war on terrorism were related to partisanship, with Democrats and independents more likely than Republicans to support increased spending.

FIGURE 5-4   Attitudes toward the War on Terrorism according to Party Identification, 2008

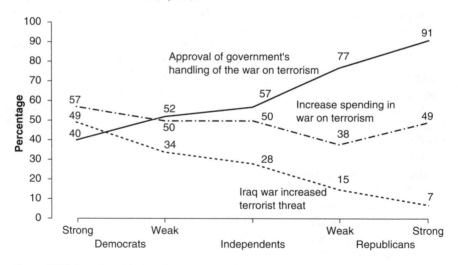

Source: 2008 American National Election Study, available at www.electionstudies.org.

International Affairs

During the cold war years (around 1947–1991), foreign policy—and the study of public opinion about foreign policy—focused on relations between the United States and the Soviet Union. Questions centered on the relative strength of the two countries, the likelihood of nuclear conflict between them, and the preference for negotiation or military strength as a strategy for keeping the peace. With the breakup of the Soviet Union, the focus of foreign policy has shifted away from superpower military relations toward involvement, or noninvolvement, in trouble spots around the world, such as the Persian Gulf in 1990 and 1991; Afghanistan and Iraq since 2001 and 2003, respectively; Libya in 2011; the ongoing violence in the Sudan; and the political disarray in Egypt and Syria.

Issues of foreign affairs vary greatly in salience, particularly in response to involvement of the nation in a military conflict. In analyzing the public's attitudes toward international events, a distinction needs to be made between brief conflicts and longer-lasting wars. A truism now in American politics says the American public will support—usually enthusiastically—brief military involvement in a foreign conflict that seems to be successful (and they will quickly forget if it is not successful). If, however, combat drags on, support will diminish, especially if there are significant U.S. casualties. In the case of Vietnam, opposition to the war developed at a sluggish pace over a considerable period of time, as did recognition of the seriousness of U.S. involvement. In the early years, opposition to the war (as measured by support for a prompt withdrawal) was low—less than 10 percent. By 1968, it had grown to 20 percent; by 1970, it was more than 30 percent; and by 1972, more than 40 percent. Clearly, as the war dragged on, support for military involvement declined dramatically. The Korean War nearly sixty years ago offers similar evidence of the failure of public support for prolonged conflicts.

In contrast, military episodes that develop rapidly command great public attention and almost always garner public support. In the Persian Gulf War, deployment of American military forces to Saudi Arabia began in the late summer of 1990, in response to Iraq's invasion of Kuwait. In the late fall, as deployment of U.S. troops continued, the public was somewhat divided in its support of this policy. Fifty-nine percent of the public polled said they believed it was the correct policy to pursue, and 39 percent said they believed it was not. These views shifted fairly dramatically after the brief and well-televised war with Iraq in early 1991. When the same people were interviewed again in June 1991 following the war, 81 percent felt the war had been the right thing to do and only 18 percent thought the United States should have stayed out.

In the beginning, support for the second war in Iraq was high among the American public. In March 2003, immediately after the invasion, 69 percent of the public thought the United States had done the right thing in taking military action against Iraq. Only a quarter of the public thought the United States should have stayed out.[24] A little over a year later, on the anniversary of the declared end of formal hostilities, the public was evenly divided on whether or not the United States had done the right thing—47 percent thought so; 46 percent did not.[25] Small bursts of support appeared after the patriotic displays at both parties' national nominating conventions in the summer of 2004 and right before the presidential election in November 2004, but generally, the trend of support was downward. By the fall of 2008, 70 percent of the public disapproved of President Bush's handling of the war in Iraq.[26]

Political analysts have long noted a "rally 'round the flag" phenomenon that occurs at times of international crisis.[27] Presidents invariably get a boost in popularity ratings in the polls in the midst of an international incident, even when the actions of the administration are not particularly successful. John F. Kennedy got such a boost after the disastrous Bay of Pigs invasion of Cuba in 1961, as did Jimmy Carter—temporarily— after a militant student group seized the American Embassy in Iran in 1979. And public approval of President George H. W. Bush's handling of the Gulf War was extremely high during and immediately following the conflict, representing a substantial increase over his earlier ratings. Similarly, George W. Bush saw an immediate gain in presidential job approval after the attacks on the World Trade Center and Pentagon on September 11, 2001. ABC News and the *Washington Post* completed a national survey the weekend before the attacks in which Bush's job approval was at 55 percent, about average for modern presidents in the first year of their first term. Immediately after the disaster, his job approval climbed to 86 percent. The change in "strong" approval was from 26 to 63 percent.[28] This enthusiasm did not survive the passage of time as President Bush left office with approval ratings that rivaled the worst evaluations of presidential performance in modern polling history.

As with domestic issues, partisan differences are apparent, with partisans of the president in office more supportive of whatever actions are taken than are partisans of the party out of power. This was seen most clearly during the war in Vietnam. Republicans were more likely to think getting involved in Vietnam was a mistake before 1969, when Democratic president Lyndon B. Johnson was in charge; thereafter, with Republican Richard M. Nixon in the White House, Democrats were more likely to view the war as a mistake.

Similarly, in 2004, 61 percent of Republicans said that Iraq was an immediate threat that required military action, whereas only 14 percent of Democrats and 26 percent of independents held that view. The partisan differences extend to many attitudes toward the Iraq war.

Republicans, for example, are much more likely than Democrats or independents to believe that the war in Iraq was a major part of the war on terrorism. Republican support for the war in Iraq remained strong, whereas the support of Democrats and independents fell faster. In March 2003, 87 percent of Republicans said that attacking Iraq was the right thing to do. A year later, their support was still at 80 percent. Democratic support, meanwhile, dropped from 50 percent to 24 percent over the same time period, and independent support declined a comparable amount, from 70 percent to 45 percent.[29] As can be seen in Table 5-9, what question was asked about Iraq did not matter much. Republicans, Democrats, and independents responded consistently. Republicans continued to support the Republican president, whereas Democrats did not. Independents were somewhere in between but became increasingly negative as time went on. Once Democrat Barack Obama took office, the percentage of Democrats who believed the war was going well jumped nearly 20 percentage points from 27 percent in September of 2008 to 46 percent in June of 2009, whereas Republican support fell from 88 percent to 76 percent during the same period.[30]

The public makes a distinction between the war in Iraq and the war in Afghanistan, although they share the characteristic of dragging on inconclusively. By the fall of 2008, 56 percent of the public thought sending military forces to Iraq had been a mistake, but only 28 percent thought it had been a mistake to send troops to Afghanistan.[31] Similarly, a little over 60 percent of the public thought the United States should keep troops in Afghanistan, while only 45 percent thought troops should be kept in Iraq. Republicans overwhelmingly thought troops should be kept in both countries, but Democrats were less sure. Fifty-three percent of all Democrats thought troops should be kept in Afghanistan, but only 25 percent felt that way about Iraq.[32] Because the war in Afghanistan has lasted longer, simple duration of a conflict does not determine the level of support. Most important, the connection between terrorism and the war in Afghanistan has not been questioned. But the cost in American lives and dollars also has been less in Afghanistan than Iraq, and news coverage of successes and failures has been more extensive in Iraq. With the Obama administration's new emphasis on Afghanistan as the right place to fight terrorism, partisan-shaped opinions were once again evident as a 2011 survey showed that while 72 percent of the public supported Obama's Afghanistan withdrawal plan, only 50 percent of Republicans liked the idea compared to 87 percent of Democrats and 74 percent of Independents.[33]

Up until Vietnam, bipartisanship was touted as the hallmark of American foreign policy—that "politics stops at the water's edge." While strictly speaking this was never true, the division between internationalist and isolationist views on the United States' role in the world tended not to follow party lines. Today, the partisan polarization extends also to

TABLE 5-9   Attitudes toward the War in Iraq according to Party
Identification, 2004 and 2008 (in percentages)

	Democrat	Independent	Republican
Think the United States did the right thing in taking military action against Iraq (2004)	24	45	80
Think the war with Iraq has been worth the cost (2008)	8	19	56
Think Iraq was a threat to the United States that required immediate military action (2004)	14	26	61
Think the Bush administration tried hard enough to reach a diplomatic solution in Iraq (2004)	12	31	64
Think the war with Iraq has decreased the threat of terrorism against the United States (2008)	12	23	49
Approve of the way President Bush is handling the war in Iraq (2008)	7	25	69
Oppose setting a deadline for the withdrawal of troops from Iraq (2008)	17	28	60

Sources: CBS News Poll, April 6–8, 2004, data provided by Inter-university Consortium for Political and Social Research; 2008 American National Election Study, available at www.electionstudies.org.

international issues, especially as they concern one or the other party's handling of them. As Table 5-10 demonstrates, although there is widespread bipartisan agreement on general principles, such as preventing the spread of nuclear weapons, there is disagreement on the role of the United Nations, combating global hunger, and assessing presidential performance on foreign policy issues.

Issues and Partisanship

As noted in previous sections, fairly strong and consistent relationships exist between partisanship and domestic and some foreign policy issues. A leading assumption is that partisan identification provides

TABLE 5-10   Attitudes toward Possible Foreign Policy Goals according to
Party Identification, 2008, 2012

	Percentage agreeing		
	Democrats	Independents	Republicans
Preventing the spread of nuclear weapons should be a very important U.S. foreign policy goal. (2008)	83	80	87
Promoting and defending human rights in other countries should be a very important U.S. foreign policy goal. (2008)	43	35	26
Strengthening the United Nations should be a very important U.S. foreign policy goal. (2008)	55	39	29
Combating world hunger should be a very important U.S. foreign policy goal. (2008)	70	59	45
The war in Afghanistan has been worth the cost. (2012)	24	26	37
Approve of Obama's handling of foreign relations (2012)	84	52	19

Source: 2008 and 2012 American National Election Study, available at www.election studies.org.

guidance for the public on policy matters—that is, most Americans adopt opinions consistent with their partisanship. It also is likely that policy positions developed independently of one's partisanship but consistent with it will reinforce feelings of party loyalty or that attitudes on issues will lead to a preference for the party most in agreement with them. Furthermore, issue preferences inconsistent with party loyalty can erode or change it. For any particular individual, it would be extremely difficult to untangle the effects of partisanship and policy preferences over a long period of time.

Even though on many issues most partisans of one party will hold a position different from that held by the majority of the other party, considerable numbers of people with issue positions "inconsistent" with their party identification remain loyal to that party. To account for this, it is variously suggested that (1) issues are unimportant to many voters; (2) only the issues most important to individuals need to be congruent with their partisanship; (3) individuals regularly misperceive the positions of the parties to remain comfortable with both their party loyalty and their policy preferences; or (4) the positions of each party are ambiguous or dissimilar enough in different areas of the country that no clear distinction exists between the parties. Undoubtedly, all these explanations have some degree of truth, and no one should expect to find extremely strong relationships between partisanship and positions on particular issues. Nevertheless, as an indication of the recent increased polarization of the parties, racial issues and so-called moral issues have joined traditional domestic economic issues to clearly differentiate Democrats from Republicans. While this has led those with consistently liberal or consistently conservative positions to be increasingly polarized from each other, it has also led to a widening "middle" of ideological libertarians, populists, and moderates—people with dissimilar views to each other *and* the parties in government in Washington, D.C. These individuals, who have a set of views that match Republicans on one issue dimension and Democrats on another, are less likely to participate in political activities, are less partisan, and are more likely to split their tickets when voting.

Political Ideology

A political ideology is a set of interrelated attitudes that fit together into some coherent and consistent view of or orientation toward the political world. Americans have opinions on a wide range of issues, and political analysts and commentators characterize these positions as "liberal" or "conservative." Does this mean, then, that the typical American voter has an ideology that serves as a guide to political thought and action, much the same way partisanship does?

When Americans are asked to identify themselves as liberal or conservative, most are able to do so. The categories have some meaning for most Americans, although the identifications are not of overriding importance. Table 5-11 presents the ideological identification of Americans over the past four decades. A consistently larger proportion of respondents call themselves conservative as opposed to liberal. At the same time, about a quarter of the population regards itself as middle-of-the-road ideologically. The question wording provides respondents with the opportunity to say they "haven't thought much about this," and fully a quarter to a third typically respond this way. The series of liberal and conservative responses has been remarkably stable over the years. Ideological identification, in the aggregate, is even more stable than party identification. The slight drop in the percentages saying they "haven't thought about" themselves in these terms, and the corresponding increase in the proportion of those calling themselves conservatives in

TABLE 5-11   Distribution of Ideological Identification, 1972–2012

	1972	1976	1980	1984	1988	1992	1996	2000	2004	2008	2012
Extremely liberal	1%	1%	2%	2%	2%	2%	1%	2%	2%	3%	2%
Liberal	7	7	6	7	6	8	7	9	9	10	10
Slightly liberal	10	8	9	9	9	10	10	9	8	9	9
Middle-of-the-road	27	25	20	23	22	23	24	23	25	22	24
Slightly conservative	15	12	13	14	15	15	15	12	12	12	13
Conservative	10	11	13	13	14	13	15	15	16	17	15
Extremely conservative	1	2	2	2	3	3	3	3	3	3	4
Haven't thought about it	28	33	36	30	30	27	25	27	25	25	23
Total	**99%**	**99%**	**101%**	**100%**	**101%**	**101%**	**100%**	**100%**	**100%**	**101%**	**100%**
(N)	(2,155)	(2,839)	(1,565)	(2,229)	(2,035)	(2,483)	(1,712)	(849)	(1,211)	(2,319)	(2,048)

Source: American National Election Studies, available at www.electionstudies.org.

1994 and beyond, may be a response to the heightened ideological rhetoric of the 1994 campaign and the increased polarization of the political parties. The overall stability of these numbers, however, should make one cautious of commentary that finds big shifts in liberalism or conservatism in the American electorate.

Table 5-12 shows the relationship between ideological self-identification and party identification. Democrats are more liberal than conservative, Republicans are disproportionately conservative, and independents are fairly evenly balanced. But conservatives are three times as likely to be Republicans as Democrats, and liberals are far more likely to be Democrats. The relationship between ideology and partisanship is shown in the low coincidence of liberal Republicans and conservative Democrats. Also, the electorate tends to perceive the Democratic Party as liberal and the Republican Party as conservative. Those who see an ideological difference between the parties believe the Republicans are more conservative than Democrats by a ratio of more than four to one.

There is also a relationship between social characteristics and ideological self-identification. Self-identified liberals are most frequent among better-educated whites who claim no religious affiliation or a non-Christian affiliation. Figure 5-5 also shows that a plurality of Hispanics (42 percent) also self-identify as liberal. Self-identified conservatives are most common among white evangelicals, but they are also found in substantial numbers among other Protestants and more educated Catholics. The major impact of education is to reduce the proportion of respondents who opt for the middle category. The better educated are more likely to call themselves either liberal or conservative than the high school educated. This tendency would be even greater if those who offered no self-identification were included.

Approximately half the public identifies itself as liberal or conservative. Do these individuals use ideological orientation to organize political

TABLE 5-12   Relationship between Ideological Self-Identification and Party Identification, 2012

	Democrats	Independents	Republicans	Total
Liberal	18%	8%	1%	27%
Middle-of-the-road	9	17	4	30
Conservative	4	16	22	42
Total[a]	**31%**	**41%**	**27%**	**99%**

Source: 2012 American National Election Study, available at www.electionstudies.org.

[a] $N = 1,524$. "No opinion" and "haven't thought about it" responses omitted.

FIGURE 5-5   Ideological Identification, by Race, Ethnicity, Religion, and
Education, 2012

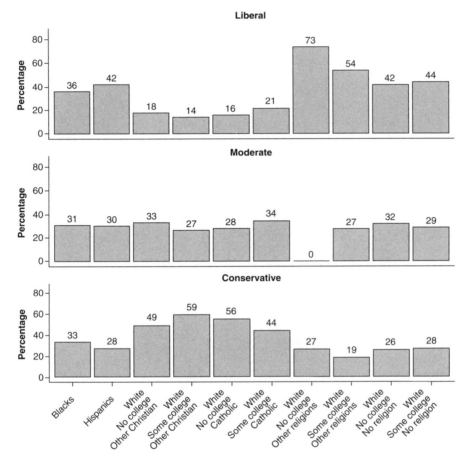

information and attitudes? Does political ideology play a role for Americans similar to the role of partisanship as a basic determinant of specific political views? Analysis has usually centered on two kinds of evidence to assess the extent of ideological thinking in the American electorate: the use of ideological concepts in discussing politics and the consistency of attitudes on related issues, suggesting an underlying perspective in the individual's approach to politics.

Data reported in *The American Voter,* by Angus Campbell, Philip E. Converse, Warren E. Miller, and Donald E. Stokes, showed that few members of the electorate discussed their evaluations of the parties and

TABLE 5-13   Distribution of the Levels of Conceptualization, 1956–2000

Levels of conceptualization	1956	1960	1964	1968	1972	1976	1980	1984	1988	2000
Ideologues	12%	19%	27%	26%	22%	21%	21%	19%	18%	20%
Group benefit	42	31	27	24	27	26	31	26	36	28
Nature of the times	24	26	20	29	34	30	30	35	25	28
No issue content	22	23	26	21	17	24	19	19	21	24
Total	**100%**	**99%**	**100%**	**100%**	**100%**	**101%**	**101%**	**99%**	**100%**	**100%**
(*N*)	(1,740)	(1,741)	(1,431)	(1,319)	(1,372)	(2,870)	(1,612)	(2,257)	(2,040)	(1,807)

Sources: Richard G. Niemi and Herbert F. Weisberg, eds., *Controversies in Voting Behavior,* 3rd ed. (Washington, DC: CQ Press, 1993), 89; Michael S. Lewis-Beck, William G. Jacoby, Helmut Norpoth, and Herbert F. Weisberg, *The American Voter Revisited* (Ann Arbor: University of Michigan Press, 2008), 279.

the candidates in ideological language; only 12 percent did so in 1956.[34] Other scholars have contributed similar analysis of subsequent years.[35] As shown in Table 5-13, a change occurred in 1964, during and after the Barry Goldwater/Lyndon B. Johnson election, with its highly ideological rhetoric. The proportions of ideologues doubled in 1964 over 1956 but still constituted only about one-quarter of the electorate. This does not mean that most voters have no notions about what the parties stand for or what they are likely to do when in office. Large proportions of the electorate evaluate the parties with group symbols: "The Democrats help the working man," and "Republicans are good for business." Still, much of the public lacks a commitment to some set of abstract principles about the role of government in society from which they can evaluate the parties.

It is possible that individuals may simply be unsophisticated in the verbal descriptions of their feelings about politics and political parties. Their ideology may guide their political decisions, but they may be unable to articulate it. In that case, the individuals' attitudes toward public issues might be expected to show a degree of coherence and consistency; they would arrive at those positions by applying a common underlying set of political ideals. If individuals are liberal on one issue, one would expect them to be liberal on other related issues; if they are conservative on one, they would be conservative on others. The most sophisticated analysis of ideological perspectives and consistency in issue positions, usually called *issue constraint,* was carried out by Philip E. Converse using data from 1956, 1958, and 1960.[36] He found that the strength of the relationship *among* domestic issues and *among* foreign policy issues was about twice as strong as that *between* domestic and foreign issues. By normal standards, even the strongest relationship among domestic issues did not suggest particularly impressive issue consistency, but consistency does increase when survey questions reference which party holds a particular position on an issue. Additionally, the degree of issue constraint on various policy matters increased in 1964 and remains at this higher level to the present.

As might be expected, the degree of consistency among attitudes on different issues varies with the level of education of the individual; the more educated are substantially more consistent in their views than the less educated. However, increasing levels of education do not appear to account for the increase in issue constraint. The work of Nie and Andersen shows convincingly that interest in politics is more critical. In other words, as members of the public become more concerned with issues and more attentive to political leaders, they perceive, and reflect, a higher degree of issue coherence. Almost certainly, the electorate has the capacity for greater issue constraint than it has shown. However, the exercise of the capacity depends much more on political leaders and events than on the characteristics of the electorate. When political leaders use ideological terms to describe themselves and the clusters of issues that they support, the electorate is capable of following suit.

The degree of issue constraint will depend on the range of issues considered. *The American Voter* documented a coherent set of attitudes on welfare policies and governmental activity, even in the 1950s. When the analysis moves to more disparate issues, such as support for welfare policies and civil liberties, the relationship weakens substantially. It can be argued that little relationship should be expected between positions in these different issue areas because they tap different ideological dimensions with no logical or necessary connections among them. For example, there is nothing logically inconsistent in a person's opposing government regulation of business and believing in racial equality. In the first half of the twentieth century, internationalist views in foreign policy were considered the liberal position and isolationist attitudes conservative. However, the cold war and Vietnam did much to rearrange these notions as liberals argued against American involvement and conservatives became more aggressive internationalists. In considering the question of issue constraint, two points should be kept in mind: (1) The meaning of the terms *liberal* and *conservative* changes with time, as do the connections between these ideologies and specific historical events, and (2) analysts, in studying issue constraint, invariably impose on the analysis their own version of ideological consistency, which, in light of the ambiguities surrounding the terms, is likely to be somewhat artificial.

A less strenuous criterion than issue constraint for assessing the impact of ideology on political attitudes is simply to look at the relationship between individuals' ideological identification and their positions on various issues taken one at a time. Here, substantial relationships are found. The relationship between ideological identification and liberal views on various policy matters over the past thirty-six years is shown in Table 5-14. Between one-fourth and one-third of the people sampled did not have an ideological position or did not profess attitudes on these issues and are, therefore, missing in the analysis. Nevertheless, the data in Table 5-14 document strong, consistent relationships between ideological identification and many issue positions. The data do not, however, demonstrate that ideology determines issue positions.

If everyone had a strong ideology, attitudes would be determined by that ideology. To a considerable extent, this appears to happen to the most politically alert and concerned in the society, but this group is only a small minority of the total adult population. To the extent that the major American political parties are ideologically oriented, then, by following the parties or political leaders in these parties, Americans have their opinions determined indirectly by ideology. American political parties are often characterized as nonideological, and the country has

TABLE 5-14   Relationship between Ideological Identification and Liberal Positions on Issues, 1972–2008

	Liberal	Somewhat liberal	Middle-of-the-road	Somewhat conservative	Conservative
Increase government services (2008)	81	55	54	29	28
Favor government health insurance (2008)	72	62	50	45	19
Pro-choice on abortion (2008)	79	50	43	34	16
Should allow gay marriage (2008)	72	53	43	28	12
Iraq war increased terrorist threat (2008)	46	45	30	22	12
Government help for blacks (2004)	48	26	20	14	11
Protect the environment (2004)	63	55	40	37	27
Oppose school vouchers (2000)	44	48	52	46	28
Protect homosexuals from job discrimination (1996)	87	79	68	63	39
Not worth it to fight in Persian Gulf (1992)	66	45	41	30	24
Support for the Equal Rights Amendment (1980)	91	78	64	48	38
Legalize marijuana (1976)	60	49	24	24	10
Oppose the Vietnam War (1972)	76	61	39	33	27

Source: American National Election Studies, available at www.electionstudies.org.

Note: The numbers in the table are the percentages taking the liberal position on each issue.

passed through substantial historical periods when the parties have seemed bent on obscuring the differences between them. At other times, such as 1964 and since the early 1990s, political leaders were more intent on drawing distinctions between themselves and the opposing party in ideological terms. At these times, the public responds by appearing more ideological as well.

Whether tightly constrained or seemingly built at random, ideology and issue preferences have to come from somewhere. For years, the dominant explanation was that preferences, ideology, and partisanship came from a process of socialization from one's parents, schools, religion, and socioeconomic status. In recent years, scholars have started to demonstrate that while socialization certainly affects our opinions, ideology, and partisanship, biological factors do as well. One study, from John Alford, Carolyn Funk, and John Hibbing, compared issue preferences of identical twins to those of fraternal twins, finding that the identical twins (ones from the same zygote, sharing 100% of their DNA) had views that were more alike than fraternal twins (from two zygotes, sharing roughly 50% of their DNA).[37] Jeffrey J. Mondak has shown how people's personality characteristics inform their ideology and preferences,[38] and other scholars, such as Peter Hatemi, Kevin Smith, James Fowler, Rose McDermott, and Hibbing have provided evidence on matters as diverse as the role that genes play in one's likelihood of identifying as a partisan (but not with which party), how physiological responses to threatening and disgusting images correlate with liberalism and conservatism, and how genes are related to voter turnout.[39] These studies have elicited plenty of controversy, with some scholars arguing that such studies are dangerous, whereas other scholars question the precision of measurements connecting deep-seated biological orientations with expressed political attitudes and behaviors.

Public Opinion and Political Leadership

The study of public opinion is of obvious relevance to public officials and political journalists who wish to assess the mood of the people on various topics, but the extent to which decision makers are influenced by public opinion on any particular policy is almost impossible to determine. Although policy makers must have some sense of the public mood, no one supposes that they measure precisely the attitudes of the public or are influenced by public opinion alone.

Political analysts and public officials both have difficulty assessing the likely impact of public opinion as measured by public opinion polls because the intensity of feelings will influence the willingness of the public to act on their views. Public officials who value their careers must be conscious of the issues that raise feelings strong enough to cause people to contribute money, to campaign, and to cast their ballots solely on the basis of that issue. As a result, public officials may be more responsive to the desires of small, intense groups than to larger, but basically indifferent, segments of the public.

In American society, public attitudes toward policies usually can be described in one of two ways: (1) as permissive opinion, whereby a wide range of possible government activities are acceptable to the public, or (2) in contrast, as directive opinion, either supportive or negative, whereby specific alternatives are definitely demanded or opposed. Ordinarily, policy alternatives advocated by both political parties are within the range of permissive opinion, a situation that does not create highly salient issues or sharp cleavages in the public, even though political leaders may present their positions dramatically. Only when many people hold directive opinions will the level of issue salience rise or issue clashes appear among the public. For example, widespread directive support exists for public education in the United States. Most individuals demand a system of public education or would demand it were it threatened. At the same time, permissive support is evident for a wide range of policies and programs in public education. Governments at several levels may engage in a variety of programs without arousing the public to opposition or support. Within this permissive range the public is indifferent.

Occasionally, the public may out-and-out oppose some programs and form directive opinions that impose limits on how far government can go. For example, the widespread opposition to busing children out of their neighborhoods for purposes of integration has perhaps become a directive, negative opinion. Political analysts or politicians cannot easily discover the boundaries between permissive and directive opinions. Political leaders are likely to argue that there are supportive, directive opinions for their own positions and negative, directive opinions for their opponents' views. One should be skeptical of these claims because it is much more likely that there are permissive opinions and casual indifference toward the alternative views. Indifference is widespread and, of course, does not create political pressure. It frees political leaders of restrictions on issue positions but, on balance, is probably more frustrating than welcome. When comparing the general ideological orientation of states to the general public policies produced by state legislatures, Robert Erikson, Gerald Wright, and John McIver have found that states with more liberal publics have state legislatures that produce more liberal public policies and vice versa.[40] At the national level, James Stimson provides evidence of federal representation, showing that as the overall public mood becomes more liberal, liberals are more likely to get elected and produce left-leaning policies, and as public mood swings to the conservative side, conservatives are more likely to enter office and produce more conservative policies.[41]

Notes

1. Edward G. Carmines, Michael J. Ensley, and Michael W. Wagner, "Political Ideology in American Politics: One, Two, or None?" *The Forum* 10, no. 4 (2012): 1–18.
2. Nolan McCarty, Keith. T. Poole, and Howard Rosenthal, *Polarized America: The Dance of Ideology and Unequal Riches* (Cambridge, MA: MIT Press, 2006). Updated data can be found at http://voteview.com/political_polarization.asp.
3. Marc J. Hetherington, "Resurgent Mass Partisanship: The Role of Elite Polarization," *American Political Science Review* 95 no. 3 (2001): 619–56.
4. Matthew Levendusky, *The Partisan Sort: How Liberals Became Democrats and Conservatives Became Republicans* (Chicago: University of Chicago Press, 2009).
5. Lydia Saad, "U.S. Debt Ceiling Increase Remains Unpopular with Americans," *Gallup Politics,* July 12, 2011, http://www.gallup.com/poll/148454/debt-ceiling-increase-remains-unpopular-americans.aspx.
6. Philip E. Converse, "The Nature of Belief Systems in Mass Publics," in *Ideology and Discontent,* ed. David Apter (New York: Free Press, 1964), 206–61.
7. John R. Zaller, *The Nature and Origin of Mass Opinion* (New York: Cambridge University Press, 1980).
8. Edward G. Carmines and James A. Stimson, "The Two Faces of Issue Voting," *American Political Science Review* 74 (1980): 78–91.
9. In the 2006 General Social Survey, for example, 38 percent said "too much" was being spent on "welfare"; however, 70 percent said "too little" was being spent on "assistance to the poor."
10. 1992 American National Election Study.
11. 2008 American National Election Study.
12. This view is most prominently associated with Paul M. Sniderman and Edward G. Carmines, *Reaching beyond Race* (Cambridge, MA: Harvard University Press, 1997). See also Paul M. Sniderman, Philip E. Tetlock, and Edward G. Carmines, *Prejudice, Politics, and the American Dilemma* (Stanford, CA: Stanford University Press, 1993).
13. A strong statement of the symbolic racism position is in Donald R. Kinder and Lynn M. Sanders, *Divided by Color* (Chicago: University of Chicago Press, 1996).
14. This position is most commonly associated with Lawrence Bobo. See his "Race and Beliefs about Affirmative Action," in *Racialized Politics,* ed. David Sears, Jim Sidanius, and Lawrence Bobo (Chicago: University of Chicago Press, 2000), chap. 5.
15. This position is represented by Jim Sidanius and Felicia Pratto in *Social Dominance: An Intergroup Theory of Social Dominance and Oppression* (Cambridge, England: Cambridge University Press, 1999).
16. Edward G. Carmines and James A. Stimson, *Issue Evolution: Race and the Transformation of American Politics* (Princeton, NJ: Princeton University Press, 1989).
17. Martin Gilens, *Why Americans Hate Welfare* (Chicago: University of Chicago Press, 1999).

18. Kinder and Sanders, *Divided by Color*.

19. Brian Montopoli, "Most Say U.S. Will Always Face Terrorism Threat," CBS News, September 9, 2011, http://www.cbsnews.com/8301-503544_162-20103461-503544/most-say-u-s-will-always-face-terrorism-threat/.

20. "America Speaks Out about Homeland Security Survey," conducted by Hart and Teeter Research Companies for the Council for Excellence in Government, February 5–8, 2004, Roper Center for Public Opinion Research.

21. Pew News Interest Index Poll, January 4–8, 2006, Roper Center for Public Opinion Research.

22. "America Speaks Out about Homeland Security Survey," Roper Center for Public Opinion Research.

23. CBS News Poll, April 2005, Roper Center for Public Opinion Research.

24. CBS News Monthly Poll 5, March 26–27, 2003.

25. CBS News/*New York Times* Poll, April 23–27, 2004.

26. 2008 American National Election Study.

27. John E. Mueller, *War, Presidents, and Public Opinion* (New York: Wiley, 1973), 208–13.

28. These data are available at www.pollingreport.com.

29. CBS News Monthly Poll 5; and CBS News/*New York Times* Poll, April 23–27, 2004. Data provided by the Inter-university Consortium for Political and Social Research.

30. Jeffrey M. Jones, "Americans Divided on How Well Iraq War Is Going for U.S.," *Gallup Politics,* August 5, 2010, http://www.gallup.com/poll/141773/Americans-Divided-Iraq-War-Going.aspx.

31. Gallup/*USA Today* Poll, July 2008, Roper Center for Public Opinion Research.

32. Pew Research Center for the People and the Press, September 2008.

33. Lydia Saad, "Americans Broadly Favor Obama's Afghanistan Pullout Plan," *Gallup Politics,* June 29, 2011, http://www.gallup.com/poll/148313/Americans-Broadly-Favor-Obama-Afghanistan-Pullout-Plan.aspx.

34. Angus Campbell, Philip E. Converse, Warren E. Miller, and Donald E. Stokes, *The American Voter* (New York: Wiley, 1960), 249.

35. John C. Pierce, "Ideology, Attitudes, and Voting Behavior of the American Electorate: 1956, 1960, 1964," Ph.D. dissertation, University of Minnesota, 1969, 63, Table 3.1; Paul R. Hagner and John C. Pierce, "Conceptualization and Consistency in Political Beliefs: 1956–1976," paper presented at the annual meeting of the Midwest Political Science Association, Chicago, 1981; and Michael Lewis-Beck, William G. Jacoby, Helmut Norpoth, and Herbert F. Weisberg, *The American Voter Revisited* (Ann Arbor: University of Michigan Press, 2008), chap. 10. See also Norman H. Nie, Sidney Verba, and John R. Petrocik, *The Changing American Voter* (Cambridge, MA: Harvard University Press, 1976), chap. 7.

36. Converse, "The Nature of Belief Systems in Mass Publics," 206–61.

37. John R. Alford, Carolyn L. Funk, and John R. Hibbing, "Are Political Orientations Genetically Transmitted?" *American Political Science Review* 99 (May 2005): 153–67.

38. Jeffery J. Mondak, *Personality and the Foundations of Political Behavior* (New York: Cambridge University Press, 2010).

39. P. K. Hatemi and R. McDermott, "The Genetics of Politics: Discovery, Challenges and Progress," *Trends in Genetics* 28, no. 10 (2012): 525–33; John R. Hibbing, Kevin B. Smith, and John R. Alford. *Predisposed: Liberals, Conservatives,*

and the Biology of Political Differences (New York: Routledge, 2013); James H. Fowler and Christopher T. Dawes, "In Defense of Genopolitics," *American Political Science Review* 107, no. 2 (2013): 362–74.

40. Robert S. Erikson, Gerald C. Wright, and John P. McIver, *Statehouse Democracy: Public Opinion, and Policy in the American States* (Cambridge, England: Cambridge University Press, 1993).

41. James A. Stimson, *Public Opinion in America: Moods, Cycles, and Swings, Second Edition* (Boulder, CO: Westview Press, 1999).

Suggested Readings

Althaus, Scott. *Collective Preferences in Democratic Politics: Opinion Surveys and the Will of the People.* New York: Cambridge University Press, 2003. A compelling demonstration that measures of public opinion do not represent the public equally.

Carmines, Edward G., and James A. Stimson. *Issue Evolution: Race and the Transformation of American Politics.* Princeton, NJ: Princeton University Press, 1989. A fascinating account of the role of racial issues and policies in American politics in recent decades.

Claggett, William J. M., and Byron E. Shafer. *The American Public Mind.* New York: Cambridge University Press, 2010. A detailed accounting of how social welfare, cultural, international, and race issue preferences structured electoral politics from 1952–2004.

Converse, Philip E. "The Nature of Belief Systems in Mass Publics." In *Ideology and Discontent,* edited by David Apter, 206–61. New York: Free Press, 1964. A classic analysis of the levels of sophistication in the American public.

Erikson, Robert S., Michael B. MacKuen, and James A. Stimson. *The Macro Polity.* Cambridge, England: Cambridge University Press, 2002. A methodologically sophisticated study of representation in the United States.

Hibbing, John R., Kevin B. Smith, and John R. Alford. *Predisposed: Liberals, Conservatives, and the Biology of Political Differences.* New York: Routledge, 2013. An in-depth look at the evidence supporting the biological roots of the notion that political opponents experience and respond to the world differently.

Hochschild, Jennifer L. *What's Fair.* Cambridge, MA: Harvard University Press, 1981. An intensive, in-depth study of the beliefs and attitudes of a few people that deals with traditional topics from a different perspective.

Lewis-Beck, Michael S., William G. Jacoby, Helmut Norpoth, and Herbert F. Weisberg. *The American Voter Revisited.* Ann Arbor: University of Michigan Press, 2008. A rich reanalysis of the themes from the classic work, using mainly 2000 and 2004 data.

Mayer, William G. *The Changing American Mind.* Ann Arbor: University of Michigan Press, 1992. Analysis of changes in issue positions between 1960 and 1988.

Sniderman, Paul M., Richard A. Brody, and Philip E. Tetlock. *Reasoning and Choice.* Cambridge, England: Cambridge University Press, 1991. A political, psychological approach to the study of issues and ideology.

Stimson, James A. *The Tides of Consent: How Public Opinion Shapes American Politics.* Cambridge, England: Cambridge University Press, 2004. A complex analysis of changing policy views and their impact.

Internet Resources

The website of the American National Election Studies, www.electionstudies.org, has extensive data on the topics covered in this chapter. After clicking on "Utilities" and then on the link for tables and graphs under "The ANES Guide to Public Opinion and Electoral Behavior," scroll down to "Ideological Self-Identification" for ideological items in a number of election years. Scroll to "Public Opinion on Public Policy Issues" for a wide range of attitudes from 1952 to the present. Each political item is broken down by an extensive set of social characteristics.

The Roper Center for Public Opinion Research, www.ropercenter.uconn .edu/, at the University of Connecticut has an enormous collection of survey data on American public opinion from the 1930s to the present.

The General Social Survey, www.norc.org/GSS+Website/, has been collecting public opinion data since 1972 on a wide range of topics. Some of these data can be analyzed online at http://sda.berkeley.edu.

C h a p t e r   S i x

Group Characteristics and Social Networks

ATTEMPTS TO EXPLAIN American voting behavior have often relied on social and economic factors to account for both stability and change in American politics. Research based on the American National Election Studies (ANES) has documented a wide range of relationships in the U.S. electorate between social and economic characteristics and political behavior. Furthermore, many descriptions of voting patterns offered by American journalists and party strategists are based on social and economic factors. Analysis regularly attributes political trends to such categories as "soccer moms" or "born-again Christians"; frequently, these explanations rely on so-called bloc voting, such as "the black vote," "the senior citizens' vote," or "the Hispanic vote," implying that some social factor causes large numbers of people to vote the same way.

The social factors that underlie partisanship reflect the partisan alignment in effect at any given time. During the New Deal alignment, partisan choices tended to fall along economic and social class lines. Blue-collar workers, those with lower incomes, those with lower education, recent immigrants, racial minorities, and Catholics were all more likely to vote Democratic. Members of the middle class, white-collar workers, the college educated, those with high incomes, whites of northern European background, and Protestants were more likely to vote Republican.

The remnants of the New Deal alignment can still be seen in the partisan choices of today. Table 6-1 displays the party identification of selected social groups in 2012. For example, income is associated with party identification, with lower-income people more likely to be Democratic than higher-income people. Blacks and Hispanics are much more Democratic than Republican. But significant differences from earlier times also have emerged. Catholics were heavily Democratic when they were recent immigrants, but as later generations moved into the middle class, their disproportionate presence among Democratic partisans has faded, and Catholics now are similar to Protestants in their party identification. Religion still has an impact on partisanship, but it has become more complicated than the difference between Protestants and Catholics. The distinction between fundamentalists and evangelicals on the one hand and more traditional mainline denominations on the other has become more important politically in recent decades, with fundamentalists and evangelicals considered a part of the Republican base. This religious distinction is complicated by race, however, given that many African Americans belong to fundamentalist and evangelical churches but remain overwhelmingly Democratic. White evangelicals and fundamentalists are heavily Republican. The importance of religion in one's life, referred to as "religiosity," is another factor that influences one's partisanship. In Table 6-1, this can be seen most starkly in the disproportionate preference for the Democrats among those who report having no religious affiliation.

Even in the heyday of the New Deal, social and economic status was hardly a perfect predictor of partisan choice. This was most obvious in the South. White southerners were overwhelmingly Democratic—a legacy from the earlier Civil War alignment—and this traditional attachment to the Democratic Party virtually wiped out the impact of any other social or economic factor on political behavior. In the 1950s, the southern middle class was about as Democratic as the working class, southern Protestants as Democratic as the relatively few Catholics in that region, and so on. Since 1956, southern whites have gone from 63 percent Democratic to 17 percent (not counting those leaning toward the Democrats), and the social factors associated with partisanship are now not distinctively different from other parts of the country.

The percentage of the overall population that a particular group comprises has also changed since the 1950s. The proportion of Hispanics has increased dramatically; the proportions of fundamentalists, evangelicals, and people with no religious affiliations have all increased, at the expense of mainline Protestants; and the proportion of people with higher education has increased, while the percentage of union households has fallen.

The Social Composition of Partisan Groups

Another way of looking at the relationship between social characteristics and partisanship is to describe Democratic and Republican Party identifiers and Independents in terms of the proportions of different

TABLE 6-1   Party Identification, by Social Characteristics, 2012

Category (percentage of sample)	Democrats		Independents			Republicans		Total percentage
	Strong	Weak	Lean Democrat	Independent	Lean Republican	Weak	Strong	
Men (48)	16	13	18	9	20	10	12	98
Women (52)	24	12	14	11	15	11	14	101
Whites (71)	13	10	15	10	22	13	17	100
Blacks (12)	56	17	17	4	5	0	1	100
Hispanics (11)	28	23	16	14	8	6	5	100
18–24 (13)	14	18	16	19	17	11	6	101
25–34 (16)	17	17	19	10	20	9	8	100
35–44 (18)	22	12	17	8	18	12	11	100
45–54 (17)	22	9	16	9	16	18	10	100
55–64 (17)	25	12	13	8	16	7	20	101
65–74 (11)	19	12	11	9	21	9	20	101
75 and over (7)	19	11	16	8	18	5	23	100
High school education or less (41)	21	15	14	15	16	7	12	100
Some college (30)	19	11	19	9	19	11	12	100
College graduate (29)	19	12	15	5	18	15	16	100
Under $12,500 (15)	23	12	15	19	12	9	10	100

Category (percentage of sample)	Democrats		Independents			Republicans		Total percentage
	Strong	Weak	Lean Democrat	Independent	Lean Republican	Weak	Strong	
$12,500–25,000 (14)	26	18	19	10	12	5	11	101
$25,000–50,000 (22)	21	12	21	10	17	6	12	99
$50,000–100,000 (30)	20	11	12	7	21	13	15	99
Over $100,000 (20)	14	11	15	7	21	17	15	100
Union households (16)	24	16	16	10	20	5	9	100
Mainline Protestants (20)	20	12	13	10	16	11	19	101
Fundamentalists, evangelicals (30)	20	13	12	6	18	15	17	101
Catholics (22)	21	13	15	10	22	8	11	100
No religion (25)	19	14	21	14	18	7	7	100
White fundamentalists, evangelicals (20)	8	9	11	7	24	19	24	102
Non-South (63)	20	14	16	11	18	10	12	101
South (37)	21	11	15	9	18	11	15	100

Source: 2012 American National Election Study, available at www.electionstudies.org.

kinds of individuals who make up their ranks. Figure 6-1 presents the social composition of Democratic, Republican, and independent identifiers, using some of the same social categories used in Table 6-1 (race and ethnicity, religion, and education). However, this way of viewing the data gives different results and answers a different set of questions. Instead of revealing to what extent particular social groups support the Democratic or Republican parties, the data show the proportion of all Democrats who are African American or Catholic. For example, the partisanship of various social groups presented in Table 6-1 shows that African Americans are heavily Democratic (73 percent in 2012 identified themselves as strong or weak Democrats). But if the proportion of all Democrats who are African American is calculated, as in Figure 6-1, African Americans are found to make up just 29 percent of the total group of Democrats. Because blacks are a relatively small proportion of the population, their contribution to the total set of Democrats is not so large, despite their lopsided preference for the Democratic Party.

Studying the partisanship of social groups has generally been regarded as the more interesting way of looking at the relationship between social characteristics and political behavior, largely because of the causal connection between social characteristics and partisanship. Thus, one is far more inclined to say that race and ethnicity, religion, or education cause an individual to select a particular political party than to say that political affiliation causes any of the others. Familiarity with the composition of the parties is useful, however, in understanding the campaign strategies and political appeals that the parties make to hold their supporters in line and sway the independents or opposition supporters to their side. For example, the fact that African Americans constitute over a quarter (29 percent) of the Democratic partisans but make up less than 1 percent of the Republican partisans is a significant factor that both parties take into account. The growing importance of the Hispanic vote for the Democrats is also reflected in Figure 6-1. In 2012, Hispanics made up 18 percent of the Democratic identifiers; in 2000, they made up only 9 percent.

The composition of the parties affects politics in another way. In an important book on the evolution of race as an issue in the United States, Edward G. Carmines and James A. Stimson argue persuasively that the composition of the parties, particularly the composition of the party activists, influences the perceptions that less involved citizens hold about the philosophy and issue stands of the parties.[1] The fact that African Americans are overwhelmingly Democratic and that vocal racial conservatives— in other words, those with a general predisposition to oppose government actions to correct racial injustices—are increasingly Republican allows the average voter to figure out which party is liberal and which is conservative on racial issues, even if race is never mentioned by candidates during the course of an election campaign.

FIGURE 6-1   Social Composition of Partisans and Independents, by Race, Ethnicity, Religion, and Education, 2012

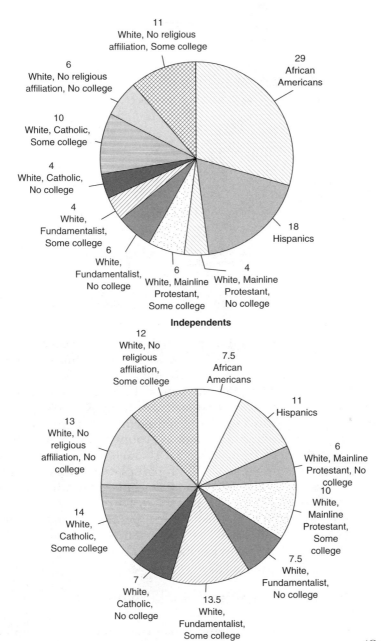

FIGURE 6-1 (Continued)

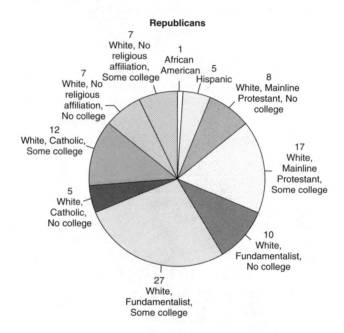

Source: 2012 American National Election Study, available at www.electionstudies.org.

As can be seen in Figure 6-1, the composition of the partisan identifiers is distinctively different. The Democrats are much more varied in racial and ethnic composition than the Republicans. Meanwhile, fundamentalist and evangelical Protestants and college-educated mainline Protestants make up significantly larger parts of the Republican Party than they do of the Democratic Party, although both parties contain substantial proportions of various religious groups and people with different educational levels. In other social characteristics, the partisan groupings are quite heterogeneous. Both parties draw substantial portions of their votes from blue-collar as well as white-collar workers, from the young, the middle-aged, the old, and so on. This diversity is also true of independents, as shown in Figure 6-1. As we pointed out in chapter 4, independent voters hold the balance of power between the major parties, and both must appeal to them to win elections.

Social Groups and Social Networks

How is it that people who share certain characteristics also tend to share the same party identification? Part of the answer is that social groups have a pronounced impact on individual attitudes and behavior.

Some of this impact occurs directly through face-to-face interactions with primary groups, such as family, friends, and coworkers. The impact can be less direct as well, especially when secondary groups are involved. Secondary groups are those organizations or collections of individuals with which one identifies, or is identified, that have some common interest or goal instead of personal contact as their major basis. Understanding the role social context plays in how people think and act when it comes to politics is essential for understanding political behavior.

Primary Groups

In some ways, it would make sense if family and friends held a wide variety of often dissimilar political attitudes. Many Americans are not interested in politics and therefore do not make it a centerpiece of their dinner discussions, or of any discussions for that matter. If politics is something these Americans want to forget exists, then it is unlikely that they would discuss politics enough to have family and friends who share their political views. On the other hand, family and friends are in close contact, they share many of the same experiences, and they care about each other. Politics might not be at the forefront of people's minds, but political topics arise and people react to what they see and hear. Whether people like it or not, the pervasiveness of politics might play out among family and friends.

Although investigations of the political behavior of primary groups are not numerous, all available evidence indicates that families and groups of friends are likely to be politically homogeneous. This is especially the case among spouses. Why are husbands and wives so similar in their political attitudes and behaviors? Researchers have offered three reasons: influence, social homogamy, and assortative mating. We discuss influence, or assimilation, first. Even if spouses hold different political views when they marry, they can become more similar over time by changing their attitudes to become more in line with each other. Laura Stoker and M. Kent Jennings found that married couples experience "mutual influence" over the course of a marriage and therefore become more similar in their political attitudes and behavior. The influence, however, does not appear to be balanced between husbands and wives. Married women are more likely to bring their views into line with their husbands, and this shift makes married women, married men, and single men very similar on average in their party identification, vote choice, ideology, racial views, and attitudes about gender equality. The outliers are single women who remain significantly more Democratic and liberal than men or married women.[2] Once married, couples share similar experiences, which tends to reinforce shared attitudes

A second explanation that might explain the similarity in the political attitudes of married couples is social homogamy, the idea that people tend to marry partners who come from the same sociocultural background and therefore share certain social characteristics, including race and ethnicity, socioeconomic status, and religion. To the extent that these social groups hold certain political views, people will tend to marry for sociocultural reasons but end up sharing political attitudes as a by-product of this process.[3] Married couples' social group characteristics can become even more similar after marriage because of their linked circumstances. They will likely, as a couple, attend the same church, have friends in the same social class, rise or fall in social status as circumstances change, and so on. These reinforcements of certain political proclivities through shared social group characteristics contribute to a high level of similarity between married couples in their political attitudes

The third explanation for couples' political similarity is assortative mating, where people choose partners because they hold similar traits. Many traits of spouses are positively correlated, including physical characteristics (such as height, weight, and even ear lobe size), social characteristics (such as education level, income, and occupation), personality (such as openness to experience), and, most important for our purposes, political ideology and party identification. Spouses share many political attitudes at the very beginning of their married life, suggesting that people choose spousal partners who share their views on such things as party identification, school prayer, the death penalty, and gay rights.[4] While politics might not be a topic people talk or care a lot about, they do care about basic political values and how society works. These values play an important role in whom people choose to marry.

Families, beyond just the spouses, tend to be politically homogeneous. Parents naturally pass on to their children some of their political values, including their ideology and party identification. It makes sense that the transmission of party identification, for example, depends on family context. As we discussed in chapter 4, children whose parents' party identifications correspond and are stable across time are more likely to hold that party identification themselves. Most important is the extent to which the family is politically engaged. The more politicized the family environment, with frequent discussions about and engagement in politics, the more signals parents send to their children. In what is equivalent to being hit over the head with politics, children in politicized families both know their parents' party identification and understand the importance of that identification. The transmission of party identification from parent to child is much higher in politicized and consistent family environments than in apolitical family environments.[5] Along these lines, it is interesting to note that party identification appears not to have much of a genetic basis but partisan strength does. That is, parents who strongly identify with a party tend to have offspring who also strongly identify with a party, although which party they identify with appears not to be based on genetics.[6]

Just as people get to choose their mates, so too do they get to choose their friends. The correlations between friends' political views tend to be fairly strong for the same reasons as spouses' similarities: being attracted to people who hold similar political values and interacting frequently, including discussing politics when the subject comes up. The tendency of people not to like conflict or disagreement increases the likelihood that friends will hold the same views and that they will not talk politics when they disagree. All of this explains why people's social networks tend to be highly homogeneous in terms of political views. Democrats rarely have Republican discussion partners (only 16 percent of all discussion partners) and Republicans are reluctant to have Democratic discussion partners (only 22 percent of all discussion partners).[7] The difference between family and friends, though, is that friends are more likely to live at a distance, less likely to be in frequent face-to-face communication, and less likely to share thoughts on politics. Friends, whether close or not, are therefore less likely to influence people's political views, including their party identification.[8] Recent research suggests, however, that friends might have a greater impact on political behavior than previously thought. Internet social networks, specifically Facebook, influence whether people vote; people who see in their Facebook newsfeed that their friends have voted are more likely to vote themselves.[9] Whether these effects can be extended to partisan attitudes and issue preferences has not been effectively studied.

Groups of coworkers appear to be somewhat more mixed politically. Presumably the social forces in families and friendship groups are more intense and more likely to be based on, or to result in, political unanimity; but in most work situations, people are thrown together without an opportunity to form groups based on common political values or any other shared traits. Friendship groups, even casual ones, may be formed so that individuals with much in common, including political views, naturally come together. Workplace groups, on the other hand, are formed with a task-oriented goal as the key, leading coworkers to be more diverse in their political leanings.

Table 6-2 presents findings from the 2000 ANES survey that illustrate the homogeneity of primary groups. Respondents were asked the political party of the people with whom they regularly discussed politics. The table shows that agreement on voting between spouses is highest, with 90 percent of the Democrats and 92 percent of the Republicans reporting that their spouses shared their vote choice. Agreement was not so high among other groups but still reflects considerable like-mindedness. Perhaps as important is the relatively low occurrence of mismatches of Democrats and Republicans in primary groups. Sixty percent of the respondents were in agreement on presidential vote choice with all of their reported primary group contacts.

TABLE 6-2   Reported Vote Preferences of Primary Groups, by Respondent's Reported Vote for President, 2000

	Respondent's vote for president	
Primary group	Democrat	Republican
Reported vote of spouse		
Democrat	90%	8%
Republican	10	92
Total	100%	100%
(*N*)	(149)	(157)
Reported vote of other relatives		
Democrat	79%	22%
Republican	21	78
Total	100%	100%
(*N*)	(282)	(254)
Reported vote of coworkers		
Democrat	62%	39%
Republican	38	61
Total	100%	100%
(*N*)	(189)	(250)
Reported vote of fellow churchgoers		
Democrat	65%	17%
Republican	35	83
Total	100%	100%
(*N*)	(49)	(103)
Reported vote of neighbors		
Democrat	75%	35%
Republican	25	65
Total	100%	100%
(*N*)	(142)	(112)

Source: 2000 American National Election Study, available at www.electionstudies.org.

Note: Respondents were asked to name four people with whom they discussed political matters, after which their relationship with those mentioned was established. The table includes only the responses of those who said they talked about political matters at least occasionally with the people they mentioned.

The homogeneity of political beliefs within primary groups increasingly extends to neighborhoods as well. This might seem odd, and researchers in this area do not suggest that an overriding reason for people to move into certain neighborhoods is partisanship, but the findings are convincing that neighborhoods are becoming more homogeneous in terms of partisanship over time. Bill Bishop and Robert Cushing argue that people are sorting themselves, through decisions about where to live, into increasingly solid Democratic or Republican counties. Whether people are choosing where to live based on race, education level, or church availability, the outcome is more counties in which the Democratic or Republican candidate wins in a landslide and fewer competitive counties. Wendy Tam Cho, James Gimpel, and Iris Hui find that most people choose where to lived based on such factors as how safe, quiet, and affordable a neighborhood is, but both Democrats (29 percent) and Republicans (39 percent) say an important factor in their choice of residence is having the neighborhood populated with fellow partisans. They further find that even taking into account neighborhood characteristics such as race and income level, people choose to move into neighborhoods that are more partisan than their old neighborhood. Republicans are especially likely to move into more Republican neighborhoods, but Democrats have a tendency to move into Democratic neighborhoods as well.[10]

Diana Mutz addresses the importance for democracies of having political discussions with people with whom one disagrees. The United States, she points out, is comparatively a highly partisan nation, with most Americans favoring a party or candidate. This partisan context opens the possibility that people could have exciting political discussions with people from the opposing party. Yet this is not what she finds.

> Highly partisan political environments [such as the United States] pose a paradox: on the one hand, the existence of large numbers of people who hold readily identifiable political preferences would tend to suggest a vibrant, active political culture. On the other hand, it appears that many citizens in such an environment will isolate themselves among those of largely like-minded views, thus making it difficult for cross-cutting political discourse to transpire.[11]

Americans talk about politics, whether among family, friends, coworkers, or neighbors, but they overwhelmingly talk to fellow partisans, not to people who might push them to think outside their partisan box. As we will see in chapter 7, this predilection is also extending to the choices people make about what news programs they prefer to watch or read.

There is nothing new in people preferring to be around or talk to people like them. What is disconcerting about the homogeneity of social networks and neighborhoods is its potential impact on democratic politics. A democratic political system in as large and diverse a nation as the United States deals with a wide variety of often contentious issues. Lawmakers need to debate competing options and reach compromises on solutions. The more constituents hear the views from just one side, the less likely they are to appreciate that the opposing side might have viable arguments as well and the less likely they are to accept compromises. They will erroneously believe that the vast majority of Americans agree with them when it comes to politics because that is what they hear from family, friends, and neighbors. Why accept debate and compromise when, as one focus group participant put it, "80 percent of the people think one way"?[12] If people understood that Americans fundamentally disagree on a lot of issues because they have frequently interacted with those who hold different views, they might better understand the need for debate and compromise in Washington.

The discussion of primary groups has implications as well for the celebrated gender gap in the political preferences of men and women, a favorite topic of political commentators since the early 1980s. Women were less favorably inclined toward Presidents Ronald Reagan, George H. W. Bush, and George W. Bush (in 2000), and toward Republicans in general, than were men. Conversely, women were more supportive of President Bill Clinton and Vice President Al Gore than were men. The gender gap disappeared in 2004, with men and women equally likely to support George W. Bush, but re-emerged in 2008 and again in 2012, when women were more likely to vote for Barack Obama than men (by about 5 percentage points in 2008 and 10 percentage points in 2012).[13] Nevertheless, as is evident from Table 6-1, the gender gap in partisanship is fairly small, with women more likely to call themselves "strong Democrats" and less likely to be independent leaners than men. This gender gap would be reduced further if controls were introduced for race and socioeconomic variables.[14] Given what was said about the influence of primary groups, the small size of the gender gap should not be surprising. Men and women interact with each other in primary groups throughout society. They select friends and spouses from among like-minded individuals; they respond, as family units, to similar social and economic forces. The views of men and women differ on certain issues, with women usually being less approving of military action in international affairs and more supportive of humanitarian aid, but given the general influence of primary groups, differences in overall political preferences are seldom large.

Lately, another gap, the "marriage gap," has gained some notoriety. It has been suggested that married people are more likely to gravitate to the Republican Party, while unmarried people, especially unmarried women, are more likely to be Democrats. The reasons alleged for this range from commitment to traditional values to the economic position of married men versus unmarried women as heads of households. In looking at a possible marriage gap, the effects of age need to be taken into account, given that younger people are both more likely to be unmarried and to identify themselves as politically independent. Figure 6-2 shows

FIGURE 6-2   Net Partisan Advantage among White Married and Unmarried Men and Women, 2012

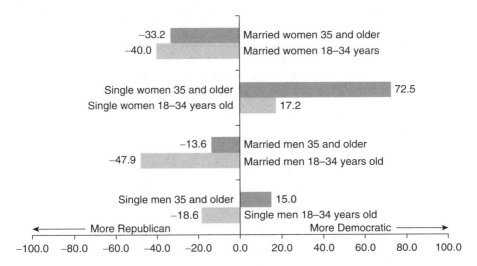

Source: 2012 American National Election Study, available at www.electionstudies.org.

Note: Values represent the difference in the percentage of Democrats (strong, weak, and leaning) minus the percentage of Republicans (strong, weak, and leaning) in each category. Negative values mean there is a higher percentage of Republicans in the category than Democrats. Positive numbers mean there is a higher percentage of Democrats in the category than Republicans.

the net difference in partisanship for white married and unmarried men and women. Married men and married women are more likely to be Republican regardless of age, and except for married men in the older age group, the slant toward the Republicans is large. Single women are much more likely to be Democrats, especially single women 35 and older. Among single men, age matters a great deal. Younger single men lean toward the Republicans, whereas older single men lean toward the Democrats. The increased interest in the marriage gap appears to be warranted, especially among women.

We have avoided use of the term *conformity* to describe the patterns of primary group behavior because these group processes are more casual and more a matter of give-and-take than the term implies. Many people care little about politics, and it plays a small part in their personal relationships. In few primary groups is politics of any consequence, so the things that happen in the group that lead to political homogeneity are of low salience. Individuals gradually create, evaluate, and revise their images of the world under the influence of social processes. Many of these processes are face-to-face exchanges of information or reassurances that others share views or consider them plausible, realistic, and acceptable. Most individuals are not pressured by primary groups to conform or to change politically, at least not nearly as much as they are influenced by casual, impromptu expressions of similar ideas and values. Ordinarily, primary groups do not tolerate high levels of political tension and conflict. Also, few people are subject to the social forces of only one or two primary groups, so conformity to group pressure would mean conformity to a large number of groups.

Social Groups

Primary groups are small and involve knowing the other group members. Interactions among primary group members are personal and often face-to-face. It is perhaps not surprising that the people within primary groups share many political attitudes and behaviors. Large, impersonal, secondary groups, however, also have an impact on people's political views and behavior, as can be seen in our earlier discussion about the shared party identification of certain social groups. What is the underlying dynamic that drives social group influence? It is not the direct influence of face-to-face interactions given the fact that people will meet only a very small handful of those who share certain social characteristics. Granted, face-to-face interactions with fellow group members can reinforce social group dynamics, but the ability of secondary social groups to influence people's political attitudes and behaviors has to come from something other than personal interactions.[15]

We discuss two interrelated phenomena that drive social group influence on party identification: social identity and partisan images. We start with social identity. People are born into a variety of social groups, such as race, gender, nationality, and social class, that might or might not become how they think of themselves. The more they identify with a group, the more they define themselves in terms of that group, the more attached they feel to the group, and the more they evaluate the group in positive terms. When a group identity is salient to an individual, that person is more likely to perceive situations from the perspective of the group and take actions that help the group, even at great personal expense. They are also more likely to take on the norms of the group, which is the most important point here. Group norms include the attitudes and behaviors that in many ways define the group and make it distinct. The more people identify with a group, the more they think and act like fellow group members when that identity is salient.[16] If the norm of a group is to support a certain party, say African Americans' support for the Democratic Party or evangelical Christians' support for the Republican Party, then people who strongly identify with their social group will be much more likely to identify with and vote for that party.

Partisan images affect whether people want to identify with a party. The political parties have become associated with certain social groups, as noted in Figure 6-1, and this social composition of the parties affects people's images, or stereotypes, of the parties. Donald Green and his colleagues put it this way: "As people reflect on whether they are Democrats or Republicans (or neither), they call to mind some mental image, or stereotype, of what these sorts of people are like and square these images with their own self-conceptions."[17] When they think about the social groups that make up the Democrats or the Republicans, they figure out which group composition best describes themselves and choose the party that is the better fit. Partisan images are not set in stone. Social groups can, for a variety of reasons, switch their party allegiance from one party to the other. An example is the South being heavily Democratic after the Civil War and then moving to the Republican Party in more recent times. The political parties are also proactive in heavily courting certain social groups they want in their voting bloc. Republicans began courting evangelical Christians in the 1980s. Democrats have stepped up their courting of Latinos and Latinas in recent years.

Early survey work done on social groups and political behavior appeared in the classic *The American Voter,* by Angus Campbell, Philip E. Converse, Warren E. Miller, and Donald E. Stokes.[18] By controlling many outside social influences with matched groups, the authors demonstrated the degree to which an individual's political behavior was influenced by secondary group membership among union members, blacks, Catholics, and Jews. They were able to show that union members, blacks, and Jews were considerably more Democratic than one would expect from the group members' other social characteristics, such as urban–rural residence, region, and occupational status. The fact that Catholics were not more Democratic in the 1950s than would be expected from their other social characteristics is consistent with what we observed earlier: as Catholics moved into the middle class, they have ceased to be disproportionately Democratic. However, union members, blacks, and Jews have remained more Democratic than expected, based on other social characteristics. In other words, group membership appears to play a role in the Democratic partisanship of union members, blacks, and Jews, but not Catholics.

The American Voter concluded that the influence was even greater if the individual identified with the group. To establish the importance of identification with the group and belief in the legitimacy of the group's involvement in politics, the authors analyzed the 1956 presidential votes of the same four social groups. The increasing impact of identification with the group and of its perceived legitimacy was associated with an increasing Democratic vote. In other words, the stronger the belief in the legitimacy of the group's political involvement and the stronger the group identification, the greater the impact of group standards on vote choice.

The behavior of union members in recent years, in contrast, illustrates a decline in group identification. Despite one-sided Democratic partisanship, union members have been volatile in voting for president and willing to ignore the announced preferences of their union leaders. After an all-out effort by union leadership for Walter F. Mondale in 1984, Mondale barely outpolled Ronald Reagan among union households. Conversely, Bill Clinton did very well among union members, despite union leaders' general lack of enthusiasm for him. In 2012, 40 percent of people in union households identified with the Democratic Party versus 14 percent with the Republican Party, and Obama outpolled Mitt Romney 52 percent to 47 percent.[19]

Among the groups usually studied, blacks and Jews are the most distinctive politically. Jews have remained strongly Democratic in their partisanship over the years in spite of social and economic characteristics more typical of Republicans. And although Jews have at times not supported the Democratic ticket, Jewish partisanship remains close to what it was in the 1950s—57 percent Democratic, 26 percent independent, and 17 percent Republican.[20] As shown in Table 6-1, African Americans also are strongly Democratic in partisanship and typically vote more than 90 percent Democratic in presidential contests. The impact of group identification was dramatically revealed by increased black turnout and near unanimous black support for Obama in both 2008 and 2012. The percentage of blacks calling themselves "strong Democrats" jumped from 31 percent in 2004 to 48 percent in 2008 and 56 percent in 2012 with a black candidate on the Democratic ticket.

For many years, the partisanship of American religious groups, other than Jews, was not seen as particularly distinctive, or at least other factors were considered more important in determining political behavior. In recent years, analysts have focused increased attention on religious groups in American society, especially within the highly varied Protestant category. Over recent decades, the composition of the Protestant category has changed dramatically. Mainline Protestant denominations such as Methodists and Presbyterians have declined from roughly 40 percent to 18 percent of the adult population. Evangelicals and fundamentalists, on the other hand, have grown to more than one-quarter (26 percent) of the electorate. Catholics are similar in size to evangelicals and fundamentalists, constituting 24 percent of the U.S. population.[21]

The Pew Forum on Religion and Public Life conducted the U.S. Religious Landscape Survey in 2007. Figure 6-3 shows the party affiliations of various religious groups. Mormons and evangelical Christians were the most likely to identify as Republicans (65 percent and 50 percent, respectively). People affiliated with historically black churches were much more likely to be Democrats (77 percent), as were about two-thirds of Jews, Muslims, Buddhists, Hindus, atheists, and agnostics. Mainline Protestants were almost evenly divided in their partisanship, with 41 percent identified as Republicans and 43 percent as Democrats. The partisan affiliations of religious groups are partially dependent, however, on religious beliefs and frequency of religious service attendance. For example, half of Jews who pray at least daily identify as Democrats compared to almost three quarters of Jews who do not pray at least daily. Only 29 percent of evangelical Protestants who attend religious service at least once a week identify as Democrats compared to 43 percent of those who attend religious services less frequently. Religious beliefs and practices are even more strongly related to ideology. People who are very religious are much more likely to be conservative than the less religious, and this holds true among evangelical Protestants, mainline Protestants, Catholics, Black Protestants, and Jews.[22]

FIGURE 6-3   Partisanship of Religious Affiliations in the United States, 2007

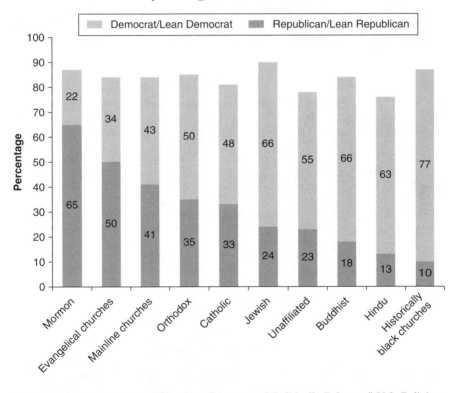

Source: "Religious Beliefs and Practices: Diverse and Politically Relevant," U.S. Religious Landscape Survey, the Pew Forum on Religion & Public Life, June 2008, at http://religions .pewforum.org/pdf/report2-religious-landscape-study-full.pdf.

Figure 6-4 looks at some political characteristics of one religious group, white fundamentalists and evangelicals, in 2012. Those who attend church most regularly are considerably more Republican and conservative than those who attend less regularly. Political strategist Karl Rove's plan to utilize the evangelical churches as a way to mobilize conservative votes for George W. Bush in 2004 was based on an understanding of the importance of group interaction in reinforcing opinions and motivating political activity. Large social groups can influence people's political attitudes and behaviors through social identity and partisan images, but group identification reinforced by social interaction has an especially potent effect on group members. Regular church attenders can more easily pick up on group norms and have their political views reinforced through casual conversations with fellow congregants. It is the interaction with like-minded individuals, represented by church attendance, that likely creates and reinforces political distinctiveness. In 2012, white evangelicals and fundamentalists who attended church regularly were more likely to identify as conservative and as strong Republicans and to vote for Mitt Romney than were those who attended church more sporadically.

Social factors, such as race, religion, or union membership, vary in their relative importance from election to election. After years of

FIGURE 6-4   Voting and Political Identification for White Fundamentalists and Evangelicals according to Church Attendance, 2012

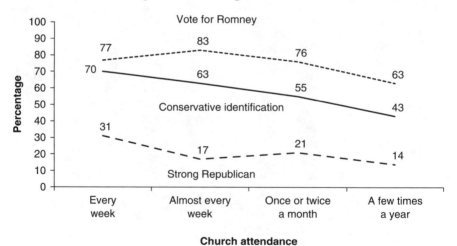

Source: 2012 American National Election Study, available at www.electionstudies.org.

Note. Protestants were determined to be evangelical or fundamentalist by their affirmative response to a question asking if they considered themselves to be born-again. Access to data that would allow a more fine-tuned measure was restricted in the 2012 ANES.

dormancy, a social factor may temporarily become significant during a political campaign and subsequently recede in importance. The 1960 presidential election provides a good example of this phenomenon. John F. Kennedy's Catholicism was a major issue throughout the campaign and of great importance to both Catholics and non-Catholics. Researchers at the University of Michigan showed that Protestant Democrats who were more regular in church attendance were more likely to defect from the Democratic candidate. Among the nominal Protestants who never attended church, Kennedy's Catholicism exerted no such negative effect.[23]

One social group not discussed in *The American Voter* but recently important to American elections is youth. As mentioned in chapter 3, young people have turned out to vote at higher rates than usual in recent elections and they have voted decidedly Democratic. Not surprisingly, eighteen- to twenty-nine-year-olds are more likely to identify as Democrats as well. According to a Pew Research Center survey of voters in 2012, 44 percent of youth voters identified as Democrats and 26 percent as Republicans. Older people, those sixty-five and over, were more evenly divided, with 36 percent identifying as Democrats and 37 percent as Republicans. There are several potential reasons for why people under thirty are more likely to identify as Democrats. One is ideology. Young people are much more likely to say they are liberal (33 percent) compared to people over sixty-five (19 percent). A second reason is that youth are less likely to be religious than older people. One out of five young people say they have no religious affiliation compared to only 6 percent of those over sixty-five. Perhaps the biggest reason for youth partisanship, though, is the racial and ethnic makeup of this age group. People under thirty in 2012 were a heterogeneous group, with 58 percent white and 42 percent people of color. The numbers look very different for those thirty and over: 76 percent were white and only 24 percent people of color.[24]

Social class, on the other hand, received a great deal of attention in *The American Voter*. In general, analysis of social class assumes that differences exist in the economic and social interests of social classes and that these conflicting interests will be translated into political forces. Given a choice between "middle class" and "working class," a majority of Americans are able to place themselves in a general social position, even to the point of including themselves in the "upper" or "lower" level of a class. Even though individual self-ratings are not perfectly congruent with the positions that social analysts would assign those individuals on the basis of characteristics such as occupation, income, and education, a general social class structure is apparent. Nonetheless, about one-third of American adults say that they never think of themselves as members of a social class, a much higher percentage than occurs in European countries.

Serious questions have been raised about whether social class still makes sense in American politics. Some people, such as Thomas Frank in his book *What's The Matter with Kansas?* argue that lower- and working-class whites are more likely to be Republicans these days because of their conservatism on social issues. When they vote Republican, they are voting against their economic interests. In an in-depth empirical analysis of Frank's claims, Larry Bartels finds that there is still a relationship between social class, economic interests, and party identification, with those in the lower and working class being more supportive of liberal economic policies and the Democratic Party. On top of this, Americans still associate the Democratic Party with the working class and poor and the Republican Party with the upper class and rich. There is some suggestion in the data, however, that being in a lower social class is related to more conservative positions on social issues.[25]

In Figure 6-5 the relationship between self-identification as a member of the working or middle class and party identification is charted from 1952 through 2012 in the nation as a whole and in the South and non-South. The values shown in the graph represent the strength of the relationship between social class and party, indicated by Somer's d. If all working-class people identified with the Democratic Party and all middle-class people with the Republican Party (with independents split evenly between the two parties), the Somer's d would be +1.0; if the reverse were true, it would be –1.0. If there were no differences in the partisan preferences of middle- and working-class people, the coefficient would be 0.0. Because working-class people have been more likely to be Democratic than have middle-class people in each year since 1952, all the values in Figure 6-5 are positive.

A number of points can be made about the data presented. Although the strength of the relationship between social class and party has varied over the years, the national trend in the relationship is downward. In other words, since 1952 the differences in partisan preference between working- and middle-class people have been getting smaller. In this context, 1964, 1976, 1988, and 2008 stand out as temporary reversals of the trend. Figure 6-5 also shows that the relationship between class and party has followed different patterns in and outside the South. Whereas the relationship has been declining elsewhere, the trend has been upward in the South. During the early 1950s middle- and working-class southerners were overwhelmingly Democratic; there were virtually no differences between them. Later, a modest, class-based partisan alignment emerged. The middle class became increasingly Republican, whereas the working class, particularly the black working class, remained solidly Democratic. This class-based alignment in the South, as well as the difference between North and

FIGURE 6-5   The Relationship between Social Class Identification and Party
Identification, 1952–2012

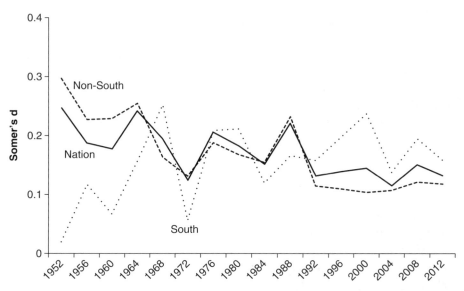

Source: American National Election Studies, available at www.electionstudies.org.

Note: The coefficients represented by points on the graph are Somer's d. The social class
identification question was not asked in 1996.

South, has disappeared temporarily across the years but was clearly
evident again in 2008. This probably results from the increase in southern blacks' identification with Obama's party.

   It is perhaps surprising that the economic crisis of 2008, featuring
themes of greedy Wall Street executives and their oversized bonuses, had
so little impact on politicizing social class differences nationwide both in
2008 and in 2012. Along with Canada, the United States is usually
regarded as an extreme case among developed democracies for the insig-
nificance of social class in political behavior; in most European democracies, social class is of greater consequence. This remains true even as the
disparity between rich and poor in the United States has reached, since
the 1980s, historically high levels. From 2009 to 2011, when many Americans were still hurting from the slow economic recovery, the net worth of
the wealthiest Americans (the top 7 percent) increased 28 percent, from
$2.4 million to $3.1 million. At the same time, the bottom 93 percent of
Americans saw their net worth decrease by 4 percent, from $139,896 to
$133,817.[26] Even with the increased disparity in wealth, social class was
less likely to be related to party identification in 2012 than it was in 2008,

before the effects of the economic crisis were keenly felt by most Americans. However, this is not to say that social inequality means nothing to Americans, nor is it to suggest that there are not political consequences to increasing perceptions of social inequality. Nolan McCarty, Keith Poole, and Howard Rosenthal have shown how increases in the divide between the rich and the poor are highly correlated with polarization in Congress.[27] This polarization has bled to the mass level as well; some argue that anger over the gap between the wealthiest 1 percent and everyone else was the impetus for the social movement Occupy Wall Street, which was supported by a strong majority of Democrats and opposed by a large majority of Republicans.[28]

Social Cross-Pressures

An interesting aspect of social characteristics is that rather than being a member of just one social group, people are members of many. A woman is not just a woman; she is also from a certain racial or ethnic group, social class, age group, religious affiliation, and so on. One of the major ideas developed in the early voting studies by Paul Lazarsfeld, Bernard Berelson, and other researchers at the Bureau of Applied Social Research of Columbia University was the "cross-pressure hypothesis."[29] The idea behind the cross-pressure hypothesis is simple: if all of your social groups lean toward one party, you are likely to hold that party identification more strongly because it is consistently reinforced; if your social groups lean toward differing parties, you are pulled in two directions and you will likely moderate your partisanship or be an independent. Basically, the hypothesis concerns the situation in which two (or more) social forces or tendencies act on the individual, one in a Republican direction and the other in a Democratic direction.

In the diagram below, we use the dimensions of rural-urban residence and age, which is taken from Brader, Tucker, and Therriault.[30] People can live in urban or rural areas, and they can be younger or older. How these two characteristics combine can make a big difference politically.

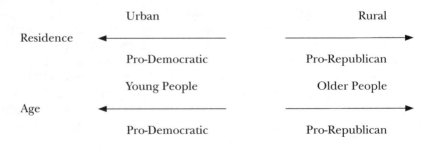

Some individuals are predisposed or pushed in a consistent way, such as urban youth, whose residence and age both predispose them in a Democratic direction, or rural older people, who are predisposed in a Republican direction.

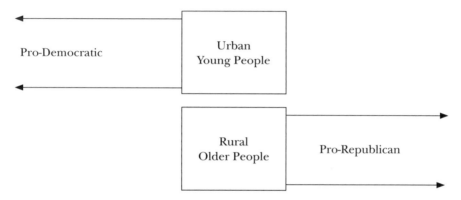

Some individuals face a social context in which they are pulled in both directions, or cross-pressured, because their social groups support different parties. Young people who live in rural areas are being pulled in different directions by the two parties, as are older people who live in urban areas.

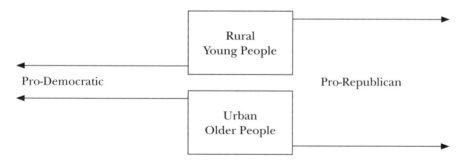

The cross-pressure hypothesis asserts that individuals under consistent pressure behave differently from individuals under cross-pressure. The predictions made under the cross-pressure hypothesis are listed below.

Consistent pressure	Cross-pressure
Straight-ticket voting	Split-ticket voting
Early decision on vote	Late decision on vote
High interest in politics	Low interest in politics
High level of information	Low level of information
Consistent attitudes	Conflicting attitudes

Receiving consistent cues from one's social groups makes thinking about and engaging in politics easy. A strong party identification makes it easier to decide for whom to vote, to decide earlier, and to care enough about electoral outcomes to get informed. When people face cross-pressures, on the other hand, dealing with politics becomes more difficult.

People who face cross-pressures in their primary or secondary groups can respond in a variety of ways. People are members of multiple secondary groups, but they do not have to feel a sense of identity with all of them. A rural young person can strongly identify with and feel strongly attached to rural America and not identify with young people. While her social groups differ in their partisan leanings, she doesn't experience the cross-pressure because her rural identity leads her to fully endorse being a Republican. People in the group with which she does not identify, in this case young people, do not hold any sway in her thinking. For others who fully recognize the cross-pressures, there are some people who embrace the conflict. People who care a great deal about politics and hold strong political views do not view the prospect of facing opposing views as a problem. They will continue to espouse their views regardless what others think. We all likely know someone who loves to argue about politics and seems to be invigorated by taking on the opposition. Many people, however, do not like conflict when it comes to politics and therefore deal with cross-pressures in different way.

One common response to cross-pressures is ambivalence. People who hear opposing viewpoints within their social contexts can end up holding opposing viewpoints themselves. When it comes to welfare, for example, people can "extol individualism and decry big government" while at the same time feel "sympathy for the poor" and support "state action to ameliorate existing social ills."[31] The more people hold ambivalent attitudes, the more intrapersonal conflict they experience. And the more uncertain they are in their political choices, the longer it takes to make decisions and the more moderate their decisions tend to be.[32] These people are the swing voters who attract so much attention during elections. When people are evenly divided between the two parties, the available voters—the voters to whom the parties must appeal to win because they hold the balance of power in elections—are in a middle position between Democrats and Republicans. The ambivalent pay attention to politics and understand the arguments; they just wait until the last minute to decide.

Another common response to cross-pressures is avoidance, specifically avoidance of politics. Among primary groups, people are often averse to the interpersonal conflict that can occur when the subject of politics comes up. They "care more about social harmony in their immediate face-to-face personal relationships than about the larger political world."[33] It is easier to dismiss politics and view it as unimportant and not interesting than to be politically engaged and face frequent conflict with friends, family, and coworkers. The cross-pressured people who respond with avoidance are less likely to form opinions about the parties or candidates and are less likely to vote. When the topic of politics arises in a social setting, they can simply tune it out or change the subject.

Fortunately for these poor souls who feel cross-pressured, it is likely that the extent to which cross-pressuring occurs is declining. As we mentioned earlier, people tend to have social networks that are quite homogeneous, which means they will have their partisanship and political attitudes reinforced rather than cross-pressured. We also know that people have sorted themselves into the two major parties along ideological grounds. Democrats are now much more likely to be liberal and Republicans are much more likely to be conservative, which means that people will feel less attitudinally cross-pressured. Matthew Levendusky argues that this partisan sorting has made people "more loyal voters of their team" in the sense that they are more likely to vote a straight party ticket and be biased in favor of their party.[34] It is also likely that partisan sorting has led to the increased partisan homogeneity of social networks. However, as discussed in chapter 5, as much as 40 percent of the public holds ideological positions on social and economic issues that are at odds with the contemporary partisan divide, leaving these people stuck in the middle of a system that does not represent the totality of their views.[35]

Cross-pressures can play an important role in moderating social conflict so long as groups are willing to get along.[36] In the current polarized environment, the political parties are increasingly hostile to each other and often appear unwilling to work together. Shanto Iyengar and Sean Westwood found that partisans increasingly view supporters of the opposing party as the outgroup and "enthusiastically voice hostility for the out party and its supporters." They find that hostility toward and discrimination against out-party supporters is higher than hostility or discrimination based on race.[37] With fewer cross-pressures to moderate the intensity of ingroup-outgroup relations, there is little to mellow partisan polarization among Americans.

Notes

1. Edward G. Carmines and James A. Stimson, *Issue Evolution: Race and the Transformation of American Politics* (Princeton, NJ: Princeton University Press, 1989).
2. Laura Stoker and M. Kent Jennings, "Political Similarity and Influence between Husbands and Wives," in *The Social Logic of Politics: Personal Networks as Contexts for Political Behavior*, ed. Alan S. Zuckerman (Philadelphia: Temple University Press, 2005), 51–74.

3. Hilde Coffé and Ariana Need, "Similarity in Husbands and Wives Party Family Preference in the Netherlands," *Electoral Studies* 29 (2010): 259–68; Alan S. Zuckerman, Jennifer Fitzgerald, and Josip Dasović, "Do Couples Support the Same Political Parties? Sometimes," in *The Social Logic of Politics: Personal Networks as Contexts for Political Behavior,* ed. Alan S. Zuckerman (Philadelphia: Temple University Press, 2005), 75–94.

4. John R. Alford, Peter K. Hatemi, John R. Hibbing, Nicholas G. Martin, and Lindon J. Eaves, "The Politics of Mate Choice," *Journal of Politics* 73 (April 2011): 362–79.

5. M. Kent Jennings and Richard G. Niemi, "The Transmission of Political Values from Parent to Child," *American Political Science Review* 62 (March 1968): 169–84; M. Kent Jennings, Laura Stoker, and Jake Bowers, "Politics across Generations: Family Transmission Reexamined," *Journal of Politics* 71 (July 2009): 782–99.

6. Peter K. Hatemi, John R. Alford, John R. Hibbing, Nicholas G. Martin, and Lindon J. Eaves, "Is There a 'Party' in Your Genes?" *Political Research Quarterly* 62 (September 2009): 584–600; John R. Alford, Carolyn L. Funk, and John R. Hibbing, "Are Political Orientations Genetically Transmitted?" *American Political Science Review* 99 (May 2005): 153–67.

7. Betsy Sinclair, *The Social Citizen: Peer Networks and Political Behavior* (Chicago: University of Chicago Press, 2012), 124. We combined strong, weak, and leaning partisans.

8. Jeffrey Levin, "Choosing Alone? The Social Network Basis of Modern Political Choice," in *The Social Logic of Politics: Personal Networks as Contexts for Political Behavior,* ed. Alan S. Zuckerman (Philadelphia: Temple University Press, 2005), 132–51.

9. Robert M. Bond, Christopher J. Fariss, Jason J. Jones, Adam D. I. Kramer, Cameron Marlow, Jaime E. Settle, and James H. Fowler, "A 61-million-person Experiment in Social Influence and Political Mobilization," *Nature* 489 (September 13, 2012): 295–98.

10. Bill Bishop and Robert Cushing, "The Big Sort: Migration, Community, and Politics in the United States of 'Those People,'" in *Red, Blue & Purple America: The Future of Election Demographics,* ed. Ruy Teixeira (Washington, DC: Brookings Institution Press, 2008); Wendy K. Tam Cho, James G. Gimpel, and Iris S. Hui, "Voter Migration and the Geographic Sorting of the American Electorate," *Annals of the Association of American Geographers* 103, no. 4 (2013): 856–70. See also Bill Bishop, *The Big Sort: Why the Clustering of Like-minded America Is Tearing Us Apart* (New York: Houghton Mifflin, 2008).

11. Diana C. Mutz, *Hearing the Other Side: Deliberative Versus Participatory Democracy* (New York: Cambridge University Press, 2006), 53.

12. John R. Hibbing and Elizabeth Theiss-Morse, *Stealth Democracy: Americans' Beliefs about How Government Should Work* (New York: Cambridge University Press, 2002), 132.

13. "Changing Face of America Helps Assure Obama Victory," Pew Research Center for the People & the Press, November 7, 2012, http://www.people-press.org/2012/11/07/changing-face-of-america-helps-assure-obama-victory/.

14. Richard A. Seltzer, Jody Newman, and Melissa Voorhees Leighton, *Sex as a Political Variable: Women as Candidates and Voters in U.S. Elections* (Boulder, CO: Lynne Rienner, 1997).

15. Katherine Cramer Walsh, *Talking about Politics: Informal Groups and Social Identity in American Life* (Chicago: University of Chicago Press, 2004).

16. See, for example, Michael A. Hogg and Dominic Abrams, *Social Identifications: A Social Psychology of Intergroup Relations and Group Processes* (London: Routledge, 1988); Naomi Ellemers, Russell Spears, and Bertjan Doosje, eds., *Social Identity: Context, Commitment, Content* (Oxford: Blackwell, 1999).

17. Donald Green, Bradley Palmquist, and Eric Schickler, *Partisan Hearts and Minds: Political Parties and the Social Identities of Voters* (New Haven, CT: Yale University Press, 2002), 8.

18. Angus Campbell, Philip E. Converse, Warren E. Miller, and Donald E. Stokes, *The American Voter* (New York: Wiley, 1960), 295–332.

19. 2012 American National Election Study.

20. 2006 General Social Survey. The number of respondents identifying themselves as Jewish in recent ANES surveys is too small for analysis. However, the Pew Research Center for the People and the Press analyzed combined surveys from September 2001 to October 2003. The combined sample had 934 Jews out of a total of some 56,000 cases. Of the Jewish respondents, 49 percent were Democrats, 19 percent were Republicans, and presumably the rest were independents.

21. The Pew Forum on Religion and Public Life, U.S. Religious Landscape Survey, May 8 to August 13, 2007, http://religions.pewforum.org/affiliations.

22. "Religious Beliefs and Practices: Diverse and Politically Relevant," U.S. Religious Landscape Survey, the Pew Forum on Religion & Public Life, June 2008, 85–87. Full report accessible at http://religions.pewforum.org/pdf/report2-religious-landscape-study-full.pdf.

23. Philip E. Converse, Angus Campbell, Warren E. Miller, and Donald E. Stokes, "Stability and Change in 1960: A Reinstating Election," in *Elections and the Political Order*, ed. Angus Campbell, Philip E. Converse, Warren E. Miller, and Donald E. Stokes (New York: Wiley, 1966), chap. 5.

24. Pew Research Center for the People & the Press, "Young Voters Supported Obama Less, But May Have Mattered More," November 26, 2012, http://www.people-press.org/2012/11/26/young-voters-supported-obama-less-but-may-have-mattered-more/.

25. Thomas Frank, *What's the Matter with Kansas? How Conservatives Won the Heart of America* (New York: Holt, 2004); Larry M. Bartels, "What's the Matter with What's the Matter with Kansas?" *Quarterly Journal of Political Science* 1 (March 2006): 201–26; Leslie McCall and Jeff Manza, "Class Differences in Social and Political Attitudes in the U.S.," in *Oxford Handbook of American Public Opinion and the Media*, ed. R. Shapiro and L. Jacobs (New York: Oxford University Press, 2011), 552–70; Stephen P. Nicholson and Gary M. Segura, "Who's the Party of the People? Economic Populism and the U.S. Public's Beliefs about Political Parties," *Political Behavior* 34 (June 2012): 369–89.

26. Richard Fry and Paul Taylor, "A Rise in Wealth for the Wealthy; Declines for the Lower 93%," Pew Research Social and Demographic Trends, Pew Research Center, April 23, 2013, http://www.pewsocialtrends.org/2013/04/23/a-rise-in-wealth-for-the-wealthydeclines-for-the-lower-93/.

27. Nolan McCarty, Keith T. Poole, and Howard Rosenthal, *Polarized America: The Dance of Ideology and Unequal Riches* (Cambridge, MA: MIT Press, 2008).

28. Pew Research Center for the People & the Press, "Frustration with Congress Could Hurt Republican Incumbents," December 15, 2011, http://www.people-press.org/2011/12/15/section-2-occupy-wall-street-and-inequality/.

29. Paul Lazarsfeld, Bernard Berelson, and Hazel Gaudet, *The People's Choice* (New York: Columbia University Press, 1944); and Bernard Berelson, Paul Lazarsfeld, and William McPhee, *Voting* (Chicago: University of Chicago Press, 1954).

30. Ted Brader, Joshua A. Tucker, and Andrew Therriault, "Cross Pressure Scores: An Individual-level Measure of Cumulative Partisan Pressures Arising from Social Group Memberships," *Political Behavior*, published electronically April 2013, http://link.springer.com/article/10.1007/s11109–013–9222–8/fulltext.html.

31. Stanley Feldman and John Zaller, "The Political Culture of Ambivalence: Ideological Responses to the Welfare State," *American Journal of Political Science* 36 (February 1992): 268–307, p. 293.

32. Diana C. Mutz, "The Consequences of Cross-Cutting Networks for Political Participation," *American Journal of Political Science* 46 (October 2002): 838–55.

33. Mutz, *Hearing the Other Side*, 106.

34. Matthew Levendusky, *The Partisan Sort* (Chicago: University of Chicago Press, 2009), 126–27.

35. Edward G. Carmines, Michael J. Ensley, and Michael W. Wagner, "Political Ideology in American Politics: One, Two, or None?" *The Forum* 10, no. 3 (2012): 1–18.

36. Robert E. Goodin, "Cross-Cutting Cleavages and Social Conflict," *British Journal of Political Science* 5 (October 1975): 516–19.

37. Shanto Iyengar and Sean J. Westwood, "Fear and Loathing across Party Lines: New Evidence on Group Polarization" (unpublished manuscript, April 2013, Stanford University).

Suggested Readings

Campbell, Angus, Philip E. Converse, Warren E. Miller, and Donald E. Stokes. *The American Voter.* New York: Wiley, 1960. A classic study of the social psychological factors influencing political behavior.

Hajnal, Zoltan L., and Taeku Lee. *Why Americans Don't Join the Party: Race, Immigration, and the Failure (of Political Parties) to Engage the Electorate.* Princeton, NJ: Princeton University Press, 2011. A provocative examination of the racial and ethnic makeup of the political parties and partisan attachments.

Huckfeldt, Robert, and Carol Weitzel Kohfeld. *Race and the Decline of Class in American Politics.* Urbana: University of Illinois Press, 1989. A study arguing that racial cleavages have become more important than social class divisions in influencing electoral decisions, with serious consequences for the Democratic Party's coalition.

Huckfeldt, Robert, and John Sprague. *Citizens, Politics, and Social Communication.* Cambridge, England: Cambridge University Press, 1995. An important study examining political attitudes and behavior within their social context.

Lazarsfeld, Paul, Bernard Berelson, and Hazel Gaudet. *The People's Choice.* New York: Columbia University Press, 1944. A classic study of Erie County, Ohio, and the first study of voting to make extensive use of survey research.

Leege, David C., and Lyman A. Kellstedt. *Rediscovering the Religious Factor in American Politics.* New York: M. E. Sharpe, 1993. A collection of articles exploring the impact of religious beliefs on political behavior.

Lewis-Beck, Michael S., William G. Jacoby, Helmut Norpoth, and Herbert F. Weisberg. *The American Voter Revisited.* Ann Arbor: University of Michigan Press, 2008. A rich re-analysis of the themes from the classic work using mainly 2000 and 2004 data.

Lipset, Seymour M., and Stein Rokkan. "Cleavage Structures, Party Systems, and Voter Alignments: An Introduction." In *Party Systems and Voter Alignments,* edited by Seymour M. Lipset and Stein Rokkan. New York: Free Press, 1967. An important conceptual statement about the role of party and social cleavages in historical perspective.

Petrocik, John. *Party Coalitions: Realignments and the Decline of the New Deal Party System.* Chicago: University of Chicago Press, 1981. An analysis of American politics that emphasizes social and economic characteristics.

Stonecash, Jeffrey M. *Class and Party in American Politics.* Boulder, CO: Westview Press, 2000. An extensive analysis of the role of class in American politics.

Walsh, Katherine Cramer. *Talking about Politics: Informal Groups and Social Identity in American Life.* Chicago: University of Chicago Press, 2004. A fascinating study of how ordinary Americans use their group identities to make sense of politics in their everyday lives.

Internet Resources

The website of the American National Election Studies, www.electionstudies.org, has extensive data on social characteristics and party identification from 1952 to the present. Click on "Utilities" and then click on the link for tables and graphs under "The ANES Guide to Public Opinion and Electoral Behavior." Scroll down to "Partisanship and Evaluation of the Political Parties." For every political item, there is a breakdown for each social characteristic in every election year.

For current data on partisans and independents, you can find analysis on websites such as the Pew Research Center for the People and the Press at www .people-press.org and the Gallup Poll at www.gallup.com.

Political Communication and the Mass Media

SINCE MOST of us will not be spending a great deal of one-on-one time with the president or members of Congress, we rely on the mass media and our personal information networks to learn about what is going on in the political world. Therefore, the content of political communication has the potential to greatly influence both attitude formation and opinion change. At the extremes, the process of influencing political opinions is labeled *brainwashing* or *propaganda*. In reality, only a matter of degree separates these forms of influence from political persuasion, campaigning, or even education. All the efforts covered by these terms are directed toward changing individuals' political ideas, values, and opinions or toward fostering some political action. Enormous amounts of time and money are expended in American society to change political views. Most of these efforts are unsuccessful. Indeed, competing efforts to influence the public mind, along with the diversity and complexity of the society itself, makes highly unlikely a quick or uniform public response to any one of these attempts. Of course, dramatic events or crises can quickly change the public's views. Although news of such events comes through the media, the impact generally results from the events themselves, not simply the media imagery. The media are often more adept at affecting views at the opinion formation stage; for example, those who watch postpresidential debate coverage about who "won" are more likely to develop views consistent with the pundits' take on the contest than those who shut off the TV and looked away from their phones after the debate ended.[1]

Political persuasion can also be effective in casual personal relationships. The impact of the mass media likely is important in shaping the contours of political discourse, but only gradually and over fairly long periods of time. At the same time, the role that the media have in making information widely available is significant in creating the conditions under which attitude change occurs. In this chapter, we consider the functions of the media, types of media, bias, the basic processes of opinion change, and the impact of the mass media and election campaigns on individual political behavior.

Functions of the News Media

Despite being a crucial intermediary that connects a diverse array of people in profound ways, the mass media are a frequent punching bag for politicians, scholars, and the public alike. Much of the ire aimed at the media stems from critiques of the ways in which the media perform their basic functions. Doris Graber has argued that there are four functions of the mass media: surveillance, interpretation, socialization, and manipulation.[2]

Surveillance is the process by which the news media inform people of important events. Since most people do not wake up asking themselves, "How do I hold my government accountable today?" journalists convey to readers, listeners, and viewers which events are important and which are not. This begins with judgments about what is newsworthy. In general, newsworthy stories are those that are timely, proximal, and familiar, and contain some kind of conflict, violence, or scandal. The surveillance function of the media is closely connected to the concept of gatekeeping—which is the power the media have to convey to the audience what is important and what isn't. Which of the fifteen items on the city council agenda merit public attention? Does a public protest merit media coverage or is it small potatoes? Which elements of the Affordable Care Act deserve emphasis in the story and which can be ignored? Surveillance is public in the sense that it brings attention to public officials, organized interests, and the like, and it is private in that it helps provide people an avenue to stay informed. Critics argue that the media's choices about what to cover rely too much on the discourse of political elites and ignore the challenges and issues facing everyday citizens.

Interpretation is the function of the media that puts an issue into context. Interpretation goes beyond surveillance to explain to the audience what an event *means*. For example, the headline for a piece on the *Washington Post* website "Why Mitt Romney's '47 percent' quote was so bad" went beyond surveillance to argue that the comment especially hurt Romney because it was captured on video; if it had only been reported to have been said, people could have easily dismissed it as the rantings of political opponents or a biased media. The interpretation function was also on full display on a *New York Times* elections blog,

214 *Political Behavior of the American Electorate*

where Nate Silver provided survey data to show that Obama's polling was on the upswing before the 47 percent comment, so it was difficult to know how much that comment really hurt Romney. While the surveillance function of the media certainly contains some biases regarding who gets covered the most (the president and other public officials compared to ordinary citizens), the interpretation function is one that is often home to charges of ideological bias in news coverage, something we consider later in the chapter.

The third media function, according to Graber, is *socialization*. This is the function in which the mass media help citizens learn basic values that prepare them to live in their society. For instance, the news media tend to cover the two major political parties, but largely ignore third parties. When third parties are covered, it is usually to speculate about which of the major parties might lose votes to the third party. Thus, news coverage helps socialize Americans to accept the two-party system of government. Broader, cultural socialization can come from the mass media as well; notable examples include changing attitudes about premarital sexual behavior, sexual orientation, and racial attitudes.

Finally, the news media engage in what is called *manipulation*. Manipulation can mean many different things, including journalists engaging in "muckraking," the digging up of dirt on government behavior designed to force lawmakers to "clean up their act." However, Graber notes that manipulation also can mean the sensationalizing of facts to try to increase an audience's interest in a story to boost ratings and profits, and it can even mean the media surreptitiously advocating for the positions of some politicians or trying to alter the preferences of other politicians.

Other scholars think about the functions of the news media with respect to whether news coverage enhances the prospects and performance of democratic citizenship. A number of scholars have pointed out that it may be rational for voters to ignore much of the political information around them. Rational choice theorists, following the lead of economist Anthony Downs, argue that the benefits derived from reaching a "correct" decision on a candidate or policy may not be worth the costs the voter incurs in finding out the information.[3] It is rational, therefore, for the voter to take a number of information shortcuts, such as relying on someone else's judgment or voting according to one's established party identification. Samuel L. Popkin uses the analogy of "fire alarms" versus "police patrols" to explain how most people view political information.[4] Instead of patrolling the political "neighborhood" constantly to make sure nothing there requires their attention, most citizens rely on others to raise the alarm when something important happens. Television news and newspaper headlines may be enough to tell average citizens whether they need to delve deeper into a particular story.

Michael Schudson, a sociologist of news, argues that a good citizen need not be fully informed on all issues of the day, but that she or he ought to be "monitorial."[5] That is, a good citizen scans the headlines for issues that might be important enough about which to form an opinion or on which to take some action. Political scientist John Zaller argues for a "burglar alarm" standard of media coverage in which reporters regularly cover nonemergency but important issues in focused, dramatic ways that simultaneously entertain and allow traditional newsmakers like political parties and interest groups to express their views about the issue.[6]

Types of Media and Their Users

For the media to have an impact on an individual's political attitudes and behavior, the individual must give some degree of attention to the media when political information is being reported. Almost all Americans have access to television and watch political news at least some of the time. In 2008, a majority of Americans (54 percent) reported reading a daily newspaper regularly, often online.[7] Somewhat fewer reported reading a newspaper for political news. This represents a decline in daily newspaper readership from more than 70 percent early in the 1990s. Occasional newspaper reading is higher. Television remains the main source of news for most Americans, but the Internet has passed newspapers and radio as the second most commonly used source.[8]

Network television news viewership is down over the past several years; about 22 million Americans watch the NBC, ABC, or CBS evening news programs on an average weeknight. Primetime viewers of CNN, Fox News, and MSNBC combined averaged 3.4 million people each weeknight. While about 92 percent of Americans listen to the radio at some point during the week, only about one-third told the Pew Research Center that they listened "yesterday." Only 20 percent of eighteen- to twenty-four-year-olds listen to radio news; the age group that listens the most is thirty- to thirty-nine-year-olds at 40 percent. The use of mobile technologies for radio listening has grown over the past decade; online listening on cell phones had nearly tripled from 2000 to 2011.[9]

In 2012, 67 percent of the public reported using television as a main source for campaign news, but the Internet jumped ahead of newspapers and into second place with 47 percent. Newspaper use as a main source for election information dropped from 35 percent in 2008 to 27 percent in 2012. Radio use held steady at 20 percent, and magazine use at 3 percent. When it came to following election returns, about 16 percent of Americans did so with friends, while 8 percent did so on social networks. For those under thirty-nine years of age, that percentage jumped to 12. Obama voters, meanwhile, were three times as likely as Romney voters to follow returns on Facebook or Twitter.[10]

One major consequence of the growth of technologies that can deliver the news is the increased choice media consumers have about what they will watch on television, read in a paper or magazine, listen to on the radio, or surf on the web. Markus Prior has called the era in which we live a period of "post-broadcast democracy," meaning that the rise of cable news and the Internet have fundamentally altered who gets the news, which, in turn, has affected citizen political knowledge, voter turnout, polarization, and congressional and presidential elections.[11] During the early age of television, there was a limited number of networks (and no cable), thus constraining the choice of what people could watch. Moreover, they all tended to air the news at the same time, so if you wanted the television to be on in your home at 5:30 p.m. on a Wednesday night in Madison, Wisconsin, you had to be watching the news. This meant that some people who were not so interested in politics, but interested in watching television, would learn a bit about what was going on in spite of their own interests. Prior calls this "by-product learning." During the 1950s and 1960s, by-product learning helped account for a more informed, moderate, and participatory electorate. The media tended to produce broad, nonideological journalism because that was the best way to appeal to the highest number of potential viewers in an era of constrained viewer choice. The moderate coverage helped produce more moderate public preferences, and the attention to politics spurred enough interest in enough people to increase voter turnout.

The development and growth of cable news, with cable networks like CNN, Fox News, ESPN, and HBO, changed all of that. Now, you can have the tube on at 5:30 p.m. and watch a movie on HBO instead of the news. You can even watch a show you digitally recorded a year ago. Thus, those with a higher preference for entertainment compared to news are now opting out of watching the news and choosing instead to watch ESPN's *SportsCenter*, Lifetime's Movie of the Week, and so forth. As the by-product learning dropped for those who preferred entertainment to hard news coverage, so did their political knowledge and civic engagement. Moreover, those who like politics do not have to watch the broad, nonideological network news anymore. They can watch Fox News or MSNBC, stations whose primetime lineup is full of ideological opinion programs hosted by strong personalities like Rachel Maddow and Sean Hannity. One consequence of the availability of these kinds of choices was that those who prefer ideological news are able to watch programs that spend more time providing justification for their points of view and attacking opposing points of view, leading to a greater polarization of the politically engaged.

What's more, Shanto Iyengar and Kyu Hahn have shown that when given the choice, conservatives are more likely to choose Fox News and liberals are more likely to reject Fox for almost anything else. This emergence of a "red media" and "blue media" could exacerbate polarization and further turn off those who find themselves in the middle.[12]

Media Bias and Audience Bias

One reason those highly interested in politics choose more ideological outlets to serve their information-consuming desires is that they believe that the mainstream media are biased. Most scholarly research investigating questions of media bias finds that the biases exhibited by the media are more structural than ideological. That is, they favor the two-party system, give more attention to the president, provide more positive coverage to parties on issues for which the parties have a strong public reputation, and cover partisan lawmakers who disagree with their party more than they cover members of the loyal rank and file. These slants in coverage, though, are a far cry from ideological bias that favors one political point of view over another.

As is usually the case, however, the research has not stopped the public from believing that ideological bias is pervasive in the mainstream news media. Nearly three times more Republican voters than Democratic voters thought that the press influenced the outcome of the 2012 presidential election.[13] A Gallup poll from September of 2012 showed distrust in the news media hitting a new high of 60 percent of the American people. Of course, there are partisan differences in media trust. About 58 percent of Democrats trust the media a "great deal" or a "fair amount" compared to 31 percent of Independents and 26 percent of Republicans. Even so, 48 percent of Republicans told Gallup they follow the news "very closely" compared to only 39 percent of Democrats and 33 percent of Independents.[14]

More recently, political scientist and economist Tim Groseclose, sometimes along with economist Jeffrey Milyo, has argued that the mainstream media are stunningly left-wing in their coverage of national and international affairs. One measure used to demonstrate this is a comparison of how often partisan members of Congress cite particular think tanks when they are speaking on the floor to how often the news media use those same think tanks in their reporting. Groseclose and Milyo found a news media far more likely in their reporting to use think tanks favored by liberals compared to those favored by conservatives.[15] Even the *Wall Street Journal,* a paper with a conservative editorial page, produced news coverage using think tanks favored by Democrats compared to those cited by Republicans. Political scientist Brendan Nyhan has argued that liberal members of Congress tend to favor nonpartisan think tanks, which fits into the media ethic of objective coverage, while conservative lawmakers speaking on the floor of the House or Senate prefer think tanks with a professed conservative point of view. Nyhan concludes that this is not evidence of media bias, but a difference in lawmakers' preference for the use of particular kinds of evidence.[16]

Despite very little empirical evidence that the media are providing ideologically biased coverage, individuals are not convinced. In fact, people tend to view the news media as hostile to their own point of view, regardless what that point of view is. Research investigating the hostile media effect has repeatedly shown that people of different ideological orientations can read the same story and think that it is biased in completely different directions. Joel Turner has shown that people also judge how balanced a news source is based on the source itself rather than the content. He found that liberals who thought they were watching a CNN story thought it was fair, while liberals who saw the exact same story, but thought they were watching Fox News, thought that the story was conservatively biased. He found the exact same relationship for conservatives: they more favorably evaluated the Fox version of the story compared to the exact same thing under the CNN banner.[17]

Social and political psychologists argue that one reason these attitudes persist is because of a concept called motivated reasoning. Motivated reasoning refers to a kind of information processing that fits conclusions about an issue to an individual's preexisting goals or views. Ironically, those with the most education are often the guiltiest of motivated reasoning because they have had more schooling and thus more training in the evaluation of evidence and the art of debate. Thus, they are more able to produce counterarguments to evidence that challenges their point of view. Indeed, conservatives who had a college education were more likely to falsely believe that President Obama was born in Kenya and not the United States. It is not hard to imagine an astute arguer countering evidence of the president's birthplace with questions about whether the birth certificate the president produced was a forgery or asking why it took as long as it did for the president to produce it, even though the fact remains that the president was born in the United States.

After President George W. Bush declared the end of "formal hostilities" in Iraq in May 2003, many surveys documented a pattern of beliefs among partisans about the factual evidence for the existence of weapons of mass destruction (WMDs) in Iraq, Iraqi nuclear arms development, and Iraqi dictator Saddam Hussein's involvement in the attacks on September 11. A year later, Bush supporters disproportionately believed that Iraq had WMDs and, to a lesser degree, that they had actually been found in Iraq. People not sympathetic to the president believed the opposite. *Newsweek* magazine polls in 2003 and 2004 showed that nearly one-half of the American people believed that Saddam Hussein was involved in the September 11th attacks on the United States. Figure 7-1 shows that views on the existence of WMDs were strongly associated with vote intention in 2004.

The motivated reasoning argument turns the traditional view—that misinformation or ignorance is the result of apathy or inattention—on its head. Rather than expecting the better educated and more interested to be accurately informed about WMDs in Iraq, the motivated reasoning argument suggests the opposite. But is the traditional view wrong? No. In fact, both the traditional view and the motivated reasoning argument are right. Among Bush supporters, those who were highly attentive and those who were least attentive to the election campaign were equally likely to believe there were WMDs in Iraq. That is, they held an inaccurate opinion. The Kerry supporters, represented by the sloping line in Figure 7-1, had different views depending on their level of interest in the campaign. The least attentive Kerry supporters had about the same views as the Bush supporters.

A study by the Program on International Policy Attitudes (PIPA) shows some evidence of a relationship between viewing Fox News and believing that WMDs had been found in Iraq.[18] A simple argument would be that Fox News's content led its audience to this belief. But that argument is too simple. Almost all of the Fox News audience also paid attention to media sources that offered a different perspective than

FIGURE 7-1   Percentages Believing Iraq Has Weapons of Mass Destruction, by Attention to the Campaign and Vote Intention, 2004

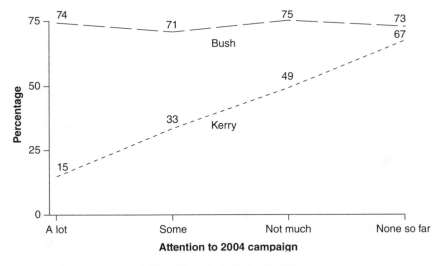

Source: CBS News/*New York Times* Monthly Poll, April 2004.

Fox.[19] Why did they appear to believe Fox News and not their other news sources? Even Fox News stories were not consistent in their bias.[20] Why did their viewers believe some stories but not others? A more plausible explanation is that people who believed that WMDs had been found in Iraq had characteristics that made them more likely to view Fox News. They may have watched Fox News because they hoped to view stories that would support their beliefs about WMDs, but probably more general orientations, such as support for President Bush and the Republican Party, led them to seek out Fox News as a conservative voice.

This pattern of behavior can be referred to as "dissonance reduction." Because these individuals supported Bush, who used the presence of WMDs as a reason for going to war, accepting the idea that these weapons did not exist might create negative feelings toward Bush. To avoid the cognitive dissonance that would result, the individuals persisted in believing that Iraq had such weapons. Over time, it doubtless became more difficult to believe that Iraq had WMDs, and a different dissonance reduction step had to be taken. In this case, the step was to change the belief that the existence of WMDs was a significant reason for going to war. Eventually, President Bush and others offered the view that the reason for going to war was not WMDs but the removal of Saddam Hussein and the establishment of democracy in Iraq. This might be considered an example of reducing dissonance through rationalization.

Scholars like Brendan Nyhan and Jason Reifler have shown how persistent misperceptions are and how difficult they can be to overcome for conservatives and liberals alike. One thing that helps people change their attitudes in the face of facts that dispute their own point of view is the presence of visual data. Nyhan and Reifler showed that when liberals saw visual evidence of fewer American soldier deaths after President Bush's "surge" plan in Iraq, they were more likely to believe the surge had worked, and conservatives who saw visual evidence of an economy adding more jobs under the Obama administration were more likely to believe that the economy was getting better.[21]

Media Coverage and the Public Agenda

As noted in the section about the surveillance function of the media, much discussion has ensued in the scholarly literature on mass media about the capacity to bring matters to the attention of the public or to conceal them.[22] This is usually referred to as *agenda setting*. The literature suggests that the media have great influence over what the public is aware of and concerned with. Television news and front-page stories in newspapers focus the public's attention on a few major stories each day. This function, sometimes called headline service, tells the

public. "Here are important developments you should be aware of."
Major events, such as the killing of Osama bin Laden; the September 11,
2001, terrorist attacks; or scandals, such as President Bill Clinton's sexual liaison with White House intern Monica Lewinsky; along with celeb-
rity milestones, such as the death of Michael Jackson, push other stories
off the agenda. The media make it almost impossible for an ordinary
American to be unaware of these events. These are examples of agenda
setting, but the concept also refers to the consequence of people finding an issue to be more important than they did before as a direct result
of increased media coverage about that issue.

Candidates for office want to set the public's agenda for a variety of
reasons. First, if you are thinking about issues a candidate wants you to
be thinking about, you are not thinking about other things that could
be damaging to the candidate. For example, in 2008, John McCain's
campaign knew that they were being tied to the Bush economy, which
had fallen off a cliff just a month before the election. McCain tried to
burnish his foreign policy credentials, hoping some voters would focus
on Barack Obama's comparative lack of foreign policy experience. Second, the issue ownership hypothesis developed by John Petrocik shows
evidence that the public thinks that each party is better at dealing with
certain issues.[23] For example, people think Democrats are strong on
health care and Republicans are better on handling crime. Thus, candidates for office want to set our agendas on issues on which we favorably
evaluate their political party. In 1988, George H. W. Bush famously aired
controversial ads on the death penalty and a prison furlough plan in
Massachusetts, the state where his opponent, Democrat Michael Dukakis, was governor. In addition to being tough, controversial attack ads,
they also reminded voters that Republicans are tough on crime. Recent
evidence shows that candidates even pivot away from tough questions in
debate settings to circle back and highlight issues they want the public
to be thinking about when they enter the voting booth.[24]

Television often plays a critical role in bringing events and issues to
the public's attention, presenting certain types of information in an
exceptionally dramatic or impressive way. The Persian Gulf War and the
start of the Iraq war were televised to an unprecedented extent. The
American public watched a real-life video arcade of modern warfare. In
January 1991, 67 percent of a national sample reported following the
Persian Gulf War "very closely."[25] Attention was not as high in 2003, but
over half the public followed the invasion of Iraq very closely.[26] In the
short run, the coverage created the impression of an overwhelming
military victory and great satisfaction with the performance of each president. In each instance, the president's job approval ratings soared and
support for the war increased dramatically.[27] Evaluations became more
mixed with the passage of time.

Perhaps nothing in television history compares with the coverage of the attacks on the World Trade Center and the Pentagon on September 11. The major news channels abandoned regular programming and focused on the attacks and their aftermath for days. Virtually everyone in the country was attentive to this coverage, and most people had strong emotional reactions to what they saw.

The news media, particularly television, can rivet public attention on certain issues and, in doing so, limit the policy-making options of political leaders. The range of subjects on which this can be done is narrow, however. Death, destruction, intrigue, or pathos are generally essential ingredients. More abstract or mundane political issues are easily ignored by most of the public.

Although the media may focus on certain news items, the public has an enormous capacity for ignoring the coverage and being highly selective about what to take an interest in. First the *Los Angeles Times Mirror* and later the Pew Research Center for the People and the Press have engaged in an extensive project to explore the public's awareness of and interest in news stories.[28] Some news stories, such as the explosion of the space shuttle *Challenger* and the 1989 San Francisco earthquake, were followed with great interest by most of the public. As shown in Table 7-1, almost all the news stories from January 1986 to August 2009 that were followed "very closely" by large percentages of the public were military operations or disasters of one sort or another. In contrast, less than 25 percent of the public paid close attention to news stories about the mapping of the human genetic code, charges that Speaker Newt Gingrich violated House ethics rules, or the U.S. Supreme Court decision on campaign finance.

As would be expected, a large percentage of the public followed news about the terrorist attacks on September 11 very closely. Some of the people who did not follow the story said they were so distraught they avoided the news. Public attention to the military activities in Afghanistan following the attacks, shown in Table 7-1 at 51 percent, is noticeably below the level of attention to the Persian Gulf War in 1991, at 67 percent. Public attention to the debate about going to war in Iraq during several months in the spring of 2003 (around 62 percent) was greater than the attention to the onset of the war itself in March of that year (57 percent).

Large numbers of Americans (70 percent) followed the news of Hurricane Katrina in the late summer of 2005.[29] Most (89 percent) relied on television coverage, especially that of cable news channels, for their news about Katrina and its aftermath. Interestingly, equally large numbers (71 percent) paid close attention to the news about high gasoline prices in the wake of the storm; Table 7-1 reflects concern about gas prices at other times as well.

Not surprisingly, in the fall of 2008 a large percentage of the public paid close attention to news about the economy, and these high levels of attention continued through early 2009. More unusual was the relatively

TABLE 7-1　Most Closely Followed News Stories and Other Selected News
Items, 1986–2009

News stories	Percentage following very closely
Ten most closely followed news stories	
Explosion of the space shuttle *Challenger* (January 1986)	80
Terrorism attacks on the United States (September/October 2001)	74
San Francisco earthquake (November 1989)	73
High price of gasoline (September 2005)	71
Condition of U.S. economy (September 2008)	70
Hurricane Katrina (September 2005)	70
Verdict in Rodney King case and subsequent violence (May 1992)	70
TWA 800 crash (July 1996)	69
Rescue of little girl in Texas who fell into a well (October 1987)	69
Columbine High School shooting (April 1999)	68
Other news stories	
End of Persian Gulf War (January 1991)	67
Increases in the price of gasoline (June 2008)	66
Hurricane Andrew (September 1992)	66
Sniper shootings near Washington, D.C. (October 2002)	65
News about situation in Iraq (May 2003)	63
Debate about war in Iraq (February 2003)	62
Debate over Wall Street bailout (October 2008)	62
Increases in the price of gasoline (October 1990)	62
Increases in the price of gasoline (June 2000)	61
News about presidential election (October 2008)	61
Increases in the price of gasoline (June 2004)	58
War with Iraq (March 2003)	57
Condition of U.S. economy (February/March 2009)	56
News about situation in Iraq (May 2004)	54
Death of Princess Diana (September 1997)	54
U.S. military effort in Afghanistan (April 2009)	52
U.S. military effort in Afghanistan (January 2002)	51
Health care reform debate (August 2009)	49
Bill Clinton's health care reform proposals (December 1993)	49
Terrorist bombings in London (July 2005)	48
Breakup of the Soviet Union (October 1991)	47
Outcome of the presidential election (November 2000)	38
George W. Bush's proposal to deal with Social Security (March 2005)	38
Charges that Newt Gingrich violated House ethics rules (January 1997)	23
Mapping the human genetic code (July 2000)	16
U.S. Supreme Court decision on campaign finance (December 2003)	8

Source: Pew Research Center for the People and the Press, available at www.people-press.org.

high level of interest in the presidential campaign throughout the fall of 2008. At its high point in October, 61 percent reported following the campaign very closely, an all-time high for interest in presidential elections from 1986 to 2009, the time covered by Pew's News Interest Index.[30] In contrast, the disputed outcome of the 2000 presidential election was followed closely by only 38 percent.

The combination of television, Internet, radio, newspapers, and magazines represents an extraordinary capacity to inform the public rapidly and in considerable depth about major political news items. Add to this the informal communication about the news of the day that most people engage in, and it is easy to see that the American public is in a position to be well informed. The fact that as many people persist in *not* informing themselves about most political news is not evidence of a failure of the mass media to make the news available in a variety of forms.

Because the most interested voters are also the most partisan, a relationship also exists between attention to the media and partisanship. The fact that strong partisans and politically interested people are most attentive to the media accounts for the somewhat paradoxical finding that those with the most exposure to the media are among the least affected by it. Philip E. Converse, in his study of the impact of mass media exposure on voting behavior in elections in the 1950s, drew several conclusions based on findings similar to those represented in Figure 7-2.[31] The voters most stable in their preferences (whether stability is measured during a campaign or between elections) would be those who are

FIGURE 7-2   Hypothetical Relationship between Mass Media Attention and Stability of Voting Behavior

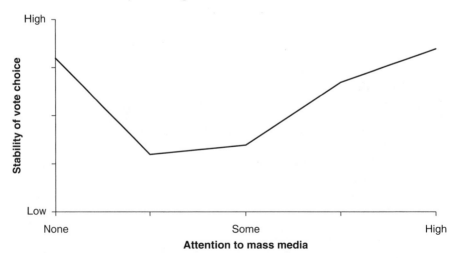

highly attentive to mass media but firmly committed to their party or candidate. Those who pay no attention to media communication remain stable in their vote choices because no new information is introduced to change their votes. The shifting, unstable voters are more likely to be those with moderate exposure to mass media. Unfortunately, efforts at replicating Converse's findings for other election years have failed to uncover similar patterns. One difficulty may be that in recent years there have been hardly any voters with no exposure to the mass media. Nevertheless, the reasoning behind this expected relationship is compelling: The impact of the media is likely to be greatest when the recipients of the message have little information and few existing attitudes or attitudes that are not strongly held.

Political Communication and Attitude Change

Individuals receive ideas and information intended to alter their political opinions from a variety of sources. Some sources are political leaders and commentators whose views arrive impersonally through the mass media; others are friends, coworkers, and family members who influence opinions through personal contact. Much remains to be learned about political persuasion and communication, but at least occasionally many Americans engage in attempts to influence others, and almost everyone is regularly the recipient of large quantities of political communication.

A useful but oversimplified perspective on the transmission of political information would have the media presenting a uniform message to a mass audience made up of isolated individuals. The audience would receive all or most of its information from the media. Thus, public opinion would be a direct product of the information and perspective provided through the media. A more complex view suggests that information is transmitted in a "two-step flow of communication."[32] Information is transmitted from "opinion elites" (leaders in society, such as politicians, organizational heads, and news commentators) to a minority of the public—the "opinion leaders"—and from them to the remainder of the public.

The information from opinion elites usually is sent through the mass media, but this view implies that only a portion of the audience— the opinion leaders—is attentive to any particular type of information such as political news. The opinion leaders, as intermediaries, then interpret, modify, and explain facts and events to those friends and neighbors who are less interested in or concerned with these happenings. In the process, the original message conveyed through the media becomes many somewhat different messages as it reaches the public.

The two-step flow model may not be strictly true in most cases, and public opinion research has generally failed to turn up many people who recognize themselves as opinion leaders. Even so, most members of the public probably receive information from the mass media in the context of their social groups. Thus, they filter the information and interpretations of the media through not only their own perceptions, experiences, and existing attitudes but also those of people around them. Only when the media have the attention of most members of the audience and a virtual monopoly over the kinds of information received by a public that has few existing attitudes about the subject can the media produce anything like a uniform change in public attitudes.

A somewhat different argument, also based on the role of social influences on the development of public opinion, has been made by Elisabeth Noelle-Neumann in *The Spiral of Silence.*[33] She argues that members of society sense that some views are increasing in popularity, even if these ascending viewpoints are held only by a minority. Under such circumstances, people become reluctant to express opinions contrary to the presumed ascending view, whereas individuals holding that view are emboldened and express themselves more freely. This furthers the illusion that one viewpoint is widely shared. People then adopt the viewpoint because of this largely imaginary public pressure. Although intriguing, the attractiveness of this argument is diminished somewhat by the almost total lack of evidence in support of it.

In the remainder of this chapter, we consider the impact of the mass media on political attitudes in the context of political campaigns. Because the media can be influential only if people are paying attention, we look at the question of the overall attentiveness of the public to political news. Because the impact of the media varies depending on the existing attitudes and information of the audience, we examine the impact of the media on different kinds of people and in different campaign contexts.

To begin, however, we need to revisit some distinctions among the various types of media. First, the impact of information may be different depending on the type of media through which it is received. Precisely the same information received through television, radio, or a newspaper may impress the recipient differently. For example, viewing a speech on television may be more dramatic than hearing it on the radio or reading the text in a newspaper. Something like this occurred in 1960 when television viewers of the first of three presidential debates between John F. Kennedy and Richard M. Nixon had a less favorable impression of Nixon than did radio listeners.[34] A difficult topic, however, may be more easily absorbed by reading and rereading an article in the newspaper than by watching a story flash by once on television.

Second, the media differ in what they offer. Simple elements of information are more quickly and dramatically presented to a large audience on television than they can be through the print media. Television, however, may systematically underinform its audience by rarely offering more than a "headline service" of a minute or two on any one story. The more the public wants information and is motivated to seek it, the more important newspapers, magazines, and the Internet become. It is easy to search for information on the Internet, more difficult but possible in the print media, and much more difficult with radio and television. The characteristics of the media give them different roles in the formation of public opinion. In general, television alerts the public to a variety of topics and newspapers inform a smaller segment of the public in greater depth. The Internet does some of both.

Third, an increasing diversity of news sources is available through television, especially over the past twenty years. CNN, MSNBC, and Fox News are genuine alternatives to the broadcast networks, especially when it comes to fast-breaking stories and to news and commentary with a political slant. Surveys done by the Pew Research Center for the People and the Press in 2008 estimated that more than half the public watched CNN at least "sometimes" and 24 percent did so "regularly."[35] The Fox News cable audience was just as large and far larger in prime time. The C-SPAN channels provide extensive coverage of both the U.S. House of Representatives and the Senate, as well as other political events, without the intermediary of network editing and commentary. Over 20 percent of the public reports watching C-SPAN at least occasionally.[36] Call-in television and radio provide lengthy discussions of public issues and, since 1992, offer a mechanism whereby candidates can bypass the normal news channels and receive unmediated coverage.

The Internet as a news source is a more recent development, with intriguing characteristics. Providing almost unlimited access to information, it requires the consumer to seek out that information actively. It also offers opportunities to "talk back" or comment on the news, and to be put in touch with other like-minded people. Few "gatekeepers" operate on the Internet, and the issues of the reliability and credibility of information are largely left to the user to determine. Opportunities abound for whispering campaigns of rumor and misinformation.

Fourth, the impact of editorial endorsements by newspapers (television and radio stations rarely make endorsements) should be assessed independently of news coverage, although editorial preferences may bias news stories. Newspaper endorsements seemingly have a minimal impact in presidential elections, given that many other sources of influence exist.[37] In less visible, local races, a newspaper editorial may influence many voters.[38] Some concern exists that major newspaper chains could wield significant power nationally by lining up their papers behind one candidate. In recent years, however, the large chains have generally left their papers free to make decisions locally. Still, additional concerns come from evidence showing that candidates who received editorial endorsements receive more favorable coverage on the news side of the paper as well.[39]

Fifth, throughout our discussion we need to make the distinction between the impact of news coverage by the media and political advertising carried by the media. This is not an easy task, especially because the news media often cover political advertising as if it were news and consciously or unconsciously pick up themes from political ads and weave them into their own coverage.[40] Placing political advertising in news programs makes it harder to separate news from ads. Even the "ad watches" that news organizations use to critique candidates' advertising may contribute to the confusion over what is news and what is paid advertising.

The Media and Presidential Approval Ratings

Presidential approval ratings, regularly measured by public opinion polling organizations, reflect both the effect media coverage can have on political attitudes and its limitations. Media polls regularly ask about and report on the public's views on how the president is handling his job.

The various polling organizations ask the question in different ways, but what they generally report—and what we report here—is the percentage of the public that approves of the way the president is doing his job, not the degree of enthusiasm they feel. The approval measure sometimes behaves oddly. For example, President Ronald Reagan's approval rating jumped 10 percent after he was shot, presumably an expression of sympathy and not an assessment of the job he was doing.

In one sense, the ratings are a function of media content, because media coverage is the only source of information about the president for most people. The most precipitous changes in approval ratings, though, result from dramatic and important events. Although media coverage colors the recipient's perception of events, the media are usually not free to ignore them; the events themselves, not just the coverage, make them compelling.

Most presidents begin a term with high ratings, a phenomenon referred to as a "honeymoon effect." Presidents usually suffer a decline in approval ratings the longer they are in office. Not only are the ratings expected to decline over time, but as the public becomes more knowledgeable about a president, the approval ratings also should become more stable and more retrospective. In other words, the more people know about the president, the less impact some new element of information has and the more their approval or disapproval represents a summary judgment. As this happens, the day-to-day events covered by the media, and the coverage itself, have less impact in shaping the attitudes of the public.

Extraordinary events can boost a president's popularity while in office. International crises usually produce an increase in approval ratings as the public rallies 'round the flag and its representative, the president. Winning a second term (or even campaigning for one), with the accompanying election fanfare, also lifts presidential approval scores. These boosts usually prove to be temporary, and popularity ratings tend to drift downward again as time in office passes. (We discuss the relationship between job approval and vote choice in chapter 8.)

The approval ratings of both George H. W. Bush and George W. Bush illustrate the transitory nature of the increase in popularity associated with international crises. Both presidents' approval ratings improved dramatically during their respective wars in Iraq, both of which started far into their first terms as president. Poll results varied, but generally the senior Bush received approval ratings as high as any president had ever received, approaching 90 percent. His son did not do as well, but his ratings went over 70 percent in early April 2003. In both cases, their approval ratings began to fall immediately after the declared end of hostilities, for much the same reason initially. The public shifted its attention and concern away from the war and to the economy. For the senior Bush, the sagging economy drove his approval ratings down for the remainder of his presidency as the Persian Gulf War became irrelevant. By the fall of 1992, he was receiving ratings about as low as any past president.[41]

President George W. Bush found his approval ratings dropping because of the economy and because of the continuing insurgency in Iraq. His ratings dropped even further (to new lows) after Hurricane Katrina in the late summer of 2005. The approval ratings of both presidents followed a remarkably similar path over the course of their respective crises, as shown in Figure 7-3.

What happened to the ratings of the two Bushes illustrates the public's shifting focus on what matters in assessing the president. Throughout 1990, 1991, and 1992, President George H. W. Bush received low ratings for his handling of the economy, so when the economy mattered most to people, his overall approval ratings were low. During the Persian Gulf War, attention shifted to foreign affairs—an area in which Bush had always enjoyed high ratings—and this translated, for a while, into high overall approval ratings.

President George W. Bush had enjoyed very high approval ratings after September 11—almost as high as his father's after the Persian Gulf War. But by early 2003, his approval ratings had dropped 30 percentage points, back to their level before the terrorist attacks. Public attention

FIGURE 7-3   Approval Ratings of Presidents George H. W. Bush and George
W. Bush before and after Middle Eastern Wars, August 1990–
January 1992 and October 2002–March 2004

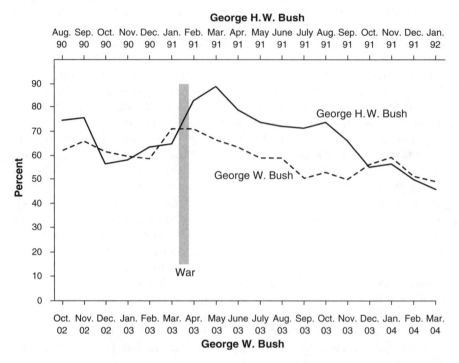

Sources: CNN/ *USA Today*/Gallup Polls, available at www.pollingreport.com and the Roper
Center for Public Opinion Research.

on the military action in Iraq raised his job approval ratings about
20 percentage points. During the next year, his ratings dropped to the
point that more people disapproved of the job he was doing than
approved. Figure 7-4 shows George W. Bush's approval ratings from the
start of his term until December 2008. His ratings differ considerably
depending on whether the question focused on his overall job performance, his handling of the situation in Iraq, or the war on terrorism.

The trend of President Clinton's approval is somewhat unusual in
that he reversed a precipitous decline in popularity on the basis of a
confrontation with Congress over domestic politics rather than on his
handling of an international crisis. Clinton ended his term in office in
January 2001 with approval ratings of 61 percent, unprecedented for a
modern president at the end of his second term. Commentators and
politicians have asked repeatedly how Clinton could maintain such high
approval ratings when the public was thoroughly aware of his personal

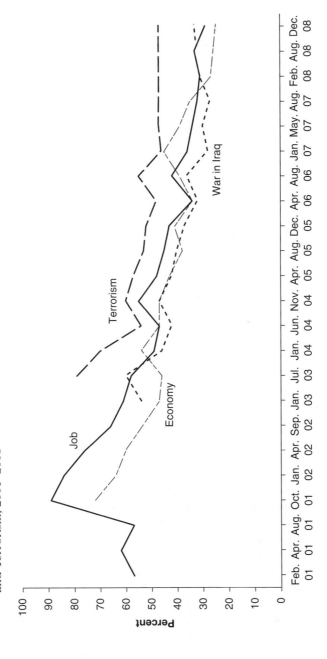

FIGURE 7-4 Approval Ratings of President George W. Bush in Handling His Job as President, the Economy, the War in Iraq, and Terrorism, 2001–2008

Sources: CNN/*USA Today*/Gallup Poll, available at www.pollingreport.com, with these exceptions: the May 2003 and the December 2008 data on "terrorism" came from CBS News Polls; the December 2008 "Iraq" data came from an NBC News/*Wall Street Journal* Poll; and the December 2008 "economy" data came from an ABC News/*Washington Post* Poll, all from the Roper Center for Public Opinion Research.

Note: The October 2001 poll was conducted immediately after 9/11. The spike in three lines in the spring of 2003 corresponded with the military phase of the war in Iraq. The spike in January 2004 followed the capture of Saddam Hussein.

misbehavior and disapproved of it. An overwhelming majority of Americans thought Clinton lacked the ability to provide moral leadership for the country and that providing moral leadership was important for a president to do. The explanation, to the extent that one exists, appears to be another dissonance reduction device—compartmentalization. Republicans made the connection between personal misbehavior and the job Clinton was doing as president and reported their disapproval. Democrats and, to a lesser extent, independents did not link the two views. In July 1998, a CBS News poll asked people whether they thought of "this whole situation [with Monica Lewinsky] more as a private matter having to do with Bill Clinton's personal life, or more as a public matter having to do with Bill Clinton's job as president."[42] Eighty percent of the Democrats and 68 percent of the independents—but only 37 percent of the Republicans—said they regarded this as a "personal matter."

In the early months of his presidency, Barack Obama's approval rating reached 69 percent, high even by "honeymoon" standards. Given his full plate of financial and economic crises, two wars, and moves to reform health care, his approval rating followed the pattern of his predecessors over the course of his first term.[43] By the end of the first year, his approval rating dropped to 49 percent. At the time of the 2010 midterms, he had dropped to 43 percent, a number that helped Republicans dominate competitive House elections and inch closer to taking the Senate. When he began the year of his final political campaign, a slowly improving economy had brought the president's numbers back up to 47 percent. Over the last few months of the 2012 campaign, Obama's approval rating, as measured by Gallup (which dramatically overestimated Romney's support in the election), hovered around 50 percent approval and 43 percent disapproval.

Campaigns and Political Communication

Political campaigns are efforts to present candidates or issues to voters with information, rationales, characterizations, and images to convince them that one candidate or position is better than the alternatives and to get them to act on that preference. Massive amounts of money are spent in modern campaigns to saturate the airwaves in an effort to influence voters. A perennial question for politicians, political commentators, and scholars is, "How much difference does a campaign make?"

Although most professional politicians take for granted the efficacy of political campaigns, scholarly analysis has often questioned their impact. In most elections, the majority of voters decide how they will vote, based on partisanship or ideological leanings, before the general election campaign begins. Beyond this, the generally low level of political information among the less politically interested throws doubt on the ability of undecided voters to absorb ideas during a campaign. Andrew Gelman and Gary King have offered an especially interesting form of this argument.[44] They contend that a voter's eventual choice can be predicted satisfactorily at the start of a campaign, well before the candidates are even known. Furthermore, because a voter may move away from this ultimate choice during the course of a campaign, intermediate predictions—so popular in media coverage and campaign organizations—are misleading.

Other analysts, using economic forecasting models, argue that the outcome of the election—and the margin of victory—can be predicted long before the election campaign from such variables as the rates of economic growth, inflation, and unemployment.[45] It may be difficult to believe that an individual voter's choice is made before the start of a campaign or is determined by economic forces; yet evidence indicates that in most years, the vote choices of most voters are not affected by the general election campaigns. The American National Election Study regularly asks voters when, during the presidential campaign, they made their voting decisions.[46] In most years, about two-thirds of the electorate reports deciding before or during the conventions, with the final one-third deciding during the campaign. Over the years, fewer people report deciding during the conventions—presumably because, in recent decades, the candidates have essentially been chosen by the end of the presidential primaries in the late spring.

The decision times of partisans and independents are different because the loyal party votes line up early behind the party's candidate. In all recent presidential elections, the strong partisans made their decisions by the end of the conventions, whereas many of the less committed partisans and independents were typically still undecided at the start of the general election campaign. In fairly close elections, this relatively uncommitted group can swing the election either way, with 10 to 15 percent of the voters making a decision in the last days of the election campaign.

The possibility clearly exists that campaigning can influence a small but crucial proportion of the electorate, and many elections are close enough that the winning margin could well be a result of campaigning. Professional politicians drive themselves and their organizations toward influencing undecided voters in the expectation that they are the key to providing, or maintaining, the winning margin. One can easily think of examples of elections in which the only explanation for the outcome was the aggressive campaign of one of the candidates. Multimillionaire publisher Steve Forbes could never have won the 1996 Republican presidential primaries in Arizona and Delaware without the expensive media advertising campaign he waged in those states. One can, however, just as easily think of examples of well-financed campaigns that failed. In early 1996, Senator Phil Gramm of Texas raised more money and won fewer delegates than any other Republican presidential candidate. The simple, if unsatisfying, answer to the question "do campaigns work?" seems to be "sometimes."

In this section, we will explore the conditions under which campaigns, and the information they seek to convey, are likely to have the most impact. In general, the effect of information provided in a campaign will depend on (1) the amount already known about the candidate or issue, (2) the extent to which the information is countered by competing claims, and (3) the extent to which the information is in a form that resonates with the concerns and life experiences of the voter.

New information has the greatest impact in situations in which little is known about the candidate or issue and in which the voters have few existing attitudes. The application of this generalization can be seen in many areas. For example, the candidate who is less well known has the most to gain (or lose) from joint appearances, such as debates. The 1960 debates between Kennedy and Nixon, the first-ever series of televised presidential debates, appear to have had a substantial impact on the election outcome, in large part because at the time Kennedy was not well known to the public. According to several different public opinion polls in 1960, about half of the voters reported that they were influenced by the debates, with Kennedy holding an advantage of three to one over Nixon.[47] Although Nixon's poor showing is often blamed on his five o'clock shadow, it is unlikely that his appearance caused many to turn against him because he had been in the public eye as vice president for eight years. Instead, Kennedy's advantage came from undecided Democrats who had little information about Kennedy (but were favorably disposed toward him because he was the Democratic candidate) and who were influenced by his attractive appearance and good performance. The immediate effect of the 1960 experience was the abandonment of presidential debates until 1976. Incumbent presidents or campaign front-runners were unwilling to offer such opportunities to their lesser-known challengers.

The 2008 debates presented a similar situation for Barack Obama. As the younger, less experienced, and less familiar candidate, he had the chance and the challenge to shape the impressions that voters had about him to a greater extent than the more familiar candidate, John McCain. Although public opinion polls generally showed that Obama "won" all the debates,[48] his greater victory was probably in reassuring those already leaning in his direction that he had the right characteristics to be president, as Kennedy had done in 1960.

In 2012, the general consensus was that Mitt Romney won the first debate. Much ink was spilled and air time was spent analyzing President

Obama's performance, looking for slight changes in the day-to-day tracking polls (which gave Romney a small, short-lived boost), and speculating about whether the first contest was a "game changer." It wasn't. The remaining debates, including Vice President Biden's lone contest with Congressman Paul Ryan, failed to meaningfully influence the polls.

Because new information has the greatest impact when little is known, voter preferences or opinions will be more volatile when candidates or public figures are not well known. When McCain plucked Sarah Palin from Alaska to be his running mate, she was viewed favorably by 22 percent of the public, with 66 percent not knowing enough about her to render an opinion. A week later, after her well-received introduction at the Republican National Convention, her "favorability" rating had doubled, to 44 percent. After her widely panned and satirized interview with Katie Couric, her rating slid to 32 percent, then bounced back to 40 percent after her debate with Joe Biden. It sunk to 31 percent thereafter, before recovering to 37 percent by Election Day.[49] In the brief two months of the general election campaign, each piece of new information had a disproportionate impact on evaluations of her as a candidate, and her ratings by the public bounced up and down as a result.

Paul Ryan had higher favorability ratings from the start, perhaps buoyed by his reputation among informed Republicans as a policy wonk. At the beginning of September 2012, his favorability rating hovered around 50 percent. By the election, it was holding steady at about 47 percent. By the summer of 2013, however, as journalists began speculating about whether he would mount a 2016 bid for the White House, his favorability rating had fallen to 41 percent. By comparison, media-anointed 2016 Democratic nomination frontrunner Hillary Rodham Clinton's favorability rating was at 58 percent in the summer of 2013.

Similarly, public opinion "trial heats" that are intended to gauge the preferences of the electorate during the course of an election campaign can be highly unstable when one or all of the candidates are not well known. In the contest for the Democratic presidential nomination in 2007–2008, Hillary Clinton began as a well-known figure, after eight years as first lady and six and a half years as senator from New York. Obama, on the other hand, was largely unknown as a first-term senator, despite his splash as keynote speaker at the 2004 Democratic National Convention. The trial heats, from September 2007 to May 2008, presented in the top half of Figure 7-5, show a steady base of support for the well-known Clinton but much greater volatility in preferences for Obama as he introduced himself to the public during the primary campaign. In contrast, the trial heats for Obama and McCain, found in the bottom half of Figure 7-5, show less volatility over the course of the campaign after both had clinched their respective nominations.

FIGURE 7-5   Trial Heat Results from the Democratic Presidential Primary and
the General Election, 2008

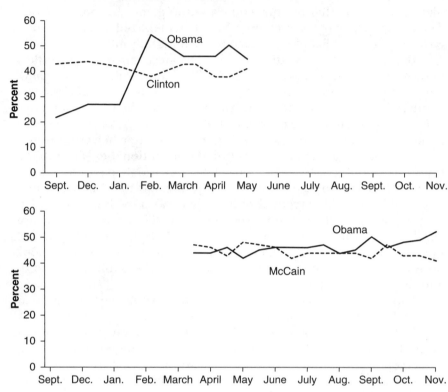

Source: Gallup Polls, available at www.pollingreport.com.

The second condition under which campaigns and the information they provide are most effective in influencing attitudes is when counter-information is not available. The obvious example is when one candidate has substantial resources for campaigning and the opponents do not. The well-financed candidate can present a favorable image of himself or herself—or an unflattering image of the opponent—without having those images contradicted. This situation is more likely to occur in primaries, when candidates must rely on their own funds and whatever they can raise from others, than in general elections, when both candidates can tap party resources. However, strategic decisions may also lead to a failure to counter information. In 2004, John Kerry delayed responding to the Swift Boat Veterans for Truth ads attacking his war record. The Swift Boat Veterans had been following him with similar accusations for years. He may have underestimated their potential harm to him when these allegations were played on a national stage, with higher stakes and an audience less knowledgeable about him than were his constituents in Massachusetts. Most major campaigns now have a "rapid response team" as part of their campaign staff to fire back when hit with unexpected and potentially damaging attacks. Obama reportedly beefed up his team after his campaign was slow to respond when allegations about his connections to 1960s radical William Ayers and indicted Chicago developer Tony Rezko surfaced in the spring of 2008. Even with the capability to respond quickly, candidates and their advisers still must make the strategic decision whether a response will be effective or will only serve to keep the story alive.

In presidential elections, the national nominating conventions offer each party the opportunity, at least temporarily, to get its message to the public without the annoyance of sharing the stage with the other party. The televised acceptance speech of the nominee, the ability to showcase rising stars and celebrate past heroes—all before a prime-time audience—offer unique opportunities for the political parties to present themselves and their campaign themes as they wish the public to see them. Although the news media interject commentary and analysis, the media's view of what is interesting generally leads them to emphasize strategy and motives instead of outright contradiction of a party's claims. The result of this nationwide opportunity for favorable publicity is the convention "bounce" that presidential nominees typically receive in their approval ratings and trial heat results immediately after their party's convention.[50] Obama had a 2008 convention bounce of about 5 percent at the end of August, and McCain's bounce was of the same amount after the Republican convention a week later. In 2012, Gallup reported a small, 3-point bounce for Obama after the Democratic National Convention and no bounce for Mitt Romney after the Republican National Convention.

The 2012 election showed that political parties have not always been able to use the nominating convention to their advantage. Many previous nominating conventions corroborate this point. The battle-marred Democratic National Convention in 1968 and George McGovern's acceptance speech long after midnight in 1972 represent dramatic failures to use this opportunity to benefit the party's nominee. Opponents within one's party may present the case against a nominee as effectively as the opposing party could. In recent years, when the nomination has been a foregone conclusion well before the nominating convention, both parties have tried to control their conventions as tightly as possible, keeping controversial issues and personalities under wraps. However, as the conventions become more staged in an effort to promote the most favorable image of the candidate, the audience and the news coverage for them have shrunk, making it less likely that those images would be conveyed to the public. In 2008, the Obama campaign sought to increase the audience appeal of the Democratic convention by showcasing the nominee's acceptance speech in a stadium filled with over eighty thousand enthusiastic supporters. Although the speech was well received, the effect was short-lived, as McCain countered by announcing his running mate the following morning.

Another, less obvious, situation in which unchallenged information has an impact is when all parties agree on the characterizations of a candidate or issue. If, for example, both candidates agree on which of them is liberal and which is conservative (although not on which position is "good" and which is "bad"), this information will be effectively conveyed to voters during the course of a campaign. Thomas E. Patterson and Robert D. McClure suggest that a major impact of television advertising may be on increasing voters' awareness of the issue stands of the candidates.[51] They conclude that television advertisements, more than television news stories, contain the most explicit information about the candidates' stands on issues and that they have a correspondingly greater impact on voters' awareness of the candidates' issue positions. Television news stories are too brief and focus too much on campaign action to convey much issue information to the viewer.

A third factor affecting whether information in a campaign will have an impact on voter attitudes is the extent to which the voters accept it as being relevant to their own concerns. In *The Reasoning Voter,* Samuel L. Popkin offers "Gresham's law of information," which states that small amounts of personal information drive out large amounts of impersonal information.[52] In other words, because personal information has more meaning to average voters—they use similar kinds of data every day in assessing friends and colleagues—they use such information about a candidate to make inferences about the kind of person that candidate is and how he or she will perform in office. In the short run, Palin's biography as "hockey mom" and mother to a special-needs child trumped her lack of knowledge about foreign policy in appealing to some voters.

Information will also be more or less effective depending on the context in which the recipient receives or understands it. Many social scientists use the concept of "framing" to study how people's preferences or decisions depend on the context or frame in which the alternatives are presented. For example, in the summer of 1979, in public opinion polls, Democrats preferred Senator Edward M. Kennedy over President Jimmy Carter by a margin of three to one as their party's nominee for president.[53] By March 1980, Carter was ahead of Kennedy by two to one among Democrats.[54] Although a number of things had intervened between these times, an important element seems to have been reminding the voters of Senator Kennedy's involvement in the accidental death of Mary Jo Kopechne a decade earlier. When the voters' frame of reference was an unpopular president viewed as responsible for high inflation, Kennedy was an attractive alternative. Later, when Kennedy was framed as a fatally irresponsible playboy, Carter was preferred. A similar situation happened to George H. W. Bush in 1992 and John McCain in 2008. When the election was framed in terms of national security, they did well; when the frame changed to the economy, their opponents prevailed.

The fact that voters respond differently to information depending on its presentation offers campaign managers opportunities to use sophisticated techniques to create favorable images of their candidates. Highly paid political consultants use an arsenal of social science knowledge and techniques in an attempt to do just that. Although some of these attempts have been notably successful, serious limitations also exist.

To successfully "sell" a candidate with advertising techniques, image makers must be able to control the information available about their candidate, thereby controlling the perceptions the voters hold about him or her. Reagan was more successfully handled in this way than most other presidential candidates. Perhaps his training as an actor made him more amenable to management by his advisers. However, to a considerable degree, maintaining his public image depended more on protecting him from the press and public exposure than on manipulating the content of publicity about him. This approach was especially effective in the 1980 campaign, when the focus of attention and public dissatisfaction rested on President Carter and not the challenger, Reagan.

For most candidates, however, manipulating a public image by controlling information is either impossible or self-defeating. For a relatively unknown challenger, such as Bill Clinton in 1992 or Obama in 2008, this type of strategy would appear self-defeating because few candidates have had the resources to become well known nationwide through advertising and staged appearances alone. (Billionaire Ross Perot in 1992 was an exception.) Instead, unknowns scramble for exposure in any forum they can find, and this prevents the careful manipulation of an image. Conversely, well-known candidates or incumbents, who can afford to sit back and let the public relations people campaign for them, probably already have images that are impossible to improve in any significant way over the relatively short period of time available in an election campaign. The most famous alleged attempt to repackage a candidate was the effort of the Nixon campaign staff in the 1968 presidential election.[55] However, the evidence suggests that more voters decided to vote for other candidates during the course of the campaign than decided to vote for Nixon. After about twenty years of nationwide public exposure, a "new Nixon" reinforced existing images, both negative and positive. He simply could not create a new, more attractive image. Mitt Romney faced criticism in 2012 for what critics called repeated attempts to change his image. Fearing his moderate record as governor of Massachusetts could hurt him in the GOP primary, Romney used one of the primary debates to refer to himself as a "severe" conservative. However, once Romney secured the nomination, a staffer of his went on television to claim that it was time to "shake" the Etch-a-Sketch and remake Romney's image for the general election.

Campaign organizations also attempt to affect the public image of their candidates by supplying the news media with favorable information. If successful, this strategy can be particularly effective, because the information arrives through the more credible medium of news coverage instead of paid advertising. Media events can be staged that provide the media—particularly television—with an attention-grabbing headline, sound bite, or photo opportunity. The campaigns of Nixon in 1968 and George H. W. Bush in 1988 were particularly successful in manipulating news coverage favorable to their candidates by staging media events and otherwise limiting access to the candidates. In 2004, the campaign of George W. Bush went to great lengths to handpick the audiences at appearances of the president or vice president, thereby ensuring an enthusiastically supportive crowd.

Limiting exposure of the candidate to staged media events works better for well-known incumbents than for challengers. Attempts by the McCain campaign to keep Sarah Palin under wraps were ultimately unsuccessful because the press and public demanded to know more about a person who might be a heartbeat away from the presidency. Furthermore, recent advances in technology make carefully controlling the image of a candidate even more daunting. A casual remark at a reception of supporters, captured by cell phone video and uploaded to YouTube, can become an overnight sensation on the Internet with catastrophic consequences for the candidate.

In recent years, campaign organizations have had difficulty getting news stories aired or printed about their issue positions and policy stands, but they have had more success with negative stories and attacks on other candidates. A key tactic is to seduce the media into covering paid political advertising, usually negative, as if it were news. In her book *Dirty Politics,* Kathleen Hall Jamieson details how, in 1988, the news media continually reinforced the premise behind the infamous Willie Horton ads that attacked Democratic candidate Michael Dukakis's position on crime.[56] For some years afterward, television and newspapers regularly featured ad watches that attempted to dissect the claims made in candidates' paid advertising; ironically, in the course of doing so they provided the ads with a wider audience.

Negative campaigning and advertising offer an effective way to hurt an opponent's image. In recent years, candidates' campaigns and independent organizations have attacked the images of candidates in personal and political terms. The volume of this particular form of negative advertising, sometimes called attack ads, has increased greatly. Many of these ads are paid for by committees, interest groups, and organizations not connected directly to a candidate or a campaign. The Supreme Court has ruled that such attack ads are issue advocacy and therefore cannot be limited because of the First Amendment.[57] As a result, a candidate can be hit with a massive campaign for which the opposing candidate need take no responsibility and that is basically outside the regulations and agreements governing the candidates and their campaign organizations. Two generalizations about negative campaigning can be made: (1) the public disapproves of negative campaigning, and (2) even so, it sometimes works. What's more, negative ads are often found to be more informative than positive ads. Because the public disapproves of negative advertising, some candidates have managed to be positive in their own ads while allowing independent organizations to trash their opponents for them, though presidential candidates in recent years have aired a high percentage of negative ads on their own.

If negative campaigning illustrates the capacity to use the mass media to accomplish political purposes, the difficulty candidates have in using the media to respond to these attacks reveals its limitations. Victims of negative campaigning have tried to ignore the attacks, attempted to answer the charges, or counterattacked with their own negative campaign. None of these responses appears to be notably successful—a fact that encourages the continued use of negative campaigning. Attacks in the form of ridicule or humor may be particularly difficult to answer. Some strategists have urged the victims of negative campaigning to respond immediately and defend themselves aggressively. This may be good advice, but following it requires much from the victim. To respond promptly with advertising requires a great deal of money (perhaps near the end of a campaign, when resources are limited) and a skilled staff. Moreover, victims of negative campaigning need to have a strong, effective answer to such attacks.

In their study of the 1992 presidential campaign, Marion R. Just, Ann N. Crigler, Dean E. Alger, Timothy E. Cook, Montague Kern, and Darrell M. West offer a useful way to look at the "construction" of a candidate's persona over the course of an election campaign.[58] Instead of the candidate's image being the creation of a campaign staff or the product of straight news coverage, it will evolve through the three-way interaction of the candidate's campaign, the news media, and the public. The candidates' initial attempts at establishing themselves face a range of reactions from the press and public—encouragement, incredulity, boredom—and the candidates adjust accordingly. Likewise, the news reporters assess and react to the response of colleagues and the public to their coverage of candidates. Finally, the public's judgments in public opinion polls, radio call-in programs, live interviews, and e-mail indicate displeasure or support of the behavior of both candidates and news media. The final picture may not be a faithful reflection of the candidate's inner being, but neither is it an artificial creation of campaign technicians nor the distortion of an overbearing press.

Presidential Primary Campaigns

Because the impact of new information is greatest when there are few existing attitudes, the impact of campaigns should be greatest in primary elections, especially with little-known candidates. In primaries, when all the candidates are of the same party, the voter does not even have partisanship to help in the evaluation of candidates. In such situations, whenever new information is provided it can have a substantial impact.

After 1968, reforms in the presidential nominating process led to an increased use of presidential primaries as a means of selecting delegates to the Democratic and Republican nominating conventions. The purpose of the reforms was to make the choice of the presidential candidates more reflective of the preferences of the party's supporters in the electorate. In fact, the increased use of presidential primaries opened the door, at least initially, to the nomination of candidates little known to the general public. Political newcomers, such as Carter in 1976, Gary Hart in 1984, Steve Forbes in 1996, and Howard Dean in 2004, had an opportunity to focus their energy and campaign resources on a few early primaries or caucuses, gain national media attention by winning or doing surprisingly well in those early contests, and generate momentum to allow them to challenge more established and well-known potential nominees. Such candidates often do not have long-term viability. Their early appeal, based on little information, dissipates as more, often less flattering, information becomes available. Nevertheless, by the time this happens, the candidate may already have secured the nomination (Carter in 1976) or severely damaged the front-runner, as Hart damaged Walter F. Mondale in 1984. Primaries can do considerable harm to candidates' images under some circumstances. Well-known front-runners such as George H. W. Bush in 1992 and Bob Dole in 1996 suffered a loss of popularity that they never recovered under the campaign attacks of fellow Republicans. Intraparty fighting is typically destructive for established candidates. Ever since 1972, segments of the Democratic Party expressed concern that the new reliance on presidential primaries was preventing the party from nominating its best or most electable candidates.

Before the 1988 election season, southern Democratic leaders decided that concentrating their states' primaries early in the election year would focus media and candidates' attention on the southern states as well as give a head start to more conservative candidates who could pick up a large bloc of delegate votes from these states. Although this strategy did not work in the short run—the Democrats nominated the liberal northeastern governor Dukakis in 1988—the creation of Super Tuesday considerably shortened the primary season by allowing candidates to amass enough delegates to secure the nomination months before the summer convention.

Every four years since 1988, additional states have moved their primaries forward, hoping to capture some media attention or, at least, to have a say before the nominations had been decided. By 2008 and 2012, this process had gone so far that half the states had their primaries or caucuses by early February, far supplanting the old Super Tuesday in early March. This "front-loading" of primaries originally had the effect of favoring the front-runner and decreasing the opportunity for lesser-known candidates. Because the primaries are so close together in time, candidates cannot concentrate their resources in a few states and use victories there to generate favorable coverage in other states. Instead, after the early states of Iowa and New Hampshire, which now have their caucuses and primary in early January, candidates must campaign all across the country in many states. Unknown candidates have almost no time to capitalize on early success in Iowa or New Hampshire by raising money and creating state campaign organizations. The established, well-known candidates again seem to have the advantage.

Although the Obama phenomenon in 2008 seems to contradict the conventional wisdom about the front-loading of primaries advantaging the front-runner, we should be careful about jumping to conclusions. Obama was unusual among lesser-known candidates because he was able to raise an enormous amount of money and create a substantial grassroots organization across many states before the primary season began in January 2008. None of the other non-front-runners (except Dean in 2004) were able to come close to that. Whether other lesser-known candidates of the future will have those fund-raising and organizational skills—and the staying power that Obama had and Dean did not—is unclear. In any event, if the Democrats had held a national primary on February 5 (a national primary being the logical outcome of the current process of moving more and more primaries to the beginning of the season), it is quite likely that Hillary Clinton, the established front-runner, would have won, according to the nationwide trial heat results of the time.

The role of the news media in influencing presidential primaries with their coverage has changed as the format of the primaries has changed. In the 1970s and 1980s, the media had considerable potential to enhance one candidate's campaign momentum and to consign others to obscurity. Thomas E. Patterson's study of the role of the media in 1976 shows that, during the primaries, Carter benefited from the tendency of the press to cover only the winner of a primary, regardless of the narrowness of the victory or the number of convention delegates won.[59] Even the accident of winning primaries in the eastern time zone gave Carter disproportionately large, prime-time coverage on evenings when other candidates enjoyed bigger victories farther west.[60] This was possible because few voters were well informed about or committed to any of the many Democratic candidates. During the same period, the media exaggerated the significance of President Gerald R. Ford's early primary victories without noticeably influencing the public's feelings about him or his challenger, then-governor of California Reagan.[61] It is much more difficult to influence voters who have well-informed preferences.

The "winner-take-all" commentary on the presidential primaries has been replaced in recent years by talk of "unexpected" winners and losers. The most favorable coverage may be given to a second- or third-place finisher, and the real winner in terms of numbers of votes or delegates may be treated as a loser if he or she has not had a big enough win. Attention focuses on who does better or worse than expected, regardless of the number of votes they receive. This was the case with Hillary Clinton's third-place finish in Iowa (which led to the media writing her candidacy off), as well as her "surprise" win in New Hampshire, where she won more votes—but ultimately fewer delegates—than Obama. The same thing happened to Rick Santorum, who won the Iowa caucus after all the votes were counted; the media named Romney the winner on the night of the caucus even though the results were not all in and too close to call. The irony of this type of commentary is that it essentially converts the errors in the media's preelection coverage into newsworthy political change. With the front-loading of the primaries, however, media coverage becomes less relevant after the first few primaries.

Inequality in the resources available to candidates in presidential primary campaigns is likely to have a greater effect than in the presidential general election, in which public financing is available to both major-party candidates. In the 2000 election campaign, George W. Bush raised more than $100 million, more money by far than any of the other candidates and more than twice as much as any previous candidates for president. He also raised his money early. Six months before the first primary, he had raised more than half his eventual total. This enormous war chest served both to discourage other potential candidates and to defeat his most serious rival for the nomination, John McCain. In 2008, Hillary Clinton followed a similar strategy of raising and spending so much money that it would create an aura of invincibility and scare off would-be rivals for the nomination. Unfortunately for the strategy, her fund-raising was more than matched by Obama's, and Clinton's campaign was chronically short of funds later in the season. Indeed, Obama's fund-raising prowess was so formidable that it enabled him to forego public financing in the general election, giving him a considerable financial advantage over Republican John McCain, who had accepted public financing. Both Romney and Obama eschewed public financing in 2012. Those choices, along with the *Citizens United* decision from the Supreme Court, led to record spending from the candidates and from outside groups.

Campaign Strategy

Those attempting to communicate with the American public on political matters face an awkward dilemma. The attentive members of the public, the individuals most likely to receive political messages, are least likely to be influenced by one or a few items of information. Meanwhile, the individuals who are open to persuasion are uninterested in politics and not likely to pay attention to politics in the media.

By way of conclusion, we can use material from this chapter as a basis for generalizing about political communication and campaign effects from the perspective of a candidate. In political campaigns, candidates stand little chance of altering the electorate's issue preferences on policies that are sufficiently prominent to affect their vote choices. In the short run, to change individuals' preferences on issues that they care about is difficult by any means, and it is particularly difficult through the impersonal content of mass media. To change an individual's preferences or pattern of behavior, personal contact is more effective than the media.

To a limited degree, candidates can alter the prominence of a few issues for some segments of the public, but their capacity to increase or decrease the importance of issues is slight compared with what will happen in the ordinary course of events. For example, a candidate cannot make corruption in government a salient issue solely through his or her campaign, but a major scandal can make it an issue whether the candidates want it to be or not. Nevertheless, it is worth some effort to increase the visibility of issues that are expected to benefit the candidate, even though that effort will probably fail. It is also worth some effort to attempt to reduce the salience of issues that hurt a candidate, though again, this strategy is not likely to succeed.

The public's perceptions of candidates' positions on issues are much more susceptible to change. News and advertising through the mass media can convey a considerable amount of information on issue stands and dramatize the differences between candidates. The more factual the information and the more the candidates agree on the respective characterizations, the more fully the information is absorbed by the public. This is the area of attitude change and public awareness in which candidates can accomplish the most.

In the final analysis, candidates are most interested in winning votes, regardless of how strong a preference each vote represents. But there are grounds for wanting large numbers of supporters with very strong preferences. Individuals with an overwhelming preference, holding no significant conflicting views, form the base of support for a candidate that yields campaign contributions and workers. These are the individuals all through society who casually influence the people around them to hold views favorable to a candidate. These are the opinion leaders who interpret and misinterpret the news on behalf of their candidate.

The Obama campaign stepped up its efforts to contact voters in 2012, overlaying various pieces of "big data" to try to determine which of their supporters were most likely to vote and vice versa. They also made predictions about who the most persuadable voters were. Armed with that information, volunteers were sent to knock on doors and make phone calls to spur strong supporters to the polls even if they were not regular voters and to win the loyalty of those who had not yet (or not strongly) made up their mind.

There are several overall implications of this discussion. A long time and probably noncampaign periods of low intensity are needed to switch individual issue stands or party loyalties. The media presentation and personal discussion of political and social conditions or events have a greater impact on attitudes than advertising or party contacts.

To a considerable degree, by the time a candidate wins nomination, he or she faces a constituency whose basic values and preferences can be changed only by events over which the candidate probably has little or no control. The only impact the candidate can have through campaigning is to make his or her issue positions known as dramatically as possible and to contrast those positions with the opponent's. No candidate will know in advance what the net effect of these efforts will be, and most will never know. But most elections are contested under conditions that give one candidate a great initial advantage in the partisan loyalty and issue preferences of the constituency. The best chance for candidates is to exploit what they believe are their advantages, but in most cases the stable party loyalties and unchanging issue preferences of a constituency impose significant constraints on how much difference campaign strategies can make.

Speculation on the nature of political communication has ranged from alarm over the mass public's vulnerability to manipulation through the media to annoyance at the difficulty of reaching the public. The American people make use of the mass media to inform themselves on matters of interest, but this does not mean that they pay attention to everything in the media. Individuals have a remarkable ability to ignore information—one as fully developed as the ability to absorb information. Influencing individuals on a subject about which they feel strongly is extremely difficult because they reject the media content, and influencing individuals on a subject about which they are indifferent offers problems because they ignore the media content.

Also, the media are difficult to use for manipulation because so many different points of view are found within them. An extremely wide range of political perspectives is available to some degree in the mass media, although some perspectives are much more frequently available and more persuasively presented than others. The media in American society allow all views to enjoy some expression, although media coverage of many topics may be expressed in a manner favorable to some viewpoints and unfavorable to others. Disentangling the bias associated with the news and commentary in the media from the distortion found in the individual's reception of political information would be difficult. Either of these conditions would be adequate to account for considerable discrepancy between political reality and the public image of that reality.

Notes

1. Kim L. Fridkin, Patrick J. Kenney, Sarah Allen Gershon, Karen Shafer, and Gina Serignese Woodall, "Capturing the Power of a Campaign Event: The 2004 Presidential Debate in Tempe," *Journal of Politics* 69, no. 3 (2007): 770–85.
2. Doris A. Graber, *Mass Media and American Politics*, 8th ed. (Washington, DC: CQ Press, 2010).
3. Anthony Downs, *An Economic Theory of Democracy* (New York: Harper and Brothers, 1957).
4. Samuel L. Popkin, *The Reasoning Voter* (Chicago: University of Chicago Press, 1991), 47–49.
5. Michael Schudson, *The Good Citizen: A History of American Public Life* (New York: Free Press, 1998).
6. John Zaller, "A New Standard for News Quality: Burglar Alarms for the Monitorial Citizen," *Political Communication* 20, no. 2 (2003): 109-130.
7. Between 15 and 20 percent report reading a newspaper online. Pew Research Center for the People and the Press, "2008 Biennial Media Consumption Survey," April 30–June 1, 2008.
8. Pew Research Center for the People and the Press, News Interest Index, "Internet Overtakes Newspapers as News Outlet," December 23, 2008, http://www.people-press.org/2008/12/23/internet-overtakes-newspapers-as-news-outlet/.

9. Pew Research Center for the People and the Press, "In Changing News Landscape, Even Television Is Vulnerable," http://www.people-press.org/2012/09/27/in-changing-news-landscape-even-television-is-vulnerable/.

10. Pew Research Center for the People and the Press, "Low Marks for 2012 Election," http://www.people-press.org/2012/11/15/section-4-news-sources-election-night-and-views-of-press-coverage/.

11. Markus Prior, *Post-Broadcast Democracy: How Media Choice Increases Inequality in Political Involvement and Polarizes Elections.* (New York: Cambridge University Press, 2007).

12. Shanto Iyengar and Kyu S. Hahn, Red Media, Blue Media: Evidence of Ideological Selectivity in Media Use, *Journal of Communication* 59, no. 1 (2009): 19–39.

13. Pew Research Center for the People and the Press, "Low Marks for 2012 Election," http://www.people-press.org/2012/11/15/section-4-news-sources-election-night-and-views-of-press-coverage/.

14. Lymari Morales, "U.S. Distrust in Media Hits New High," September 21, 2012, http://www.gallup.com/poll/157589/distrust-media-hits-new-high.aspx.

15. Tim Groseclose and Jeffrey Milyo, "A Measure of Media Bias," *Quarterly Journal of Economics* 120, no. 4 (2005): 1191–1237.

16. Brendan Nyhan, "Does the US Media Have a Liberal Bias? A Discussion of Tim Groseclose's Left Turn: How Liberal Media Bias Distorts the American Mind," *Perspectives on Politics* 10, no. 3 (2012): 767–71; and http://www.brendan-nyhan.com/blog/2005/12/the_problems_wi.html.

17. Joel Turner, "The Messenger Overwhelming the Message: Ideological Cues and Perceptions of Bias in Television News," *Political Behavior* 29 (April 2007): 441–464.

18. Steven Kull, "Misperception, the Media, and the Iraq War," Program on International Policy Attitudes and Knowledge Networks, October 2, 2003, http://www.pipa.org/OnlineReports/Iraq/IraqMedia_Oct03/IraqMedia_Oct03_rpt.pdf.

19. Pew Research Center for the People and the Press, "2004 Biennial Media Consumption Survey."

20. "The State of the News Media 2005," Project for Excellence in Journalism, available at www.stateofthemedia.org.

21. Brendan Nyhan and Jason Reifler, "When Corrections Fail: The Persistence of Political Misperceptions," *Political Behavior* 32, no. 2 (2010): 303–30.

22. For an early statement of this point, see Bernard C. Cohen, *The Press and Foreign Policy* (Princeton, NJ: Princeton University Press, 1963).

23. John R. Petrocik, "Issue Ownership in Presidential Elections, with a 1980 Case Study," *American Journal of Political Science* 40 (August 1996): 825–50.

24. Amber E. Boydstun, Rebecca A. Glazier, and Claire Phillips, "Agenda Control in the 2008 Presidential Debates." *American Politics Research* (forthcoming).

25. Times Mirror Center for the People and the Press, "The People, the Press, and the War in the Gulf," January 31, 1991.

26. Pew Research Center for the People and the Press, early April 2003 War Tracking Poll, available at http://www.people-press.org/2003/03/25/march-20-april-7-2003-iraq-war-tracking-poll/.

27. CBS News/*New York Times* Poll, press release, January 17, 1991, and CNN/*USA Today*/Gallup Poll, March–April 2003, available at www.pollingreport.com.

28. A variety of publications, including monthly reports, are available on the website of the Pew Research Center for the People and the Press at www.people-press.org.
29. These data on attention to news stories can be found in the "Hurricane Katrina Survey," September 6–7, 2005, available at www.people-press.org.
30. Pew Research Center for the People and the Press, News Interest Index, December 23, 2008.
31. Philip E. Converse, "Information Flow and the Stability of Partisan Attitudes," *Public Opinion Quarterly* 26 (Winter 1962): 578–99.
32. Elihu Katz and Paul F. Lazarsfeld, *Personal Influence: The Part Played by People in the Flow of Mass Communications* (New York: Free Press, 1964).
33. Elisabeth Noelle-Neumann, *The Spiral of Silence* (Chicago: University of Chicago Press, 1984).
34. James N. Druckman. "The Power of Television Images: The First Kennedy-Nixon Debate Revisited," *Journal of Politics* 65 (2003): 559–71.
35. Pew Research Center for the People and the Press, "2008 Biennial Media Consumption Survey," April 30–June 1, 2008, available at www.people-press.org.
36. Ibid.
37. Everette E. Dennis, *The Media Society* (Dubuque, IA: Wm. C. Brown, 1978), 37–41.
38. Michael B. MacKuen and Steven L. Coombs, *More Than News* (Beverly Hills, CA: Sage, 1981).
39. Kim Fridkin Kahn and Patrick J. Kenney, "The Slant of the News: How Editorial Endorsements Influence Campaign Coverage and Citizens' Views of Candidates," *American Political Science Review* 96 (2002): 381–94.
40. Kathleen Hall Jamieson, *Dirty Politics: Deception, Distraction, and Democracy* (New York: Oxford University Press, 1992).
41. Pew Research Center for the People and the Press, "Modest Bush Approval Rating Boost at War's End, Economy Now Top National Issue," April 18, 2003, available at www.people-press.org.
42. CBS News Poll, July 30, 1998. Data provided by the Inter-university Consortium for Political and Social Research.
43. CBS News/*New York Times* surveys, available at www.pollingreport.com.
44. Andrew Gelman and Gary King, *Why Do Presidential Election Campaign Polls Vary So Much When the Vote Is So Predictable?* (Cambridge, MA: Littauer Center, 1992).
45. Michael S. Lewis-Beck and Tom W. Rice, *Forecasting Elections* (Washington, DC: CQ Press, 1992). These economic forecasts limit themselves to two-party races and cannot accommodate third-party candidates such as Ross Perot.
46. American National Election Studies, 1948–2004.
47. Recomputed from Elihu Katz and Jacob J. Feldman, "The Debates in the Light of Research: A Survey of Surveys," in *The Great Debates: Background, Perspective, Effects,* ed. Sidney Kraus (Bloomington: Indiana University Press, 1962), 212.
48. Post-debate polls by *USA Today*/Gallup and CNN/Opinion Research Corporation, available at www.pollingreport.com.
49. CBS News Surveys, August 29–November 2, 2008, available from the Roper Center for Public Opinion Research.
50. James E. Campbell, Lynna L. Cherry, and Kenneth A. Wink, "The Convention Bump," *American Politics Quarterly* 20 (July 1992): 287–307.

51. Thomas E. Patterson and Robert D. McClure, "Television News and Televised Political Advertising: Their Impact on the Voter," paper presented at the National Conference on Money and Politics, Washington, DC, 1974; and Thomas E. Patterson and Robert D. McClure, *Political Advertising: Voter Reaction to Televised Political Commercials* (Princeton, NJ: Citizens' Research Foundation, 1973).
52. Popkin, *The Reasoning Voter,* 73.
53. *Gallup Opinion Index* 183 (December 1980): 51.
54. "Opinion Roundup," *Public Opinion* 3 (April/May 1980): 38.
55. Joe McGinniss, *The Selling of the President* (New York: Trident Press, 1969).
56. Jamieson, *Dirty Politics,* chap. 1.
57. Federal legislative attempts to curb negative ads, such as the McCain-Feingold Act, have generally been thwarted by the courts. In 2007, the Supreme Court ruled in *FEC v. Wisconsin Right to Life, Inc.* (551 U.S. 449) that issue ads may not be banned.
58. Marion R. Just, Ann N. Crigler, Dean E. Alger, Timothy E. Cook, Montague Kern, and Darrell M. West, *Crosstalk: Citizens, Candidates, and the Media in a Presidential Campaign* (Chicago: University of Chicago Press, 1996).
59. Thomas E. Patterson, "Press Coverage and Candidate Success in Presidential Primaries: The 1976 Democratic Race," paper presented at the annual meeting of the American Political Science Association, Washington, DC, 1977.
60. James D. Barber, ed., *Race for the Presidency* (Englewood Cliffs, NJ: Prentice-Hall, 1978), chap. 2.
61. Thomas E. Patterson, *The Mass Media Election* (New York: Praeger, 1980), 130–32.

Suggested Readings

Graber, Doris. *Processing the News.* New York: Longman, 1988. An in-depth study of a few respondents on the handling of political information from the media.

Jamieson, Kathleen Hall. *Dirty Politics: Deception, Distraction, and Democracy.* New York: Oxford University Press, 1992. A blistering commentary on political advertising strategies and the interaction between advertising and news coverage.

Just, Marion R., Ann N. Crigler, Dean E. Alger, Timothy E. Cook, Montague Kern, and Darrell M. West. *Crosstalk: Citizens, Candidates, and the Media in a Presidential Campaign.* Chicago: University of Chicago Press, 1996. A multimethod study of the 1992 presidential election campaign.

Neuman, W. Russell, Marion R. Just, and Ann N. Crigler. *Common Knowledge.* Chicago: University of Chicago Press, 1992. An interesting analysis of mass media and political attitudes.

Pew Research Center for the People and the Press. *Audience Segments in a Changing News Environment: Key News Audiences Now Blend Online and Traditional Sources,* 2008. A rich analysis of media behavior that continues Pew's biennial survey. Available at www.people-press.org/reports/pdf/444.pdf.

Popkin, Samuel L. *The Reasoning Voter.* Chicago: University of Chicago Press, 1991. A wide-ranging discussion of campaigning and presidential vote choice.

Sides, John, and Lynn Vavreck. *The Gamble: Choice and Chance in the 2012 Presidential Election.* Princeton, NJ: Princeton University Press, 2013. A political science-oriented election book produced as the 2012 campaign was occurring.

Vavreck, Lynn. *The Message Matters: The Economy and Presidential Campaigns.* Princeton, NJ: Princeton University Press, 2009. A creative and original account of when and how candidates' campaign messages ought to include economic messages as compared to messages on other issues.

West, Darrell M. *Air Wars: Television Advertising in Election Campaigns, 1952–2008.* Washington, DC: CQ Press, 2009. The fifth edition of a study of many aspects of television advertising in presidential elections.

Internet Resources

The Pew Research Center for the People and the Press conducts numerous political surveys throughout the year as well as the best study of American media behavior done in the spring of even-numbered years. The center not only makes the data available freely, at www.people-press.org, but the website also offers extensive analysis of many political and media topics. For information, click on "Commentary," "Survey Reports," and "News Interest Index." During election years, most major news organizations have websites with survey data on many political items, but poll aggregating websites such as elections.huffingtonpost.com/pollster provide stronger estimates of candidate support and changes thereof in real time.

C h a p t e r   E i g h t

Vote Choice and Electoral Decisions

A CENTRAL FOCUS of research on American political behavior is vote choice, especially presidential vote choice. Most Americans follow presidential campaigns with greater attention than they give other elections, and eventually over 50 percent of the electorate expresses a preference by voting. The results of presidential balloting are reported and analyzed far more extensively than any others. This chapter explores the main determinants of vote choice and the interpretation of election outcomes in light of these determinants. We attempt to generalize the discussion beyond presidential choice, but inevitably most of the illustrations are drawn from recent presidential election studies.

In their pioneering work *The American Voter,* Angus Campbell, Philip E. Converse, Warren E. Miller, and Donald E. Stokes introduced the metaphor of the "funnel of causality" to depict the way multiple factors have an impact on an individual's vote choice.[1] As they envision it, at the narrow end of the funnel is the dependent variable, vote choice. At the wide end of the funnel are social characteristics, like race, gender, social class, and level of education—factors that shape many facets of an individual's life and that are related to political attitudes and, ultimately, vote choice. These relationships, however, are not especially strong. Next in the funnel are long-term predispositions, like partisanship and ideology, that orient and predispose an individual to view the world and act in particular ways. These predispositions are more strongly related to vote choice than are the social characteristics, but by no means do they determine it. They are themselves related to the social characteristics but, again, are not wholly determined by them. Moving further toward the narrow end of the funnel, we find attitudes toward issues that are important to the individual as well as evaluations of the current parties and of particular candidates. Again, these attitudes are related to the long-term predispositions of party and ideology and, to a lesser extent, to the individual's social characteristics. They are also more closely linked to, and more predictive of, how the individual will vote. We can think of the funnel of causality as a diagram of factors of varying proximity to final vote choice, with more distant factors influencing those that are more proximate, but having a weaker overall relationship to vote choice itself. As we get closer to the narrow end of the funnel, the connection to vote choice becomes stronger.

The funnel of causality is not offered as a statistical model or a predictive theory of vote choice. However, it is a convenient way to conceptualize the factors that influence vote choice, and we use it to organize the material in this chapter. The preceding chapters have looked in depth at the various factors. In this chapter, we bring them all together to answer the question, "Why do people vote the way they do?"

Social Characteristics and Presidential Vote Choice

Social characteristics like an individual's race, religion, social class, or education are unlikely to change over the course of a campaign. They are, rather, a set of long-term factors that both analysts and politicians link to vote choice. Social analysis of the 2012 presidential election reveals striking patterns of behavior, shown in Figure 8-1, which uses the same social characteristics as those introduced in chapter 6.

A key feature of the 2012 election was the changing demographics of the American people and how this played out in support for the two major-party candidates. According to the 2010 U.S. Census, the American population consists of 72 percent whites (down from 75 percent in 2000), 16 percent Hispanics (up from 13 percent), 13 percent African Americans (up from 12 percent), and 5 percent Asians (up from 4 percent).[2] The United States has a more diverse population than it did even a decade ago. If the various racial and ethnic groups looked the same in terms of vote choice, the changing demographics would be politically uninteresting. Instead, they are highly interesting. Whites were much more likely to support Republican Mitt Romney than Democrat Barack Obama, whereas every other racial and ethnic group was much more likely to support Obama than Romney.

In 2012, African American voters were nearly unanimous in their support of Democratic candidate Barack Obama. Recall that African American voters have overwhelmingly supported the Democratic

FIGURE 8-1   Vote for President, by Race, Ethnicity, Religion, and Education, 2012

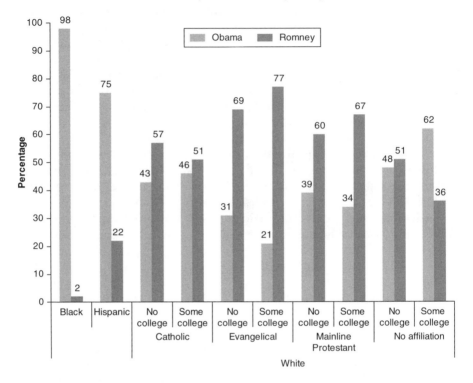

Source: 2012 American National Election Study, available at www.electionstudies.org.

candidate—usually by 90 percent or more—for decades. The impact that a black candidate had on black voting behavior was seen more in heightened turnout and enthusiasm than in actual vote choice.

Obama also did very well among other minority groups, especially Hispanics and Asian Americans. In recent years, Republicans have had hopes of making inroads among Hispanic voters, but in 2012 Hispanics voted 75 percent for Obama, according to the ANES data, which was an increase over Democrat John Kerry's share of 61 percent in 2004 and even higher than the 67 percent of the Hispanic vote Obama received in 2008. In data not shown in Figure 8-1, Asian Americans have turned to the Democratic Party in leaps and bounds over the past couple of decades. The Democratic share of the Asian American vote was 31 percent in 1992, 62 percent in 2008, and 73 percent in 2012.[3]

White Americans were much more supportive of Republican Romney than were the other major racial and ethnic groups, with 58 percent voting for Romney and 41 percent voting for Obama. We further break down the white vote by religion and education, two social characteristics that differentially drive the white vote. White Protestants were Romney's strongest supporters, with better-educated evangelicals giving him 77 percent of their vote. Less educated evangelicals were not far behind with 69 percent voting for Romney. He also gained majority support from mainline Protestants and Catholics. Among the better educated with no religious affiliation, support was high for Obama.

In the nation as a whole, Obama received 41 percent of the white vote, but this overall figure hides a deep regional divide. In the South, Obama had just 30 percent of the white vote compared to the 45 percent he had in the rest of the country. There was very little in terms of a gender gap among white voters, with 42 percent of men and 39 percent of women supporting Obama. A bigger marriage gap appeared, with 35 percent of married white men and women voting for Obama, in comparison with 52 percent of unmarried whites.

We can also look at the ways various social groups contributed to the vote totals of the two candidates. Shown in Figure 8-2, this analysis of the "composition" of Obama's and Romney's votes—in contrast to how the social groups voted—is similar to our analysis of partisanship in chapter 6. The composition of Obama's vote total reflects his appeal to diverse groups in American society: Blacks made up 28 percent of Obama's vote, Hispanics 13 percent, and whites 58 percent. Among these white supporters, Obama received an equal percentage of votes from better educated Catholics and from better educated people with no religious affiliation, each contributing 13 percent to Obama's total. Obama even received 10 percent of his votes from fundamentalist and evangelical Protestants (combining the less and better educated). The composition of Romney's vote total is less diverse: Blacks constituted only 0.5 percent of Romney's vote and Hispanics only 5 percent. Fully 95 percent of Romney's vote was made up of white non-Hispanics; almost 60 percent were mainline or fundamentalist/evangelical Protestants. Religious groups were an important part of Romney's camp, yet he received 15 percent of his vote from those with no religious affiliation.

The Republican Party, in assessing its loss in the 2012 election, pointed to the problem of diversity within the party as a possible culprit. Republican National Committee Chairman Reince Priebus argued that Americans viewed the party as a "'narrow-minded, out-of-touch' party of 'stuffy old men'" and that the GOP needed to do something about this party image. Young Republicans, in the College Republican National Committee, were especially blunt in arguing that the party needed to

FIGURE 8-2   Social Composition of the Vote for President, by Race, Ethnicity, Religion, and Education, 2012

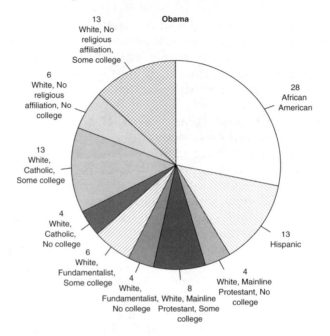

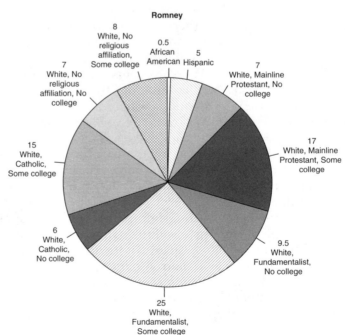

take steps to broaden its appeal, including reaching out to women, minorities, gay voters, and Millenials. Of particular concern to Republicans is the trend toward the Democratic Party of Latinos and Latinas. Some Republicans, including U.S. Senator Marco Rubio of Florida, have tried to push the Republican Party to support immigration reform that is more sensitive to Latinos and Latinas in the United States.[4] Political scientist Sergio Wals's research points to potential positives of the Republican Party courting Hispanic voters. Wals found that Mexican immigrants aren't guaranteed Democrats. They span the ideological spectrum and, as a bonus to the Republican Party, those on the right are more likely to be politically engaged than those on the left.[5] Not all Republicans are on board with the idea that the party needs more diversity, however. Conservative and Tea Party Republicans countered the plan to diversify by pointing to what they saw as the real reason for the party's loss—that it had not stuck to principles.

Partisanship and Ideology

As seen in earlier chapters, party loyalty is a basic characteristic that influences many aspects of an individual's political behavior, including vote choice, and is itself influenced by an individual's social characteristics. In Table 8-1, we see the relationship between partisanship and vote choice in 2012. As strength of partisanship increases, so does the likelihood of voting for one's party so that strong Democrats and strong Republicans are nearly unanimous in supporting their respective party's nominee. As strength of partisanship declines, so does the impact on vote choice.

Ideology works in much the same way as partisanship as a long-term predisposition that shapes attitudes and behavior. When voters have a clear ideological view, it is highly related to vote choice, as can be seen in Table 8-2. Among those who call themselves "moderate" or who disclaim any ideology, it offers no guide to how they might vote.

As we have seen in chapter 5, partisanship and ideology are related to each other, and increasingly so given the partisan sort, and it would be very difficult to untangle the causal connections between the two. No doubt some individuals adopt a party because it fits their ideological world view or because their admired party leaders are so labeled. Partisanship—or party identification—takes a more central role in explaining voting behavior in part because more Americans think of themselves as partisans or independents than as ideologues. Also important analytically, candidates are more clearly connected to their party than to their ideology because the candidate usually has chosen a party label under which to run (while possibly avoiding or obfuscating an ideological label for another one like "reformer," "maverick," or "outsider"). Nonetheless, as we think about the factors that influence a

TABLE 8-1 Presidential Vote, by Party Identification, 2012

	Strong Democrat	Weak Democrat	Independent Democrat	Independent	Independent Republican	Weak Republican	Strong Republican
Barack Obama	99%	84%	85%	44%	13%	13%	4%
Mitt Romney	1	15	12	51	84	86	96
Other	*	1	3	6	3	1	0
Total	**100%**	**100%**	**100%**	**101%**	**100%**	**100%**	**100%**
(N)	(340)	(164)	(203)	(73)	(238)	(168)	(230)

Source: 2012 American National Election Study, available at www.electionstudies.org.

* Less than 0.5 percent.

TABLE 8-2 Presidential Vote, by Ideological Identification, 2012

	Strong liberal	Liberal	Slightly liberal	Moderate	Slightly conservative	Conservative	Strong conservative
Barack Obama	91%	97%	85%	59%	26%	12%	6%
Mitt Romney	3	2	14	38	72	88	94
Other	6	1	1	3	2	0	0
Total	**100%**	**100%**	**100%**	**100%**	**100%**	**100%**	**100%**
(N)	(34)	(173)	(116)	(314)	(210)	(266)	(48)

Source: 2012 American National Election Study, available at www.electionstudies.org.

person's vote, we can think of ideology as holding a similar place in the chain of factors—or funnel of causality—that leads to the final voting decision, especially now that the parties have more clearly become ideologically sorted.

Short-Term Forces

In seeking to understand vote choice, an individual's partisanship can be construed as a long-term predisposition to vote for one party or another, other things being equal. In other words, in the absence of any information about candidates and issues or other short-term forces in an election, individuals can be expected to vote according to their partisanship. However, to the extent that such short-term forces have an impact on them, they may be deflected away from their usual party loyalty toward some other action. The more short-term forces there are in an election—or the more a voter is aware of them—the less will be the impact of partisanship. This idea is crucial for understanding the relative impact of partisanship in different types of elections. In highly visible presidential elections, when information about candidates and at least some issues is widely available, partisanship will typically be less important to the voter's decision than in less visible races down the ticket. Furthermore, more potent short-term forces would be required to cause a very strong partisan to vote for another party than would be necessary to prompt a weak partisan to defect. An individual's vote in an election can be viewed as the product of the strength of partisanship and the impact of short-term forces on the individual.

In most elections, both candidates and political commentators give their attention to short-term forces, such as the candidates' personalities, the issues, and the parties' records, because these elements might be modified by the actions of candidates and campaign strategies. Although in many respects partisanship and the state of the economy are the most important elements, they are taken as constants because, in the short run, they are not likely to change. This section considers the impact of the short-term forces of candidate image, current party images, and issues within a setting of stable party loyalties.

Candidate Image

The appeal of candidates has been given more attention in recent elections than any other short-term influence. During the past sixty years, national samples have been extensively questioned about likes and dislikes concerning the presidential candidates. During this period, several very popular candidates, such as Republican Dwight Eisenhower and Democrat Lyndon Johnson, had extremely favorable images, and several others, such as Republican Barry Goldwater and Democrat George McGovern, were rejected by the electorate in part on the basis of their personal attributes.

Figure 8-3 displays the mean ratings of presidential candidates since 1968 on the American National Election Studies "feeling thermometer," which asks respondents to rate how "warmly" or favorably they feel toward a candidate on a scale of 0 to 100, with 100 being very warm and 0 being very cold. Perhaps the most prominent feature of this series is its downward trend for the Republican candidates. Democratic candidates experienced something of a downward trend as well until Barack Obama became their candidate in 2008 and again in 2012. Other indicators of candidate image show that the downward trend would be even steeper if elections in the 1950s and early 1960s were included. The disenchantment with government and politics, catalogued in chapter 1, clearly extends to the personal images of the presidential candidates.

In light of subsequent events, it may be surprising how favorably Richard Nixon was viewed in 1968 and 1972 and how relatively unfavorably Ronald Reagan was seen in his initial election of 1980. In recent

FIGURE 8-3   Democratic and Republican Presidential Candidate Feeling Thermometers, 1968–2012

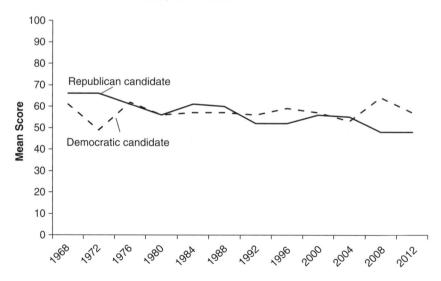

Source: American National Election Studies, available at www.electionstudies.org.

Note: The values in the figure represent "thermometer scores," in which respondents are asked to rate the candidates on a scale of 0 to 100, where 0 is a very negative view and 100 is very positive.

elections, Democratic presidential candidates have been rated slightly more positively than Republican candidates. Obama's mean rating in 2008 was significantly higher than has been the norm for Democratic candidates over the past three decades, but by 2012 he was back to the norm; McCain's rating in 2008 and Romney's in 2012 were on the low end of the evaluations of past Republican candidates.

Throughout its long history, the ANES has asked respondents open-ended questions to ascertain their likes and dislikes about the candidates, giving an idea of the specific content of the candidates' images. These opinions range widely in seriousness—from "he's too old" to "he's dishonest"—but they often give a clear indication of how the candidates are viewed. For example, President George H. W. Bush's reneging on his 1988 campaign promise of "read my lips, no new taxes" showed up as a damaging contributor to his image problem in 1992.

Respondents' comments also illustrate a complication in thinking about the concept of candidate image. For some candidates, the "likes" mentioned often have to do with issues—"I like what he's saying about health care"; "I hate that he got us into Iraq"—feelings quite far removed from the candidate's personality. This was especially true about Bill Clinton's image in both 1992 and 1996. He was not viewed so favorably in personality terms (for example, on his honesty or for his avoidance of military service during Vietnam), but this perception was more than offset by positive comments about his vigorous discussion of issues. Similarly, in 2000 Al Gore drew both unfavorable reactions to his personal style and many favorable comments about his positions on a wide range of issues. In 2004, the most frequent reason given for liking John Kerry was that he wasn't George W. Bush. Clearly, the voter sees more than the personal traits of the candidate when asked for an evaluation, and this complicates the idea of candidate image.

Incumbent presidents face a different situation from challengers in that voters have the previous four years to judge whether the president has been doing a good job or not. If the president is doing a bad job, it doesn't make a lot of sense to put him back in office for another four years. Part of voters' calculus when deciding for whom to vote when an incumbent is running includes an assessment of the president's performance in office. One question asked by many polling organizations and included in the ANES survey is the presidential approval question, which asks if people approve or disapprove of the way the president is handling his job. While presidential approval is not a direct measure of candidate image, it acts as a gauge of the perceived leadership ability of the incumbent president. Since 1972, there have been seven elections in which an incumbent is running for reelection. Of those seven, the incumbent has won reelection five times and lost two times. Table 8-3 shows the presidential approval level in the preelection survey and whether the incumbent won reelection or not.

TABLE 8-3   Presidential Approval and Reelection, 1972–2012

Year	Incumbent president	Approval level	Won/lost reelection
1972	Richard Nixon	65	Won
1976	Gerald Ford*	56	Lost
1980	Jimmy Carter	39	Lost
1984	Ronald Reagan	59	Won
1988	Open seat	57	Incumbent party won
1992	George H. W. Bush	42	Lost
1996	Bill Clinton	68	Won
2000	Open seat	66	Incumbent party lost
2004	George W. Bush	51	Won
2008	Open seat	22	Incumbent party lost
2012	Barack Obama	54	Won

Source: American National Election Studies, available at www.electionstudies.org.

*Gerald Ford became president after Richard Nixon resigned in the aftermath of the Watergate scandal. He ran for election to the presidency for the first time in 1976 but was defeated; 1976 is therefore neither an open-seat election nor a reelection election.

When the incumbent president's approval level dips below 50 percent, the likelihood of winning reelection is slim. Jimmy Carter was originally elected in 1976. When he came up for reelection in 1980, he was associated with both a bad economy and the Iran hostage crisis. With only 39 percent approval, he lost his reelection bid to Ronald Reagan. George H. W. Bush, who had been Ronald Reagan's vice president and won his bid for the presidency in 1988, similarly had to try to get past a struggling economy to be reelected. His approval rating was only 42 percent as the 1992 election approached, and he was defeated by Bill Clinton. These are the only two cases in recent history in which an incumbent ran and lost reelection. All other incumbents have had better approval ratings, including Barack Obama in 2012, who had a 54 percent approval rating. It should be pointed out that the public's image of a president does not automatically revert to the commander in chief's vice president. Bill Clinton's vice president Al Gore sought the Oval Office during an era in which his boss was very popular and the economy was fairly strong. Gore was able to eke out a popular vote victory, but he lost the Electoral College, and the White House. While positive feelings toward a president do not necessarily translate into an open-seat winner from the same party, negative images of a president can wrap themselves around the neck of the party's next presidential candidate. Though John McCain had run against George W. Bush in the 2000 Republican primaries and though he had been an occasional antagonist of President George W. Bush, Democratic candidate Barack Obama tied McCain to Bush every chance he got, helping to link voters unusually negative perceptions of Bush to the McCain candidacy.

Analysts have tried to get at how the electorate evaluates candidates on a more personal level. Every presidential election year, political reporters try to gauge with which candidate people would rather have a beer or with whom they would rather spend casual time. In 2012, ABC News polled voters asking them with whom they would rather have dinner, which candidate they would want to take care of them if they were ill, and which candidate they would want to captain a ship in a storm. Respondents were much more likely to choose Obama for the caregiver role (49 percent Obama, 36 percent Romney) and as a dinner guest (52 percent Obama, 33 percent Romney) and slightly more likely to pick him as the captain of the ship (46 percent Obama, 43 percent Romney).[6] With which candidate people would rather have dinner might seem frivolous—the best dinner date is not necessarily a good president—but candidate image can help people assess what kind of a job the candidates would do in office and if they would understand the needs and concerns of everyday Americans.

On average, presidential candidates score higher on traits associated with their political party. That is, people assume a party's candidate is characterized by the traits they associate with the party. People assume Republican candidates are stronger leaders and more moral, whereas Democratic candidates are assumed to be more compassionate and empathetic.[7] In 2012, the Democratic candidate scored higher than the Republican candidate on all of these traits. The ANES survey asked respondents the extent to which a variety of traits—moral, leadership, caring, knowledgeable, intelligent, and honest—describe the two major presidential candidates. The response options ranged from "not well at all" to "extremely well." Figure 8-4 shows the means for Obama and Romney for each of the traits. Barack Obama received significantly higher trait ratings than Mitt Romney on each of the traits but especially on knowledgeable, intelligent, honest, and caring. Romney had to convince people that he was not an out-of-touch elitist given the news stories about his plans to build a $12 million expansion on his house in California that included a car elevator in the garage, his reluctance to release his tax information, and his comments about the 47 percent who don't pay federal income taxes and are dependent on government.[8] Obama had less to deal with in terms of personality traits and more to deal with in terms of issues, in particular the state of the economy and negative public reactions to health care reform.

FIGURE 8-4   Democratic and Republican Candidate Image, 2012

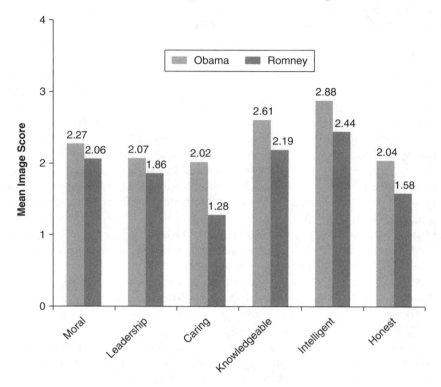

Source: 2012 American National Election Studies, available at www.electionstudies.org.

Note: Candidate image is based on people's assessments of the extent to which Obama and Romney are moral, have leadership qualities, care, are knowledgeable, are intelligent, and are honest.

Part of Obama's advantage came from being the incumbent president. Americans had already had four years to get to know Barack Obama, and they generally liked what they saw, whereas Mitt Romney was much less well known at the beginning of the election season. A major question is whether candidates can manipulate their image to their advantage. That is, do campaign managers come up with an ideal image for their candidate and then create that image in the mind of the American public? It is highly unlikely that candidate image is created and altered at the will of the candidate or campaign manager, and this is especially true for well-established candidates about whom voters are reasonably well informed. Overall, the public's impressions of candidates for major office seem to be realistic, gained primarily through ordinary news coverage. This is not to say that these images are accurate, fair, or sophisticated, but they are not fictitious pictures created by public relations personnel. In 2012, Romney was viewed as able to work in a bipartisan way with Democrats, and this perception was based on the time he was governor of Massachusetts. Romney was also viewed as wealthy, which was also true. There was little he could do about these two perceptions.

Few candidates for other offices are as well-known or as well publicized as candidates for the presidency. Most candidates in most elections are unknown quantities for the average voter. Typically, voters will be aware of the candidate's party affiliation and whether he or she is an incumbent, but not much more. In fact, these pieces of information may come to the voter's attention only if they are indicated on the ballot. Lynn Vavreck has shown that messages candidates promote and images they try to cultivate are the most effective when they coincide with broader, structural forces that shape electoral outcomes (as discussed in chapter 2).[9] For example, having empathy and focusing on economic issues served Bill Clinton well in the 1992 campaign season, which occurred during an economic recession.

Normally, the impact of candidate image on vote choice declines as one goes farther down the ticket to less visible and less well-known offices. This does not mean that the candidate's personal qualities are unimportant in winning election to these offices. They may be of paramount importance in obtaining the nomination or endorsement of the party organization, in raising financial support, in putting together a campaign staff, in performing well in a debate, and in gaining backing from the leadership of influential organizations. But these personal attributes are unlikely to influence the decisions of the average voter simply because the voter is unlikely to be aware of them. What does seem to matter in these low-information races is the order of candidate names on the ballot. Candidates whose names come first on the ballot tend to get more votes than candidates whose names appear further down on the list.[10]

Party Image

The images of the parties are another short-term factor that can influence the voting decisions of the electorate. Even though party images are strongly colored by long-standing party loyalties, the focus of this analysis is a set of potentially variable attitudes toward the parties that can be viewed as short-run forces at work in an election. These attitudes usually have to do with the ability of the parties to manage government, to keep the economy healthy, and to keep the country out of war. Party images also affect and are affected by the images of the candidates running under the party label and by the attitudes toward issues espoused by the candidates or the party platforms. These factors can be kept distinct conceptually, though disentangling the effects may be impossible in any actual situation.

Traditionally, the Republican Party has been viewed as the party best able to keep the country out of war; the Democratic Party held a similar advantage as the party of prosperity. Figure 8-5 shows the trends in these party images in recent years. The Democrats briefly lost their traditional advantage as the party best able to handle the economy in 1994, and the Republicans lost their foreign affairs advantage in 2000 and beyond. The post–September 11 atmosphere has created a paradox. The Republican Party is seen as best able to handle the threat of terrorism, even as it is seen as less able to keep the country out of war. However, about one-third of the electorate does not perceive a difference between the parties on these items.

FIGURE 8-5   Party Better Able to Handle the Nation's Economy and Keep the Country Out of War, 1988–2012

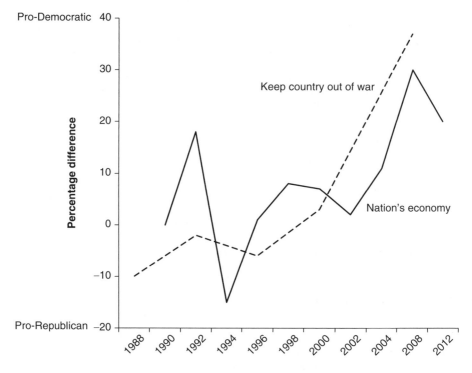

Source: 2012 American National Election Study, available at www.electionstudies.org.

Note: The data points in the figure represent the percentage of respondents answering "Democrats" minus the percentage answering "Republicans."

The role of party images in vote choice has been labeled "retrospective voting" by Morris P. Fiorina, who argued that voters continuously evaluate the performance of the political parties, especially the president's party.[11] Voters use the evaluation of past performance as an indicator of future performance, and they take this retrospective assessment into account when making their vote choices. Because these assessments are likely to involve the performance of the current administration, questions about the incumbent president's handling of certain policy areas have been used as indicators of the extent of retrospective voting. Among incumbents running for reelection in recent years, Bill Clinton came into the 1996 presidential race with fairly positive evaluations of his performance in office. In 2004, George W. Bush's approval ratings offered a mixed bag. His negative ratings on handling the economy and the war in Iraq were offset by positive evaluations of his handling of the threat of terrorism, which was enough of a boost to get him reelected. By 2008, the negative evaluations of the Bush administration had a strong impact on the fortunes of his party's nominee, John McCain. Barack Obama came into 2012 with mixed assessments of his first four years in office but with the Democratic Party's image still stronger than the Republican Party's image on the economy, a key issue coming into the election.

Party images and presidential evaluations are strongly related to partisanship, with partisans more likely to embrace positive images of their party and to reject negative ones than independents or partisans of the opposition. Partisanship and party image are not synonymous, however, because individuals often hold unfavorable perceptions of their party without changing party identification. Yet at some point, negative images of one's own party or positive perceptions of the other party undoubtedly lead to partisan change. One of the difficulties for the Republican Party in 2008 (as well as a complicating factor for the analysis of voting in that year) was that the unpopularity of the Republicans over the last two years of the Bush administration carried with it a slight but noticeable shift along the party identification continuum in the direction of the Democrats—slightly higher numbers of Democrats, including strong Democrats, and slightly fewer Republicans. This Democratic "bump" had disappeared by 2012 when party identification returned to a level more consistent with previous years.

The images of local or state parties may be considerably different from and independent of those of their national counterpart. A state or local party organization may be perceived in different terms from the national party, and many a local or state party has gained a reputation for ineptitude or corruption that did not influence voting decisions for national offices. At the same time, such local images may become increasingly important in voting for offices at lower levels because party labels become a more important identifying characteristic in those races.

Issue Impact

Candidate images and party images may be closely related to issues, and under some circumstances they are indistinguishable. The perception of the stands of candidates and parties on issues is a basis for making vote choices, a basis usually distinct from either personality characteristics or long-standing symbolism. Most significant, candidates can establish issue positions or alter their appeals through their presentation of issues in ways that are not applicable to personal images or party characteristics. In the short run, candidates cannot change their job experience, religion, or party, but they can take new stands on issues or attempt to change the salience of issues. Therefore, candidates can attempt to appeal for votes on the basis of issues.

Over the years, considerable commentary has focused on the rise of single-issue voting. Collections of voters, caring intensely about a particular issue, vote for whichever candidate is closest to their views on that issue, regardless of the candidate's party, personal characteristics, or positions on other issues. There is nothing new about this phenomenon. The classic example of single-issue voting in American politics was abolition, an issue so intense that it destroyed the Whig Party, launched several new parties including the Republican Party, and was a major contributing factor to the Civil War. Abortion is currently an issue that determines the way many people will vote.

Although organizational sophistication and increased opportunities for dissemination of information make single-issue groups a potent force in American politics today, politically ambitious candidates have always searched for issues of this type to help them gain a following. At the same time, incumbent candidates and the broadly based political parties have seen advantages in avoiding or glossing over such issues. Intense concentration on a single issue is potentially divisive and damaging to parties that must appeal to a broad range of voters or to those in office who must cast votes on a wide range of issues. Nevertheless, the political opportunity for the candidate who can capture a group of voters willing to vote on the basis of a single issue or cluster of issues is so great that it is unlikely that any intense concern in the electorate will be long ignored.

Several characteristics of electoral behavior conflict with this description of the role of issues in influencing vote choice. For one thing, in most elections many voters are unaware of the stands candidates take on issues. Voters commonly believe that the candidates they support agree with them on issues. This suggests that voters may project their issue positions onto their favorite candidate more often than they decide to vote for candidates on the basis of their position on issues. Furthermore, when voters agree on issues with the candidate they support, they may have adopted this position merely to agree with their candidate. Candidates and other political leaders frequently perform this function for members of the electorate; they provide issue leadership for their following. Within the enormous range of possible issues at any given time, complete indifference to many is common. Most issues important to political leaders remain in this category for the general public.

The extent to which voters are concerned with issues in making vote choices is a subject of considerable debate.[12] There was a rise in issue voting associated with the election of 1964, when the correlation between attitudes on issues and vote choice peaked in the ideological Johnson/Goldwater campaign, but issue voting remained through 1972 at a considerably higher level than in the "issueless" 1950s.[13] What makes these elections stand out is the clear contrast the candidates offered in their issue positions. If candidates take highly divergent stands on important issues of the day, people will be able to vote on the basis of issues. If, however, candidates' issue stands are quite similar, people will have a difficult time being issue voters. This was the case in the elections of 1988 and 1992.[14] Even if people don't vote on the basis of candidates' issue stands, they could vote using the heuristic, or shortcut, of party issue image. Candidates and their issue stands come and go and are more or less transparent, but the reputations parties develop within certain issue areas can easily be used by voters when determining which party's candidate is likely to pursue which policy areas. When people have low information about the candidates' issue stands, they can be issue voters indirectly by voting for the candidate whose party's issue positions come closest to their own.[15] Benjamin Highton has found that candidate issue contrast has a much bigger impact on vote choice from election to election than party issue contrast, but both play a role in elections.[16]

In 2012, as in most years, a strong relationship existed between a variety of issues and the vote for president. We quickly examine a handful of issues that were relevant to the presidential election. A major issue that has divided the two major parties for many decades is the extent to which government spending and services should be increased or decreased. As Figure 8-6 shows, those who favored increasing governmental services and spending voted overwhelmingly for Obama over Romney, and those who favored decreasing services and spending preferred Romney over Obama by an even greater margin.

On another domestic issue—whether the government should help blacks versus letting blacks help themselves, shown in Figure 8-7—Obama voters were fairly evenly distributed across the issue, with many of his supporters placing themselves in the middle of the scale. Romney voters, on the other hand, overwhelmingly supported the position that blacks should help themselves. Over 60 percent of Romney voters placed themselves at 6 or 7, the end of the scale supporting the position that

FIGURE 8-6   Presidential Vote and Attitude toward Government Services, 2012

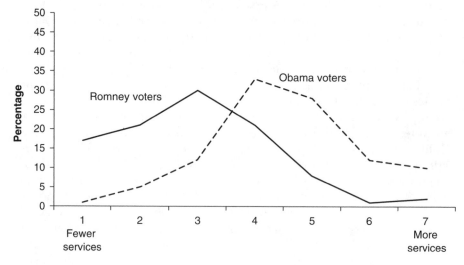

Source: 2012 American National Election Study, available at www.electionstudies.org.

FIGURE 8-7   Presidential Vote and Attitude toward Government Help for Blacks, 2012

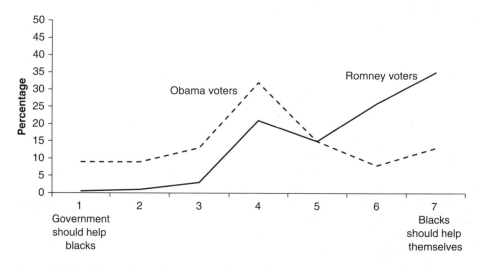

Source: 2012 American National Election Study, available at www.electionstudies.org.

blacks should help themselves. Only 1.5 percent placed themselves at 1 or 2, that government should provide help for African Americans. If one looks at this relationship only among white voters, the relationship remains very strong.

Because both these issues deal with themes that have long divided the parties, it is not surprising that substantial relationships exist between holding a certain view and supporting a particular candidate. The issue of abortion has not always been so closely related to vote choice. The strong relationship found in 2012 and shown in Figure 8-8, also true in 2000, 2004, and 2008, suggests increasing polarization between the major parties on social issues. Romney's supporters were more likely to be on the pro-life side of the issue, although almost 30 percent of his supporters were pro-choice; Obama voters were overwhelmingly on the pro-choice side. Respondents taking the two moderate positions on the abortion issue divided in Romney's favor.

One of the questions asked in the 2012 ANES was whether people thought global warming was mostly caused by human activity, mostly the effect of natural causes, or an equal combination of the two. Figure 8-9 shows the partisan split between Obama and Romney voters on this issue. Fewer than one in ten Obama voters pointed solely to natural causes and fewer than two in ten Romney voters pointed to human activity. Most voters, whether for Obama or Romney, pointed to a combination of causes, but when they made a choice, Obama voters were much more likely to view global warming as the outcome of human activity, whereas Romney voters were more likely to view global warming as a natural occurrence.

Two issues were at the forefront of the 2012 election. One of these was the state of the economy. As explained in Chapter 2, economic conditions are highly correlated with presidential election results and midterm election results in congressional contests. People naturally want the economy to be strong and for whoever is elected to the presidency to make sound decisions that will lead to or shore up a healthy economy.

FIGURE 8-8   Presidential Vote and Attitude toward Abortion, 2012

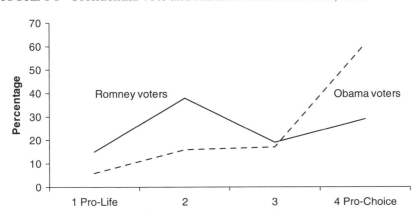

Source: 2012 American National Election Study, available at www.electionstudies.org.

FIGURE 8-9   Presidential Vote and Attitude toward the Cause of Global Warming, 2012

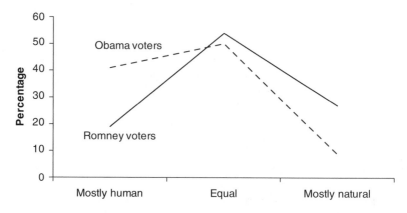

Source: 2012 American National Election Study, available at www.electionstudies.org.

Both of the major party candidates must work to convince voters that they will increase jobs, keep inflation in check, and increase economic growth if they are elected. Guessing what might happen in the future is obviously largely based on speculation, but when an incumbent is running for reelection, voters have more information on which to base their decision. Presidents tend to be held responsible, or at least partially responsible, for the state of the economy. When the economy is strong, people are more likely to reward the incumbent president with reelection. When the economy is weak, on the other hand, punishing the president at the polls is an obvious option people can readily take.[17]

In 2012, Americans were fairly evenly divided in their perception of the state of the economy. About one-third thought the economy was worse off than one year earlier, about one-third thought it had stayed about the same, and about one-third thought it was better off. Figure 8-10 shows that these perceptions had a strong impact on vote choice. Almost 9 out of 10 Americans who thought the economy was better off voted for Barack Obama, compared to only 19 percent who thought the economy was worse off. Mitt Romney did best among those who thought the economy was worse off, getting 81 percent of those voters. People who thought the economy had stayed about the same over the previous year were almost evenly divided between the two candidates.

The second major issue in the 2012 election was the Affordable Health Care Act of 2010, known as Obamacare. Health care reform was one of Obama's major accomplishments in his first term, but the legislation was highly controversial. Republicans in Congress tried to get the act repealed, and Republican candidates running in 2012 took aim at

FIGURE 8-10   Presidential Vote and Perceptions of the National Economy, 2012

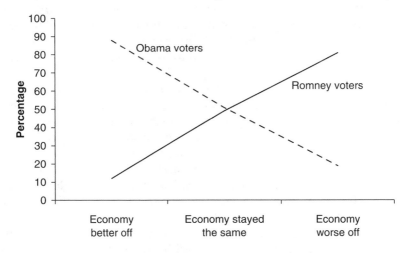

Source: 2012 American National Election Study, available at www.electionstudies.org.

Obamacare. Mitt Romney came out strongly opposed to Obamacare, but he faced questions about his support for health care reform in Massachusetts when he was governor. Figure 8-11 shows the strong relationship between support for Obamacare and presidential vote choice. Almost half of Romney supporters (48 percent) opposed the 2010 health care law a great deal, and almost as many Obama supporters (44 percent) favored it a great deal. Democratic and Republican voters also differed in

FIGURE 8-11   Presidential Vote and Attitude toward the 2010 Health Care Law, 2012

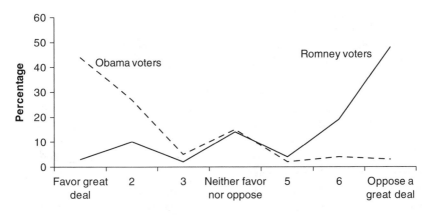

Source: 2012 American National Election Study, available at www.electionstudies.org.

their assessment of the impact of the health care law. ANES asked respondents if, after the health care law is fully implemented, they think the law will have improved, worsened, or had no effect on the quality of health care services in the United States. Eighty percent of Romney voters said the quality of health care services will have worsened, whereas 69 percent of Obama voters said it will have improved.

Figure 8-12 looks at vote choice in a somewhat different manner by illustrating the electorate's perceptions of the ideological positions of Obama and Romney, as well as the relationship between the voters' own ideological positions and their vote choices between the two candidates. In the 2012 ANES survey, voters were asked to locate each candidate on a seven-point scale ranging from "extremely liberal" to "extremely conservative." In Figure 8-12 the frequency distributions in the lower half of the chart illustrate the voters' perceptions of the two candidates' ideological positions. For example, 24 percent of the respondents labeled Obama as extremely liberal and only 3 percent labeled him as extremely conservative; 17 percent placed Romney in the most extreme conservative position. Most voters placed Obama on the liberal and Romney on the conservative ends of the scale.

Voters were also asked about their own ideological position using the same seven-point scale. The distributions in the upper half of Figure 8-12 indicate the self-placements of those who voted for Obama and Romney. They show that Romney drew most of his support from conservative voters, and Obama received most of his from liberals. Obama also gained a greater share of the votes of those in the middle of the ideological spectrum. Figure 8-12 also reinforces a point we made earlier: The electorate sees itself as more middle-of-the-road but views the leaders of the respective parties as more ideologically extreme.

A number of factors must be present for issues to have an impact on vote choice. First, voters must be informed and concerned about an issue; second, candidates must take distinguishable stands on an issue; and third, voters must perceive the candidates' stands in relation to their own. These conditions often are not achieved. Voters may be unable to locate themselves or the candidates on one or more issues. In 2012, 13 percent of Americans had no opinion on the issue of cutting government services and spending versus increasing government spending and services. Three percent were unable to locate the position of Obama on this issue, and 8 percent could not locate the position of Romney. Similar proportions of the electorate could not locate themselves or the candidates on the issue of government help for blacks. Voters may also misperceive the candidates' positions. For example, a few voters viewed Obama as an extreme conservative or Romney as an extreme liberal, although most perceptions appeared accurate.

FIGURE 8-12   Vote for President according to Voters' Ideological Identification and Perceptions of the Candidates' Ideology, 2012

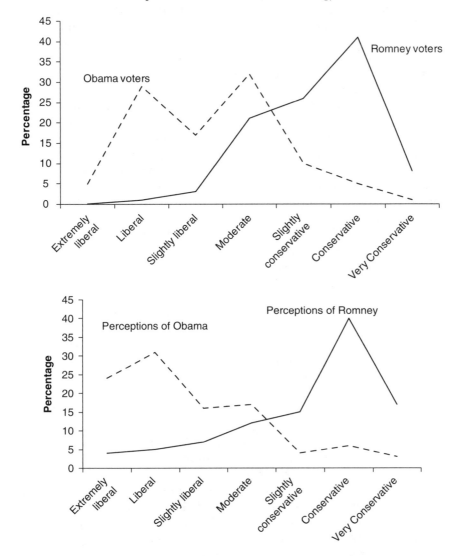

Source: 2012 American National Election Study, available at www.electionstudies.org.

A weak relationship between an individual's issue positions and vote choice may result from the fact that the analyst chooses the issues for analysis, and these might be issues that are not important to the individual. A person who votes on the basis of agriculture policy but is never asked about this issue in a survey will appear not to be an issue voter when she actually is one. If voters are allowed to define what they see as the most important issue, a somewhat stronger relationship between their position on issues and voting decisions is found.[18] Another problem with the generic approach to issue voting is that candidates are strategic actors who play up (or try to ignore) certain issues if doing so will win votes. Lynn Vavreck found that incumbent party candidates talk a lot about the economy when it is strong, whereas challengers talk a lot about the economy when it is weak. It is strategically advantageous for both sides to do so.[19] Candidates even pivot toward or away from these kinds of positions during presidential debates. [20]

This analysis also does not reveal what causes these relationships. Positions on issues may cause an individual's vote choice. Alternatively, a preference for a candidate on other grounds may lead individuals to adjust their positions on issues in support of their vote choice. Analysts have tried to resolve this question, but it has been impossible to do so conclusively. Regardless of the causal relationship, it is significant that although many voters lack opinions on issues or on the candidates' positions, those who do have opinions show considerable consistency between issue positions and vote choice.

Determinants of Vote Choice

The preceding sections considered candidate images, party images, and issues as short-term forces that either reinforce or deflect voters from their long-term party loyalty. An interesting, but far more difficult, question is the relative impact of these factors on vote choice. Because all these factors are strongly interrelated and almost certainly all influence each other, disentangling their effects using the kinds of data available in nationwide surveys is virtually impossible. If one assumes that issues are all-important in determining vote choice, most voting behavior can be accounted for by issues alone, ignoring other factors. However, if one assumes that party identification and a few social characteristics are all-important, most voting behavior can be accounted for with these variables, ignoring issues. The conflicting conclusions that are reached are largely a matter of the theoretical assumptions with which one starts.

In Table 8-4, we offer an analysis of the determinants of the choice between Obama and Romney in 2012. For simplicity, we consider nine possible factors influencing vote choice reflecting the important impacts on vote choice discussed above. We include party identification and ideology as long-term forces. We also include candidate image and issues as short-term forces. The first column of the table shows the odds ratios, which basically indicate the probability of voting for Obama or

Romney given that variable while holding everything else equal. Odds ratios over 1 show a net gain for Obama, and odds ratios under 1 show a net gain for Romney. We show the net shift of votes in the last two columns to indicate the increased probability of voting for Obama or Romney given the odds ratios. The only two variables that didn't have a significant impact on vote choice were attitudes about government services and spending and government help in ensuring the fair treatment of blacks. We therefore did not compute the net shift in votes for these two variables.

Table 8-4 shows that party identification and ideology benefited Romney. As we saw earlier in Table 8-1, partisans tended to vote for their party's candidate. When holding all of the other variables in Table 8-4 equal, moving one unit on party identification (from Democrat to independent or from independent to Republican) increased the odds of voting for Romney by 1.7. For example, independents were 1.7 times more likely than Democrats to vote for Romney. Ideology had

TABLE 8-4   Determinants of Presidential Vote Choice, Barack Obama versus Mitt Romney, 2012

| | | Net shift of votes | |
	Odds ratio	Pro-Obama	Pro-Romney
Party identification	0.59		1.7
Ideological identification	0.38		2.6
Obama's handling of the job of the presidency	2.93	2.9	
Obama's candidate image	1.19	1.2	
Romney's candidate image	0.84		1.2
Policy positions			
Fewer government services and spending	1.11		
Less government help for blacks	0.86		
Support 2010 health care law	1.39	1.4	
Perception of the state of the economy	2.73	2.7	

Source: 2012 American National Election Study, available at www.electionstudies.org.

Note: The odds ratios are used to represent the strength and direction of the relationship between each variable and presidential vote choice controlling for the other variables. These variables correctly predict 95 percent of the votes.

an even bigger impact than party identification. Moderates were 2.6 times more likely than liberals to vote for Romney. Party identification and, to a lesser extent, ideology are good long-term predictors of vote choice. In 2012, Romney benefited from the votes of independents and moderates.

Candidate image also had an impact on vote choice in 2012, although neither candidate had an advantage in this realm. A one-unit increase in Romney's leadership image increased the likelihood people would vote for him by 1.2, which is the same boost Obama got from having a more positive image. Overall, Obama's image was more positive than Romney's image. The candidate image scales range from 0 (extremely negative image) to 24 (extremely positive image). The mean on Obama's image scale was 14 compared to 11.5 on Romney's image scale. Nonetheless, the more people thought either candidate was moral, a good leader, caring, honest, knowledgeable, and intelligent, the more likely they were to vote for him.

Obama was helped a great deal by his presidential approval ratings. People who were slightly approving of Obama's job performance were 2.9 times more likely to vote for him than people who were slightly disapproving. The strength of this retrospective assessment makes sense; the best way to predict how a president will perform in office is to look at how he did in his previous four years. The more people approved of the job Obama had already done, the more likely they were to vote him in for another four years.

The impact of issues on people's vote choice depends heavily on the issue. Table 8-4 shows that the traditional issues of government spending and help for African Americans did not play much of a role in 2012. The two issues discussed extensively throughout the campaign— the state of the economy and Obamacare—had big impacts on vote choice, especially the former. People who thought the economy had stayed about the same over the past year were 2.7 times more likely to vote for Obama than were those thought the economy had gotten worse. Obama benefited greatly from the slight boost in the economy that occurred prior to the election. If the economy had been getting worse, it is likely Obama would have been a one-term president. The president also benefited from his health care reform law passed in 2010, although to a much lesser extent than the boost he received from the improved economy. People who were neutral toward Obamacare were 1.4 times more likely to vote for Obama than those who slightly opposed it. The state of the economy and the health care reform law were the only two issues included in Table 8-4 that had an impact on people's vote choice. Not coincidentally, these were the issues that received the most air time during the election year. The more issues are played up in a campaign, the more people use those issues when deciding for whom to vote.

The Popular Vote and the Electoral College

One aspect of the American electoral system that often raises questions is the Electoral College. If one requirement of a democracy is a reasonably faithful translation of popular votes into governmental control, then the Electoral College is a potential impediment to democracy. Americans' presidential vote choices do not necessarily determine the outcome of the election.

Under the constitutional system adopted in 1787 and amended in 1804, the president is selected by the Electoral College, with each state having electoral votes equal to the combined seats that it has in the U.S. House of Representatives and Senate. Voters cast a ballot for one or the other party's presidential and vice presidential nominees. Legally, however, the voter is casting a ballot for that party's slate of electors, which was certified months before by the party's formal submission of the slate to a state official. The electors of the winning party in each state meet in their respective state capitals on the Monday following the second Wednesday in December and cast their votes for president and vice president. Almost without exception they respect their pledge and vote for their party's nominees. A majority of the electoral votes is required to elect a president—270 electoral votes at this time.

In 2000, for the first time in more than one hundred years, the Electoral College chose a president who was not the winner of the popular vote. Al Gore won the popular vote and George W. Bush won the Electoral College vote. In 2004, the possibility loomed again, although it did not happen—in part because of Republican strategists' efforts to mobilize extra voters in safe Republican states to prevent a second popular vote loss for Bush. In a system that purports to be a democracy, it is a significant occurrence when the candidate with fewer votes is declared the winner. To understand how the Electoral College could produce a winner who is not the popular vote winner, it is important to remember that all states (except Maine and Nebraska) use a winner-take-all procedure for deciding who wins the states' electoral votes. In other words, it does not matter whether a candidate wins the state narrowly or by a wide margin—all of the electoral votes go to the winner. If one candidate wins many states narrowly and the other candidate wins states by a wide margin, the first candidate can win in the Electoral College while the second candidate can have more popular votes. Usually the second candidate is said to have wasted votes by winning by a larger margin than needed to carry the state.

In 2000, Gore won by large margins in a number of big states such as California and New York, accumulating a huge number of popular votes, while Bush won some big states, such as Florida, narrowly. In 2000, another factor was at work to a degree. Bush won a large share of the small states, in which the two electoral votes assigned to every state to represent their seats in the U.S. Senate create something of a bonus. If turnout is comparable, each electoral vote in a small state represents fewer voters than in a large state. In 2000, each electoral vote in Wyoming represented seventy thousand popular votes, and in California each electoral vote represented more than 200,000 popular votes.

Although only rarely does the Electoral College produce a winner who has not won the popular vote, the consequences of a winner-take-all system are well known to campaign strategists in presidential elections. The Electoral College arrangement strongly influences presidential campaign strategy. The closer the expected margin in a state and the larger the number of electoral votes available, the more resources the campaigns will put in the state and the more aggressively the candidates will attempt to respond to the political interests in the state. These are the battleground states, where both candidates have a chance to win and much is at stake. In contrast, safe states are relatively unimportant to both candidates in a general election campaign—taken for granted by one and written off by the other—although they may be visited by one or both candidates to raise funds to spend in competitive states. The 2000 presidential election was deceptive in making every state appear crucial because the result was so close, but in fact, a winning strategy in this and other presidential elections calls for slighting most states. This strategy clearly played out in both 2008 and especially 2012, as can be seen in Figure 8-13, which shows the states where ads were aired. Television ads supporting Obama or Romney were almost exclusively aired in the swing states. States that were safe for one candidate or the other were virtually, if not completely, ignored.[21]

In retrospect, it may seem odd that the founders created such a peculiar scheme for selecting a president. Their main concern was to devise a method for selecting the president that would result in the selection of George Washington as the first president. The allocation of electoral votes simply combined the state representation in the Senate and the House of Representatives, an easy decision after the Great Compromise had been reached. In the context of the Constitutional Convention, the Electoral College had another virtue: it treated the states as they viewed themselves—as sovereign entities. In the current climate, retaining the states as meaningful units in a federal system is one rationale for maintaining the Electoral College.

The fact that the Electoral College was extremely indirect democracy was not a concern for the founders; most of them were wary of too much democracy and approved the idea of state legislatures selecting the electors. The founders did not anticipate the emergence of political parties that quickly changed the process of selecting electors into a completely partisan endeavor. By 1824, most state legislatures had turned the selection process over to the public to avoid the political hassle.

FIGURE 8-13   The Strategic Placing of Ads in Swing States, 2008 and 2012

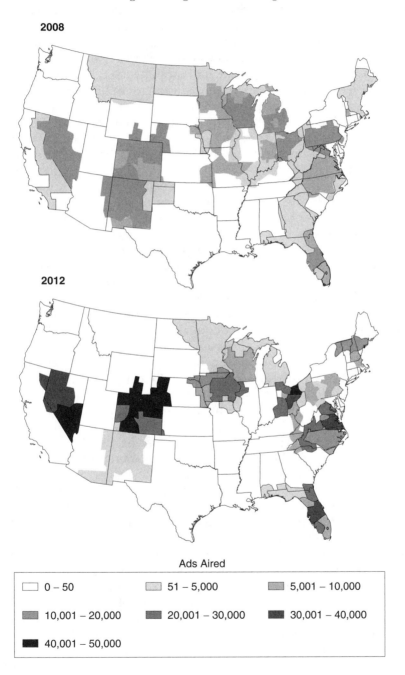

2008

2012

Ads Aired

☐ 0 – 50	◻ 51 – 5,000	▨ 5,001 – 10,000
▨ 10,001 – 20,000	▨ 20,001 – 30,000	▨ 30,001 – 40,000
■ 40,001 – 50,000		

Source: Wesleyan Media Project, http://mediaproject.wesleyan.edu/2012/10/24/2012-shatters-2004-and-2008-records-for-total-ads-aired/#more-2150.

Over the years, proposals have been put forth to change or abandon the Electoral College.[22] Some proposals are modest, such as getting rid of the slate of electors (who occasionally do not vote the way they are pledged) and have the secretary of state simply certify each state's electoral votes. Proponents of greater change have resisted this proposal, though in itself noncontroversial, for fear that adopting it would reduce the incentive to make more substantial changes in the system.

The most sweeping proposal, and the one most commonly discussed by political commentators, would be electing the president in a nationwide popular election and getting rid of the Electoral College. This is an obvious alternative method of selecting the president, answering the main criticism of the Electoral College—the potential that the popular vote winner is not the Electoral College winner. A nationwide popular election, however, has problems of its own. It is generally believed that a national popular election would attract more and more candidates—third-party candidates, independent candidates, and major-party candidates who failed to get their party's nomination. Candidates with a small but crucial constituency could threaten to take votes away from the major-party nominees as a way to win concessions. But presumably more candidates would stay in the race to demonstrate their strength, so gradually the percentage of the vote needed to win would shrink. The popular vote winner could have 35 percent or 25 percent of the total vote, and arguably this would undermine the legitimacy of the winner. As a consequence, most proposals for a national popular election have included provisions for a run-off election if the winner's percentage was below, say, 40 percent. The prospect of two presidential elections and the political maneuvering associated with run-off elections has reduced enthusiasm for making such a change.

The current interest in adopting an "instant run-off" in some local elections offers a possible solution. Under instant run-off arrangements, if there are more than two candidates in a race, voters rank their preferences among them. When the votes are counted, the candidate with the fewest number of votes is eliminated and the second choices of the voters who voted for the eliminated candidate are then counted and added to those candidates' totals. This process is continued until one candidate has a majority (50 percent plus one) of all votes cast. Such a system would produce a majority winner without a run-off. There are a number of objections and potential problems with instant run-off, some of which may become apparent when it is adopted in local elections around the country. If it proves workable, however, it might answer some of the perennial concerns about a direct popular vote for president.

Two other proposals have been advanced that would not require a constitutional amendment, although a constitutional amendment would be required to adopt them uniformly across the country. The district method, now used in Maine and Nebraska, allows two electors to be selected statewide and the remainder to be selected within congressional districts. The proposal does not eliminate the winner-take-all characteristic, but it does allow for a distribution of electoral votes that is more reflective of the popular vote. Maine has never divided its Electoral College vote in the 40 years it has had the congressional district system. Nebraska, which has five electoral votes, has divided its votes only once since the congressional district system was put in place in 1991. In 2008, John McCain won the popular vote in two congressional districts and in the state as a whole. Barack Obama won the popular vote in the 2nd congressional district. McCain therefore won four of Nebraska's electoral votes and Obama one electoral vote. Some Republicans in the Nebraska state legislature, unhappy with this outcome, have introduced legislation to go back to the winner-take-all system but have been unsuccessful thus far in getting this legislation passed. The state legislature's efforts at redistricting that took place after the 2010 Census added several thousand Republicans to the congressional district that Obama won in 2008, contributing to Obama's losing the district in 2012 to Mitt Romney.

The proportional method would allocate all of the electoral votes on a statewide basis, but through proportional representation instead of to the plurality winner. Given the typical margin of victory in the popular vote in a state, a winning candidate would be unlikely to gain more than a one-vote electoral margin from a state using proportional representation. No individual state is likely to adopt this method because, with only one electoral vote at stake, it would become the least attractive state in the nation for presidential candidates to campaign in.

For years, political scientists and some political commentators predicted that the Electoral College would be immediately abandoned if, in the modern age, it produced a nonpopular vote winner. Why, then, has so little happened to jettison the Electoral College since the 2000 election? One would think Democrats would have pushed hard to change the Electoral College system given their candidate's loss in 2000. Instead of focusing on Electoral College reform, however, Democrats pushed for reforms to take care of more pressing issues that came to the surface in the 2000 election—notably ballot type and vote-counting procedures. The 2000 election also raised questions about the viability of a nationwide popular vote. After the debacle of the Florida recount, the possibility of a nationwide recount became highly unattractive.

What movement there has been in the area of Electoral College reform has come not from Democrats but from Republicans in some of the swing states. In 2012, Barack Obama won both the popular and the Electoral College vote, receiving 51 percent of the popular vote and 332 electoral votes to Mitt Romney's 47 percent of the popular vote and 206 electoral votes. Obama won in six states that have both a Republican governor and a state legislature controlled by Republicans: Michigan, Wisconsin, Ohio, Pennsylvania, Florida, and Virginia. If these six states used the congressional district system used by Maine and Nebraska, Obama would have won with 270 electoral votes to Romney's 268. A plan discussed in Virginia would have distributed the two at-large votes not to the state's popular vote winner but to the candidate who won the most congressional districts. If all six states used this modified congressional district system, Romney would have won 280 electoral votes and the presidency while losing the popular vote. The Virginia legislature voted against adopting the modified plan, and some Republicans have questioned trying to game the Electoral College system for electoral advantage. Republican Speaker of the Florida House William Weatherford said, "To me, that's like saying in a football game, 'We should have only three quarters, because we were winning after three quarters and they beat us in the fourth.' I don't think we need to change the rules of the game, I think we need to get better."[23]

State legislatures are reluctant to change Electoral College rules because a rule change that benefits the majority party one year could end up hurting the party in a following year. Most people agree that the Electoral College system has major problems, including electing the less popular candidate, but there is no agreement on a clean fix, and the two major parties do not want to alter the system in a way that will hurt their party in the future.

Vote Choice in Other Types of Elections

Vote choice can be thought of as the product of a voter's long-term partisanship and the impact of the campaign's short-term forces of candidate characteristics, evaluation of the party's performance, and issue positions. In presidential elections, in which information about the candidates and issues is widespread and easily available, short-term forces often overcome partisanship and cause substantial numbers of voters to defect from a party. In less prominent races, voters make choices with less information and fewer factors influencing their decisions.

In voting for members of Congress, most of the electorate has relatively little information about the candidates, especially candidates challenging incumbents. Party-line voting becomes stronger for less visible offices, including Congress, because issues and personal attributes of the candidates are less likely to have an impact on the voter in less publicized races.

Another significant factor in congressional elections is incumbency. Studies have shown that voters are about twice as likely to be able to identify the incumbent as the challenger in congressional races, and almost all the defections from partisanship are in favor of the more familiar incumbent.[24] Both Republicans and Democrats seem strongly susceptible to voting for incumbents, with more than one-third typically abandoning their usual party for an incumbent representative of the other party. Strong partisans of both parties frequently defect to incumbents of the other party but, on balance, support the challengers from their own party more often than not. Both Democratic and Republican weak partisans, in contrast, are more likely to defect for incumbents than to vote for challengers from their own party.

The advantage that incumbents have does not mean that congressional districts are invariably safe for one party, though many are. Instead, it suggests that even in those districts in which the outcome is virtually a toss-up when two nonincumbents face each other, the representatives who manage to survive a term or two find reelection almost ensured. This tendency becomes accentuated as the opposition party finds it increasingly difficult to field an attractive candidate to challenge a secure incumbent. Thus, many incumbent representatives are elected again and again by safe margins from districts that may fall to the other party once the incumbent no longer seeks reelection. Put another way, the existence of a safe incumbent in a district may say little about the underlying partisan division in that district. It may simply reflect short-term forces that were at work in the last election in which two nonincumbents faced each other.

A Senate election has relatively high visibility and, unlike most congressional races, is amenable to a mass media campaign using television. The more information about the election that gets through to the voters, the less they rely on either partisanship or the familiarity of the incumbent's name. The visibility of a Senate race makes an incumbent senator vulnerable to a well-financed campaign by an attractive opponent. Incumbency may even become a disadvantage in such circumstances, because the incumbent has a voting record to defend.

Despite the advantages of incumbency, national electoral tides can make enough of a difference in enough districts to change the balance of power in one or both houses of Congress. The elections of 2006 and 2008 saw such nationwide tides in favor of the Democrats, significantly increasing the Democratic numbers in both the House and Senate. Especially noteworthy is that these Democratic tides occurred in successive elections. Usually, an electoral sweep brings into the House narrow winners in marginal districts who are vulnerable to defeat in the next election. The nationwide tides swept in with a vengeance, though, in the elections of 2010.

In the midterm House elections of 2010, the Democrats lost a whopping 63 seats and their majority in the House, dropping from 256 seats to only 193 seats. A total of 54 incumbents lost reelection that year, and only two of them were Republicans. Even with this turnover, it was much safer to be an incumbent than not. Just under nine out of ten House incumbents (86 percent) won reelection to the House. But the people hit the hardest by the shifting tides were freshman Democrats who had first been elected in 2008. Only 44 percent of the freshman Democrats running for reelection in 2010 won, compared to 92 percent of freshman Republicans. Democrats did not do well in open seats either. While only 15 of 43 open seats changed party hands (with the rest going to the same party that had held the seat previously), all but one of the 15 changed from a Democratic to a Republican seat. Democrats picked up only one open seat.

In the 2010 Senate elections, Democrats lost six seats, dropping from 57 to 51, but they maintained their majority. Overall, Senate incumbents did quite well in 2010, winning 91 percent of the time. Two incumbent Democrats lost reelection: Democrat Blanche Lincoln of Arkansas lost to Republican John Boozman and Democrat Russ Feingold of Wisconsin lost to Republican Ron Johnson. Of the four open seats that changed party hands, all switched from the Democratic to the Republican Party.

Given the volatility of the past three midterm elections and given the large number of freshman representatives in the House, 2012 could have continued the tidal waves. Instead, 2012 was a quiet year for members of Congress running for reelection. The Democrats gained eight seats in the House, increasing their number of seats to 201 but not coming anywhere near the Republicans' 234 seats. Only 27 incumbents were defeated (10 Democrats and 17 Republicans), in five cases to someone in their own party due to redistricting. Some congressional districts were drawn so that an incumbent had to run against an incumbent. Open seat switches were evenly divided between Democrats and Republicans. In the Senate, Democrats gained only two seats, increasing their majority to 53. Republicans picked up an open seat in Nebraska but lost a seat in both Massachusetts (incumbent Republican Scott Brown lost to Democrat Elizabeth Warren) and Maine (Republican Olympia Snowe retired and independent Angus King won the election). Democrats won a seat in Connecticut when independent Joe Lieberman retired and Democrat Chris Murphy won the seat.

When people are asked if they approve or disapprove of the job Congress is doing, only about 15 percent say they approve. Nearly four out of five Americans say they disapprove. When asked about the job being done by Democrats or Republicans in Congress, the percentage approving goes up (about one-third approve of the job the Democrats are doing and about one-quarter approve of the job the Republicans are doing), but a vast majority disapprove.[25] Americans clearly do not like what Congress is doing, and it would make perfect sense to "throw the rascals out." Instead, 90 percent of representatives running for reelection to the House and 91 percent of senators running for reelection to the Senate won their races in 2012.[26] Why are so many members of Congress reelected when people are so dissatisfied with Congress? Richard Fenno, Jr., has pointed out the interesting paradox that people hate Congress but love their own member of Congress. Members of Congress take great pains to make sure their constituents are happy, including cultivating trust and being seen as "one of us."[27] John Hibbing and Elizabeth Theiss-Morse questioned what it is about Congress that people hate. They found that most Americans approve of Congress as an institution (88 percent) but are highly disapproving of the members of Congress, the 435 House members and the 100 Senators. Only 24 percent approved of the members of Congress.[28] People might like their own representative and senators, although even this has declined in recent years, but they heartily dislike the other members of Congress. They are limited, though, in only being able to vote for or against their own representatives. This helps explain why reelection rates remain so high even though people are so thoroughly disgusted with Congress.

The Meaning of an Election

Politicians and news commentators spend much time and energy interpreting and explaining the outcome of an election. The difficulties in assigning meaning to election results are easy to exaggerate. The most important element is usually clear—the winner. Elections are primarily a mechanism for selecting certain governmental leaders and, just as important, for removing leaders from office and preventing others from gaining office. Nevertheless, an effort is often made to discover the policy implications of patterns of voting and to read meaning into the outcome of elections. This effort raises two problems for analysis: first, the issue content of the voters' decisions and, second, the policy implications of the winning and losing candidates' issue stands.

It is very difficult to establish that the voters' preferences have certain policy meanings or that the votes for a particular candidate provide a policy mandate. After all, people do not vote for "Obama, pro-choice, and opposed to the tax increase on the wealthy." The only information they provide is the vote they cast for a particular candidate and not why they voted that way. Several obstacles lie in the way of stating simply what policies are implied by the behavior of the voters. In many elections, the voters are unaware of the candidates' stands on issues, and sometimes the voters are mistaken in their perceptions. Furthermore, many voters are not concerned with issues as such in a campaign but vote according to their party loyalty or a candidate's personality. Their votes have no particular policy significance but reflect a general preference for one candidate. And as John Sides points out, voters "choose a candidate based on party or whatever, and then line up their views on issues to match the candidates."[29] Voters who supported Reagan in 1980 had an unfavorable view of Carter's performance as president, especially his handling of the Iranian hostage crisis. The dissatisfaction with Carter was clear enough. However, the expectations about Reagan were vague and perhaps limited to the hope that he would strengthen national defense and balance the budget. Reagan's supporters came around to support his issues but not liking Carter and liking Reagan were the bigger drivers behind people's votes in 1980. In 2012, having an incumbent in the race meant that voters could base their votes on major policy initiatives of the Obama administration. People who liked Obamacare and wanted to see this health care law implemented by the Obama administration could cast their vote for the president. Those opposed to the health care reform could vote for Romney. As noted above, this is precisely what many voters did. Three-quarters of Obama voters (76 percent) supported his health care reform and almost as many Romney voters (71 percent) opposed it. But as we discussed earlier, voters were influenced not just by the health care issue; they were also heavily influenced by party identification, Obama's job approval, and the state of the economy.

The extent to which mandates occur depends more heavily on politicians than on voters.[30] Candidates run on certain policy stands, but the vote is a blunt instrument that leaves it unclear what the voters intended. Newly elected presidents, especially those who win decisively, play up the idea that the voters gave them a mandate to pursue their policy interests. Presidents quickly push their policy agenda in Congress, usually trying to get as much done as possible in the first one hundred days, because it is during this period that members of Congress are still trying to figure out what message the voters were sending. When members of Congress perceive election returns to be significant, they are willing to change their voting behavior to go along with the new president's agenda. This does not happen often—clear cases are Lyndon B. Johnson's election in 1964 and his Great Society policy agenda, Ronald Reagan's election in 1980 and the subsequent Reagan Revolution, and the 1994 congressional elections putting in place the

Contract With America—but when it does, policy changes are dramatic. The window of opportunity is narrow and most elections are not perceived to be significant, but at times mandates do happen. Did a mandate happen in 2012? There is no evidence to support a mandate interpretation of the election. Americans were deeply divided in their candidate choice and issue stands. Even as they agreed that the economy was the number-one problem facing the nation, they disagreed over what needed to be done.

One factor that can help new presidents is their popularity with the general public. Presidents can use their popularity to let members of Congress know what a mistake it would be to vote against their policy agendas. Presidents tend to get a boost in their approval ratings right after an election, and President Obama was no exception. As Figure 8-14 shows, Obama's approval ratings were in the mid-40s until September when he got a small bump. This bump lasted through his swearing in for his second term and through February of 2013. By March, however, Obama's approval had dropped to the upper 40s, and by June it was back to its preelection level.

On the one hand, American elections are hardly a classic model of democracy with rational, well-informed voters making dispassionate

FIGURE 8-14   President Obama's Approval Ratings, January 2012–June 2013

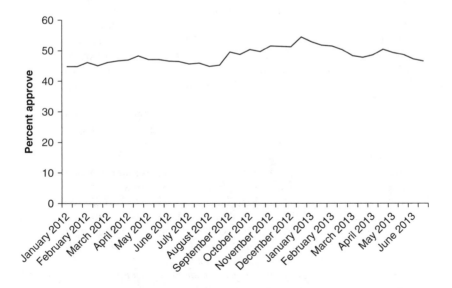

Source: Gallup Poll Daily Job Approval, http://www.gallup.com/poll/113980/Gallup-Daily-Obama-Job-Approval.aspx.

decisions. On the other hand, American elections provide an acceptable opportunity for parties and candidates to attempt to win or hold public office. Despite the polarization of the political elite and political activists, a sizable portion of the electorate is moderate or unconcerned about ideology and lacking in firm partisan attachments. For the present at least, this segment of the electorate holds the key to electoral victory. The political parties, their officeholders, and their candidates ignore this situation at their peril.

Notes

1. Angus Campbell, Philip E. Converse, Warren E. Miller, and Donald E. Stokes, *The American Voter* (New York: Wiley, 1960), chap. 2.
2. Karen R. Humes, Nicholas A. Jones, and Roberto R. Ramirez, "Overview of Race and Hispanic Origin: 2010," United States Census Bureau (March 2011), http://www.census.gov/prod/cen2010/briefs/c2010br-02.pdf.
3. Taeku Lee and Karthick Ramakrishnan, "Asian Americans Turn Democratic," *Los Angeles Times*, November 23, 2012, http://articles.latimes.com/2012/nov/23/opinion/la-oe-lee-asian-american-voters-20121123. The ANES sample had too few Asian Americans to analyze.
4. Susan Heavey, "Republicans Aim to Rebrand Party, Attract Voters," Reuters, March 18, 2013, http://www.reuters.com/article/2013/03/18/us-usa-republicans-idUSBRE92H0HL20130318; Katie Glueck, "Reince Priebus Hails College GOP Report," *Politico*, June 3, 2013, http://www.politico.com/story/2013/06/reince-priebus-college-gop-report-92146.html; Ron Elving, "RNC Post-Election Report a Line in the Sand for Divided GOP," *It's All Politics*, NPR, March 19, 2013, http://www.npr.org/blogs/itsallpolitics/2013/03/18/174689113/ rnc-chairs-postmortem-report-a-line-in-the-sand-for-divided-gop.
5. Sergio C. Wals, "Made in the USA? Immigrants' Imported Ideology and Political Engagement," *Electoral Studies* 32 (December 2013): 756–67.
6. Gregory J. Krieg, "Poll: Americans Pick President Obama over Mitt Romney for Dinner Date," ABC News, September 11, 2012, http://abcnews.go.com/blogs/politics/2012/09/poll-americans-pick-president-obama-over-mitt-romney-for-dinner-date/.
7. Danny Hayes, "Candidate Qualities through a Partisan Lens: A Theory of Trait Ownership," *American Journal of Political Science* 49 (October 2005): 908–23.
8. Ashley Parker, "For Romney, a Four-Car Garage with Its Own Elevator," *New York Times Blogs*, March, 27, 2012, http://thecaucus.blogs.nytimes.com/2012/03/27/for-romney-a-four-car-garage-with-its-own-elevator/?_r=0; Michael D. Shear and Michael Barbaro, "In Video Clip, Romney Calls 47% 'Dependent' and Feeling Entitled," *New York Times*, September 18, 2012, p. A1.
9. Lynn Vavreck, *The Message Matters: The Economy and Presidential Campaigns* (Princeton, NJ: Princeton University Press, 2009).
10. Joanne M. Miller and Jon A. Krosnick, "The Impact of Candidate Name Order on Election Outcomes," *Public Opinion Quarterly* 62 (Autumn 1998): 291–330; Jonathan G. S. Koppell and Jennifer A. Steen, "The Effects of Ballot Position on Election Outcomes," *Journal of Politics* 66 (February 2004): 267–81.

11. Morris P. Fiorina, *Retrospective Voting in American National Elections* (New Haven, CT: Yale University Press, 1981).

12. A good discussion of this topic in a single source is the collection of articles and commentary by Gerald Pomper, Richard Boyd, Richard Brody, Benjamin Page, and John Kessel in *American Political Science Review* 66 (June 1972): 415–470. See also Benjamin I. Page, *Choices and Echoes in Presidential Elections* (Chicago: University of Chicago Press, 1978).

13. Norman H. Nie, Sidney Verba, and John R. Petrocik, *The Changing American Voter* (Cambridge, MA: Harvard University Press, 1976), chap. 10; see also Benjamin I. Page and Richard A. Brody, "Policy Voting and the Electoral Process: The Vietnam War Issue," *American Political Science Review* 66 (September 1972): 979–95.

14. J. Merrill Shanks and Warren E. Miller, *The New American Voter* (Cambridge, MA: Harvard University Press, 1996).

15. James M. Snyder, Jr., and Michael M. Ting, "An Informational Rationale for Political Parties," *American Journal of Political Science* 46 (January 2002): 90–110; Jonathan Woon and Jeremy C. Pope, "Made in Congress? Testing the Electoral Implications of Party Ideological Brand Names," *Journal of Politics* 70 (July 2008): 823–36.

16. Benjamin Highton, "The Contextual Causes of Issue and Party Voting in American Presidential Elections," *Political Behavior* 32 (December 2010): 453–71.

17. Gerald H. Kramer, "Short-Term Fluctuations in U.S. Voting Behavior, 1896–1964," *American Political Science Review* 65 (March 1971): 131–43; Thomas J. Rudolph, "Who's Responsible for the Economy? The Formation and Consequences of Responsibility Attributions," *American Journal of Political Science* 47 (October 2003): 698–713.

18. David RePass, "Issue Salience and Party Choice," *American Political Science Review* 65 (June 1971): 368–400.

19. Vavreck, *The Message Matters: The Economy and Presidential Campaigns.*

20. Amber E. Boydstun, Rebecca A. Glazier, and Claire Phillips, "Agenda Control in the 2008 Presidential Debates" *American Politics Research* 41 (September 2013): 863–99.

21. "2012 Shatters 2004 and 2008 Records for Total Ads Aired," Wesleyan Media Project, October 24, 2012, http://mediaproject.wesleyan.edu/2012/10/24/2012-shatters-2004-and-2008-records-for-total-ads-aired/#more-2150.

22. See Lawrence D. Longley and Alan G. Braun, *The Politics of Electoral College Reform* (New Haven, CT: Yale University Press, 1972) for a survey of the proposals for Electoral College reform.

23. Alan Greenblatt, "Some in GOP Want New Electoral College Rules," *It's All Politics,* NPR, January 28, 2013, http://www.npr.org/blogs/itsallpolitics/2013/01/25/170276794/some-in-gop-want-new-electoral-college-rules; see "Gaming the Electoral College," http://www.270towin.com/alternative-electoral-college-allocation-methods/, to see how changing the Electoral College rules would affect who wins the presidential elections.

24. Donald E. Stokes and Warren E. Miller, "Party Government and the Saliency of Congress," *Public Opinion Quarterly* 26 (Winter 1962): 531–46.

25. The job approval ratings are taken from the Gallup Poll administered June 1–4, 2013, for Congress as a whole (http://www.pollingreport.com/CongJob1.htm).

and June 20–24, 2013, for the parties in Congress (http://www.pollingreport .com/cong_dem.htm and http://www.pollingreport.com/cong_rep.htm).

26. Chris Cillizza, "People Hate Congress, But Most Incumbents Get Re-elected. What Gives?" *Washington Post*, May 9, 2013, http://www.washingtonpost.com/ blogs/the-fix/wp/2013/05/09/people-hate-congress-but-most-incumbents-get-re-elected-what-gives/.

27. Richard F. Fenno, Jr., "If, as Ralph Nader Says, Congress Is 'The Broken Branch,' How Come We Love Our Congressmen So Much?" in *Congress in Change: Evolution and Reform*, ed. Norman J. Ornstein (New York: Praeger, 1975), 277–87; Richard F. Fenno, Jr., *Home Style: House Members in Their Districts* (New York: Pearson, 2002).

28. John R. Hibbing and Elizabeth Theiss-Morse, *Congress as Public Enemy* (New York: Cambridge University Press, 1995), 45.

29. John Sides, "The 2012 Election Was Not a Mandate," *The Monkey Cage* (blog), November 7, 2012, http://themonkeycage.org/2012/11/07/the-2012-election-was-not-a-mandate/.

30. David A. M. Peterson, Lawrence J. Grossback, James A. Stimson, and Amy Gangl, "Congressional Response to Mandate Elections," *American Journal of Political Science* 47 (July 2003): 411–26; Lawrence J. Grossback, David A. M. Peterson, and James A. Stimson, *Mandate Politics* (New York: Cambridge University Press, 2007).

Suggested Readings

Abramowitz, Alan I., and Jeffrey A. Segal. *Senate Elections*. Ann Arbor: University of Michigan Press, 1992. An extensive analysis of the factors contributing to election outcomes in Senate races.

Bartels, Larry M. *Presidential Primaries and the Dynamics of Public Choice*. Princeton, NJ: Princeton University Press, 1988. The best available analysis of public opinion and vote choice during presidential primaries.

Fiorina, Morris P. *Retrospective Voting in American National Elections*. New Haven, CT: Yale University Press, 1981. An important conceptual argument for viewing vote choice as judgments about the past.

Jacobson, Gary C. *The Politics of Congressional Elections*, 6th ed. New York: Longman, 2006. An authoritative survey of a broad topic and the literature surrounding it.

Lau, Richard R., and David P. Redlawsk. "Voting Correctly." *American Political Science Review* 91 (September 1997): 585–98. An intriguing analysis of whether people vote "correctly," that is, in line with their interests, on Election Day.

Lewis-Beck, Michael S., William G. Jacoby, Helmut Norpoth, and Herbert F. Weisberg. *The American Voter Revisited*. Ann Arbor: University of Michigan Press, 2008. A rich reanalysis of the themes from the classic work, using mainly 2000 and 2004 data.

Mayer, William G., ed. *The Swing Voter in American Politics*. Washington, DC: Brookings Institution Press, 2008. A collection using several definitions of "swing voters" to analyze them currently and over time.

Niemi, Richard G., and Herbert F. Weisberg, eds. *Classics in Voting Behavior.* Washington, DC: CQ Press, 1993. Niemi, Richard G., and Herbert F. Weisberg, eds. *Controversies in Voting Behavior,* 4th ed. Washington, DC: CQ Press, 2001. These two collections offer the best readings from decades of research on public opinion and voting behavior.

Shanks, J. Merrill, and Warren E. Miller. *The New American Voter.* Cambridge, MA: Harvard University Press, 1996. A sophisticated analysis using an elaborate model of vote choice.

Internet Resources

The website of the American National Election Studies, www.electionstudies.org, has extensive data on topics covered in this chapter. Click on "Utilities" and then click on the link for tables and graphs under "The ANES Guide to Public Opinion and Electoral Behavior." Scroll down to "Evaluation of the Presidential Candidates," "Evaluation of Congressional Candidates," and "Vote Choice" for a variety of political items from 1952 to the present. In addition, all of these items can be broken down by social characteristics.

Pollingreport.com and Pollster have current political information on elections as well as public opinion data. Major news organizations like CNN and the *New York Times* post results of exit polls on their websites. Candidates for office, like the political parties, have websites that can be located with search engines.

Survey Research Methods

MANY OF THE DATA in this book have come from survey research, and most of the analysis cited has been based on findings from survey research. For more than sixty years, the data from the American National Election Studies (ANES), as well as from other major survey projects in political science, have been available through the Inter-university Consortium for Political and Social Research and have formed the basis for countless research projects in many fields by scholars, graduate students, and undergraduates. Given this widespread use of survey data, it is appropriate to give some description of the data collection methods that underlie them.

During the past eighty years, social scientists have developed an impressive array of techniques for discovering and measuring individual attitudes and behavior. Basically, survey research relies on giving a standard questionnaire to the individuals to be studied. In most major studies of the national electorate over the years, trained interviewers ask the questions and record the responses in a face-to-face interview with each respondent. A few studies depend on the respondents themselves filling out the questionnaires. Recently, the rising costs of survey research, the pressure for quick results, and the availability of random-digit telephone dialing have led both commercial and academic pollsters to rely increasingly on telephone interviewing. The ANES used both face-to-face and telephone interviewing in 2000 but returned to using face-to-face interviews exclusively in 2004 and 2008. In 2012, the ANES once again used face-to-face interviews, but they also had a sample of respondents answer the survey on the Web. Web-based surveys are increasingly common, with organizations having respondents fill out questionnaires on a survey organization's website. Also, for several decades, news organizations have conducted exit polls on Election Day to give an early estimate of the outcome and gather additional information about voters that election statistics do not provide.

Survey Data Collection

We describe four data-collection phases in the survey research process, noting the ways these steps vary depending on whether the surveys are face-to-face, telephone, Internet, or an exit poll. The four phases are sampling, questionnaire constructing, interviewing, and coding.

Sampling

The key to survey research is probability sampling. It may seem inappropriate to analyze the entire American electorate using studies composed of fewer than two thousand individuals, which is about the average number of respondents in the studies used in this book. But it would be prohibitively expensive to interview the entire electorate, and the only way to study public opinion nationally is by interviewing relatively few individuals who accurately represent the entire electorate. Probability sampling is the method used to ensure that the individuals selected for interviewing will be representative of the total population. Probability sampling attempts to select respondents in such a way that every individual in the population has an equal chance of being selected for interviewing. If the respondents are selected in this way, the analyst can be confident that the characteristics of the sample are approximately the same as those of the whole population.

It would be impossible to make a list of every adult in the United States and then draw names from the list randomly. All survey organizations depart from such strict random procedures in some way. The ANES surveys, the General Social Survey, and other high-quality surveys using face-to-face interviews employ stratified cluster samples, based on households.

Stratification means that random selection occurs within subpopulations. In the United States, the sample is customarily selected within regions to guarantee that all sections are represented and within communities of different sizes as well. *Clustering* means that relatively small geographical areas, called primary sampling units, are randomly selected within the stratified categories so that many interviews are concentrated within a small area to reduce the costs and inconvenience for interviewers. Finally, the ANES samples *households* instead of individuals (although within households individuals are randomly selected and interviewed), which means that within sampling areas households are enumerated and selected at random. (This sampling procedure means that no respondents are selected in military bases, hospitals, hotels, prisons, or other places where people do not live in households. However, after the enfranchisement of eighteen-year-olds, the ANES and General Social Survey began to include college dormitories as residences to be sampled.)

Increasingly, the commercial polling organizations have turned to telephone interviewing as a faster and cheaper alternative to field interviewing. Random-digit dialing is typically used by these polling operations to select both listed and unlisted numbers and to give each residential number the same chance of being called. Telephone sampling has an advantage over field surveys because it does not require clustering.

Telephone sampling only recently added cell phone–only households and still ignores individuals without telephones. Otherwise, no major obstacles prevent drawing an excellent sample of telephone numbers. The problems begin at that point. Success in finding someone at home and completing a telephone interview is uneven, and failures may run as high as 50 percent. Some polling organizations make repeated callbacks, as the chances of getting an answer increase with the number of callbacks. Repeated callbacks, however, slow the data collection and increase the costs. Because an important reason for using the telephone is speed and low costs, most polling organizations do not call back.

Once the telephone is answered, or the household is contacted for a face-to-face interview, a respondent from the household must be selected. Some randomizing procedure is typically used to select the respondent. There are two methods for selecting respondents, and they have different consequences. The best sampling procedure, but a costly and time-consuming one, is to identify all the eligible members of the household and select one at random. If the respondent selected is not at home, an appointment is arranged for a callback. In a high-quality survey such as the ANES, many attempts are made to interview the individual randomly selected, but no substitutions are made. Telephone surveys typically allow a huge proportion of their respondents to be substitutes for the respondents who should have been interviewed. The alternative, and more common, method of selection identifies the respondent among those eligible who are at home, and the interview is conducted immediately. This further compromises the sample, making it a selection among those people who happen to be at home when the interviewer calls.

The more often the randomly selected respondents cannot be contacted or refuse to be interviewed, the more the sample departs from its original design. Probability samples, with either face-to-face or telephone interviews, can result in unrepresentative samples if the *nonresponse rate* is high. The nonresponse rate refers to the number of respondents originally selected who, for whatever reason, are not interviewed and thus do not appear in the sample.[1] Should these nonrespondents share some characteristic disproportionately, the resulting sample will underrepresent that type of person. For example, residents of high-crime neighborhoods and the elderly may be reluctant to answer the door for a face-to-face interview; busy people with multiple jobs may not be at home enough to be reached by telephone. When this happens, the sample will have fewer of these people than occur in the population and thus the sample will be biased. All the polling organizations take steps to counter these tendencies by weighting the results to compensate for various demographic biases.[2] This is a difficult problem to solve, however. The likelihood is high that the people who consent to be interviewed are different from, and therefore not representative of, those who refuse. If this is the case, counting those who are interviewed more heavily (which is essentially what weighting the sample does) does not eliminate the bias.

Internet polls and exit polls have their own sampling problems. Self-administered Internet polls are still relatively new and uncommon. Random-digit dialing is used to draw a sample of residential telephones, similar to a telephone poll, and create a "panel"—a large group of individuals who agree to answer a questionnaire and participate in future studies. These individuals are provided with Internet access and a computer, if necessary, so the panel is not limited to those who already have such access. Each study draws a sample from the larger panel, and these respondents are informed of the opportunity to go online to answer a questionnaire at a secure website. Although the sampling design initially produces a representative set of potential respondents, people who are willing to join the panel and participate in particular studies may be different from the rest of the public. The ANES has started to use Internet surveys in addition to the traditional face-to-face method. Given the potential differences of these two methods with respect to comparability over time, we report only the face-to-face results in this book.

Internet polls have nothing in common with the self-selected "vote on the Internet" polls favored by some television programs. When people take the initiative to respond, instead of being chosen to respond through a random selection procedure, there can be no claim that it is a representative sample of the public.

Exit polls involve random selection of polling places. Then interviewers go to each of the randomly selected polling places and are instructed to select, say, every tenth voter emerging from the polling place for an interview. At midday, the interviewers call in the results of the first set of completed interviews, and at this time the central office may adjust the interval of voters to speed up or slow down the pace of interviewing. A number of biases can be introduced in the sampling process, as busy voters refuse to be interviewed and other voters avoid interviewers on the basis of age or race.

Questionnaire Constructing

In survey questionnaires, several types of questions will ordinarily be used. Public opinion surveys began years ago with forced-choice questions that a respondent was asked to answer by choosing among a set of offered alternatives. For example, forced-choice questions frequently take the form of stating a position on public policy and asking the respondent to "agree" or "disagree" with the statement. The analysis in chapter 5 was based in part on the answers to forced-choice questions on public policy that were used in ANES questionnaires in which respondents were asked to "agree strongly," "agree," "disagree," or "disagree strongly." Some respondents either gave qualified answers that did not fit into these prearranged categories or had no opinions.

A major innovation associated with the Survey Research Center at the University of Michigan is the use of open-ended questioning. Open-ended questions give respondents the opportunity to express their opinions in their own way without being forced to select among categories provided by the questionnaire. Questions such as "Is there anything in particular you like about the Democratic Party?" or "What are the most important problems facing the country today?" permit the respondents to answer in their own terms. Interviewers encourage respondents to answer such questions as fully as they can with neutral "probes" such as "Could you tell me more about that?" or "Anything else?" or similar queries that draw forth more discussion. Open-ended questions are a superior method of eliciting accurate expressions of opinion, but open-ended questioning has two major disadvantages: (1) it places more of a burden on interviewers to record the responses, and (2) the burden of reducing the many responses to a dimension that can be analyzed is left for the coders. For example, if Americans are asked, "Do you think of yourself as a Democrat, a Republican, or an independent?" almost all the responses will fit usefully into the designated categories:

Democrat

Independent

Republican

Other party

I'm nothing; apolitical

Don't know

Refused to say

Not ascertained

If a relatively unstructured, open-ended question is used, however— such as "How do you think of yourself politically?"—some people would answer with "Democrat," "Republican," and so forth, but many others might give answers that were substantially different, such as "liberal," "conservative," "radical," "moderate," "pragmatic," or "I hate politics"— and these could not easily be compared with the partisan categories.

Analysts often intend to force responses into a single dimension, such as partisanship, whether the respondents would have volunteered an answer along that dimension or not. This is essential if researchers are to develop single dimensions for analytic purposes. Modern survey research includes questions and techniques considerably more complex than these examples for establishing dimensions.

Questionnaires differ a great deal in their complexity and sophistication. Face-to-face interviews with well-trained interviewers may have many open-ended questions or questions with branching, conditional on the responses to previous questions. Telephone interviews using computer-assisted telephone interview (CATI) technology and online Internet polls can also be complex, relying on computer branching to guide the respondent through the questionnaire. At the other extreme, exit polls are entirely forced-choice questions that can be completed quickly by the voter without instruction.

Writing good interview questions is an art. The questions should be clear, direct, and able to be understood in the same way by all respondents, regardless of age, education, or regional or subcultural differences. They need to avoid various technical mistakes, like asking two things in one question (a so-called double-barreled question). A professionally done poll that seeks accurate results—whether an academic survey, a journalistic poll, or a political poll that wants both the good news and the bad news for its client—will try very hard to ask unbiased questions that reflect the actual opinions of the respondents rather than leading them to answer in any particular way. Not all survey operations have this as a goal, however. The following example comes from the "True Patriot Survey," conducted in August 2008:

> *Question:* "Now I'm going to read you some proposals that a candidate for president might make because he says they embody America's best, most patriotic ideals. After each one, please tell me whether it is a good way or bad way to express America's patriotism. . . . Protect the right to keep and bear arms, which our Founders knew would let law-abiding citizens protect themselves against both crime and tyranny."[3]

Amazingly, 26 percent of the sample didn't take the hint and answered that it was a "bad way."

Interviewing

The selection of the sample can depend in part on the interviewer, but even more important is the role of the interviewer in asking questions of the respondent and in recording the answers. Motivated, well-trained interviewers are crucial to the success of survey research. The interviewer has several major responsibilities. First, the interviewer must select the respondent according to sampling instructions. Second, the interviewer must develop rapport with the respondent so that he or she will be willing to go through with the interview, which may last an hour or more. Third, the interviewer must ask the questions in a friendly way and encourage the respondent to answer fully without leading the respondent to distort his or her views. Fourth, the interviewer must record the answers of the respondent fully and accurately. The best survey organizations keep a permanent staff of highly trained interviewers for this purpose.

A technological innovation used in telephone interviewing is the CATI system. The interviewer sits at the telephone, with the questionnaire appearing on a computer screen. As the interviewer moves through the questionnaire, responses are entered directly into the computer and automatically coded. Complicated branching to different questions, conditional on the responses given to preceding questions, is possible.

Telephone interviewing has some real advantages. The travel costs of a field staff are eliminated. Having interviewing conducted from a call-room allows for direct supervision of the interviewing staff, enhancing the uniformity of the administration of the questionnaires. Within-interview "experiments" are possible with the CATI system. Also, changing the content of the questionnaire during the course of the study is easy and inexpensive. The great disadvantage is that face-to-face interviews yield higher-quality data.

In Internet polling, on the one hand, there are no interviewers, which is a great saving in cost. On the other hand, there is no interviewer to help the respondent navigate the questionnaire or to keep the respondent motivated—or to make judgments about the plausibility of the responses.

Exit polls generally use a combination of self-administered questionnaires with interviewers available to read the questionnaires and record responses for those voters who need assistance. Given that exit polls might provide one day of work every couple of years, exit poll interviewers are not seasoned professionals. They also work in scattered locations with no direct supervision. Errors in implementing the sampling technique or in administering the questionnaires would rarely be caught and unlikely to be corrected in the short time span of Election Day.

Coding

Once the interviewers administer the questionnaires to respondents, the verbal information is reduced to a numerical form, according to a code. Numeric information, unlike verbal information, can be processed and manipulated by high-speed data-processing equipment. The coder's task may be simple or complex. For example, to code the respondent's gender requires a simple code: 1 = male, 2 = female. A data field that contains information on the respondent will have a location designated for indicating the respondent's gender. A value of 1 will indicate male, and a value of 2 will indicate female. The list of partisan categories above gives the coding numbers that would stand for various responses. Printed questionnaires for face-to-face interviews are precoded for many of the more straightforward questions, and the CATI system allows precoded categories to be assigned automatically as the interviewer records the respondent's answers.

Some coding is complicated, with elaborate arrays of categories. For example, coding the responses to a question such as "Is there anything in particular you like about the Democratic Party?" might include hundreds of categories covering such details as "I like the party's farm policies," "I like the party's tax program," and "I've just always been a Democrat." Some codes require coders to make judgments about the respondents' answers. In political surveys, these codes have included judgments on the level of sophistication of the respondents' answers and about the main reason for respondents' vote choices.

After the verbal information has been converted into numbers according to the coding instructions, the data are ready for analysis by computer. At this point, the survey research process ends and the political analysts take over to make what use of the data they can.

Validity of Survey Questions

A frequent set of criticisms directed at public opinion research questions the validity of the responses to survey items. *Validity* simply means the extent to which there is correspondence between the verbal response to a question and the attitude or behavior of the respondent that the question is designed to measure. There is no one answer to doubts about validity, because each item has a validity applicable to it alone. Some items are notoriously invalid; others have nearly perfect validity. Many survey items have not been independently tested for their validity, and for practical purposes, the researcher is forced to say that he or she is interested in analyzing the responses, whatever they mean to the respondent. In other instances, the sample result can be compared with the known population value.

The items with the most questionable validity in political studies come from those situations in which respondents have some incentive to misrepresent the facts or when their memories may not be accurate. Questions about voter turnout or level of income are noteworthy in this regard. Validity checks reveal that respondents are about as likely to underestimate their income as overestimate it, and a noticeable percentage of respondents claim to have voted when they did not.[4]

Advantages and Disadvantages of Different Types of Surveys

Face-to-face interviews with respondents drawn from a sample of households

Advantages	High-quality data Allows for longer, more in-depth interviews
Disadvantages	High cost Slow data collection and processing

Telephone interviews of respondents drawn from a sample of residential and cell phone numbers

Advantages	Lower cost Fast turnaround, especially using a computer-assisted telephone interview system Allows direct supervision of interviewing process
Disadvantages	No-phone households are excluded Call-screening and resistance to stranger calls further degrades the sample

Self-administered Internet polls

Advantages	Less expensive once the panel is set up Subsamples with particular characteristics can be drawn from the panel
Disadvantages	Those who agree to participate may be unrepresentative of the population

Exit polls

Advantages	Provides a large number of journalists with material for reporting and commentary immediately after an election
Disadvantages	Lack of training and supervision of interviewers With increase in absentee and mail-in voting, poll needs to be supplemented with telephone survey of voters who do not go to a polling place

---

Recall of past voting behavior falls victim to failing memories and intervening events. Changes in party identification, past votes cast, the party identification of one's parents—all may contain substantial error. For example, during November and December immediately after the 1960 election, respondents were asked how they had voted for president. Most remembered voting for either John F. Kennedy or Richard M. Nixon, and as shown in Table A-1, they were divided about evenly between the two. (The slight deviation of 1 percent from the actual results is within sampling error by any reasonable standards.) The 1962 and 1964 sample estimates of the 1960 vote reveal increasing departures from the actual outcome. Granting that some change in the population over four years may affect vote-choice percentages, a substantial proportion of the 1964 sample gave responses to the question of 1960 presidential vote choice that misrepresented their vote. The validity of this item always declines over a four-year period, but President Kennedy's assassination in the intervening years created an unusually large distortion in recalled vote.

TABLE A-1 Recalled Vote for President in 1960, 1962, and 1964

Recalled vote	1960	1962	1964	Actual vote in 1960[a]
John F. Kennedy	49%	56%	64%	49.7%
Richard M. Nixon	51	43	36	49.5
Other	[b]	[b]	[b]	0.7
Total	**100%**	**99%**	**100%**	**99.9%**
(*N*)	(1,428)	(940)	(1,124)	

Sources: National Election Studies, available at www.electionstudies.org, and U.S. House of Representatives, Office of the Clerk, clerk.house.gov.

[a] The 1960 popular vote can be tallied in a number of ways, including those that show Nixon with a slight popular vote majority. No matter how the votes are counted, the election was very close.

[b] Less than 0.5 percent.

Validity versus Continuity

One of the important features of the ANES is its continuity over a sixty-year time span. Samples of the American population have been asked the same questions during every national election campaign throughout this period, offering an extraordinary opportunity for studying trends in the attitudes of the American electorate. The development of this valuable, continuous series does have one unfortunate aspect, however. Because the value of the series depends on the comparability of the questions, researchers are reluctant to alter questions, even when doubts about their validity arise. Improving the questions undermines compara-bility. Therefore, a choice between continuity and validity must be made.

The ANES questions concerning religious preference provide a recent example in which validity was chosen over continuity. For years, respondents were simply asked, "What is your religious preference?" Although a small percentage in each survey answered "None," it was clear that a significant number of those answering "Protestant," and fewer numbers citing other religions, had no meaningful religious affiliation. In the 1992 survey, the ANES began asking the question differently. Respondents were first asked, "Do you ever attend religious services, apart from occasional weddings, baptisms, and funerals?" Those who answered "no" were asked an additional question about their religious preference: "Regardless of whether you now attend any religious services, do you ever think of yourself as part of a particular church or denomina-tion?" Those who did not answer "yes" to one of these two screening questions were not asked the traditional question about religious affilia-tion that then followed. As a result, the percentage of the population categorized as having no religious affiliation increased dramatically. This new question more validly reflects the religious sentiments of the Ameri-can public, but it is now impossible to compare these later results with those of previous years. We cannot infer a large drop in religious affilia-tion on the basis of the responses to these new and different questions. In this instance, continuity has been sacrificed in favor of validity.

Despite inevitable concerns about validity, survey research pro-vides the best means of investigating the attitudes and behavior of large populations of individuals such as the American electorate.

Notes

1. See John Brehm, *The Phantom Respondents* (Ann Arbor: University of Michigan Press, 1993).
2. *Public Opinion* 4 (February/March 1981): 20.
3. True Patriot Survey, by Eric Liu and Nick Hanaver, conducted by Greenberg Quinlan Rosner Research, August 12–14, 2008; data available from the Roper Center for Public Opinion Research, http://www.ropercenter.uconn.edu/.
4. Paul Abramson and William Claggett, "Race-Related Differences in Self-Reported and Validated Turnout," *Journal of Politics* 46 (August 1984): 719–38.

Suggested Readings

Asher, Herbert. *Polling and the Public*, 5th ed. Washington, DC: CQ Press, 2001. A good discussion of how polls are conducted and how they are used.
Groves, Robert M., et al. *Survey Methodology*, Hoboken, NJ: Wiley, 2009. Excellent coverage of the many topics of survey methods.

Kish, Leslie. *Survey Sampling.* New York: Wiley, 1965. By far the most authoritative work on survey sampling.

Mann, Thomas E., and Gary R. Orren, eds. *Media Polls in American Politics.* Washington, DC: Brookings Institution Press, 1992. An excellent collection of essays on the use of polls in contemporary media analysis.

Weisberg, Herbert F. *The Total Survey Error Approach.* Chicago: University of Chicago Press, 2005. A comprehensive treatment of survey research methods.

Weisberg, Herbert F., Jon Krosnick, and Bruce D. Bowen. *An Introduction to Survey Research and Data Analysis.* San Francisco: W. H. Freeman, 1989. A good, methodological textbook on survey research and the interpretation of statistical analysis.

Internet Resources

The website of the American National Election Studies, www.electionstudies.org, has extensive information on survey methodology.

Some other websites with methodological information are the Gallup Poll, www.gallup.com, and the General Social Survey, www.norc.org/GSS+Website.

The Pew Research Center for the People and the Press, www.people-press.org, has done interesting methodological analysis, most recently on sampling cell phone–only households.

Index

description of, 12
elections and, 13–21
power in, 13
Republican Party
  in 2010 midterm elections, 2, 6, 54–55
  in 2010 Senate elections, 286
  in 2012 presidential election, 255
  Affordable Health Care Act and, 272
  awarding of delegates by, 56
  campaign spending by, 15–16
  candidate image, 264
  civil rights and, 151
  conservatism of, 124
  government activity advocated by, 141
  health care and, 147
  identification with, 100
  ideological self-identification, 170
  image of, 266
  immigration reform and, 257
  Iraq war and, 164–165
  liberalism of, 141
  in nineteenth century, 121
  participation by, 91
  partisan division, 99
  primary elections in, 56
  social characteristics of, 184–186
  social class and, 202
  spending cuts and, 145–146
  young people in, 201
Restore Our Future, 59
Rezko, Tony, 237
Roe v. Wade, 153
Romney, Mitt
  2012 presidential campaign by, 1–6,
    16–17, 48–49, 62–66, 113, 153,
    234, 239–240, 255, 283–284
  campaign debates by, 234–235
  campaign spending by, 15, 58
  economy and, 272
  47 percent comment by, 5, 66, 164,
    213–214, 263
  government assistance programs
    and, 269–270
  image of, 278
  leadership image of, 278
  Obamacare opposition by, 273–274
  party identification effects on, 277
  political party traits and, 263

popular vote for, 283–284
in presidential primaries, 244
social groups and, 255–256
television advertising by, 62–63
vote choice determinants for,
  276–277
voter demographics, 253–255
Roosevelt, Franklin D., 122
Roosevelt, Theodore, 11, 122
Rosenthal, Howard, 204
Rove, Karl, 2
Rubio, Marco, 4, 257
Russia, 42
Ryan, Paul, 4, 49, 235

Sabato, Larry, 5
Sampling, 295–297
Sanders, Lynn M., 152
Santorum, Rick, 2–3, 244
Saudi Arabia, 163
Schattscheider, E. E., 98
Schlozman, Kay L., 32–33
Schudson, Michael, 215
Secondary groups, 197, 206
Secret ballot, 71–72
Senate elections, 285
September 11, 2001
  description of, 7, 161
  George W. Bush's approval ratings
    after, 229–230
  media coverage of, 222
  political tolerance affected by, 25, 40
  trust in government after, 29
Service learning, 33
Shelby County v. Holder, 84
Short-term forces, 101
Sides, John, 53, 288
Silver, Nate, 1, 5, 51, 214
Single-issue voting, 268
Smith, Kevin, 39, 176
Sniderman, Paul, 143
Snowe, Olympia, 286
Social capital, 32–33
Social characteristics
  of Democratic Party, 184–186
  political behavior and, 186
  of Republican Party, 184–186
  vote choice and, 253–257

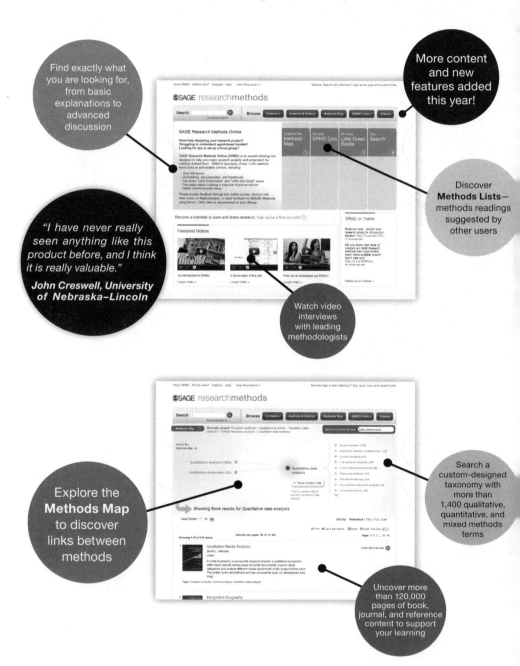

ⓈSAGE researchmethods

The essential online tool for researchers from the world's leading methods publisher

Find exactly what you are looking for, from basic explanations to advanced discussion

More content and new features added this year!

Discover **Methods Lists**— methods readings suggested by other users

"I have never really seen anything like this product before, and I think it is really valuable."

John Creswell, University of Nebraska–Lincoln

Watch video interviews with leading methodologists

Explore the **Methods Map** to discover links between methods

Search a custom-designed taxonomy with more than 1,400 qualitative, quantitative, and mixed methods terms

Uncover more than 120,000 pages of book, journal, and reference content to support your learning

Find out more at
www.sageresearchmethods.com